The Economics of Food
Price Volatility

A National Bureau of
Economic Research
Conference Report

The Economics of Food
Price Volatility

Edited by **Jean-Paul Chavas, David Hummels,
and Brian D. Wright**

The University of Chicago Press

Chicago and London

JEAN-PAUL CHAVAS is the Anderson-Bascom Professor of
Agricultural and Applied Economics at the University of Wisconsin–
Madison and a member of the Board of Directors of the National
Bureau of Economic Research. DAVID HUMMELS is professor
of economics in the Krannert School of Management at Purdue
University and a research associate of the National Bureau of
Economic Research. BRIAN D. WRIGHT is professor of agricultural and
resource economics at the University of California, Berkeley.

The University of Chicago Press, Chicago 60637
The University of Chicago Press, Ltd., London
© 2014 by the National Bureau of Economic Research
All rights reserved. Published 2014.
Printed in the United States of America

23 22 21 20 19 18 17 16 15 14   1 2 3 4 5
ISBN-13: 978-0-226-12892-4 (cloth)
ISBN-13: 978-0-226-12908-2 (e-book)
DOI: 10.7208/chicago/9780226129082.001.0001

Library of Congress Cataloging-in-Publication Data

The economics of food price volatility / edited by Jean-Paul Chavas,
    David Hummels, and Brian D. Wright.
        pages cm — (A National Bureau of Economic Research
    conference report)
        "The conference was organized by the three editors of this book
    and took place on August 15–16, 2012, in Seattle."—Preface.
    Includes bibliographical references and index.
    ISBN 978-0-226-12892-4 (cloth : alkaline paper) —
    ISBN 978-0-226-12908-2 (e-book) 1. Food prices—Congresses.
    2. Agriculture—Economic aspects—Congresses. I. Chavas,
    Jean-Paul, editor. II. Hummels, David, editor. III. Wright, Brian,
    1948 January 1–, editor. IV. Series: National Bureau of Economic
    Research conference report.
    HD9000.5.E27 2014
    338.1'9—dc23

                                                    2013040592

Relation of the Directors to the Work and Publications of the National Bureau of Economic Research

1. The object of the NBER is to ascertain and present to the economics profession, and to the public more generally, important economic facts and their interpretation in a scientific manner without policy recommendations. The Board of Directors is charged with the responsibility of ensuring that the work of the NBER is carried on in strict conformity with this object.

2. The President shall establish an internal review process to ensure that book manuscripts proposed for publication DO NOT contain policy recommendations. This shall apply both to the proceedings of conferences and to manuscripts by a single author or by one or more co-authors but shall not apply to authors of comments at NBER conferences who are not NBER affiliates.

3. No book manuscript reporting research shall be published by the NBER until the President has sent to each member of the Board a notice that a manuscript is recommended for publication and that in the President's opinion it is suitable for publication in accordance with the above principles of the NBER. Such notification will include a table of contents and an abstract or summary of the manuscript's content, a list of contributors if applicable, and a response form for use by Directors who desire a copy of the manuscript for review. Each manuscript shall contain a summary drawing attention to the nature and treatment of the problem studied and the main conclusions reached.

4. No volume shall be published until forty-five days have elapsed from the above notification of intention to publish it. During this period a copy shall be sent to any Director requesting it, and if any Director objects to publication on the grounds that the manuscript contains policy recommendations, the objection will be presented to the author(s) or editor(s). In case of dispute, all members of the Board shall be notified, and the President shall appoint an ad hoc committee of the Board to decide the matter; thirty days additional shall be granted for this purpose.

5. The President shall present annually to the Board a report describing the internal manuscript review process, any objections made by Directors before publication or by anyone after publication, any disputes about such matters, and how they were handled.

6. Publications of the NBER issued for informational purposes concerning the work of the Bureau, or issued to inform the public of the activities at the Bureau, including but not limited to the NBER Digest and Reporter, shall be consistent with the object stated in paragraph 1. They shall contain a specific disclaimer noting that they have not passed through the review procedures required in this resolution. The Executive Committee of the Board is charged with the review of all such publications from time to time.

7. NBER working papers and manuscripts distributed on the Bureau's web site are not deemed to be publications for the purpose of this resolution, but they shall be consistent with the object stated in paragraph 1. Working papers shall contain a specific disclaimer noting that they have not passed through the review procedures required in this resolution. The NBER's web site shall contain a similar disclaimer. The President shall establish an internal review process to ensure that the working papers and the web site do not contain policy recommendations, and shall report annually to the Board on this process and any concerns raised in connection with it.

8. Unless otherwise determined by the Board or exempted by the terms of paragraphs 6 and 7, a copy of this resolution shall be printed in each NBER publication as described in paragraph 2 above.

Contents

Preface

The year 2008 saw large swings in food prices. The causes and effects of such swings have generated much interest around the world. The effects of food price volatility on farmers, consumers, and food market participants are complex. For example, while high food prices benefit farmers, they hurt consumers. The linkages between food price volatility and the functioning of food markets remain poorly understood, and so are the implications for agricultural and trade policy. This motivated us to organize a conference to study these issues and provide an updated evaluation of current knowledge.

The conference was held in Seattle on August 15–16, 2012. It was jointly sponsored by the National Bureau of Economic Research (NBER) and the American and Applied Economics Association (AAEA) and was funded by a grant from the Economic Research Service (ERS) at the US Department of Agriculture (USDA). The economics of food price volatility was the focus of the conference, which involved the presentation and discussion of papers by distinguished researchers and experts on the subject. The objective of this book is to make this information widely available.

Following the conference in Seattle, all papers were subject to external reviews and revised. The revised versions of the papers along with their associated discussions are the ones presented in this book. As such, the book reports and assesses the latest research on central issues related to recent food price volatility. This research evaluates current knowledge on the causes and effects of food price volatility, examines the extent to which particular current economic conditions contribute to this volatility, and identifies issues that are in need of further investigation. By disseminating new research on food price volatility, the book intends to help both private and public decision makers develop improved management strategies and policies that can address current and future food market instability.

Introduction

Jean-Paul Chavas, David Hummels, and Brian D. Wright

Introduction

Historically, food markets have been subject to much instability, and the last few years have seen very large swings in food prices. This price volatility has had large effects on farmers, market participants, and consumers. Higher commodity prices benefit sellers (including grain farmers), but they hurt buyers (including consumers, and dairy/livestock farmers who face higher feed cost). Lower prices have the opposite effects. Market instability makes anticipating future price patterns difficult and creates significant price risk/ uncertainty for market participants. It can also lead to hasty and injudicious policy responses that might be difficult to reverse. This puts a premium on understanding the factors that contribute to large price swings as a prelude to designing policy schemes that can help reduce this uncertainty or to ameliorate its effects.

The recent increase in food price volatility raises three important sets of questions:

- What are the main causes of food price instability? Does instability arise primarily from technological or weather-related supply shocks or from demand shocks such as those induced by biofuels? Does financial speculation and globalization lead to increased or decreased volatility?

Jean-Paul Chavas is the Anderson-Bascom Professor of Agricultural and Applied Economics at the University of Wisconsin–Madison and a member of the Board of Directors of the National Bureau of Economic Research. David Hummels is professor of economics in the Krannert School of Management at Purdue University and a research associate of the National Bureau of Economic Research. Brian D. Wright is professor of agricultural and resource economics at the University of California, Berkeley.

For acknowledgments, sources of research support, and disclosure of the authors' material financial relationships, if any, please see http://www.nber.org/chapters/c12803.ack.

Is the current market instability just a short-term phenomenon or is it the beginning of a longer-term trend?

- What are the welfare effects of increased food price volatility for farmers, traders, and consumers? How does it affect the welfare of poor households in developed as well as developing countries?
- What are the management and policy implications of increased volatility in agricultural markets? What is the role of private stockholding in reducing price instability? How can financial markets help improve the allocation of food price risk? Do existing agricultural, energy, climate, and trade policies mitigate or exacerbate volatility and can reforms of those policies lead to better management of food price volatility and the reduction of food insecurity around the world?

Providing better answers to these questions is the main motivation for this book. This book presents and assesses the latest research on central issues related to recent food price volatility. This research evaluates current knowledge on the causes and effects of food price volatility, examines the extent to which particular current economic conditions contribute to this volatility, and identifies issues that are in need of further investigation. By disseminating new research on food price volatility, it intends to help both private and public decision makers to develop improved management strategies and policies that can address current and future market instability.

Food Price Volatility: Historical Evidence

The evolution of food prices over the last decade is shown in figure I.1 for three agricultural commodities: corn, wheat, and rice. This figure, drawn from the Food and Agriculture Organization (FAO 2010), shows very large changes in food prices in 2008. In a period of few months, grain prices basically doubled, followed by a very sharp decline. The changes were most dramatic for rice. These rapid price fluctuations are quite unsettling for any market participant.

Figure I.2, which presents data from the Economic Research Service of the United States Department of Agriculture (ERS USDA 2010) , shows longer-term annual data on agricultural prices. It shows the real price of food (nominal dollar prices divided by the US Consumer Price Index [CPI]) over the last century for three farm commodities: corn, milk, and wheat. There is a long-term declining trend in real prices. Over the last ninety years, the average annual rate of change in real price was –1.8 percent for corn, –1.9 percent for wheat, and –0.8 percent for milk. This is a remarkable fact: agriculture has been able to feed the growing world population at a lower price for consumers.

Figure I.2 also shows that prices exhibit substantial variability. Two periods are particularly noteworthy: the 1930s (during the Great Depression)

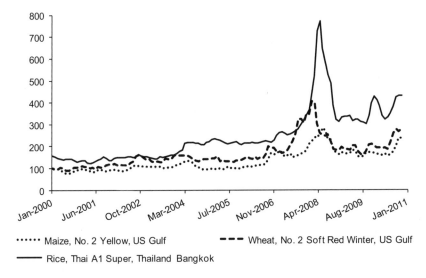

.... Maize, No. 2 Yellow, US Gulf   ━ ━ ━ Wheat, No. 2 Soft Red Winter, US Gulf

━━━━ Rice, Thai A1 Super, Thailand Bangkok

Fig. I.1   Nominal prices of food, 2000–2010 (US $/ton)

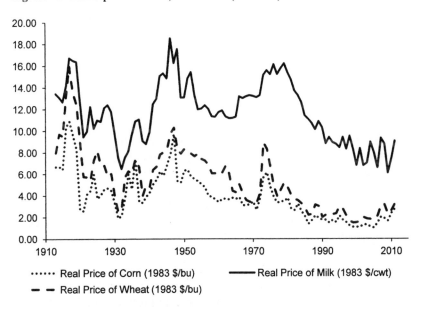

.... Real Price of Corn (1983 $/bu)   ━━━ Real Price of Milk (1983 $/cwt)

━ ━ Real Price of Wheat (1983 $/bu)

Fig. I.2   Real prices of food, 1913–2011 (US 1983$)

when food prices were very low, and the early 1970s when food prices were
very high. The 1970s was a period exhibiting high population growth and
increased resource scarcity. But it was followed by three decades of fairly
steady decline in real prices for food, which has been good news for consumers. However, the last few years have seen a large increase in price variability.

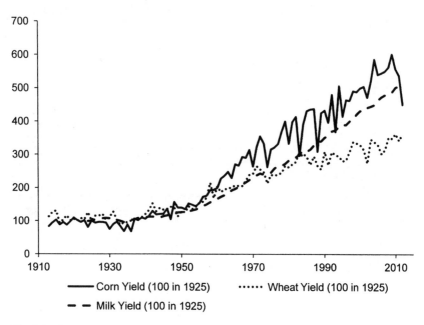

Fig. I.3   Evolution of agricultural yields, United States, 1913–2012
Source: ERS USDA (2012).

For example, the real price of milk in the United States has declined by 34 percent from 2007 to 2009, followed by a 48 percent increase from 2009 to 2011. Similarly, the real price of corn in the United States has doubled from 2005 to 2007, followed by a 19 percent decline from 2007 to 2009, and then by a 70 percent rise from 2009 to 2011. These large fluctuations create significant challenges to market participants. They also raise questions about what is coming next.

Since the Great Depression, the main source of the long-term decline in real food prices has been improvements in agricultural productivity. Figures I.3 and I.4 illustrate the evolution of agricultural yields over the last few decades. Figure I.3 shows how US yields have changed for three commodities: corn, wheat, and milk. Over the last eighty years, the average annual growth rate in yield was 2.0 percent per year for corn and 1.4 percent per year for wheat, reflecting very large increases in land productivity. Similarly, the last eighty years have seen an average annual growth rate in milk production per cow of 1.9 percent per year. Recently, we have seen several unusual shortfalls in grain yields. For example, the US Corn Belt suffered a widespread drought in 2012: US corn yield in 2012 was 16 percent lower than in 2011 and 25 percent lower than in 2009. To the extent that such supply shocks are associated with climate change, they may become more frequent and contribute to greater instability in agricultural markets. Figure I.4 shows the

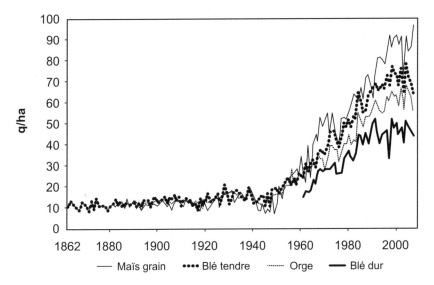

Fig. I.4   Evolution of agricultural yields, France, 1862–2007
Source: The figure is from Agreste Primeur (2008).
Note: The yields are in quintals (100 kg) per hectare. "Maïs grain" is corn/maize, "Blé tendre" is bread wheat, "Orge" is barley, and "Blé dur" is durum wheat.

evolution of yield for selected farm commodities in France. Like figure I.3, it shows a large and steady increase in land productivity over the last fifty years. Since 1930, the average annual growth rate in yield was 2.3 percent per year for corn and 1.9 percent per year for soft wheat. These are very large increases that were crucial in increasing food production.

How much of these increases came from technological change? Part of the historical increases in food production came from increased input use (e.g., fertilizer, pesticides, capital). But the evidence shows that most of these increases came from technological improvements (Ball et al. 1997; Gardner 2002; Fuglie 2008). For example, Ball et al. (1997) documented that US agricultural production grew at an average rate of 2 percent annual rate over the last few decades, most of it (1.94 percent) coming from productivity growth (as measured by a total factor productivity [TFP] index). Remarkably, such changes took place while US agricultural labor input was declining at an average rate of 2.7 percent a year (reflecting both rural-urban migration and increased mechanization). In addition, Fuglie (2008) found that, over the last four decades, agricultural productivity has been growing at fairly high rates in most regions of the world. This reflects the important role played by innovations in farming systems, fertilizer use, pest control methods, mechanization, and genetic improvements. It means that technological change has been the principal factor responsible for increased food production around the world. Although the rates of growth in yields of rice and wheat appear to have declined recently, at this point there is no definitive evidence of a general slowdown in agricultural productivity growth. What is less clear is what is coming next. Is the recent increase in food price volatility a short-term issue? Or is it a sign of significant and longer-term changes in agricultural markets? To the extent that climate change is contributing to increasing both the frequency and severity of adverse weather shocks on crop yields and food supply, increased price volatility may become a permanent feature of food markets. In addition, other factors (besides supply shocks) may also play a role. Could financial speculation and globalization also be contributing factors? What can be done to improve the functioning of food markets? How does food price volatility affect welfare and income distribution? What are the policy implications? The objective of this book is to present the latest research and inquiries addressing these questions.

Overview of the Book

The book includes nine chapters that investigate the economics of food price volatility along five directions of inquiry. First, they document the recent and historical patterns in food price volatility, including the evolving food supply and demand conditions. Second, they study how food price volatility relates to linkages between food markets and energy markets, with special attention given to the role of biofuel policy. Third, they assess the impact of storage and speculation on food price volatility. Fourth, they examine the role of international markets, with a focus on the role of trade policy. Finally, they evaluate the distributional and welfare effects of food price volatility and their effects on the poor around the world.

The role of innovation and technological progress in agriculture has been significant. As noted above, large productivity gains in the food sector have been major drivers of the long-run decline in food price. The chapter by Alston, Martin, and Pardey evaluates the role of agricultural technology and its effects on food price volatility. Technological change affects the variability of food prices by changing the sensitivity of aggregate farm supply to external shocks. After reviewing patterns of production, yields, and prices for the major cereal grains—wheat, maize, and corn—over the last fifty years, the Alston, Martin, and Pardey chapter studies how technological change can help reduce food price variability. It also shows how technical change has contributed to reducing the importance of food price variability for the poor, especially by reducing the number of poor.

The chapter by Berry, Roberts, and Schlenker presents estimates of the elasticity of aggregate supply and demand for food and the implications for agricultural price volatility. These estimates are important because price volatility depends not just on the magnitude of shocks but the elasticity of response to them. The chapter also provides important insights on two sets of issues: (a) the effects of ethanol and biofuel policy on the food sector, and (b) the effects of weather shocks on food supply. The first issue is timely given current biofuel policy. The United States is now diverting about 30 percent of the food or feed value of corn to bioethanol production, and Europe and the United States are using a substantial amount of oilseeds to generate biodiesel. This new demand contributes to diverting agricultural land away from food production, thus reducing food supply and increasing food prices. Finally, the issue of evaluating weather shocks is particularly relevant as agriculture is a sector most vulnerable to climate change. The chapter examines how adverse weather conditions in 2012 have contributed to a 14 percent decline in US maize production. It predicts that such effects may become the new normal under anticipated climate change.

The chapter by Abbott provides a refined analysis of the effects of recent biofuel policy and its implications for linkages with the food and energy markets. The chapter argues that current biofuel policy has created incentives to increase ethanol plant capacity, thus creating a new and persistent demand for corn and upward pressure on corn and food prices. It also provides evidence that these effects vary over time, depending in part on whether the capacity of ethanol plants is binding or not. The chapter argues that apparent corn price volatility is due in part to switching between alternative policy regimes.

In a period of globalization, market linkages across sectors are important. The dynamic linkages between agricultural, energy, and other markets are studied in the chapter by Enders and Holt. Relying on refined multivariate time series models, the chapter examines the factors that contributed to recent changes in the grain markets. It documents how energy prices, exchange rates, and interest rates have affected grain prices. It also examines how the introduction of ethanol as an important fuel source has contributed to the run-up in grain prices. Finally, economic growth in emerging economies such as China, India, and Brazil is identified as a contributing factor.

The recent increase in food price volatility has raised questions about its relationship with the functioning of markets. One question is about the role of storage as a means of reducing price volatility. The chapter by Bobenrieth, Bobenrieth, and Wright examines what the theory of stock holding offers on this issue. The chapter studies the implications of storage behavior for the time series properties of market prices. In this context, the analysis rules out "bubbles" as defined in financial economics. Yet, it shows the presence of price runs that could be characterized as "explosive" and might seem to be bubble-like. This warns us not to interpret observations of large price increases as evidence of excessive speculation.

With the rapid development of financial markets over the last decade, there have been some concerns about the "financialization" of commodity futures markets (Domanski and Heath 2007). This has generated a debate on the role of financial markets in the recent increase in market volatility.

The chapter by Irwin, Garcia, and Aulerich examines this issue in the context of the food markets. It provides a refined analysis of the market impact of financial index investment on agricultural futures markets. The analysis is applied to twelve agricultural markets. It shows that buying pressure from financial index investment in recent years did not cause massive bubbles in agricultural futures prices.

In a period of globalized exchange, the role of trade and its effects of food price volatility has been the subject of much interest. If domestic shocks are large and uncorrelated with foreign shocks, trade can reduce domestic volatility. But trade can also transmit volatility from foreign shocks into an otherwise tranquil domestic market. When food price spikes in countries with large numbers of poor people, public interventions involving both domestic and trade policies can help alleviate hunger and malnutrition. This has raised many questions. How effective can domestic economic policy be in reducing price instability? How does trade liberalization relate to price volatility? What has been the quantitative impact of ad hoc export restrictions in transferring volatility from domestic to foreign markets? Are certain trade instruments especially problematic in transmitting or helpful in diminishing volatility? Are temporary trade restrictions beneficial to individual nations even as they distort and destabilize global markets?

The chapter by Gouel evaluates the relationships between food price volatility and domestic stabilization policies in developing countries. The chapter analyzes the trade-off existing between government interventions in the domestic markets to stabilize food prices (e.g., storage and restrictive trade policies) and greater reliance on international trade. It evaluates the economic and policy challenges to balance the benefits of greater integration in world markets and the domestic welfare effects of economic and trade policy. It stresses the need for better integration between public and private agents involved in food markets.

The chapter by Anderson, Ivanic, and Martin investigates the effects of the 2008 world food price crisis, with implications for welfare distribution. Many governments pursued policies intended to insulate domestic prices from changes in world prices. But such policies also substantially increased world prices for key food crops such as rice, wheat, maize, and edible oilseeds. High food prices benefit food sellers but hurt food buyers and consumers. In the absence of domestic policy interventions, the consequences are particularly severe for low-income households who spend a large share of their income on food. The Anderson, Ivanic, and Martin presents evidence showing that once we account for equilibrium effects on prices, insulation is not effective in reducing poverty. Indeed, its net effect was to increase global poverty in 2008 by 7.5 million persons. This raises the challenge of designing effective policies that can reduce the impact of higher food prices on the poor.

Finally, the chapter by Do, Ravallion, and Levchenko provides a theoretical analysis of this issue. It evaluates conditions under which trade insulation can provide social protection against food price volatility. It shows that in the presence of consumer preference heterogeneity, implementing an optimal social protection policy can potentially induce higher food price volatility. The chapter urges caution against policy positions that would condemn trade insulation practices, and it calls for a reassessment of food stabilization policies.

Challenges Ahead

The recent increase in food price volatility has stimulated much academic research. The chapters presented in this book provide a broad overview of the current state of academic inquiries on the economics of food price volatility. They document the progress made in identifying the factors that have contributed to the 2008 food crisis, along with their economic and policy implications. Yet more research is needed to refine our understanding of evolving food markets and to address current challenges to improving food security around the world. Below, we briefly discuss a few directions for future inquiries.

It is important to distinguish between price volatility and high prices. Under price instability, prices are at times high (benefiting producers and hurting consumers) and at times low (benefiting consumers and hurting producers). It is possible to have an increase in the price level without changes in price volatility. It is also possible to have both simultaneously (which may have been the case in the food crisis of 2008). The distinction appears to be important for at least two reasons.

First, price changes might or might not be anticipated by market participants. If price changes are anticipated, economic and econometric analyses can focus on analyzing structural change issues. But the situation becomes more complex when (at least part of the) price changes are not anticipated by producers, consumers, or traders. In this case, the econometrician needs to distinguish between what is known versus what is not known to market participants. The changes in what is not known can be captured by changes in the distribution of price volatility. In econometrics, this means examining changes in variance (or higher moments) of the price distribution, as seen from the viewpoint of market participants. This raises the issue of empirically evaluating both changes in market conditions and changes in the information available to market participants. For example, how much of the 2008 food crisis was due to poor information available to market participants about food stocks? To the extent that there was no obvious food shortage in 2008, could better information about food stocks have prevented the large increase in food prices observed in 2008? These questions stress the need to have good information about the causes and nature of evolving market conditions. Unfortunately, access to such information by economists and policymakers is often limited. This reduces our ability to provide an in-depth analysis and evaluation of price volatility issues. This argument emphasizes that future progress on understanding the economics of food price volatility must rely on access to good data.

Second, the distinction between anticipated versus nonanticipated price changes is important for an economic and policy viewpoint. Anticipated changes are easier to manage by both private agents and policymakers. For example, if a supply shock is anticipated, then production, consumption, and storage behavior can adjust ahead of time and reduce the economic and welfare effects of the shocks on market participants. But if the shock is not anticipated, the economic implications are quite different. First, the welfare and distributional effects can be stronger. Second, the adjustments must be contingent on the particular shock, implying state-contingent decisions that are in the realm of insurance and risk markets. But insurance and risk markets are known to be incomplete. For populations for whom food constitutes a minor share of the budget, this is not important. For people so poor that food has a major expenditure share, why such markets tend to be incomplete remains an interesting question. Recent experience indicates that insurance markets in agriculture do not develop easily (in the absence of heavy government subsidies). This suggests that the welfare costs of volatility are not large enough to justify paying the full cost of insurance, including administrative expenses. If this is so, there is no problem of underprovision of insurance. Is it possible to improve on the welfare outcome-associated current food price volatility? What is the role of markets? What is the role of government policies (including both domestic policy and trade policy)? As discussed above, free trade can help reduce the welfare effects of location-specific shocks in food supply (e.g., the case of a drought, flood, heat wave, or cold spell in a given region). But it would be less effective in addressing the effects of worldwide shocks to the food sector.

Two sources of shocks are of particular interest. First, globalization has strengthened the linkages between food markets, energy markets, and financial markets. It means that shocks to the energy or financial markets now have stronger effects on the food sector. How are the food markets adjusting to these shocks? Second, climate change is increasing the prospects of seeing significant weather shocks in agriculture. The implications for food markets and agricultural and trade policies remain unclear. While we know that markets and free trade can help improve aggregate efficiency, the issue of private and public risk management schemes associated with unanticipated shocks to the food sector needs further investigation. This is particularly crucial when considering that large food price increases can have devastating effects on the welfare of poor households around the world.

References

Agreste Primeur. 2008. *La Statistique Agricole*. Numéro 210. Montreuil-sous-Bois, France: Service Central des Enquêtes et Etudes Statistiques, Ministère de l'Agriculture et de la Pêche.

Ball, V. E., J. C. Bureau, R. Nehring, and A. Somwaru. 1997. "Agricultural Productivity Revisited." *American Journal of Agricultural Economics* 79:1045–63.

Domanski, D., and A. Heath. 2007. "Financial Investors and Commodity Markets." *BIS Quarterly Review* March:53–67.

Economic Research Service, United States Department of Agriculture. (ERS USDA). 2010. *Data Sets*. Washington, DC: ERS USDA. http://www.ers.usda.gov/Data.

Food and Agriculture Organization (FAO). 2010. *Global Information and Early Warning Systems*. Rome: Food and Agriculture Organization, United Nations. http://www.fao.org/giews/pricetool2.

Fuglie, K. O. 2008. "Is a Slowdown in Agricultural Productivity Growth Contributing to the Rise in Commodity Prices?" *Agricultural Economics* 39:431–41.

Gardner, B. L. 2002. *American Agriculture in the Twentieth Century*. Cambridge, MA: Harvard University Press.

1

Influences of Agricultural Technology on the Size and Importance of Food Price Variability

Julian M. Alston, William J. Martin,
and Philip G. Pardey

1.1 Introduction

Innovation and technological change in agriculture have contributed to profound changes in the structure of agricultural production, markets, and trade. Significant technological changes have been made both on farms and in the industries that store, transport, process, distribute, and market farm products and supply inputs used by farmers (e.g., see Pardey, Alston, and Ruttan 2010).

These changes have affected the size and importance of food price variability in three main ways. First, innovations can change the sensitivity of aggregate farm supply to external shocks—for instance, if farmers adopt improved crop varieties that have higher expected yields but more- or less-variable yields, if individual farmers are induced through innovation to

Julian M. Alston is professor in the Department of Agricultural and Resource Economics at the University of California, Davis; associate director of science and technology at the University of California Agricultural Issues Center; and a member of the Giannini Foundation of Agricultural Economics. William J. Martin is research manager in agriculture and rural development in the Development Research Group at the World Bank. Philip G. Pardey is professor in the Department of Applied Economics and director of the International Science and Technology Practice and Policy (InSTePP) Center at the University of Minnesota.

The work for this project was partly supported by the University of California; the University of Minnesota; the HarvestChoice initiative, funded by the Bill and Melinda Gates Foundation; and the Giannini Foundation of Agricultural Economics. The authors gratefully acknowledge excellent research assistance provided by Jason Beddow, Maros Ivanic, Connie Chan-Kang, Kabir Tumber, and Wei Zhang, and helpful comments and advice from various colleagues including Jock Anderson, Steve Boucher, Brian Buhr, Derek Byerlee, Michael Carter, Doug Gollin, Terry Hurley, Travis Lybbert, James Roumasset, Ed Taylor, and Daniel Sumner, as well as Jim MacDonald and other participants at the NBER conference. For acknowledgments, sources of research support, and disclosure of the authors' material financial relationships, if any, please see http://www.nber.org/chapters/c12804.ack.

become more specialized in particular outputs, or if the adoption of innovations results in less variation among farmers in the timing of farm operations (e.g., the date of planting of crops) or an increase in the geographical concentration of production. Second, technological innovations on or off farms can result in changes in the price elasticity of supply or demand (of both farm inputs and outputs), changing the sensitivity of prices to a given extent of underlying variability of supply or demand or both. This can happen both directly, as a consequence of particular innovations, or indirectly because of the broader economic implications of technological changes—for example, by increasing incomes. Third, food price volatility is less important to richer people and, by increasing the general abundance of food and reducing the share of income spent on food, agricultural innovation has made a given extent of volatility less important.

The recent evidence of a slowdown in agricultural productivity growth in many parts of the world, combined with the rise of biofuels, has coincided with a reversal of the trend of rising abundance of food, and a corresponding increase in vulnerability of a greater number of poor people to food price volatility.[1] Moreover, as poor farmers respond to food scarcity by increasing the intensity of production practices and moving farther into marginal areas, we may see an increase in vulnerability of their production to weather and other shocks for some farmers. This chapter explores these different dimensions of the role of agricultural technology in contributing to or mitigating the consequences of variability in agricultural production, both in the past and looking forward.

1.2   A Simple Model of Technology and Prices

A simple supply and demand model can be used to illustrate the various ways in which changes in technology influence food price variability.[2] In the following model of the farm-level market for a staple food commodity, subscripts s and d refer to supply and demand respectively, Q represents quantity, P represents price, and η represents the absolute value of the elasticity of supply or demand.[3] In each equation, α, the "intercept" comprises a deterministic part and a random part, which is the source of variability:

1. Whether measures of growth of total factor productivity (TFP) or multifactor productivity (MFP) in agriculture are exhibiting a slowdown is the subject of a continuing debate among agricultural economists, but the participants in that debate have agreed that growth rates of partial factor productivity measures such as crop yields have slowed for the world as a whole and for most producing countries (e.g., see Alston, Babcock, and Pardey 2010).

2. Although the general discussion is pertinent to a broader set of circumstances, for concreteness we have in mind a model of the national or global market for a particular food commodity, as represented by aggregate farm-level annual supply and demand. To emphasize the important first-round effects the analysis is mainly partial, although the empirical simulations in section 1.5 explicitly link the farm sector to the broader economy.

3. Some more-detailed results will be conditioned by the use of constant elasticity forms as a local approximation to represent supply and demand equations that could take some other shape, but the main results here will not be sensitive to this approximation, which allows us to represent the key relationships in terms of familiar parameters.

(1) $$\ln Q_s = \alpha_s + \eta_s \ln P_s \text{ (supply)}$$

(2) $$\ln Q_d = \alpha_d - \eta_d \ln P_d \text{ (demand)}$$

Assuming $Q_s = Q_d$ and $P_s = P_d$, solving equations (1) and (2) for market clearing prices and quantities yields:

(3) $$\ln P = (\alpha_d - \alpha_s)/(\eta_s + \eta_d),$$

(4) $$\ln Q = (\eta_s\alpha_d + \eta_d\alpha_s)/(\eta_s + \eta_d).$$

Taking variances of $\ln P$ and $\ln Q$ in equations (3) and (4) yields:[4]

(5) $$\text{Var}(\ln P) = [\text{Var}(\alpha_d) + \text{Var}(\alpha_s) - 2\text{Cov}(\alpha_d,\alpha_s)]/(\eta_s + \eta_d)^2,$$

(6) $$\text{Var}(\ln Q) = [\eta_d^2\text{Var}(\alpha_s) + \eta_s^2\text{Var}(\alpha_d) + 2\eta_s\eta_d\text{Cov}(\alpha_d,\alpha_s)]/(\eta_s + \eta_d)^2.$$

Hence, price volatility, as represented by the variance of logarithms of prices in equation (5), increases with either (a) increases in the variability of demand or supply, as represented by $\text{Var}(\alpha_d)$ and $\text{Var}(\alpha_s)$; (b) reductions in the covariance between shocks to supply and demand; or (c) decreases in the elasticity of supply or demand. The corresponding measure of quantity variability in equation (6) increases with increases in variability of supply or demand or decreases in the covariance, but the signs of the effects of the elasticities depend on their relative sizes and the relative sizes of the variance and covariance terms.

Technology enters equations (5) and (6) in several ways, both on the demand side and the supply side. Specifically, the intercepts (α_s and α_d) and elasticities (η_s and η_d) are all functions of technology along with other variables, which are also left implicit, some of which may interact with technology and modify its effects on price volatility. In many contexts, for practical purposes the covariance terms in equations (5) and (6) will be negligible.[5] On the other hand, the mechanization of agriculture, the introduction of chemical fertilizers, and the rise of biofuels have tended to make the supply and demand for agricultural products more elastic (agriculture using a larger share of highly elastically supplied petroleum-based products as inputs makes supply more elastic, and biofuels demand makes demand for agricultural products more elastic unless it is driven by binding mandates). These factors also make agricultural supply and demand potentially more variable (because they are now vulnerable to oil price shocks in a way that was not true in the era of the horse), and the linkage of agriculture to the oil economy

---

4. Alternative measures of variability were considered. Many studies have used a coefficient of variation to remove the influence of differences in average levels or in units of measurement (e.g., Hazell 1989; Gollin 2006). The variance of log-transformed data has similar characteristics—it is unit-free and invariant to multiplicative transformations of the data—and has the further advantage that statistical tests developed for comparing variances between populations can be applied directly to it, as discussed by Lewontin (1966).

5. Sudden health epidemics, like bird flu or SARS, affect demand and could also affect supply if the affected labor is a major input into agricultural production, as it is in economies with agriculturally oriented economies and labor-intensive farming systems.

makes for a negative covariance between demand shocks and supply shocks (higher oil prices increase demand for biofuels and reduce agricultural supply). Much of the motivation for the present interest in commodity price volatility relates to this nexus. Table 1.1 summarizes the channels by which changes in technology can affect price variability as expressed in equation (5). The discussion that follows puts flesh on these bones.

1.2.1   On-Farm Agricultural Technology and Price Variability— The Supply Side

The primary role of technical change in agriculture has been to increase the supply of farm commodities, which we can think of as a decrease in the intercept of the supply equation, α_s in equation (1), reflecting a downward (or outward) shift in supply stemming from the use of new and better farming techniques or inputs.[6] As a result of innovations of this nature, global growth in supply over the second half of the twentieth century significantly outpaced growth in demand, arising mainly from growth in population and income, to the extent that since 1975 real prices of cereals have fallen by roughly 60 percent (see appendix A). These changes in turn have changed the implications for farm and nonfarm families of a given extent of price variability, an issue to which we will return later. They may have also served to change the extent of price variability as discussed next.

More variable supply of farm outputs? Clearly on-farm innovations (and other changes, some of which were not simply changes in technology, such as a change in the structure, size, and specialization of farms) have profoundly changed the supply function. As well as changing the position of the supply function, the same innovations may have entailed changes in the vulnerability of farm production to biotic and abiotic stresses, reflected as changes in $\text{Var}(\alpha_s)$. A widespread view of technological innovation is that it leads to the introduction of monocultures that—while higher yielding— are more vulnerable to output shocks from disease or other sources. Some economists have proposed that "Green Revolution" technology, for instance, increased cereal yields on average but also led to increases in relative yield variability for individual producers or in aggregate (e.g., Hazell 1989).[7] However, more recent studies have tended to find that Green Revolution technol-

---

6. Much of what we refer to here as "on-farm" technology is developed and produced "off-farm" for adoption by farmers. These on-farm innovations (including seeds, chemical fertilizers and pesticides, machinery, and methods not embodied in physical inputs) themselves reflect important changes in technology used by the agribusiness firms that supply inputs used by farmers—including everything from ballpoint pens and telephones through to satellite navigation systems, the Internet, and everything in between, which are also used by farmers. Off-farm technologies also include the technologies to process farm output, which may change the composition of and intensity of farm output used in food, fiber, feed, and fuel products.

7. Even if yield variance does not increase for individual farmers, an increased covariance of yield (or yield risk) among farmers implies an increase in variance of production and prices globally.

Table 1.1   Channels through which agricultural and other technology affects food price variability

Parameter in equation 5	Effect on price variability	Type of technological change and examples
Variability of supply of farm product: $Var(\alpha_s)$	+	*On-farm technology* • New crop varieties: e.g., Bt maize is less vulnerable to extreme pest pressure • Green Revolution technologies using modern varieties with modern inputs (fertilizer, irrigation) have less-variable yields • Integrated pest management allows better-informed decisions that reduce vulnerability to pests and diseases • Mechanization reduces vulnerability to farm labor shortages; increases vulnerability to some weather shocks • Other technology-induced changes in input mix may increase importance of inputs with more variable supply • Intensive livestock production may be more vulnerable to disease contagion but better able to contain outbreaks *Technology-induced changes in location of production* • Shift of geographic locus of production to places with different climate or other factors that influence variability
Elasticity of supply of farm product: η_s	−	*Pre-farm technology* • New technology (e.g., transportation, manufacturing) may influence variability of supply of factors to farmers *More elastic supply of farm products could result from changes in pre-farm or on-farm technology* • Increased use of more elastically supplied inputs—e.g., intensive livestock production uses feed grains • Induced reductions in relative importance of home consumption reduce the elasticity of supply of marketable surplus • Improved on-farm storage technology increases elasticity of supply to the market
Variability of demand for farm product: $Var(\alpha_d)$	+	*Changes in post-farm technology (storage, preservation, transport, handling, processing, food manufacturing, marketing)* • Improved storage and preservation technology likely to reduce variability of demand *Technology that allows markets to be better-integrated over space and time* • Can make market vulnerable to government intervention (trade barriers, "stabilization" policies) • May increase the risk of volatility from effects of invasive pests and diseases
Elasticity of demand for farm product: η_d	−	*Changes in post-farm technology could make demand for farm products more elastic* • Technology that allows markets to be better integrated over space and time makes demand more elastic *Changes in on- or off-farm technology could make demand for farm products less elastic* • Technology that contributes to increases in per capita incomes makes demand for food commodities less elastic
Covariance of supply and demand shocks: $Covar(\alpha_d, \alpha_s)$	−	*Various technologies increase the strength of the link between agriculture and oil prices and increase the covariance between demand and supply shocks affecting agriculture* • Increased use of mechanical technologies and petroleum-based inputs such as chemical fertilizers • Increased production of biofuels

Note: The symbol + indicates a positive effect of an increase in the parameter on variability of food prices, and the symbol − indicates a negative effect.

ogies reduced the relative variability of maize and wheat yields over time (e.g., as suggested by Gollin 2006).

A more subtle but still substantial influence is that changes in technology have contributed to changes to where production takes place—for instance, enabling wheat production to shift from the eastern United States into the Great Plains states and north into Canada (e.g., see Olmstead and Rhode 2002, 2010)—with implications for variability of yield and production.[8] More recently Beddow (2012) estimated that from 1899 to 2007 the centroid of corn production—essentially the geographical pivot point of US corn production—moved about 440 kilometers in a northwesterly direction. In 1899 the centroid of production was located in central Illinois; by 2007 it had migrated to southeastern Iowa.

On the other hand, some new technologies have equipped farmers to better match technology to environments, to make them potentially less vulnerable to stresses, or to be more resistant to some types of stress. The most recent revolution in crop varietal technology uses genetically modified (GM), herbicide-tolerant (HT), or insect-resistant (IR) varieties that substitute for chemical pesticides. These varieties change the yield profile of the crops in ways that have specific implications for variability of production. In particular, insect-resistant varieties avoid the severe yield losses that can arise with conventional technology in seasons with extreme pest pressure, especially in those areas where access to chemical pesticides is limited. Unlike the chemical pesticide technologies they substantially replace in many settings, yields of genetically engineered insect-resistant crop varieties are less vulnerable to insect damage because the technology does not rely on farmers anticipating pest problems and spraying in advance or observing infestations and spraying when they are under way (Qaim and Zilberman 2003; Hurley, Mitchell, and Rice 2004).[9] The insecticide is inherent in the plant.

In a similar vein, integrated pest management (IPM) technologies involve monitoring pest populations and applying pesticides at an optimal rate and time according to pest pressure, rather than according to the calendar. These and other information technologies allow farmers to apply inputs more flexibly and more precisely in ways that can reduce vulnerability to both biotic and abiotic stresses. Further, thinking more broadly about the change in paradigms associated with technological advance, we have improved methods for the early detection and management of pests and diseases using both

8. Beddow et al. (2010) document dramatic shifts in the location of agricultural production around the world during recent decades.

9. From the evidence presented by Hurley, Mitchell, and Rice (2004) it is evident that *Bt* corn technologies unambiguously reduced the relative variability of crop yields. However, the effects on the variability of corn supply could be ambiguous, depending on the fee charged for the use of the *Bt* technology. Qaim and Zilberman (2003) reported significant reduction in pest damage and higher average yield for *Bt* cotton in India; their results would also appear to imply reduced variance of yields.

current technology on farms and induced adaptive innovation as private and public research institutions respond to information about pest and disease threats.

More elastic supply of farm outputs? Second, technical change on farms may have resulted in changes in the elasticity of supply of agricultural outputs and the food, feed, fuel, and fiber products derived from agricultural outputs. One way this can happen is if new technologies emphasize the use of inputs that are relatively elastically supplied, such as agricultural chemicals, energy inputs, seed, or agricultural machinery (or, more precisely, the services from them), rather than inputs that are comparatively inelastically supplied, such as land and water, and in some cases, labor (see, for example, Schultz 1951). If relatively elastically supplied inputs represent an increased share of the cost of production, then the elasticity of supply will be greater (e.g., see Muth 1964); likewise, supply will be made more elastic if an innovation allows greater substitutability among inputs.

In the US poultry and hog industries, for instance, the introduction of intensive production systems made supply comparatively elastic. The primary inputs are feed grains and oilseeds, which are highly elastically supplied to each of these industries; there are not really any constrained specialized factors of production, and the producing units are replicable at efficient size such that the industry is characterized by constant returns to scale. In the richer countries at least, this industrial structure replaced an industry based on smaller, less-specialized operations, in which hogs and poultry were often raised as sidelines on dairy and grain-producing farms. As documented by Key and McBride (2007) and MacDonald and McBride (2009), livestock agriculture in the United States has undergone a series of striking transformations that affected the structure of the industry and the nature of supply response. Production has become more specialized, such that nowadays farms usually confine and feed a single species of animal, often with feed that has been purchased rather than grown on site, and they typically specialize in a specific stage of production. The scale of operations has increased, and economies of scale have contributed along with technological innovations to rapid growth of productivity. Contracting over production and the use of hired labor have both grown in importance.[10] Similar innovations have taken place in many other countries and are underway in others. These innovations that have tended to make livestock supply in these markets more elastic (at least over the medium to long run), might at the same time have made production more (or less) vulnerable to shocks such as

10. These technical changes have coincided with the move toward the pervasive use of contract farming and vertically integrated structures in most rich-country livestock supply chains. These institutional and structural developments may have muted short-run quantity responses to changes in market prices for farm commodities because of fixities in these complex supply systems, while enabling greater medium- to long-run response to price changes.

disease epidemics that may be spread more rapidly within closely confined systems, but they might also be easier in some cases to prevent, detect, and contain for similar reasons and given the use of better hygiene and access to improved veterinary medicines and practices.

Another way in which changes in technology on farms may have affected the elasticity of supply to the market is by changing the cost of on-farm storage or by causing (through effects on incomes, the extent of specialization, or other variables) changes in the importance of farm-household consumption as a share of the total use of farm output. The elasticity of supply of marketable surplus is an inverse-share-weighted average of the elasticity of farm production response with respect to price and the (absolute) elasticity of farm-household consumption response to price, such that changes in technology that reduce the relative importance of farm-household consumption will tend to reduce the elasticity of supply to the market.

In principle, changes in technology in the agribusiness sector that supplies inputs used by farmers might affect the variability in supply of key inputs, or the elasticity of supply of key inputs, to an extent that either the elasticity of farm output supply or the variability of farm output supply would be affected. For example, the rise of genetically engineered proprietary seed technologies represents an instance where a change in the technology of crop varieties (i.e., genetic engineering) has given rise to a substantial change in the conditions of input supply to the industry. Seed costs now represent a significant share (say, 10 percent) of total costs in North American corn, cotton, canola, and soybean production (e.g., see Alston, Gray, and Bolek 2012), with the technology supplied by a relatively concentrated sector with monopoly privileges. These developments in the conditions of seed supply might have implications for variability in supply in addition to those implied by the seed technology itself given their important consequences for the cost shares of different categories of inputs and the process by which input prices are determined.

1.2.2   Postfarm Agricultural Technology and Price Variability

Changes in technology in the postfarm agribusiness sector might change the elasticity of demand or the variability of demand, or both, as well as contributing to the growth of demand for farm outputs. The characteristics of demand for the farm product might also be affected by *on-farm* changes in technology that have had profound effects on incomes of the poor, which would be expected in turn to contribute to increases in demand for most farm products (though with a shift in the balance toward livestock products), and to make demands for farm commodities generally less elastic, and perhaps less variable.

The main factors driving growth in demand for farm products have been changes in the share and structure of on- versus off-farm consumption (associated with increases in farm size and specialization, part-time farming and urbanization), and increases in population and per capita incomes. The same factors have influenced the structure of demand. As per capita incomes rise, a greater share of food is consumed away from home or in more-processed and more-convenient forms for within-home consumption (e.g., Senauer, Asp, and Kinsey 1991). This reduces the farm component of retail food costs, thus muting the food price effects of fluctuations in farm-level commodity prices. All of these factors have been driven to some extent by on-farm innovations, which made food much cheaper while increasing farm incomes and freeing up labor, hitherto used on farms, for other pursuits. Complementary changes in technology off the farm have included improved technology for processing, storing, preserving, and handling food products, which, from the farmers' perspective, are also manifest as increases in demand.

Transportation and storage (notably refrigeration) technologies that increased demand for farm commodities also served to integrate markets over space and time.[11] Our simple market model abstracts from these relationships, but we can easily imagine what would happen if we expanded it from one country to two countries. In a two-country model, if we introduce trade (as a result of improved technology, increasing effective price transmission) we will make the effective demand (and supply) for food commodities facing each country more elastic, and we will make the prices in each country less variable, compared with the autarky prices, unless the shocks that are the sources of variability are perfectly correlated between the two countries. From this perspective, technology that improves transportation, facilitating interregional and international trade, would be expected to serve to reduce price variability unless it somehow increases the correlation of shocks between countries.[12]

While freer international trade in commodities does allow arbitrage to play its role in buffering prices from supply or demand shocks, it also facilitates the international movement of pests and diseases that could contribute to increases in volatility—for instance, the losses already experienced from the citrus greening disease *Huanglongbing* (known as HGB, and spread by the Asian citrus psyllid), which is already a serious problem in Brazil and now threatens the US citrus industry. Of course, the Columbian Exchange was necessary to create the possibility of "antigains" from trade in citrus

11. Information technologies that make for more efficient markets, including futures and options markets as well as spot markets, should play a complementary role in facilitating markets to better anticipate and absorb or accommodate shocks, and in enabling individuals to cope better generally with variability.

12. However, closer market integration means prices of individual inputs and outputs are more closely correlated spatially and this may have contributed to an increased covariance in prices of outputs both of the same crops among places and across crops. In turn this would add to the variance of production and prices.

and other crops by North America today, so the counterfactual is not easy to make sensible, but the point is that trade has sometimes made food prices both less volatile in the normal short-run sense and potentially more volatile in a longer-run sense because of the concomitant increases in the risk of losses from exotic pests and diseases.[13]

A more subtle implication is introduced when we consider the role of government. While international and interregional trade enabled by innovations in product preservation and transport technologies may have reduced on- and off-farm price variability ceteris paribus, it also creates new possibilities for government intervention in trade. Government intervention can make price variability worse, and it can do so in ways that are particularly damaging (such as active interventions in times of price spikes—e.g., see Martin and Anderson [2012]). The combined effect of trade and government could conceivably make volatility worse compared with autarky, an outcome that would not have happened without the creation of trade facilitated by technology. A similar argument applies in the context of improved storage technologies, which enable prices and consumption to be smoothed over time, and thereby generate net social benefits. But the development of storage technologies also enabled governments to introduce buffer stock schemes, which have historically proven to be very expensive policies. The Australian wool industry fiasco in the late 1980s is a telling example. Massy (2011) estimated that the collapse of the wool reserve price scheme in 1991 imposed social costs worth at least AU $12 billion at today's prices, more than five times the recent annual gross value of Australian wool production. Of course, the main issue here is not the storage or transport technology itself; rather, it is the unhappy decisions made by governments. But technology is involved and conditions the possibilities for damaging or desirable government policies.

Much could be said about technologies for food processing and preservation, but we will restrict attention here to fermentation technology (see Zilberman and Kim 2011). Fermentation has served as a means of converting perishable food products—such as fruit, grain, milk, and vegetables—into less perishable, more palatable, and safer forms—such as wine, beer, cheese, yogurt, sauerkraut, and kimchi among others. It also has enabled the transformation of food commodities into biofuels products. The net implications of these manifold changes are difficult to decipher, but of great immediate interest is the consequential linking of food commodity markets to fossil fuel and thus the broader economy in new ways that surely will have implications for food price volatility.

---

13. The widespread exchange of animals, plants, culture, human populations, communicable disease, and ideas between the American and Afro-Eurasian hemispheres following the voyage to the Americas by Christopher Columbus in 1492 is known as the "Columbian Exchange."

1.3   Effects of Technology on the Implications of Price Variability

As noted, the most important effects of changes in technology are through their cumulative effects on reducing the expected value of prices, rather than their impacts on price variability. By increasing real incomes through higher producer incomes at any given price and lower costs of living, and by inducing and enabling some people to leave production agriculture, technology changes the welfare implications of agricultural variability. A simple heuristic model can be used to illustrate how this works.

1.3.1   Elements of Benefits and Determinants of Beneficiaries

Productivity-enhancing changes in technology for the production of a staple crop give rise to benefits (B_i), accruing to the ith household, approximately equal to

$$(7) \qquad B_i = -P_i C_i \Delta \ln P_i + (k_i + \Delta \ln P_i) P_i Q_i,$$

where P_i is the price paid by the household for its consumption, C_i (and received for its production, Q_i) of the crop, and k_i is its household-specific proportional cost reduction associated with the improvements in technology giving rise to the proportional price change, $\Delta \ln P_i < 0$. The first element of the equation represents the consumer benefit. Households that consume but do not produce the crop obtain a benefit equal to the reduction in their cost of consumption—a real income effect of the research-induced price fall. The second element represents the producer benefit. Households that produce but do not consume the crop obtain a gain equal to the difference between their proportional cost reduction and the proportional fall in price ($k_i + \Delta \ln P_i$) times the value of their production.

More generally, households that both produce and consume the good receive a net gain equal to the sum of two gains, as shown in the following version of the above equation:

$$(7') \qquad B_i = k_i P_i Q_i - (P_i C_i - P_i Q_i) \Delta \ln P_i.$$

The first term in equation ($7'$) is the household's cost saving on production (their proportional cost saving times their value of production). The second is their gain from the reduction in their *net* costs of food purchases (the difference between their expenditure on consumption and the value of their production) resulting from the fall in price. The size of the first term in equation ($7'$) will depend on the nature, as well as the size, of the shift in technology (Martin and Alston 1997). For food deficit households, the fall in price means a benefit; for food surplus households, it means a loss. Gainers include all households who produce less of the good than they consume, regardless of whether they adopt the new technology or not. Potential losers are those surplus households (i.e., who produce more than they consume) that are not able to achieve a per unit cost reduction equal to the market-wide reduction in price associated with the technology. Among these, in this analysis, those surplus households that are unable to adopt the technology are the only sure net losers. Some of these households might be induced to leave agriculture and find employment elsewhere.[14]

The above analysis might be interpreted as a medium-term or partial analysis. A more general or longer-run analysis could take more explicit account of linkages with the broader economy and this might change the story. Gardner (2002, 328–333) presented evidence that, over a thirty-year period 1960 to 1990, changes in average county-level US farm household incomes were not related to changes in agricultural productivity (or any other agriculture-specific variable). The general idea is that, given enough time for adjustments of employment to take place, it is expected that incomes of farm households will be determined by their education, skills, and other endowments and economy-wide prices of factors, notably the opportunity cost of household farm labor. In the US example, agriculture is now such a small share of the total economy that the economy-wide factor prices can be taken as exogenous (with the possible exception of agricultural land). In less-developed countries, events in agriculture may change the economy-wide prices of factors as well, but the general point remains relevant: linkages with the rest of the economy through the integration of labor and capital markets (e.g., through changes in occupational choice, migration to the cities, and remittances) mean that events in agriculture are not the sole determinants of farm household incomes.

1.3.2 Effects of a Change in Technology on the Distribution of Household Incomes

In what follows we have in mind a model in which changes in agricultural technology induce changes in the distribution of income among house-holds through a multitude of direct and indirect effects and the optimizing responses of the households. These optimizing responses include the choice of whether to adopt the technologies in question and how best to respond to the consequences of others having adopted the technologies. The consequences are reflected both in the income distribution of the households—incomes of all producers are affected regardless of whether they adopt the new technology—and in the purchasing power of that income, since the technological innovations change the consumer cost of food.

Consider the effects of a productivity-enhancing innovation in the pro-

14. The calculations in equations (7) and (7′) refer to what de Janvry and Sadoulet (2002) termed the "direct" welfare effects of agricultural innovation. The first term in equation (7′) will capture the aggregate welfare impacts of the change except where it changes the volumes of trade passing over existing distortions (Martin and Alston 1994) while induced changes in prices and general equilibrium adjustments influence the distribution of the resulting benefits. See also Byerlee (2000).

duction of staple crops. We can write a reduced-form equation for the "full income" accruing to the ith farm household in the population of interest as:[15]

$$(8) \qquad Y_i(\tau) = Y(H_i, P, W \mid \tau),$$

where τ is an index of the *available* technology, H_i is a vector of characteristics of the household including its endowments of physical as well as human assets, P is a vector of prices of inputs and outputs, and W is a vector of environmental factors influencing production, including abiotic factors like weather and biotic factors such as pests and diseases. The elements of P and W are random variables, some of which may be contingent on the technology. The particular ex post outcome reflects the household's optimizing choices given the available technology and its assets and its expectations of prices and environmental factors, as well as the actual outcomes for prices and environmental factors.

Hence the household faces an ex ante probability distribution of income, Y_i, that is conditional on the state of available technology, regardless of whether the household does or does not adopt a new technology when it becomes available. Using equation (8) we can consider the probability distribution of income for the ith farm household in two states: under a baseline technology set, τ_0 (e.g., traditional grain varieties and related technologies as in 1962), and under an alternative technology set, τ_1 (e.g., modern high-yielding grain varieties and related technologies and other innovations introduced over the subsequent fifty years, as they apply in 2012). The new technology regime may imply a larger or smaller expected value of income for a particular farmer; likewise, the variance of income may be larger or smaller depending on whether the farmer is a technology adopter, among other things.

Even if agricultural technology has no direct effect on household incomes, it affects food security or poverty through its effects on the price of food. Figure 1.1 compares two stylized distributions of ex post household income across households, conditional on the state of technology, and assuming all realized values of random environmental variables and prices are at their expected values for each technology scenario. In each case the income distribution reflects a particular random draw of exogenous factors held constant between the scenarios and the resulting ex post prices, which differ between the scenarios.

The ex post income distribution across households, given technology τ_0, is denoted Y_0^e. Associated with this distribution, and defined by the corresponding prices is a "poverty line," reflecting the cost of a minimal quantity of food (or food calories) and other necessities, drawn at L_0^e. We wish to

---

15. Here, "full income" refers to total consumption by the household, including market goods and services, home-produced goods and services, and leisure, plus net savings. It reflects, as an accounting identity, endowment income plus variable profits—the total value of production minus costs of variable inputs (including household labor).

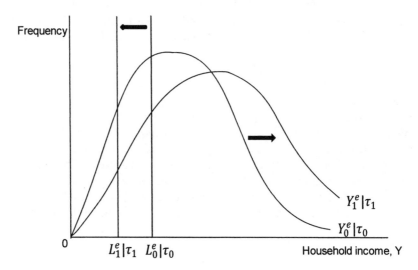

Fig. 1.1   Agricultural technology and household income distributions

compare this outcome with its counterpart under the alternative technology scenario, τ_1, given the same draw of the random environmental factors. Under the new technology, food prices are lower and the poverty line is shifted to L_1^e, reducing the fraction of the population living in poverty for a given income distribution. This can be a big effect if we have a big change in the price of food (say, a 50 percent increase from the present price if the past thirty-five years of research-induced productivity gains were eliminated—see appendix A), even with no direct changes in household incomes. In addition, if the distribution of income shifts to the right from, say, Y_0^e to Y_1^e as a result of shifting from technology regime τ_0 to τ_1, then the fraction of the population living in poverty is further reduced.[16]

1.3.3   Consequences of Income Effects of Technology for Implications of Variability

Richer people are affected less by a given shock to prices of staple grains. When the distribution of incomes has shifted substantially to the right, fewer people will suffer severe consequences from a given price shock. This idea is illustrated in figure 1.2, which shows the distribution of household income under two alternative technologies, Y_0^e and Y_1^e under τ_0 and τ_1, with the corresponding poverty lines, L_0^e and L_1^e—all conditional on a particular draw

16. Even though some farmers will be made worse off (if, for instance, they are surplus producers and cannot adopt the new technology), the distribution generally shifts to the right, as drawn, reflecting the general improvement in incomes for households although some have shifted to the left within the distribution.

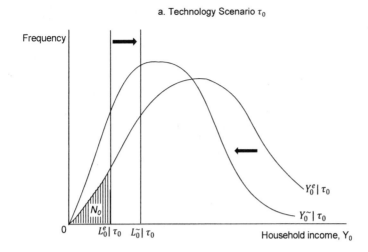

a. Technology Scenario τ_0

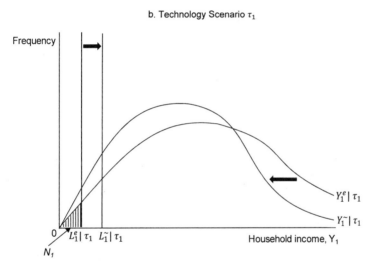

b. Technology Scenario τ_1

Fig. 1.2   **Consequences of a negative shock under alternative technology scenarios**

of exogenous environmental factors that gives rise to particular price outcomes, P_0^e and P_1^e. The corresponding numbers of people in poverty are indicated by the shaded areas, N_0 and N_1, with $N_0 > N_1$.

Now, suppose we have a negative environmental shock to the agricultural economy, such as a widespread drought, which under either technology scenario shifts the distribution of income to the left, to $Y_0^\sim$ and $Y_1^\sim$, and shifts the poverty line to the right, to $L_0^\sim$ and $L_1^\sim$. Intuitively, the consequences are expected to be much smaller under technology τ_1 because (a) a smaller number of people were already poor, (b) staple food commodities represent a smaller share of incomes generally such that the proportion of the population driven into poverty is smaller under technology τ_1, and (c) farmers represent a smaller share of the population such that the direct effects on farm incomes from the shock are less important for the overall picture.

In section 1.5 of this chapter, we explore these aspects using a computable general equilibrium model. Before doing that, in section 1.4 we consider recent past agricultural innovations, their consequences for technologies and productivity, and their implications for variability. In this work, we take the view that the relevant concern is not with day-to-day price variability, but some other form of variability that is more important for human outcomes, such as year-to-year, multiyear or secular price shifts representing substantial changes in the odds of serious food poverty.

1.4   Agricultural Technology: Past Accomplishments and Consequences

In this section we speculate about the implications for variability stemming from some particular past changes in agricultural technology. We begin with an overview of changes in the structure of agriculture before turning to trends in productivity and prices and what they might imply for poverty and vulnerability.

1.4.1   Changes in the Number of Farmers

A major consequence of technological change has been to reduce the total amount of labor employed in farming and people living on farms. In the United States, the total farm population peaked at 32.5 million people, 31.9 percent of the total US population in 1916. Since then the US population has continued to grow while the farm population declined to 2.9 million in 2006, just one percent of the total population of 299.4 million (Alston, Andersen, James, and Pardey 2010). With less than 1 percent of Americans now on farms, the consequences of farm price variability are very different than when a third of the population was on farms, one hundred years ago. Now, 99 percent of Americans are affected only as consumers, and most of them are rich enough to be relatively unconcerned by relatively large fluctuations in prices of comparatively cheap staple foods. This effect of changes in farming technology on the implications of price variability, through reducing the number of farmers while making food generally much more affordable, is comparatively significant. This transformation of agriculture in the United States, reflecting technological change in the rest of the economy pulling labor off farms as well as on-farm labor-saving innovations, was mirrored in other higher-income countries. In many low-income countries this transformation is still in progress, and often still in its early stages, but it is well advanced in middle-income countries such as Brazil and China.

Currently, the majority of the world's poor are rural. In many parts of the world farmers and consumers of staple crops are relatively insulated from world markets—price transmission is at best partial (see, for example, Minot 2011)—and the effects on world trading prices resulting from changes in agricultural technology elsewhere have limited effects on poverty for poor producers and consumers in the hinterland where the economic (and physical) distance from reasonably sized markets is high. Over the coming decades, an increasing proportion of the world's poor will be found in cities in Asia and Africa, and the numbers of rural poor will shrink in relative if not absolute terms. For the urban poor, unless governments intervene to prevent it, price transmission is relatively good. In addition, changes in technology and improvements in infrastructure will enhance the effectiveness of price transmission to those places that are relatively insulated at present.

Given an improvement in the effectiveness of price transmission to the poor and with an increasing proportion of the poor not being engaged directly in farm production, the predominant way in which agricultural innovations will reduce poverty in the long run will be through shifting the poverty line in a secular fashion by making food generally more affordable. At the same time, the poor will be more exposed to the effects of shorter-term changes in world market prices, transitory shifts of the poverty line.

1.4.2   Longer-Term Changes in Prices and Productivity

The World Bank (2012, 1) noted that "In 2011 international food prices spiked for the second time in three years, igniting concerns about a repeat of the 2008 food price crisis and its consequences for the poor." These recent events represent a reversal of the longer-term trends. Over the past fifty years and longer, the supply of food commodities has grown faster than the demand, in spite of increasing population and per capita incomes. Consequently, the real (inflation-adjusted) prices of food commodities have generally trended down. We use US commodity price indexes as indicators of world market prices. Table 1.2 includes measures of rates of change in real and nominal prices of maize, wheat, and rice over the entire period 1950–2010 and several subperiods.[17] Figure 1.3 plots the same prices in real and nominal terms, in levels and logarithms. The period since World War II includes three distinct subperiods. First, over the twenty years between 1950 and 1970, deflated prices for rice and maize declined relatively slowly while wheat prices declined fairly rapidly. Next, following the price spike of the early 1970s, over the years 1975 to 1990, prices for all three grains declined relatively rapidly and more or less in unison. Finally, over the years 1990 to 2011, prices increased for all three commodities, especially toward the

17. The measures in this table are averages of annual percentage changes, and therefore sensitive to end-points. Trend growth rates imply slightly different patterns.

Table 1.2   Average annual percentage changes in US commodity prices, 1950–2011

	Commodity			Commodity		
Period	Maize	Wheat	Rice	Maize	Wheat	Rice
	(average annual percentage change			(trend growth rate, percent per year)		
Nominal prices						
1950–2011	2.25	2.15	1.59	1.73	1.79	1.26
				(8.78)	(8.86)	(6.21)
1950–1970	–0.67	–2.04	0.08	–1.53	–2.65	–0.07
				(–3.71)	(–7.99)	(–0.36)
1975–2005	–0.87	–0.20	–0.29	–0.49	0.07	–0.90
				(–1.48)	(0.22)	(–1.82)
1975–1990	–0.72	–2.05	–1.47	–0.61	–0.19	–2.68
				(–0.61)	(–0.19)	(–2.06)
1990–2011	4.62	4.99	3.32	2.78	3.23	3.03
				(3.07)	(3.98)	(2.99)
2000–2011	10.70	9.70	7.86	9.75	8.71	11.27
				(6.37)	(6.20)	(6.35)
Deflated prices						
1950–2011	–1.63	–1.73	–2.29	–2.46	–2.40	–2.94
				(–15.85)	(–15.00)	(–14.58)
1950–1970	–2.67	–4.04	–1.92	–3.10	–4.22	–1.64
				(–8.96)	(–11.30)	(–8.55)
1975–2005	–4.32	–4.07	–4.94	–3.61	–3.04	–4.01
				(–11.41)	(–9.09)	(–7.95)
1975–1990	–5.89	–7.22	–6.64	–5.44	–5.02	–7.51
				(–6.66)	(–6.11)	(–6.56)
1990–2011	1.19	1.56	–0.10	–0.48	–0.03	–0.23
				(–0.65)	(–0.04)	(–0.27)
2000–2011	5.92	4.92	3.08	4.76	3.71	6.27
				(3.41)	(2.86)	(3.76)

Notes: Values in parentheses are *t*-statistics. Deflated prices were computed by deflating nominal commodity prices by the Consumer Price Index.

end of that period. This reflected a generally slowing rate of price decline throughout the period prior to the price spike in 2008—in fact, essentially from 2000 forward, prices increased in real terms.

These three crops provide about two-thirds of all energy in human diets (Cassman 1999). Data from the Food and Agriculture Organization of the United Nations (FAO 2013) for 2009 (Food Balance Sheets) show a global total food supply of 2,831 kcal/capita/day of which 43 percent was in the form of wheat, rice, and maize, but this does not include the contribution of feed grains to dietary energy through livestock. The direct contribution of these three crops to dietary energy stays reasonably constant in absolute terms but declines in proportional terms as incomes grow, total food con-

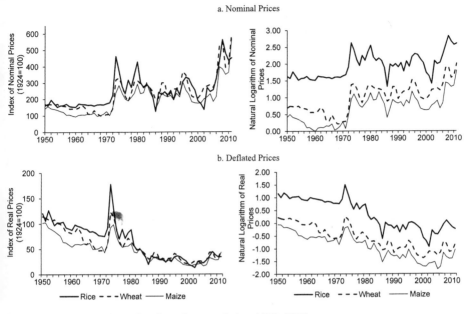

Fig. 1.3   US prices of maize, wheat, and rice, 1950–2011

Note: Nominal prices were deflated using the US Consumer Price Index.

sumption increases, and the share from livestock increases. For the "least-developed countries" group the total food supply for 2009 was 2,298 kcal/capita/day, of which 47 percent was from wheat, rice, and maize, and for India and China the shares were 52 percent and 47 percent, respectively. For high-income countries (such as the United States or the European Union) total caloric consumption was greater (3,688 or 3,456 kcal/capita/day) and the share of calories *directly* in the form in the form of wheat, rice, and maize was smaller (more like 25 percent), but the share of calories from grain-fed livestock is much larger. In 1961 global per capita energy consumption was lower (2,189 kcal/capita/day), but the share from cereals at 41 percent was similar to that in 2009.

Growth in agricultural productivity, fueled by investments in agricultural research and development (R&D), has been a primary contributor to the long-run trend of declining food commodity prices and the slowdown in the decline of real commodity prices since 1990, itself a dual measure of productivity growth, reflected a slowdown in the rate of growth of crop production and yields, among other things. Global annual average rates of crop yield growth for maize, rice, wheat, and cereals are reported in table 1.3, which includes separate estimates for various regions and for high-, middle-, and low-income countries, as well as for the world as a whole, for

Table 1.3   Global and regional yield growth rates for selected crops, 1961–2010

	Maize		Wheat		Rice, paddy	
Group	1961–1990	1990–2010	1961–1990	1990–2010	1961–1990	1990–2010
			percent per year			
World	2.33	1.82	2.73	1.03	2.14	1.09
Geographical regions						
North America	2.19	1.75	1.38	0.98	1.22	1.33
Western Europe	3.73	1.32	3.21	0.83	0.62	0.70
Eastern Europe	2.54	1.93	3.19	0.18	0.51	3.49
Asia & Pacific (excl. China)	1.96	2.88	2.96	1.39	1.83	1.49
China	4.39	0.81	5.76	2.05	3.06	0.64
Latin America & Caribbean	2.01	3.22	1.67	1.52	1.39	3.10
Sub-Saharan Africa	1.30	1.70	2.88	1.84	0.83	1.03
Income class						
High income	2.24	1.68	2.02	0.68	1.03	0.79
Upper middle (excl. China)	1.85	3.04	2.22	1.19	0.99	2.23
China	4.39	0.81	5.76	2.05	3.06	0.64
Lower middle income	1.79	3.06	3.27	1.42	2.36	1.36
Low income	1.19	0.36	2.08	2.02	1.50	2.18

Source: Pardey, Alston, and Chan-Kang (2013).

two subperiods: 1961 to 1990 and 1990 to 2010. In both high- and middle-income countries—collectively accounting for between 78.8 and 99.4 percent of global production of these crops in 2007—average annual rates of yield growth for cereals were lower in 1990 to 2010 than in 1961 to 1990. The growth of wheat yields slowed the most and, for the high-income countries as a group, wheat yields barely changed over 1990 to 2010. Global maize yields grew at an average rate of 1.82 percent per year during 1990 to 2010 compared with 2.33 percent per year for 1961 to 1990. Likewise, rice yields grew at 1.03 percent per year during 1990 to 2010, less than half their average growth rate for 1960 to 1990.

1.4.3   Global Crop Yield Variability, 1960 to 2010

Green Revolution varieties of wheat and rice (and other crops) combined with complementary fertilizer and irrigation technologies contributed to very significant growth of grain yields in the latter part of the twentieth century. Did they also contribute to greater variability of yields, production, and prices? And what is the appropriate measure of variability in this context? Competing views have been published on this question.[18] The earlier studies tended to find an increase in variability associated with the adoption of modern varieties. However, more-recent studies have reported that the predominant effect has been to reduce variability of yields and production, as documented in detail by Gollin (2006). Gollin (2006) combined country-level data on the diffusion of modern varieties (MVs) of wheat and maize with corresponding data on aggregate production and yields over the period 1960 to 2000. Using these data he depicted changes in national-level yield variability for wheat and maize across developing countries, and related these changes to the diffusion of MVs.[19] He found "the outcomes strongly suggest that, over the past 40 years, there has actually been a *decline* in the relative variability of grain yields—that is, the absolute magnitude of deviations from the yield trend—for both wheat and maize in developing countries. This reduction in variability is statistically associated with the spread of MVs, even after controlling for expanded use of irrigation and other inputs." (Gollin [2006], 1, emphasis in original).

In our broader context, given an interest in price variability, we are interested in whether changes in technology affected variability of yield per unit area and production as they affect prices, including yield and production in high- and middle-income countries as well as in the low-income countries emphasized by Gollin (2006). A first step toward answering that question is to ask whether yield variability has changed. Table 1.4 provides some more up-to-date measures of variability corresponding to those reported by Gollin (2006), based on data from FAO (2012).[20] The measures in table 1.4 are ten-year moving variances of logarithms of global total annual production and average yields (computed as total annual production divided by total harvested area), whereas Gollin (2006) computed ten-year moving coefficients of variation, but they are otherwise similar in concept. The last two columns of the table include the coefficient from regression of this measure of variability against a linear time trend, and the corresponding *t*-statistic.

As can be seen in table 1.4, variability of global production and average yields trended down over the half century ending in 2010 (the trend coefficients are all negative numbers, and all statistically significantly different from zero). The decade-by-decade figures in the table also tend to

18. For example, see Hazell (1989); Anderson and Hazell (1989); Singh and Byerlee (1990); Naylor, Falcon, and Zavaleta (1997); Gollin (2006); and Hazell (2010).
19. Gollin (2006) presented various measures of variability, including ten-year moving coefficients of variation, but his main results rest on measured changes over time in the relative variability of yields calculated as the change in the absolute deviation of yields relative to a trend value derived using a Hodrick-Prescott filter.
20. Appendix B contains more detailed results, by crop and region of production. It also includes plots of first differences of logarithms of production, yield, and prices, which provides an alternative, visual indication of the changes in variability over time.

Table 1.4   Variability of global production and average crop yields, 1961–2010

	10-year moving variance, logarithms, 10 years ending					Trend regression	
	1970	1980	1990	2000	2010	coefficient	t-stat
Production							
Wheat	0.0173	0.0101	0.0055	0.0022	0.0047	−0.0003	−10.99
Maize	0.0128	0.0134	0.0107	0.0081	0.0152	−0.0002	−4.49
Rice	0.0140	0.0071	0.0057	0.0032	0.0044	−0.0002	−10.41
Cereals	0.0116	0.0065	0.0035	0.0019	0.0056	−0.0002	−8.67
Yield							
Wheat	0.0121	0.0053	0.0078	0.0020	0.0023	−0.0003	−10.18
Maize	0.0074	0.0081	0.0059	0.0055	0.0040	−0.0002	−7.08
Rice	0.0057	0.0032	0.0043	0.0012	0.0020	−0.0001	−4.03
Cereals	0.0081	0.0042	0.0037	0.0029	0.0032	−0.0001	−9.67

Notes: Entries are ten-year moving variances of logarithms of global total production or logarithms of yield (total production divided by total harvested area), with the ten years ending on the year shown in the column heading. The time-trend coefficient is from the regression of the annual observations of the ten-year moving variance against a linear time trend, and the t-stat is for the test of the null hypothesis that the coefficient is zero.

decline with time, although the variability of production increased (roughly doubling) for every crop between 2000 and 2010. Variability of yield also increased in the last decade in table 1.4 for wheat, rice, and cereals as a group (though not for maize), but generally by a smaller proportion than the corresponding increase in variability of production.

The global aggregate figures mask some interesting regional variation in these measures. Figure 1.4 graphs the annual observations of the ten-year moving variances for the global measure of production (panel a) and yields (panel b), along with counterpart observations for the low-income countries as a group (panels c and d). In the world as a whole, variability of both production and yields trended down, but in the low-income countries the converse was true, especially since 1990: the measures of variability of production increased four- to fivefold between the mid-1990s and 2010. The reasons for this dichotomy between patterns in the higher- versus low-income countries remain uncertain, but a significant factor might have been slower growth of the means of yield and production in the low-income countries. The pattern everywhere changed toward the end of the series. The variability of global production of cereals increased after 2007 (panel a) but the variability of yields did not increase nearly as much (see panel b). The difference probably reflects supply response to commodity prices that became more variable in the same period.

We computed ten-year moving variances of the real and nominal prices of maize, rice, and wheat as counterparts to the measures of variability of yield and production thus discussed, and these are plotted in figure 1.5 and

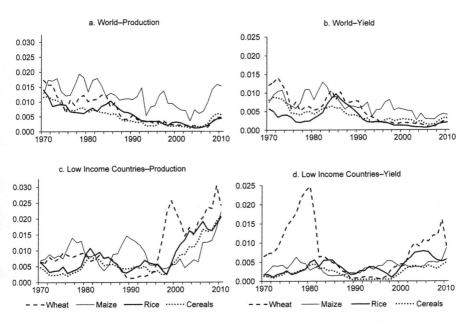

Fig. 1.4   **Variability of grain production and yield, ten-year moving variances of logarithms, 1970–2010**

Note: See table 1.3 and associated text for details.

summarized in table 1.5. As can be seen in figure 1.5, in both nominal and real terms, prices were comparatively stable through the 1950s and 1960s. The pattern changed in the 1970s, reflecting the price spike and its aftermath. Thereafter the patterns for wheat and maize are quite similar but rice is more distinct, with generally higher variability and greater variation in variability over time. Variability of deflated prices was lower in the 1990s than in the 1980s for all three grains but then increased in the early twenty-first century—especially for rice. The changes in price variability—especially in the mid-1970s and in the mid to late years of the first decade of the twenty-first century—do not appear to be clearly associated with changes in technology; they are more likely linked to other market phenomena that have been widely documented and discussed (see, for example, Wright 2011).

Of course, these prices of grain commodities are different from final consumer prices of food that may or may not include grain as an ingredient. Using data from FAO (2013) we computed the country-specific variances of the logarithms of annual average food Consumer Price Indexes (CPI) for the ten-year period of 2001 to 2010 (conceptually comparable to the variances of logarithms of annual average commodity prices in table 1.5, in the column labeled 2010). If we include only the variances for the 172 countries for which we have data for every year, the mean of the logarithmic variances across countries is 0.12, but the median is 0.025 (the distribution

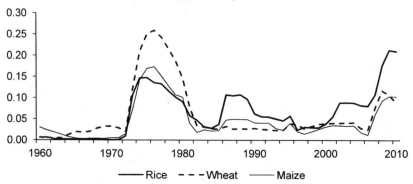

a. 10-Year Moving Variance of Logarithms of Nominal Prices
(US Dollars)

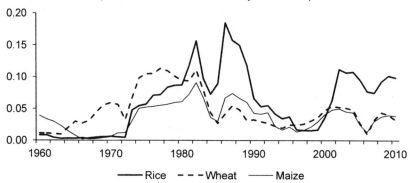

b. 10-Year Moving Variance of Logarithms of Real Prices
(Nominal US Dollars Deflated by the US CPI)

Fig. 1.5   Variability of prices of maize, wheat, and rice, 1951–2010

Source: These are based on updated versions of prices reported by Alston, Beddow, and Pardey (2009).

Note: The ten-year moving variance is plotted against the last year of the corresponding ten-year period, such that a shock in 1971 is reflected in the measures for 1971 through 1980.

is very skewed to the left, and for 75 percent of the countries the variance is less than 0.06); this remains true if we exclude a few extreme outliers from either end of the distribution. The corresponding variances of logarithms of international (US) prices of rice, wheat, and maize in table 1.5 are 0.21, 0.09, and 0.10, somewhat larger generally than the counterparts for food CPIs. We would expect domestic prices to be less variable than international prices for grains, depending on country-specific price transmission relationships, and we would expect food prices to be less variable than grain prices. Our general observations are consistent with this expectation. However, the variability of CPIs varies tremendously among countries and, while the pat-

Table 1.5   **Variability of prices of rice, maize, and wheat, 1951–2010**

Crop	Ten-year moving variance of logarithms of prices, 10 years ending						Time-trend coefficient (t-values in italics)	
	1960	1970	1980	1990	2000	2010	1960–2010	1980–2010
	A. Nominal values							
Rice	0.0061	0.0005	0.0906	0.0620	0.0380	0.2095	0.0019	0.0026
							4.22	*3.00*
Wheat	0.0062	0.0327	0.1456	0.0277	0.0386	0.0875	−0.0002	0.0007
							−0.23	*1.09*
Maize	0.0302	0.0052	0.1010	0.0409	0.0312	0.1027	0.0003	0.0006
							0.61	*1.20*
	B. Deflated values							
Rice	0.0082	0.0064	0.0874	0.0664	0.0361	0.0988	0.0015	−0.0013
							3.76	*−1.48*
Wheat	0.0111	0.0595	0.0946	0.0328	0.0475	0.0325	−0.0003	−0.0013
							−0.88	*−3.11*
Maize	0.0392	0.0063	0.0612	0.0431	0.0409	0.0387	0.0003	−0.0012
							1.24	*−3.55*

Notes: Entries are ten-year moving variances of logarithms of prices, with the ten years ending on the year shown in the column heading. The time-trend coefficient is from the regression of the annual observations of the ten-year moving variance against a linear time trend, and the t-value is for the test of the null hypothesis that the coefficient is zero.

terns of variation among the country-specific measures of variability seem generally plausible and consistent with expectations (e.g., very low for Japan and Switzerland), to say anything more specific would require a substantial dedicated research effort.

1.5   Implications of Alternative Productivity Paths

As discussed above, recent evidence indicates that agricultural productivity growth rates have slowed significantly in many (especially rich) countries over the past twenty years or so (e.g., see Alston, Beddow, and Pardey 2009, 2010, Alston, Babcock, and Pardey 2010), especially in the higher-income countries. In addition, rates of growth in investment in productivity-enhancing agricultural R&D that slowed earlier have turned negative in many (especially high-income) countries, suggesting a worsening of the agricultural productivity slowdown in years to come, given the long R&D lags (e.g., see Pardey and Alston 2010; Pardey, Alston, and Chan-Kang 2013). Both the slowdown in agricultural productivity patterns generally and the divergent patterns among countries in rates of research investments and productivity will have implications for future paths of agricultural prices, price variability, and consequences of variability. These outcomes might be moderated by a restoration of research investments and revitalization of productivity growth. To explore these possibilities we conducted simulations using a computable general equilibrium framework.

1.5.1   The Model and the Simulations

Our analysis uses a model and approach developed and applied by Ivanic and Martin (2012) (see also Ivanic and Martin 2008; Ivanic, Martin, and Zaman 2011) to evaluate the impacts of agricultural productivity growth on poverty. Using this model, we extend the analysis of Ivanic and Martin (2012) to evaluate the effect of agricultural productivity growth on vulnerability of the poor. To do this we simulate the global economy from 2010 to 2050 under two alternative agricultural technology scenarios: (a) a pessimistic (slower growth) scenario, with equal productivity growth rates in agriculture and other sectors; and (b) an optimistic (faster growth) scenario, with agricultural productivity growing by one percentage point per year faster than in the rest of the economy. The higher growth scenario involves global average rates of agricultural productivity growth that are broadly in line with the projections of Fuglie (2008). Then, for each scenario we simulate the effects of a negative agricultural shock and compare the impacts on the number of people in poverty in a selection of less-developed countries between the optimistic and pessimistic productivity scenarios.

Here we provide a summary description of the key features of the model, which is described in more complete detail by Ivanic and Martin (2012). The simulations were carried out using an aggregated version of the latest Global Trade Analysis Project (GTAP) model that contains the geographical regions defined by the World Bank (East Asia and Pacific, Europe and Central Asia, Developed, Latin America, Sub-Saharan Africa, the Middle East, and South Asia). The thirty-four nonagricultural and nonfood GTAP commodities were aggregated into five categories relevant for this work (agricultural farm output, energy, nondurables, durables, and services). The food-related sectors remain disaggregated. Because most of our simulations relate to long-term changes, we applied a long-run closure that allows complete flexibility of employment of capital and labor and limited flexibility of land use. Poverty assessment is based on the household survey data sets collected at the World Bank for twenty-nine developing countries that span the developing world, but notably exclude China. All of the surveys used in this study are relatively recent, and they contain detailed information on the patterns of households' incomes from and expenditures on agricultural products.[21] Behavioral responses of the households in the model are represented using

---

21. The information on household consumption expenditures, including any own-produced consumption, was separated into seven broad categories: agricultural (food) products, nondurables, energy goods, durables, services, financial expenses, and taxes and remittances paid by the household. The category of agricultural products was further divided into thirty-nine individual commodities, which roughly follow the GTAP commodity classification with some additional crops that may be important to the poor, such as sorghum, cassava, coffee and tea, and potatoes.

expenditure functions to characterize consumption responses, and profit functions to represent output decisions and input responses.[22] When prices change, we identify those households whose cost of living less any changes in income moved them across the poverty-line level of utility. We then recalculate the poverty rate for each country following each simulation and the income and expenditure shares that are the primary determinants of the impacts of price and productivity shocks. Of specific interest is the difference in the effects of a commodity supply shock on poverty outcomes between the optimistic and pessimistic productivity growth scenarios.

1.5.2   The Simulation Results

The baseline projections are intended not as forecasts but as a plausible backdrop against which to examine policy alternatives. These particular results appear to be consistent with the widespread view that substantial growth in agricultural output will be required over the next forty years to meet increasing demand. Under the pessimistic scenario of uniform productivity growth across the agricultural and nonagricultural sectors, the prices of many foods rise substantially: food prices at the household level increase by an average of 48 percent by 2050 (63.3 percent in developing countries). Under the optimistic scenario, with productivity growing 1 percent per year faster in agriculture than in other sectors, food prices rise by a modest 1.4 percent over the same period (8 percent in developing countries).[23]

Table 1.6 shows the total population in column (1) and the initial baseline percentage poverty rate (at US$1.25 per person per day) in each of the twenty-nine countries of interest in column (2). The next two columns show the effects of 1 percent higher productivity growth over forty years, 2010 to 2050, in reducing the poverty rate in column (3) and the number of people in poverty in column (4). The new poverty rate under the high-productivity growth scenario is shown in column (5). Thus, for example, in India the initial poverty rate of 43.83 percent applied to a population of 1.17 billion implies a total of some 513 million people in poverty. If global agricultural productivity grew by 1 percent per year faster for forty years, this number would be reduced by 89 million and the poverty rate would be reduced by 7.6 percentage points. The reductions in poverty rates would be even more pronounced in some countries. Across all of the countries in this sample poverty rates would be reduced by an average of 4.75 percentage points and a total of more than 135 million people would be lifted above the poverty

---

22. The consumer expenditure functions of the households were calibrated to make the elasticities of demand derived from them consistent with those in the macro model. The profit functions were similarly calibrated to ensure that the elasticities of supply that they imply are consistent with those in the macro model.

23. Ivanic and Martin (2012) also examined a scenario with one percent per year higher productivity in agriculture in developing countries only, under which food prices increase by 13.5 percent (19.2 percent in developing countries). This highlights the importance of productivity growth in developed countries for prices and poverty in less-developed countries as well as showing the central role of productivity growth in less-developed countries.

Table 1.6   Baseline scenario: Changes in poverty from 1 percent per year higher
                   agricultural productivity growth over 2010–2050

| | | | Change in poverty | | |
Country	Population (1)	Initial poverty rate, percent (2)	Percentage points (3)	Headcount (4)	New poverty rate, percent (5)
	number	percent	percent	number	percent
Albania	3,204,284	0.85	–0.13	–4,104	0.72
Armenia	3,092,072	10.63	–1.27	–39,176	9.36
Bangladesh	148,692,100	50.47	–4.29	–6,372,561	46.18
Belize	344,700	33.50	–1.73	–5,962	31.77
Cambodia	14,138,260	40.19	–18.96	–2,680,020	21.23
Cote d'Ivoire	19,737,800	23.34	–3.94	–777,204	19.40
Ecuador	14,464,740	15.78	–3.27	–473,067	12.51
Guatemala	14,388,930	12.65	–5.02	–722,634	7.63
India	1,170,938,000	43.83	–7.59	–88,868,501	36.24
Indonesia	239,870,900	7.50	–1.54	–3,682,462	5.96
Malawi	14,900,840	73.86	–12.71	–1,894,637	61.15
Moldova	3,562,062	8.14	–4.04	–143,983	4.10
Mongolia	2,756,001	22.38	–6.30	–173,642	16.08
Nepal	29,959,360	55.12	–4.46	–1,337,469	50.66
Nicaragua	5,788,163	45.10	–5.62	–325,177	39.48
Niger	15,511,950	65.88	–2.10	–326,292	63.78
Nigeria	158,423,200	64.41	–3.47	–5,493,147	60.94
Pakistan	173,593,400	22.59	–6.97	–12,094,064	15.62
Panama	3,516,820	9.48	–1.94	–68,181	7.54
Peru	29,076,510	7.94	–1.77	–514,516	6.17
Rwanda	10,624,010	76.56	–2.26	–239,671	74.30
Sri Lanka	20,859,950	14.00	–3.20	–668,386	10.80
Tajikistan	6,878,637	21.49	–8.67	–596,488	12.82
Tanzania	44,841,220	67.87	–3.62	–1,621,932	64.25
Timor-Leste	1,124,355	52.94	–3.29	–37,033	49.65
Uganda	33,424,680	51.53	–6.78	–2,267,582	44.75
Viet Nam	86,936,460	13.70	–2.10	–1,824,816	11.60
Yemen	24,052,510	17.53	–5.25	–1,263,621	12.28
Zambia	12,926,410	61.87	–5.30	–684,590	56.58

Notes: In the "low-productivity" scenario, productivity grows at the same rate in agriculture as in the rest of the economy; in the "high-productivity" scenario, productivity grows 1 percent per year faster in agriculture than in the rest of the economy in all countries. The changes in poverty in this table reflect 49 percent higher productivity in agriculture as a result of 1 percent higher growth over forty years.

line under the faster productivity growth scenario. Results such as this are the focus of the study by Ivanic and Martin (2012). Our purpose here is to explore the implications of the same difference in baseline productivity growth rates for the vulnerability of people to changes in food markets, as represented by price shocks.

Table 1.7 shows the impacts of a substantial externally generated (say, drought- or crop-pest-induced) price shock on poverty rates under the pes-

Table 1.7   Changes in poverty rates resulting from a supply shock in the industrial
                   countries causing agricultural commodity prices to double

	Low productivity state of the world		High productivity state of the world		Reduction in poverty impact: High versus low productivity state	
	Initial rate (1)	Change (2)	Initial rate (3)	Change (4)	Rate (5) = (2) – (4)	Headcount (6)
	percentage points					*thousands*
Albania	0.85	0.11	0.72	–0.26	0.37	11.9
Armenia	10.63	0.92	9.36	0.14	0.78	24.1
Bangladesh	50.47	1.74	46.18	0.06	1.68	2,498.0
Belize	33.50	2.43	31.77	0.44	1.99	6.9
Cambodia	40.19	–2.85	21.23	–3.09	0.24	33.9
Côte d'Ivoire	23.34	–0.26	19.40	–0.63	0.37	73.0
Ecuador	15.78	2.25	12.51	0.19	2.06	298.0
Guatemala	12.65	6.59	7.63	0.42	6.17	887.8
India	43.83	4.70	36.24	1.74	2.96	34,659.8
Indonesia	7.50	0.77	5.96	0.15	0.62	1,487.2
Malawi	73.86	1.14	61.15	–0.59	1.73	257.8
Moldova	8.14	3.99	4.10	0.55	3.44	122.5
Mongolia	22.38	2.31	16.08	0.57	1.74	48.0
Nepal	55.12	–0.67	50.66	–1.27	0.6	179.8
Nicaragua	45.10	3.16	39.48	–0.35	3.51	203.2
Niger	65.88	–0.75	63.78	–1.29	0.54	83.8
Nigeria	64.41	0.32	60.94	–0.10	0.42	665.4
Pakistan	22.59	3.02	15.62	0.73	2.29	3,975.3
Panama	9.48	1.20	7.54	–0.42	1.62	57.0
Peru	7.94	0.93	6.17	–0.50	1.43	415.8
Rwanda	76.56	0.49	74.30	0.21	0.28	29.7
Sri Lanka	14.00	2.45	10.80	0.72	1.73	360.9
Tajikistan	21.49	6.14	12.82	0.37	5.77	396.9
Tanzania	67.87	1.61	64.25	0.05	1.56	699.5
Timor-Leste	52.94	0.00	49.65	–0.43	0.43	4.8
Uganda	51.53	–0.07	44.75	–0.95	0.88	294.1
Viet Nam	13.70	–0.58	11.60	–0.84	0.26	226.0
Yemen	17.53	3.35	12.28	0.33	3.02	726.4
Zambia	61.87	0.77	56.58	–0.27	1.04	134.4
Average	34.18	1.56	29.43	–0.15	1.71	39,460.4

Notes: In the "low-productivity" scenario, productivity grows at the same rate in agriculture
as in the rest of the economy; in the "high-productivity" scenario, productivity grows one
percent per year faster in agriculture than in the rest of the economy in all countries. The external price shock is represented by a 100 percent increase in the prices of all agricultural
commodities. The numbers in column (6) are derived by applying the rates in column (5) of
table 1.6 to the total population given in column (1) of table 1.5.

simistic agricultural productivity scenario (columns [1] and [2]) and the optimistic scenario (columns [3] and [4]). In most cases the price shock causes an
increase in the poverty rate (positive signs on entries in columns [2] and [4])
but in other cases—where there are many poor net-selling households—the
price shock causes a decrease in the poverty rate (negative signs on entries in

columns [2] and [4]). However, in every case the entry in column (2) is more positive than the entry in column (4), such that the difference (in column [5], given by column [2] minus column [4]) is positive—the poverty rate increases by less (from a lower base) or decreases by more in the high-productivity scenario, compared with the low-productivity scenario. This means that the effect of the price shock on poverty is always more favorable given the high-productivity scenario than the low-productivity scenario. On average across countries in the high-productivity scenario, the external price shock results in a *reduction* in poverty by 0.15 percentage points, whereas in the low-productivity scenario, the poverty rate increases by 1.56 percentage points. The difference reflects a benefit from higher productivity in providing some insulation against the impoverishing effects of price variability, and—in most cases—reductions in the proportion of the population vulnerable to poverty.

In general, we find that the high-productivity scenario leaves households less vulnerable to price shocks. Higher productivity growth lowers real prices and—given the small price elasticities of demand for staple foods—leaves households with smaller shares of their income spent on food. The high-productivity scenario also leads to a decline in the global share of income from food production given the low price elasticities of demand. For most countries, the reduction in poverty associated with higher productivity reduces the fraction of the population vulnerable to poverty. This is not always the case, however. In countries like Malawi, where the poor fraction of the population was initially more than half, the reduction in the poverty rate may increase the fraction of the population near the poverty line. The numbers are substantial. As shown in column (6) of table 1.7, across the twenty-nine countries, a total of 39.5 million fewer people would be cast into poverty by a doubling of food commodity prices in the high-productivity growth scenario compared with the low-productivity growth scenario. This total benefit—that is, the reduced poverty impact of the price change in the high-productivity growth scenario—reflects the effects of (a) having a smaller shift of the income distribution induced by the price change in the high-productivity state, and (b) generally having a smaller share of the population close to the poverty line as illustrated in the heuristic analysis using figures 1.1 and 1.2.

1.6 Conclusion

Technological change in agriculture can affect the variability of food prices both by changing the sensitivity of aggregate farm supply to external shocks and changing the sensitivity of prices to a given extent of underlying variability of supply or demand. At the same time, by increasing the general abundance of food and reducing the share of income spent on food, agricultural innovation makes a given extent of price variability less important. This chapter has examined these different dimensions of the role of agricultural technology in contributing to or mitigating the consequences of variability in agricultural production, both in the past and looking forward.

A review of patterns of production, yields, and prices for the major cereal grains—wheat, maize, rice, and corn—over the period since World War II indicates that technological change has contributed significantly to growth of yields and production and to reducing real prices, but has probably not contributed to increased price variability. Rather, it seems more likely that technological changes in agriculture may have contributed to an underlying trend of production, yield, and prices that was generally less variable—as measured by moving averages of variances of logarithms of real prices, production, and yields—with other factors giving rise to periodical increases in variability, such as in the early 1970s and late in the first decade of the twenty-first century. The patterns are not uniform across countries and regions. In particular, production and yields have become more variable in the low-income group of countries during the past decade or so, in contrast to the high- and middle-income groups of countries, with some variation among countries within the groups and across crops. Further work remains to be done to analyze these patterns more formally, and to see whether differences in agricultural technology, or its location-specific impacts, might have contributed to these seemingly systematic differences.

We have emphasized the role of agricultural technology in reducing the importance of food price variability for food security of the poor by reducing the number of farmers, the number of poor, and the importance of food costs in household budgets. An illustrative analysis uses simulations of the global economy to 2050. The results show that the vulnerability of households to poverty is lower following a sustained period of higher productivity growth.

Appendix A
Prices and Productivity

Between 1975 and 2010, deflated US dollar prices of maize, wheat, and rice fell by about 2.8 percent per year (this is a simple average of the individual rates as reported in the text—see table 1.1), a cumulative decline of about 63 percent of the 1975 prices over the period.[24] Over the same interval total global production of cereals (wheat, rice, and coarse grains) grew from about 1,360 million metric tons in 1975 to about 2,430 million metric tons in 2010,

---

24. The trend growth rate over this period was –2.5 percent per year. Prices fell faster and farther over the interval from 1975 to 2005, after which they increased in real terms.

an increase of about 79 percent relative to 1975 production, and the world's population increased from about 4 billion to almost 7 billion.

Suppose we assume that the medium-term elasticity of supply of grain is $\varepsilon = 0.5$ and the elasticity of demand is $\eta = -0.2$. The proportional growth of supply (g) required to achieve a proportional increase in crop output of $q = d \ln Q$ ($= 79$ percent), in spite of a negative proportional change in price of $p = d \ln P$ ($= -63$ percent), is equal to $g = q - \varepsilon p = 79 + (0.5) \times 63 = 110.5$ percent. Now, let us suppose conservatively, for the sake of argument, that half of the past thirty-five years' growth in supply is attributable to research-induced productivity improvements (i.e., in round numbers a proportional increase of $j = 0.5$ such that $100j = 55$ percent is half of $g = 110$ percent growth).

What would the world be like today in the absence of those productivity gains? This can be analyzed by examining the price and quantity effects of a $100j/(1 + j) = 35$ percent reduction in current supply against the given demand. Given $j^* = -0.35$, $\varepsilon = 0.5$ and $\eta = -0.2$, the equations for proportional changes in price and quantity are $p = 100 \, j^*/(\varepsilon - \eta) = 50$ percent and $q = -100 \, \eta j/(\varepsilon - \eta) = -10$ percent. Hence, eliminating thirty-five years of research-induced productivity gains would imply an increase of the current price of cereals by about 50 percent (19 percent of the 1975 price) and a reduction in the current quantity produced and consumed of about 10 percent (18 percent of the 1975 quantity). These numbers refer to "with" and "without" the research-induced productivity gains. Although they are quantitatively related and of similar orders of magnitudes, they are conceptually different from the price and quantity changes over time, the "before" and "after" figures, which reflect the effects of all the variables that changed.

Appendix B

More-Detailed Evidence on Variability of Production and Yield

The following tables report measures of ten-year moving variances of yield and production and regressions of those measures against a time trend, using data for 1961 to 2010.

Table 1B.1   **Yields**

	Average 2010 yield tonnes/ha	10-year moving variance					Time-trend coefficient	t-stat
		1970	1980	1990	2000	2010		
A. Wheat yield								
World	3.00	0.0121	0.0053	0.0078	0.0020	0.0023	−0.0003	−10.18
Australia & New Zealand	1.67	0.0290	0.0463	0.0486	0.0328	0.0976	0.0012	3.73
North America	3.02	0.0147	0.0033	0.0063	0.0042	0.0099	0.0000	−1.25
Western Europe	6.11	0.0115	0.0084	0.0106	0.0032	0.0036	−0.0003	−6.87
China	4.75	0.0615	0.0295	0.0157	0.0067	0.0087	−0.0011	−6.12
Asia & Pacific (excl. China)	2.56	0.0084	0.0099	0.0060	0.0032	0.0013	−0.0003	−15.10
Eastern Europe	3.61	0.0231	0.0088	0.0082	0.0059	0.0166	−0.0003	−3.15
Latin America	3.33	0.0124	0.0065	0.0100	0.0042	0.0127	−0.0002	−2.16
USSR	1.85	0.0488	0.0237	0.0266	0.0113	0.0097	−0.0006	−5.51
Northern Africa	2.43	0.0198	0.0094	0.0402	0.0105	0.0103	0.0000	0.12
Sub-Saharan Africa	2.05	0.0115	0.0105	0.0212	0.0075	0.0076	−0.0001	−1.46
High income	3.66	0.0080	0.0019	0.0047	0.0021	0.0037	−0.0001	−5.37
Upper middle income	2.79	0.0224	0.0108	0.0140	0.0031	0.0041	−0.0004	−9.41
Lower middle income	2.70	0.0186	0.0053	0.0088	0.0036	0.0013	−0.0006	−8.31
Low income	1.92	0.0065	0.0247	0.0008	0.0044	0.0092	−0.0001	−1.52
B. Maize yield								
World	5.22	0.0074	0.0081	0.0059	0.0055	0.0040	−0.0002	−7.08
Australia & New Zealand	6.75	0.0197	0.0182	0.0195	0.0069	0.0054	−0.0009	−7.07
North America	9.60	0.0117	0.0118	0.0199	0.0114	0.0051	−0.0002	−2.93
Western Europe	9.42	0.0433	0.0099	0.0039	0.0072	0.0039	−0.0007	−6.76
China	5.46	0.0359	0.0205	0.0120	0.0037	0.0029	−0.0007	−15.16
Asia & Pacific (excl. China)	3.22	0.0027	0.0046	0.0085	0.0036	0.0130	0.0002	5.43
Eastern Europe	5.34	0.0277	0.0111	0.0187	0.0539	0.0396	0.0011	8.18
Latin America	4.21	0.0047	0.0058	0.0009	0.0117	0.0095	0.0002	3.60
USSR	4.08	0.0294	0.0126	0.0104	0.0170	0.0202	0.0004	3.50
Northern Africa	6.10	0.0201	0.0063	0.0169	0.0236	0.0031	0.0001	1.59
Sub-Saharan Africa	1.92	0.0102	0.0134	0.0263	0.0226	0.0077	−0.0003	−3.97
High income	9.44	0.0131	0.0102	0.0138	0.0094	0.0044	−0.0002	−5.20
Upper middle income	4.92	0.0102	0.0106	0.0021	0.0048	0.0066	−0.0001	−4.28
Lower middle income	2.74	0.0027	0.0050	0.0061	0.0117	0.0104	0.0002	8.38
Low income	1.70	0.0016	0.0029	0.0021	0.0038	0.0086	0.0000	2.58

(continued)

Table 1B.1   (continued)

	Average 2010 yield tonnes/ha	10-year moving variance					Time-trend coefficient	t-stat
		1970	1980	1990	2000	2010		
C. Rice yield								
World	4.37	0.0057	0.0032	0.0043	0.0012	0.0020	−0.0001	−4.03
Australia & New Zealand	10.84	0.0102	0.0139	0.0227	0.0129	0.0199	0.0001	1.27
North America	7.54	0.0088	0.0010	0.0070	0.0016	0.0012	0.0000	0.13
Western Europe	6.74	0.0045	0.0128	0.0013	0.0031	0.0005	−0.0002	−4.88
China	6.55	0.0234	0.0085	0.0059	0.0020	0.0008	−0.0003	−3.87
Asia & Pacific (excl. China)	3.85	0.0037	0.0031	0.0050	0.0014	0.0029	−0.0001	−2.86
Eastern Europe	4.98	0.0089	0.0238	0.0468	0.0280	0.0139	0.0000	0.11
Latin America	4.55	0.0015	0.0019	0.0100	0.0143	0.0072	0.0003	6.74
USSR	4.30	0.0349	0.0019	0.0015	0.0140	0.0178	0.0002	1.71
Northern Africa	9.38	0.0035	0.0022	0.0074	0.0045	0.0008	0.0001	1.64
Sub-Saharan Africa	2.15	0.0020	0.0006	0.0040	0.0014	0.0111	0.0001	3.10
High income	6.88	0.0027	0.0042	0.0020	0.0045	0.0009	0.0000	−1.26
Upper middle income	5.42	0.0148	0.0044	0.0051	0.0022	0.0010	−0.0002	−3.49
Lower middle income	3.83	0.0072	0.0048	0.0081	0.0014	0.0033	−0.0002	−5.44
Low income	3.61	0.0017	0.0049	0.0019	0.0037	0.0056	0.0001	4.58
D. Cereals yield								
World	3.56	0.0081	0.0042	0.0037	0.0029	0.0032	−0.0001	−9.67
Australia & New Zealand	1.76	0.0249	0.0321	0.0353	0.0218	0.0682	0.0007	3.24
North America	6.34	0.0113	0.0092	0.0111	0.0100	0.0088	−0.0001	−1.76
Western Europe	5.82	0.0100	0.0055	0.0076	0.0044	0.0026	−0.0002	−6.98
China	5.52	0.0341	0.0147	0.0086	0.0029	0.0028	−0.0005	−6.51
Asia & Pacific (excl. China)	3.06	0.0034	0.0048	0.0056	0.0027	0.0032	0.0000	−3.55
Eastern Europe	3.78	0.0157	0.0044	0.0027	0.0142	0.0157	0.0001	0.92
Latin America	3.97	0.0027	0.0044	0.0008	0.0075	0.0082	0.0001	2.81
USSR	1.96	0.0366	0.0215	0.0220	0.0106	0.0081	−0.0004	−5.07
Northern Africa	2.77	0.0242	0.0075	0.0241	0.0103	0.0055	0.0000	−0.63
Sub-Saharan Africa	1.34	0.0026	0.0073	0.0066	0.0046	0.0044	−0.0001	−5.10
High income	5.32	0.0078	0.0037	0.0054	0.0041	0.0042	−0.0001	−6.46
Upper middle income	3.76	0.0182	0.0065	0.0072	0.0041	0.0041	−0.0003	−8.17
Lower middle income	2.69	0.0055	0.0054	0.0064	0.0033	0.0032	−0.0001	−7.45
Low income	2.07	0.0013	0.0042	0.0003	0.0022	0.0049	0.0000	1.81

Note: Cereals include the following commodities: barley, buckwheat, canary seed, cereal nes, fonio, maize, millet, mixed grain, oats, popcorn, rice, rye, sorghum, triticale, and wheat.

Table 1B.2   **Production**

	2010 production share	10-year moving variance					Time-trend coefficient	t-stat
		1970	1980	1990	2000	2010		
		A. Wheat production						
World	1.00	0.0173	0.0101	0.0055	0.0022	0.0047	−0.0003	−10.99
Australia & New Zealand	0.03	0.0646	0.0783	0.0573	0.1160	0.1229	0.0013	4.35
North America	0.13	0.0159	0.0199	0.0199	0.0020	0.0173	−0.0001	−1.01
Western Europe	0.16	0.0120	0.0088	0.0118	0.0065	0.0060	−0.0002	−2.34
China	0.18	0.0628	0.0475	0.0218	0.0058	0.0121	−0.0013	−7.22
Asia & Pacific (excl. China)	0.24	0.0239	0.0200	0.0088	0.0043	0.0030	−0.0009	−13.99
Eastern Europe	0.05	0.0276	0.0097	0.0186	0.0179	0.0322	0.0002	2.29
Latin America	0.05	0.0246	0.0288	0.0139	0.0177	0.0109	−0.0005	−3.20
USSR	0.13	0.0510	0.0264	0.0147	0.0241	0.0324	0.0001	0.94
Northern Africa	0.02	0.0306	0.0114	0.0474	0.0451	0.0287	0.0010	5.90
Sub-Saharan Africa	0.01	0.0422	0.0041	0.0235	0.0145	0.0153	−0.0005	−2.93
High income	0.36	0.0130	0.0096	0.0046	0.0033	0.0074	−0.0002	−4.56
Upper middle income	0.43	0.0271	0.0129	0.0088	0.0038	0.0082	−0.0003	−5.78
Lower middle income	0.19	0.0463	0.0164	0.0147	0.0084	0.0041	−0.0015	−8.36
Low income	0.02	0.0064	0.0091	0.0012	0.0221	0.0242	0.0004	5.61
		B. Maize production						
World	1.00	0.0128	0.0134	0.0107	0.0081	0.0152	−0.0002	−4.49
Australia & New Zealand	0.00	0.0216	0.0310	0.0232	0.0457	0.0148	−0.0007	−4.26
North America	0.39	0.0132	0.0230	0.0574	0.0233	0.0171	−0.0003	−1.37
Western Europe	0.04	0.0646	0.0145	0.0101	0.0140	0.0062	−0.0015	−6.55
China	0.21	0.0585	0.0487	0.0221	0.0145	0.0250	−0.0008	−5.97
Asia & Pacific (excl. China)	0.08	0.0127	0.0126	0.0175	0.0050	0.0340	0.0003	2.98
Eastern Europe	0.04	0.0225	0.0137	0.0292	0.0448	0.0467	0.0011	7.79
Latin America	0.14	0.0243	0.0054	0.0034	0.0108	0.0200	0.0001	1.48
USSR	0.02	0.0720	0.0207	0.0327	0.0983	0.1223	0.0039	7.67
Northern Africa	0.01	0.0176	0.0113	0.0185	0.0142	0.0065	0.0001	0.75
Sub-Saharan Africa	0.07	0.0155	0.0164	0.0476	0.0233	0.0217	−0.0004	−2.59
High income	0.44	0.0146	0.0194	0.0390	0.0192	0.0126	−0.0004	−3.01
Upper middle income	0.42	0.0153	0.0136	0.0027	0.0069	0.0182	0.0001	−1.92
Lower middle income	0.09	0.0126	0.0082	0.0325	0.0053	0.0330	0.0003	2.62
Low income	0.04	0.0069	0.0081	0.0136	0.0057	0.0220	0.0000	0.94

(*continued*)

Table 1B.2   (continued)

	2010 production share	10-year moving variance					Time-trend coefficient	t-stat
		1970	1980	1990	2000	2010		
		C. Rice production						
World	1.00	0.0140	0.0071	0.0057	0.0032	0.0044	−0.0002	−10.41
Australia & New Zealand	0.00	0.0813	0.1067	0.0380	0.0333	1.9633	0.0214	3.64
North America	0.02	0.0353	0.0380	0.0267	0.0078	0.0053	−0.0007	−5.15
Western Europe	0.00	0.0083	0.0114	0.0155	0.0148	0.0043	−0.0001	−2.31
China	0.29	0.0456	0.0059	0.0050	0.0021	0.0034	−0.0005	−6.28
Asia & Pacific (excl. China)	0.61	0.0074	0.0082	0.0083	0.0048	0.0056	−0.0001	−4.03
Eastern Europe	0.00	0.0435	0.0250	0.0424	0.1513	0.2766	0.0049	2.92
Latin America	0.04	0.0156	0.0213	0.0110	0.0123	0.0079	−0.0001	−1.62
USSR	0.00	0.3507	0.0362	0.0029	0.0535	0.0487	−0.0038	−4.28
Northern Africa	0.01	0.0640	0.0020	0.0120	0.0306	0.0223	0.0003	0.97
Sub-Saharan Africa	0.03	0.0159	0.0077	0.0280	0.0041	0.0314	0.0001	0.56
High income	0.05	0.0043	0.0076	0.0021	0.0047	0.0021	−0.0001	−3.48
Upper middle income	0.39	0.0354	0.0067	0.0037	0.0021	0.0032	−0.0005	−8.01
Lower middle income	0.40	0.0124	0.0106	0.0145	0.0052	0.0049	−0.0003	−6.62
Low income	0.17	0.0062	0.0089	0.0037	0.0095	0.0204	0.0003	6.45
		D. Cereals production						
World	1.00	0.0116	0.0065	0.0035	0.0019	0.0056	−0.0002	−8.67
Australia & New Zealand	0.01	0.0551	0.0515	0.0420	0.0756	0.0798	0.0007	3.01
North America	0.18	0.0105	0.0113	0.0299	0.0099	0.0128	−0.0001	−1.24
Western Europe	0.08	0.0114	0.0060	0.0055	0.0064	0.0038	−0.0002	−5.28
China	0.20	0.0381	0.0137	0.0086	0.0036	0.0091	−0.0005	−8.33
Asia & Pacific (excl. China)	0.27	0.0076	0.0087	0.0076	0.0034	0.0049	−0.0001	−7.08
Eastern Europe	0.04	0.0115	0.0025	0.0030	0.0179	0.0215	0.0003	3.96
Latin America	0.08	0.0175	0.0080	0.0015	0.0077	0.0116	−0.0001	−1.95
USSR	0.06	0.0316	0.0235	0.0115	0.0461	0.0211	0.0003	1.90
Northern Africa	0.01	0.0396	0.0094	0.0289	0.0247	0.0164	0.0002	2.20
Sub-Saharan Africa	0.05	0.0075	0.0059	0.0233	0.0087	0.0143	0.0000	0.13
High income	0.31	0.0091	0.0055	0.0087	0.0053	0.0061	−0.0001	−6.94
Upper middle income	0.40	0.0216	0.0086	0.0043	0.0010	0.0062	−0.0004	−7.70
Lower middle income	0.21	0.0122	0.0076	0.0136	0.0045	0.0055	−0.0002	−5.89
Low income	0.08	0.0047	0.0067	0.0044	0.0067	0.0207	0.0003	6.58

Note: Cereals include the following commodities: barley, buckwheat, canary seed, cereal nes, fonio, maize, millet, mixed grain, oats, popcorn, rice, rye, sorghum, triticale, and wheat.

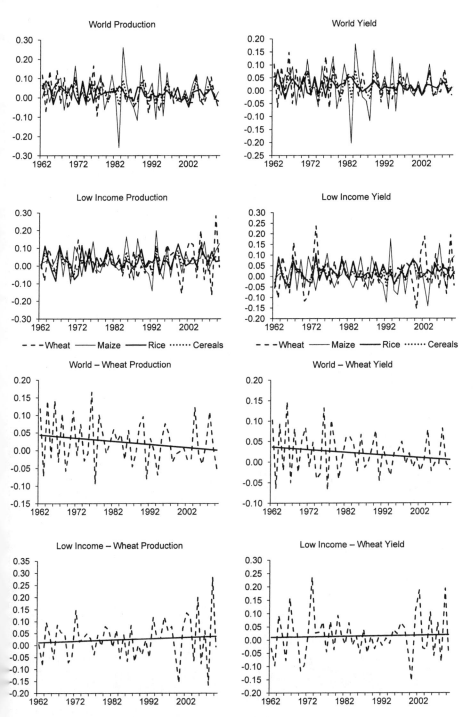

Fig. 1B.1 Variability of grain production and yield, first differences of logarithm of production, yield and prices

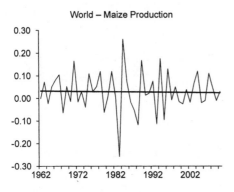

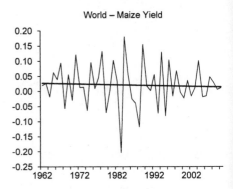

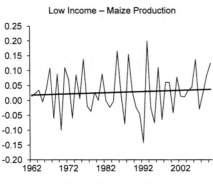

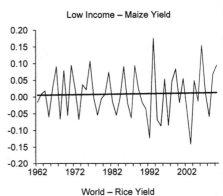

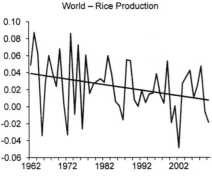

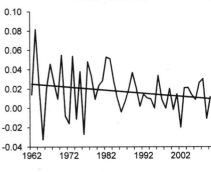

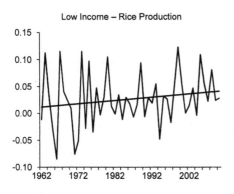

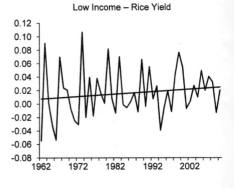

Fig. 1B.1 (cont.)

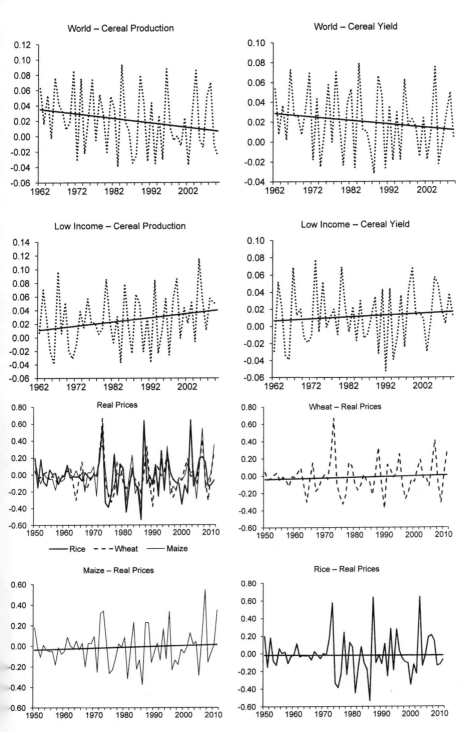

Fig. 1B.1   (cont.)

References

Alston, J. M., M. A. Andersen, J. S. James, P. G. Pardey. 2010. *Persistence Pays: U.S. Agricultural Productivity Growth and the Benefits from Public R&D Spending*. New York: Springer Publishers.

Alston, J. M., B. A. Babcock, and P. G. Pardey, eds. 2010. *The Shifting Patterns of Agricultural Production and Productivity Worldwide*. CARD-MATRIC Electronic Book. May. Ames, IA: Center for Agricultural and Rural Development. http://www.matric.iastate.edu/shifting_patterns/.

Alston, J. M., J. M. Beddow, and P. G. Pardey. 2009. "Agricultural Research, Productivity, and Food Prices in the Long Run." *Science* 325 (4): 1209–10.

———. 2010. "Global Patterns of Crop Yields, Other Partial Productivity Measures, and Prices." In *The Shifting Patterns of Agricultural Production and Productivity Worldwide*, edited by J. M. Alston, B. A. Babcock, and P. G. Pardey. CARD-MATRIC Electronic Book. May. Ames, IA: Center for Agricultural and Rural Development. http://www.matric.iastate.edu/shifting_patterns/.

Alston, J. M., R. S. Gray, and K. Bolek. 2012. "Farmer-Funded R&D: Institutional Innovations for Enhancing Agricultural Research Investments." Canadian Agricultural Innovation and Regulation Network Working Paper, University of Saskatchewan, Saskatchewan, March. http://www.ag-innovation.usask.ca/cairn_briefs/publications20for20download/CAIRN_2012_FarmerFundedRD_AlstonGrayBolek.pdf.

Anderson, J. R., and P. B. R. Hazell, eds. 1989. *Variability in Grain Yields: Implications for Agricultural Research and Policy in Developing Countries*. Baltimore: Johns Hopkins University Press (published for the International Food Policy Research Institute).

Beddow, J. M. 2012. "A Bio-Economic Assessment of the Spatial Dynamics of US Corn Production and Yields." PhD diss. St Paul: University of Minnesota.

Beddow, J. M., P. G. Pardey, B. Koo, and S. Wood. 2010. "The Changing Landscape of Global Agriculture." In *The Shifting Patterns of Agricultural Production and Productivity Worldwide*, edited by J. M. Alston, B. A. Babcock, and P. G. Pardey. CARD-MATRIC Electronic Book. May. Ames, IA: Center for Agricultural and Rural Development. http://www.matric.iastate.edu/shifting_patterns/.

Byerlee, D. 2000. "Targeting Poverty Alleviation in Priority Setting for Agricultural Research." *Food Policy* 25:429–55.

Cassman, K. G. 1999. "Ecological Intensification of Cereal Production Systems: Yield Potential, Soil Quality, and Precision Agriculture." *Proceedings of the National Academy of Sciences* 96:5952–9.

de Janvry, A., and E. Sadoulet. 2002. "World Poverty and the Role of Agricultural Technology: Direct and Indirect Effects." *Journal of Development Studies* 38:1–26.

Food and Agriculture Organization of the United Nations (FAO). 2012. FAOSTAT database. Retrieved July 2012 from http:/faostat.fao.org.

———. 2013. FAOSTAT database. Retrieved January 2013 from http:/faostat.fao.org.

Fuglie, K. 2008. "Is a Slowdown in Agricultural Productivity Growth Contributing to the Rise in Agricultural Prices?" *Agricultural Economics* 39:431–44.

Gardner, B. L. 2002. *American Agriculture in the Twentieth Century: How it Flourished and What it Cost*. Cambridge, MA: Harvard University Press.

Gollin, Douglas. 2006. *Impacts of International Research on Intertemporal Yield Stability on Wheat and Maize: An Economic Assessment*. Mexico: D.F. CIMMYT.

Hazell, P. B. R. 1989. "Changing Patterns of Variability in World Cereal Production." In *Variability in Grain Yields: Implications for Agricultural Research and Policy in Developing Countries*, edited by J. R. Anderson and P. B. R. Hazell. Baltimore: Johns Hopkins University Press (published for the International Food Policy Research Institute).

———. 2010. "Asia's Green Revolution: Past Achievements and Future Challenges." In *Rice in the Global Economy: Strategic Research and Policy Issues for Food Security*, edited by S. Pandey, D. Byerlee, D. Dawe, A. Doberman, S. Mohanty, S. Rozelle, and B. Hardy. Los Baños (Philippines): International Rice Research Institute.

Hurley, T. M., P. D. Mitchell, and M. E. Rice. 2004. "Risk and the Value of Bt Corn." *American Journal of Agricultural Economics* 86 (2): 345–58.

Ivanic, M., and W. J. Martin. 2008. "Implications of Higher Global Food Prices for Poverty in Low-Income Countries." *Agricultural Economics* 39:405–16.

———. 2012. "Agricultural Productivity Growth and Poverty Reduction." Draft Working Paper, World Bank, Washington, DC, August 6.

Ivanic, M., W. J. Martin, and H. Zaman. 2011. "Estimating the Short-Run Poverty Impacts of the 2010–11 Surge in Food Prices." Policy Research Working Paper series 5633, World Bank, Washington, DC.

Key, N., and W. McBride. 2007. "The Changing Economics of US Hog Production." Economic Research Report no. 52. December. Washington, DC: USDA Economic Research Service.

Lewontin, R. C. 1966. "On the Measurement of Relative Variability." *Systematic Zoology* 15 (2): 141–2.

MacDonald, J. M., and W. D. McBride. 2009. "The Transformation of US Livestock Agriculture: Scale, Efficiency, and Risks." Economic Information Bulletin no. 43. January. Washington, DC: USDA Economic Research Service.

Martin, W. J., and J. M. Alston. 1994. "A Dual Approach to Evaluating Research Benefits in the Presence of Trade Distortions." *American Journal of Agricultural Economics* 76 (1): 26–35.

———. 1997. "Producer Surplus Without Apology? Evaluating Investments in R&D." *Economic Record* 73 (221): 146–58.

Martin, W. J., and K. Anderson. 2012. "Export Restrictions and Price Insulation During Commodity Price Booms." *American Journal of Agricultural Economics* 94 (2): 422–7.

Massy, C. 2011. *Breaking the Sheep's Back: The Shocking True Story of the Decline and Fall of the Australian Wool Industry*. St. Lucia: University of Queensland Press.

Minot, N. 2011. "Transmission of World Food Price Changes to Markets in Sub-Saharan Africa." Discussion Paper no. 01059. January. Washington, DC: International Food Policy Research Institute.

Muth, R. 1964. "The Derived Demand Curve for a Productive Factor and the Industry Supply Curve." *Oxford Economic Papers* 16:221–34.

Naylor, R., W. Falcon, and E. Zavaleta. 1997. "Variability and Growth in Grain Yields, 1950–94: Does the Record Point to Greater Instability?" *Population and Development Review* 23 (1): 41–58.

Olmstead, A. L., and P. W. Rhode. 2002. "The Red Queen and the Hard Reds: Productivity Growth in American Wheat, 1800–1940." *Journal of Economic History* 62 (4): 929–66.

———. 2009. *Creating Abundance: Biological Innovation and American Agricultural Development*. New York: Cambridge University Press.

Pardey, P. G., and J. M. Alston. 2010. *US Agricultural Research in a Global Food*

Security Setting. A Report of the CSIS Global Food Security Project. January. Washington, DC: CSIS. http://csis.org/publication/us-agricultural-research
-global-food-security-setting.
Pardey, P. G., J. M. Alston, and C. Chan-Kang. 2013. "Public Agricultural R&D over
the Past Half Century: An Emerging New World Order"*Agricultural Economics*
44, in press, http://onlinelibrary.wiley.com/doi/10.1111/agec.12055/abstract.
Pardey, P. G., J. M. Alston, and V. W. Ruttan. 2010. "The Economics of Innovation
and Technical Change in Agriculture." In *Handbook of Economics of Technical
Change*, edited by B. H. Hall and N. Rosenberg. Amsterdam: Elsevier.
Qaim, M., and D. Zilberman. 2003. "Yield Effects of Genetically Modified Crops
in Developing Countries." *Science* 299 (5608): 900–2.
Schultz, T. W. 1951. "The Declining Economic Importance of Agricultural Land."
Economic Journal 61 (244): 725–40.
Senauer, B., E. Asp, and J. Kinsey. 1991. *Food Trends and the Changing Consumer*.
St. Paul, MN: Egan Press.
Singh, A. J., and D. Byerlee. 1990. "Relative Variability in Wheat Yields across Coun-
tries and Over Time." *Journal of Agricultural Economics* 41:2–32.
World Bank. 2012. *Food Prices, Nutrition, and the Millennium Development Goals:
Global Monitoring Report 2012*. Washington, DC: The World Bank.
Wright, B. D. 2011. "The Economics of Grain Price Volatility." *Applied Economics
and Public Policy* 33 (1): 32–58.
Zilberman, D., and E. Kim. 2011. "The Lessons of Fermentation for the New Bio-
economy." *AgBioForum* 14 (3): 97–103.

Comment   James M. MacDonald

Alston, Martin, and Pardey (AMP) provide a rich and useful framework for
thinking about the links among technology, food prices, and the impacts of
food price changes on welfare. Innovations in technology work through four
channels and can alter:

1. price elasticities of demand and supply for farm commodities, changing
the sensitivity of prices to given shifts in supply or demand;

2. the sensitivity of farm supply to external shocks, such as weather or
pests, and can therefore influence the degree to which such shocks affect
farm prices;

3. agricultural productivity, and the level of farm prices; and

4. economy-wide productivity and real incomes, which leads to falling
shares of income spent on food and hence leaves populations less exposed
to food price fluctuations.

James M. MacDonald is chief of the Agricultural Structure and Productivity Branch of the
Economic Research Service, US Department of Agriculture.

For acknowledgments, sources of research support, and disclosure of the author's material
financial relationships, if any, please see http://www.nber.org/chapters/c12805.ack.

AMP provide examples of each of these channels, but devote most attention to the third and fourth. Given expected future growth in world population, as well as the likely impact on global meat and feed demand occasioned by rising incomes and dietary shifts in some countries, this is appropriate. Failure to meet historic rates of agricultural productivity growth could lead to sharply higher commodity prices, with attendant risks to hunger and food security, political stability, and environmental outcomes, particularly in the poorest countries.

The chapter refers to previous work involving two of the authors, which makes the case that agricultural productivity growth has already slowed, as manifested in their own analyses of productivity data and in slowing growth in global crop yields. They argue that the slowdown is in large part due to reductions in public spending on research and development, and that without major new investments in R&D, the consequences of increased demand matched to productivity failures will be on us, but most severely on the developing world, soon (Alston, Beddow, and Pardey 2009).

This is an important issue, but one that is subject to considerable controversy. In particular, the United States Department of Agriculture (USDA) productivity accounts show no such slowdown in the United States, while other work finds no global slowdown, using the Food and Agriculture Organization of the United Nations (FAO) data (Fuglie 2008). Now, the answer to that question—has a slowdown occurred in the last ten to twenty years?—is not sufficient to answer the big question for the future—whether we can and will continue to achieve high rates of productivity growth over the next several decades. But the slowdown question does provide a framing for current analyses—its use here—and policy discussions, and the present chapter suggests that there is more consensus around the issue than I think really exists.

AMP focus most of their analysis on production of staple crops, which are the primary focus of concern in the least developed countries, and for which there are extensive data on production, acreage, and yields. They devote little attention to livestock. But growing incomes in middle-income countries such as China, India, and Brazil will lead to substantial ongoing increases in meat consumption, and increased derived demand for feed grains and oilseeds. The impact of increased meat consumption on feed demand, on land use for feed production, and ultimately on crop prices will depend, among other things, on how animals convert feed to meat. Here, there are significant data problems; data on livestock feed conversion to meat and milk are scattered across many sources, poorly documented, and often unreliable. I will focus my comments on what we do know about feed conversion for livestock and how that affects our judgment about future growth possibilities.

In one well-known assessment, Vaclav Smil (2000) provides a wide-ranging analysis of what is needed to meet food consumption needs in the future.

To assess the feed and land requirements needed for increased consumption of meat and dairy products, he starts with estimates of feed conversion for three main species in the United States: chickens require 2.5 pounds of feed for one pound of live-weight gain, while hogs require 4.0 pounds, and beef cattle require 8.0 pounds of feed for each pound of live-weight gain in a feedlot (nearly half their total).

Smil (2000) further finds very little improvement in feed conversion for hogs or cattle in data extending back to 1910, and no improvement for poultry after the early 1970s. These data support a sobering picture of the impact of future demand growth on prices and resource use, since they suggest relatively high feed requirements and little historic improvement.

However, the data used, from the USDA's annual *Agricultural Statistics* (USDA 2011), are not based on surveys of farms, feed providers, or animal scientists, but on feed formulas that have not been updated in many years. The temporal variations over time do not reflect changes in breeding and feed conversion, which are held constant since 1970, but rather in the size of animals.

Smil is an informed observer who used what was available, but that is not what is needed. The Economic Research Service (ERS) has added new evidence on US practices with data from the Agricultural Resource Management Survey (ARMS), an annual farm survey that is the USDA's primary source of data on the financial and productive performance of US farms. I will focus initially on what we have learned about poultry and hog production.[1]

United States hog production underwent a dramatic transformation in the last two decades: fewer but larger farms now specialize in single stages of production, with a tight system of coordination among stages, and with close attention paid to breeding, feeding, and production practices. One major outcome of that transformation was a sharp improvement in feed conversion: Key and McBride (2007) estimate that feed conversion in finishing operations improved to 2.14 (pounds of feed to produce one pound of weight gain) in 2004, from 3.83 in 1992.

Poultry production has displayed ongoing incremental improvements in breeding, feed formulations, and housing. In 1980, it took the industry fifty-two days to produce a four-pound broiler (the standard for the time), at an average feed conversion of 2.08 pounds of feed per pound of weight gain (MacDonald and McBride 2009). In 2011, four-pound birds were produced in thirty-six days, on average, at an average feed conversion of 1.75.[2]

---

1. We do not do specialized cattle feedlot surveys as part of ARMS, and therefore do not have estimates of feed conversion for beef. But Belasco, Ghosh, and Goodwin (2009), with access to feedlot records from large Kansas feedlot firms, estimate mean feed conversion for fed cattle at those sites to be 6.2 pounds, well below the Smil estimate.

2. I use a four-pound bird for comparison to the 1980 standard. The industry standard in 2011 was closer to a six-pound bird, with an average cycle time of forty-nine days and average feed conversion of 1.95 pounds of feed per pound of gain. The 2011 data are drawn from the 2011 ARMS version 4 (broilers), a representative national survey of commercial broiler operations.

These estimates are well below those provided in Smil (2000), and they show substantial improvements over time. They suggest that increased global meat consumption can have much less impact on feed and land use, and crop prices, than Smil's estimates suggest, and they also give reason to expect continuing efficiency improvements. Moreover, recent developments in genomics allow for much more rapid, inexpensive, and targeted selection in breeding, and also suggest that there may be more variation in animal populations than was previously realized. These developments are having important impacts in dairy production, and may lead to further applications in hogs, in poultry, and particularly in beef cattle. There is, therefore, reason to expect that further innovations can improve feed efficiency and can also be targeted to water use, disease susceptibility, heat stress, and meat attributes.

The ARMS data are not ideal for these purposes. I believe that they are an improvement on what was available, and they provide a useful perspective on the spread of a variety of production practices among US producers. The samples are designed to be representative of commercial production, but the survey is designed to focus on annual financial and production outcomes and not the collection of performance data; all the more reason to gather better data on applications of the science and on developments in actual practices.[3]

These measures largely reflect innovations in genetics, feeds, and housing. But management also matters for thinking about feed conversion in emerging economies. Large firms, such as Tyson Foods from the United States and CP Group from Thailand, are developing production complexes in several countries with growing meat consumption. These firms have access to the latest genetic and mechanical technology—that is, the knowledge is globally transferable within the companies. But management organization may still be a challenge.

Production complexes include feed mills and processing plants, as well as farms for egg laying, egg hatching, replacement birds, and grow-out to slaughter weights (with the equivalent stages for pork production). In the United States, farmers contract with poultry companies to raise their birds for grow-out; the farmers provide labor, capital, and energy, while the companies provide them with chicks, feed, transportation, and veterinary service. Independent growers appear to realize higher productivity and lower costs than company-owned farms, but it remains to be seen whether the US model will work in other settings, or whether the companies will come to rely more on full integration and company-owned farms.

---

3. For example, the hog estimates are based on the ratio of total feed provided to the respondent (farmer) in a year, divided by output, which is total live-weight gain in hog production. Output is measured with little error, but annual feed deliveries may not match production closely. Moreover, some contract farms do not know how much feed is delivered. As a result, the treatment of extreme values, and the treatment of missing values, matters for the estimates. In more recent surveys, we have asked directly for feed conversion data, and that provides tighter estimates, with missing values still a problem.

References

Alston, J. M., J. M. Beddow, and P. G. Pardey. 2009. "Agricultural Research, Productivity, and Food Prices in the Long Run." *Science* 325:1209–10.

Belasco, E. J., S. K Ghosh, and B. K. Goodwin. 2009. "A Multivariate Evaluation of Ex Ante Risks Associated with Fed Cattle Production." *American Journal of Agricultural Economics* 91:431–43.

Fuglie, Keith O. 2008. "Is a Slowdown in Agricultural Productivity Growth Contributing to the Rise in Commodity Prices?" *Agricultural Economics* 39:431–41.

Key, N., and W. McBride. 2007. *The Changing Economics of US Hog Production.* Economic Research Report no. 52. Washington, DC: Economic Research Service, US Department of Agriculture.

MacDonald, J., and W. McBride. 2009. *The Transformation of US Livestock Agriculture: Scale, Efficiency and Risks.* Economic Information Bulletin no. 43. Washington, DC: Economic Research Service, US Department of Agriculture.

Smil, V. 2000. *Feeding the World: A Challenge for the 21st Century.* Cambridge, MA: The MIT Press.

US Department of Agriculture. 2011. National Agricultural Statistics Service. *Agricultural Statistics.* http://www.nass.usda.gov/Publications/Ag_Statistics/.

2

Corn Production Shocks in 2012 and Beyond
Implications for Harvest Volatility

Steven T. Berry, Michael J. Roberts, and
Wolfram Schlenker

Historically, 25 percent of an average year's global corn production is held in inventories to buffer weather shocks and allow for a smooth consumption between years. As inventory levels are drawn down, prices increase, thereby giving farmers an incentive to increase production in the following years to refill depleted inventory levels.

While individual countries might face significant production shocks, these idiosyncratic shocks average out over the globe. Global corn production shocks (deviations from a trend) ranged from −13 percent to +7 percent in 1961 to 2010, with a standard deviation of 4 percent (Roberts and Schlenker 2013). International trade smoothes production shocks between countries unless these countries institute export bans.

There are, however, certain exceptions to this rule. The production of some crops is highly spatially correlated and subject to the same common weather shocks. A prime example is corn production in the United States, which is grown in the Midwest. Since the US produces roughly 40 percent of the world's corn, any impact to US production has the potential to significantly affect global production and global price levels.

Current and future corn price volatility depends directly on production shocks. One of the main drivers of production shocks are weather fluctua-

Steven T. Berry is the James Burrows Moffatt Professor of Economics at Yale University and a research associate of the National Bureau of Economic Research. Michael J. Roberts is associate professor of economics and an affiliate with Sea Grant at the University of Hawaii at Manoa. Wolfram Schlenker is associate professor at the School of International Public Affairs at Columbia University and a research associate of the National Bureau of Economic Research.

For acknowledgments, sources of research support, and disclosure of the authors' material financial relationships, if any, please see http://www.nber.org/chapters/c12806.ack.

tions. An accurate model that translates weather fluctuations into production fluctuations is hence a crucial first step in examining food price volatility.

In this chapter we extend earlier work on the effects of weather on corn production (Schlenker and Roberts 2009). We previously allowed for a highly nonlinear effect of weather on corn yields, but assumed the effect of various temperatures to be *constant* throughout the growing season that we fixed to March through August. The main innovations of this chapter are: First, we allow the effect of various weather measures to evolve over the growing season. Second, we no longer keep the growing season fixed to March through August, but rather use annual state-level data on planting and harvest dates to capture weather measures over the actual growing season. Third, we predict yields for 2012 using the traditional as well as the new model. Since the 2012 heat wave happened during the part of the growing season when it is most harmful, the new model predicts larger production shortfalls. Fourth, we contrast 2012 to what is expected under climate change.

2.1   Model

We start by estimating a baseline model of yields that assumes a fixed growing season (March through August) and a constant effect of weather variables over the growing season. This baseline replicates a specification from earlier research (Schlenker and Roberts 2009). In a second step, following Ortiz-Bobea and Just (2013), we consider models that account for planting date and temperature effects that vary over the growing season.

2.1.1   Baseline Model 1

The baseline model relates log yield y_{it} in county i and year t to four weather variables:

$$(1) \qquad y_{it} = \beta_1 m_{it} + \beta_2 h_{it} + \beta_3 p_{it} + \beta_4 p_{it}^2 + c_i + f_s(t) + \epsilon_{it},$$

where m_{it} is growing degree days between 10°C and 29°C, accounts the beneficial effects of moderate temperatures, h_{it} are degree days above 29°C that capture the damaging effect of extreme heat, and p_{it} and p_{it}^2 are season-total precipitation and its square.[1] County fixed effects c_i account for baseline differences between counties and state-specific time trends f_s account for

---

1. *Growing degree days* are based on cumulative heat exposure above a threshold temperature, which is sometimes also truncated by an upper bound. Degree days 10°C–29°C count all temperatures below 10°C as zero, temperatures between 10°C and 29°C as the difference between the observed temperature and 10°C, and temperatures at or above 29°C as 19. For example, twenty-four hours of exposure to a temperature of 11°C counts as one growing degree day while twenty-four hours of exposure to a temperature of 12°C counts as two degree days, and so on. In our weather data, we incorporate the entire distribution of temperatures between the daily minimum and maximum, thereby counting fractions of a day (see the data in section 2.2). Degree days above 29°C put the lower bound at 29°C and have no upper bound.

technological progress as average yields have been trending upward over time. Errors are clustered at the state level to adjust for spatial correlation.

The data underlying these regressions is constructed using daily fine-scaled weather measures on a 2.5 × 2.5 mile grid for the contiguous United States. We follow the same algorithm as Schlenker and Roberts (2009), but update the data through 2012. We use only counties east of the 100-degree meridian (excluding Florida) in the regression because the response function might be different for highly irrigated areas.[2] The data set spans the years 1950 to 2012.

2.1.2   Model 2: Time-Varying Parameters

Model 2 allows the effect of weather variables to vary over the growing season. Ortiz-Bobea and Just (2013) extend our earlier work by separating the growing season into three subintervals, and then estimate separate (constant) coefficients for each of the subintervals. This chapter allows the effect of weather variables to vary continuously over time. To make locations comparable, we use yearly data on planting and harvesting dates and normalize the season to have length 1. A value of 0.5 stands for the day that occurred in the middle of the growing season.

In a first step we only allow the coefficient β_2 that measures the effect of extreme heat to vary over the growing season. The reason is that extreme heat has consistently been found to have the largest influence on year-to-year variability of crop yields. There is agronomic evidence that heat matters especially during the flowering period, and the effect of weather measures might hence evolve over time. Model 2 is defined as:

$$(2) \qquad y_{it} = \beta_1 m_{it} + g_2(h_{0it},...,h_{D_iit}) + \beta_3 p_{it} + \beta_4 p_{it}^2 + c_i + f_s(t) + \epsilon_{it}.$$

In the baseline model we summed daily degree days above 29°C over all days of the fixed growing season $\sum_{d=\text{March 1}}^{\text{August 31}} h_{dit}$, while $g_2()$ now allows the effect of h_{dit} to vary over the growing season. Note that we also no longer fix the growing season to March 1st through August 31st, but allow it to vary year to year. Different places might have different growing season lengths, and there is year-to-year variation in planting and harvesting dates at a given location. We define a growing season to last from planting (time 0) to harvest (time 1).

We construct a restricted cubic spline with k knots over the growing season, which will result in $k - 1$ spline variables $s_j()$. We consider models with between 3 and 7 knots, with the knots placed at standard fractions of the growing season.[3] We normalize the growing season to length one, so the

---

2. Table 2.1 shows that these counties account for 91 percent of US production.

3. Spline knots locations are as follows: $k = 3$ indicates 3 knots set at 0.1, 0.5, and 0.9 fractions of the total growing season; $k = 4$ indicates knots set at 0.05, 0.35, 0.65, and 0.95; $k = 5$ spline knots set at 0.02, 0.26, 0.5, 0.74, and 0.98; $k = 6$ knots are set at 0.02, 0.212, 0.404, 0.596, 0.788, and 0.98; $k = 7$ knots are set at 0.02, 0.18, 0.34, 0.5, 0.66, 0.82, and 0.98.

"weighted" sum of daily degree days above 29°C (h_{dit}) over all days d of the growing season $d = 0,1,2 \ldots D_{it}$ in county i in year t depends on the phase of the growing season $x_{dit} = (d - 1)/(D_{it} - 1)$.

$$g_2(h_{it}) = \sum_{d=0}^{D_{it}} h_{dit} \underbrace{\sum_{j=1}^{k} s_j(x_{dit})}_{\text{weight(time)}} = \sum_{j=1}^{k-1} \underbrace{\sum_{d=1}^{D_{it}} s_j(x_{dit}) h_{dit}}_{H_{jit}} = \sum_{j=1}^{k-1} \beta_{2j} H_{jit}$$

The second equality simply exchanges the order of summation. We are ultimately left with $j = 1 \ldots k - 1$ variables H_{jit}, which are the sum of daily degree days above 29°C (h_{dit}) weighted by the value of the spline function $s_j(x_{dit})$ for each day (phase) of the growing season.

We also estimate an extended model that allows the effect of other weather variables to vary over the growing season. It includes a fifth variable, which is the interaction of daily degree days above 29°C and daily precipitation

$$(3) \qquad y_{it} = g_1(m_{0it}, \ldots, m_{D_{it}it}) + g_2(h_{0it}, \ldots, h_{D_{it}it}) + g_3(p_{0it}, \ldots, p_{D_{it}it})$$

$$+ g_4(p_{0it}^2, \ldots, p_{D_{it}it}^2) + g_5(h_{0it} \times p_{0it}, \ldots, h_{D_{it}it} \times p_{D_{it}it})$$

$$+ c_i + f_s(t) + \varepsilon_{it}.$$

Besides the time-varying effect of additional weather variables, the extended model differs in an another aspect: earlier models use season-total precipitation and season-total precipitation squared. The extended model uses *daily* precipitation as well as *daily* precipitation squared, and allows the effects of these variables to vary over the growing season.

2.2   Data

We pair data on annual county-level corn yields with fine scaled-weather measures that were constructed on a 2.5 × 2.5 mile grid for the entire United States. We follow the same algorithm of Schlenker and Roberts (2009), but update the data through 2012. These data give daily minimum and maximum temperature, as well as precipitation for each grid cell. Degree days above a threshold b are calculated by fitting a sine-curve between the daily minimum and maximum temperature in each cell and integrating over the difference between the temperature curve and the threshold (Snyder 1985). Daily weather measures for all grids in a county are weighted averages, where the weights are the cropland area in each grid cell that were obtained from a satellite scan. This gives daily weather measures for each county.

In the baseline model, we sum degree days over all days of the growing season, which was fixed to March 1st through August 31st for all counties and years. These variables were calculated using all counties east of the 100-degree meridian (excluding Florida). The second row of table 2.1 displays the fraction of the US growing area and production that falls in these countries for the three most recent years before the heat wave occurred; that

Table 2.1   **Descriptive statistics of county samples**

	Production		Area harvested		Yield	
	Billion bushels	Percent of US total (%)	Million acres	Percent of US total (%)	Bushel per acre	Percent of US total (%)
US Total	12.63		81.64		154.73	
Eastern counties	11.44	90.53	73.28	89.76	156.07	100.87
Planting dates	10.95	86.72	69.49	85.12	157.63	101.87

Notes: Table summarizes the subsets of counties used in this study. Data are given for the three years before the 2012 heat wave; that is, 2009 to 2011. Eastern counties are all counties east of the 100-degree meridian except Florida. Counties with planting dates are all eastern counties where state-level planting dates are available.

is, 2009 to 2011. With approximately 90 percent of the growing area and total production, these counties account for the largest share of US corn production. Given this large coverage, average yields from these counties closely match overall US yields as shown in the last two columns of the table.

2.2.1 Weather Anomalies for a Fixed Growing Season (Model 1)

Weather measures for counties east of the 100-degree meridian (excluding Florida) that grow corn are displayed on the maps in figure 2.1. The top graph shows 2012 anomalies of season-total degree days above 29°C for a fixed growing season of March through August; that is, the difference between 2012 and the average from 1950 to 2011. The bottom graph shows the 2012 anomalies for season-total precipitation. There is a lot of heterogeneity across counties, with some counties experiencing above normal conditions while others experience below-normal conditions for both weather variables. The Corn Belt was hotter and drier than usual, while southern counties had a cooler and wetter than average year. Note the variation in extreme heat: some highly productive counties in the Corn Belt experienced up to 100 extra degree days above 29°C. As we show below, each degree day above 29°C reduces log yields by 0.006, so the effect of an extra 100 degree day above 29°C is a decrease of 60 log points.

For comparison, the production-weighted average exposure to degree days above 29°C is 33 among all eastern counties in 1950 to 2011. Since bad weather in highly productive areas can cause a loss that is not compensated by better-than-average weather in less productive areas, we summarize weather outcomes by constructing the production-weighted average of all eastern counties. Production weights are the product of actual area (which is known at the beginning of the season) and predicted yields according to a trend.[4]

4. We fit a restricted cubic spline with 3 knots to the yield history of each county.

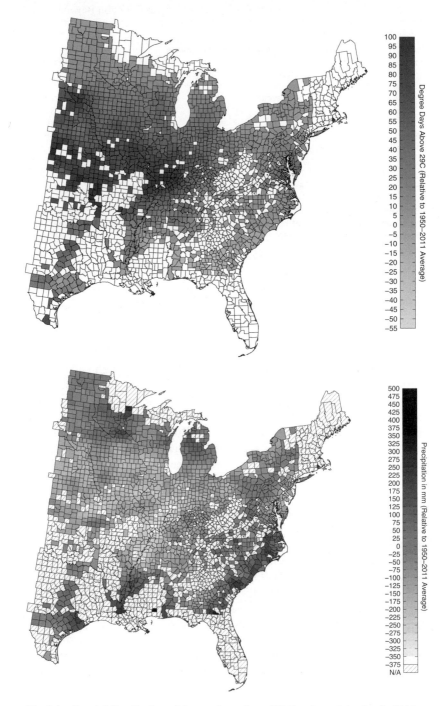

Fig.2.1   Spatial distribution of degree days above 29°C and precipitation in 2012

Notes: Spatial distribution of weather anomalies over the fixed 2012 growing season (March–August). Top panel shows degree days above 29°C, while the bottom panel shows precipitation totals.

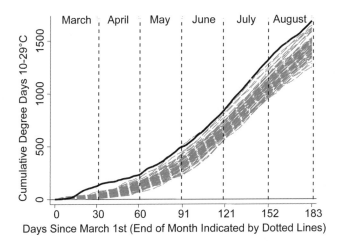

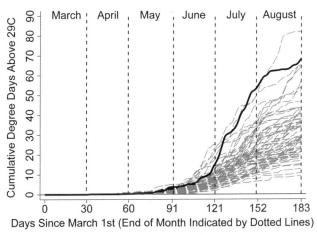

Fig. 2.2   Degree days 10°C–29°C and degree days above 29°C in 2012 relative to 1950–2011

Notes: Panels show cumulative total of degree days 10°C–29°C and cumulative total of degree days above 29°C for the eastern United States except Florida. Weather measures are the weighted average of all counties east of the 100-degree meridian excluding Florida, where the weights are predicted yields along a trend line (restricted cubic spline with 3 knots) times the actual growing area. Cumulative totals for the years 1950 to 2011 are added as thin dashed lines, while 2012 is shown as a thick solid line.

Figure 2.2 shows the evolution of the cumulative season total degree days measures over the 184 days of the growing season, ranging from March 1st (day 0) to August 31st (day 183). We average cumulative season totals up to a given day of the growing season. Historic exposures for the years 1950 to 2011 are shown as gray dashed lines, while the outcome for 2012 is shown as a thick solid line.

The top panel of figure 2.2 shows degree days 10°C–29°C. Degree days above 10°C–29°C start to increase earlier than usual in 2012, since the United States had a warm spring. The beneficial side effect of a warmer spring is that it allows for earlier planting. The bottom graph of figure 2.2 shows degree days above 29°C. July and August are traditionally the months where temperatures climb above 29°C most frequently and degree days above 29°C increase most rapidly. July 2012 was exceptionally hot by historic standards. At the beginning of July, the measures were slightly above normal, but by the end of July, it had superseded the hottest year among the 1950 to 2011 historic baseline, which was 1988. Note that 1988 had a hotter August than 2012, and as a result the season total degree days above 29°C was highest in 1988, followed by 2012.

The top graph of figure 2.3 displays the cumulative season-total precipitation. Precipitation was below normal in 2012, and the only year with drier conditions in the 1950 to 2011 historic baseline is again 1988. Note, however, that the relative deviation from the mean is much lower for precipitation than for degree days above 29°C. Finally, the bottom graph of figure 2.3 shows cumulative vapor pressure deficit, which is the difference between how much water the air can hold when it is saturated and how much water is currently in the air. This measure is used in agronomic crop models and has also been shown to predict yields in a statistical model (Roberts, Schlenker, and Eyer 2013). Similar to precipitation, this measure indicates that crops were adversely affected (a higher than usual deficit is bad for crops), yet the relative deviation from the mean was less than for degree days above 29°C.

2.2.2 Planting and Harvest Dates (Model 2)

The second model relaxes two assumptions: first, we no longer fix the growing season to March through August, but instead used data from the National Agricultural Statistics Service (NASS) on planting and harvesting dates. The NASS reports on a weekly level what fraction of the corn area in major corn-producing states was planted and harvested. We define the beginning of the growing season as the Monday of the week by the end of which at least 50 percent of the corn area in a state had been planted. Similarly, the end of the growing season is the last day of a week when at least 50 percent of the growing area had been harvested in a state.

The average planting date for each county is shown in the top graph of figure 2.4. Southern places tend to plant earlier, as they are not limited by the probability of late freezes. Northern places also have a larger intrayear cycle in solar radiation, which is an important component of crop growth that limits farmers from shifting the planting date too far forward. We do not fix the growing season in each place but allow it to vary between years according to annual NASS reports. In case only the planting date is available for a state, but not the harvest date, we approximate the harvest date by adding the average growing season length to the reported planting date. By the

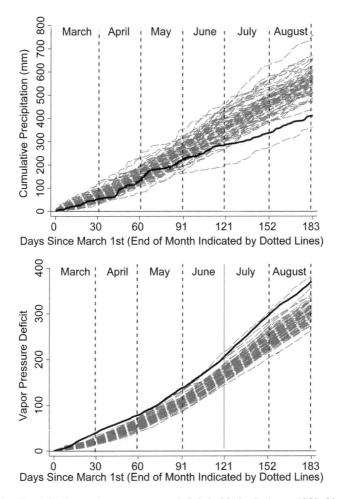

Fig. 2.3   Precipitation and vapor pressure deficit in 2012 relative to 1950–2011

Notes: Panels show precipitation and vapor pressure deficit for eastern United States except Florida. Weather measures are the weighted average of all counties east of the 100-degree meridian excluding Florida, where the weights are predicted yields along a trend line (restricted cubic spline with 3 knots) times the actual growing area. Cumulative totals for the years 1950 to 2011 are added as thin dashed lines, while 2012 is shown as a thick solid line.

same token, if the harvest date is reported but the planting date is missing, we approximate the latter by subtracting the average growing season length from the harvest date.

Southern places have a longer growing season as shown in the bottom graph of figure 2.4. As mentioned above, we make the different growing seasons comparable by rescaling them such that the first day is 0, while the last day is 1. After fitting spline polynomials over the season, we aggregate the variables to an annual level.

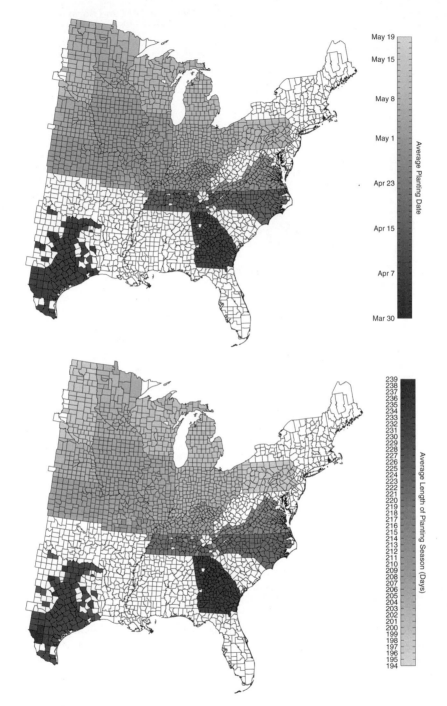

Fig. 2.4   Average planting date and growing season length (1979–2011)

Notes: Top graph shows average planting date in 1979 to 2011, while bottom graph shows average growing season length. Both planting dates and growing season length are reported annually for each state. Counties within each state might have different values because they grew corn in different years.

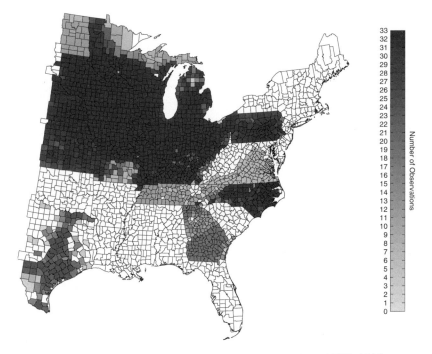

Fig. 2.5   Counties with yearly state-level data on planting dates (1979–2011)

Notes: Figure displays counties for which annual planting and/or harvesting dates as well as yields were reported. Counties are shaded by the number of yearly observations that are available for 1979 to 2011. Planting and harvest dates are reported on a state level, while yields are reported for each county. The number of observations can differ within a state because yields are not reported for all counties in a state.

The number of yearly observations for which we have yield and planting data in a county is shown in figure 2.5. The first year in which data on planting and harvesting dates is available is 1979, but many states started to report planting dates at a later time. Counties in the eastern United States (excluding Florida) that report planting and/or harvest dates are summarized in the third row of table 2.1. States that report planting dates account for 85 percent of the corn growing area and 87 percent of the US corn production in the most recent three years before the 2012 heat wave (2009 to 2011).

The second innovation of model 2 is to relax the assumption that the effect of some, and eventually all, weather variables are constant over the growing season. As outlined in section 2.1, we interact daily measures of the weather variables with spline polynomials. This allows the effect to differ over the growing season in a flexible way.

Figure 2.6 displays the average daily exposure over the growing season for four weather variables: degree days 10°C–29°C, degree days above 29°C, precipitation, and vapor pressure deficit. We use either restricted cubic splines

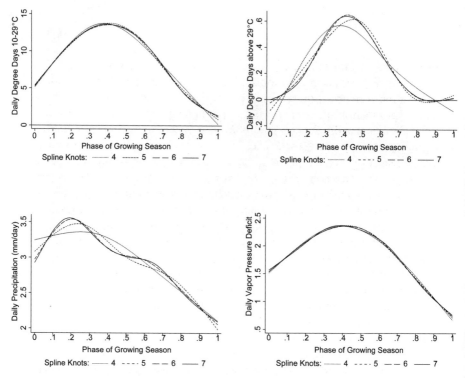

Fig. 2.6   Exposure to various weather variables over the growing season

Notes: Panels show the average exposure to various weather measures over the growing season. We use year- and state-specific estimates of the National Agricultural Statistical Service (NASS) to define the growing season: the week in which the planted area exceeds 50 percent is the start (*x*-value of 0) and the week that the harvested area exceeds 50 percent is the end (*x*-value of 1). Daily values are smoothed using restricted cubic splines with 4, 5, 6, or 7 knots.

with 4, 5, 6, or 7 knots. The results seem fairly stable as long as we include at least 5 knots.

2.3   Empirical Results

We start by replicating the results for a fixed growing season (March through August) that assume constant marginal effects of the weather variables before relaxing both assumptions.

2.3.1   Baseline Model 1

Results for a panel analysis for eastern counties (excluding Florida) for the years 1950 to 2011 is given in table 2.2. All columns use the same set of observations, but vary the set of time controls that are used to capture overall trends in yields. Columns (a), (b), and (c) use state-specific restricted cubic

Table 2.2 The effect of weather on maize yields using a fixed growing season, March through August

	(1a)	(1b)	(1c)	(2a)	(2b)	(2c)
	A. Time invariant variables					
Thousand degree days 10–29°C	0.314***	0.301***	0.303***	0.346***	0.343***	0.361***
	(0.068)	(0.066)	(0.063)	(0.082)	(0.079)	(0.074)
Hundred degree days above 29°C	−0.622***	−0.616***	−0.625***	−0.580***	−0.583***	−0.584***
	(0.068)	(0.066)	(0.065)	(0.069)	(0.068)	(0.067)
Precipitation (m)	1.028***	1.016***	1.029***	1.092***	1.061***	1.095***
	(0.212)	(0.208)	(0.198)	(0.217)	(0.216)	(0.209)
Precipitation (m) squared	−0.806***	−0.800***	−0.818***	−0.807***	−0.787***	−0.814***
	(0.165)	(0.160)	(0.153)	(0.163)	(0.161)	(0.156)
	B. Impact of 2012 weather outcome					
Total production impact (%)	−14.43	−14.65	−14.74	−13.29	−13.46	−13.12
	C. Prediction error for 2012					
RMSE—2012 county prediction	0.3250	0.3442	0.3437	0.3514	0.3476	0.4732
Pred. error total prod. 2012 (%)	3.36	8.82	10.22	10.86	9.96	36.89
R^2	0.7734	0.7784	0.7810	0.7920	0.7955	0.7972
Observations	115,205	115,205	115,205	115,205	115,205	115,205
Counties	2,276	2,276	2,276	2,276	2,276	2,276
Spline knots	3	4	5	3	4	5
Year fixed effects	No	No	No	Yes	Yes	Yes

Notes: Table regresses log maize yields for counties east of the 100-degree meridian (except Florida) in the years 1950 to 2011 on four weather variables as well as time controls. Columns (a), (b), and (c) include state-specific restricted cubic splines in time with 3, 4, and 5 knots, respectively, as time controls. The last three columns additionally include year fixed effects. Panel B gives the predicted production shortfall below trend from the 2012 weather outcomes in percentage points. Panel C compares prediction for 2012 to actual observed yields. The first row shows the root mean squared prediction error of all county-level log yields, while the second row gives the prediction error of total production for all counties combined. Errors are clustered at the state level.

***Significant at the 1 percent level.
**Significant at the 5 percent level.
*Significant at the 10 percent level.

splines with 3, 4, and 5 knots, respectively. On top of that, columns (2a), (2b), and (2c) also include year-fixed effects to capture overall shocks, like changes in global food prices or technological breakthroughs. The results are very stable across specifications. Moderate heat (degree days 10°C–29°C) is beneficial, while extreme heat (degree days above 29°C) is highly damaging. Note that 2,000 degree days 10°C–29°C increase expected yields by as much as 100 degree days above 29°C decrease them. Moreover, a coefficient of –0.6 on degree days above 29°C implies that the 100 additional degree days are lowering expected yields by 60 log points. Recall that several counties in the Corn Belt experienced heat anomalies of that magnitude in 2012 (see figure 2.1). Finally, precipitation and precipitation squared suggest that the relationship is hill-shaped (both too little and too much rain are harmful). The optimum is around 0.63m, or 25inches, which matches closely the estimate of optimal rainfall from agronomic studies.[5]

The effect of the 2012 weather outcomes on expected yields are shown in figure 2.7. The top graph depicts predicted deviations from the time trend in log points (using the specification from column [1a] in table 2.2). There is significant heterogeneity: some counties are predicted to be as much as 56 percent below normal, while others experience yields up to 32 percent above normal. Unfortunately, yield declines are concentrated in the more productive areas. The bottom graph of the figure does not show relative impacts, but predicted *total impacts*. We multiply the observed harvest area in 2012 by the predicted production shortfall per area.[6] While northern and southern areas experience small absolute increases, counties of the Corn Belt are predicted to experience large declines. The overall impact for our sample is a 14.4 percent production shortfall below trend as shown in column (1a), panel B, in table 2.2.

The observed yields in 2012 have been published after an earlier version of this chapter gave our predicted production shortfalls. Panel C therefore compares the how well our prediction compares to the actual observed yields in 2012. The first row gives the root mean squared error, which is the square root of the sum of the squared difference between the prediction in each county and the observed outcomes in 2013. The second row derives the percent error when predicted total production for all counties in the sample is compared against the observed outcome for 2012. All numbers are positive, suggesting that our model overpredicted yields, or underpredicted the damaging effects of extreme heat. Note that the error on predicted production is

---

5. Ozone pollution is correlated with high temperatures and one might wonder whether the coefficient on extreme temperatures captures the reduced form effect of both temperature and ozone. Boone, Schlenker, and Siikamäki (2013) estimate a model that includes both degree days above 29°C as well as various ozone measures. While ozone is very damaging for maize yields, its inclusion only slightly changes the coefficient on degree days above 29°C as the latter is a highly nonlinear transformation of temperature and hence not directly related to ozone exposure.

6. We obtain similar results if we instead use the average harvest area for the previous three years 2009 to 2011.

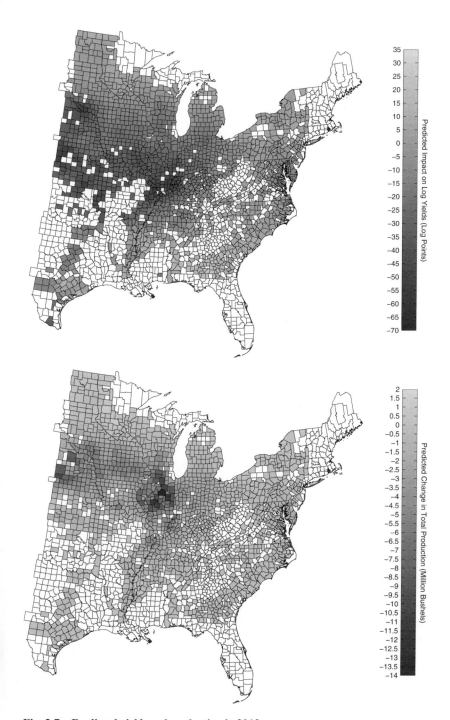

Fig. 2.7 Predicted yields and production in 2012

Notes: Predicted yield and production impacts in 2012 by county using the regression specification in column (1a) of table 2.2. The top panel shows changes in predicted yields in log points, while the bottom shows predicted changes in total production (using the average area of 2009 to 2011 as growing area). Total predicted production in the shown counties was 11.4 billion bushels, and the production shortfall was 1.7 billion bushels, or 15 percent.

quiet large if we use a fifth-order time polynomial, but not for the weather impacts. While the predicted production impact is comparable among all columns in panel B, the error on predicted total production is large when we use more flexible time trends. The reason is that the predicted trend is badly estimated for years outside the range observed in the data in a flexible model, which uses the last few years of observed data to interpolate the trend out of sample.

2.3.2   Model 2: Time-Varying Growing Season and Parameters

When we allow the effect of weather variables to vary over the growing season, we have to restrict the data set to a smaller set of counties for which annual planting and harvest dates are available. Column (1) of table 2.3, therefore, still forces the effect of each weather variable to be constant over the growing season, but runs the regression on the subset of counties for which planting dates are available and uses the weather measures when they are averaged over the actual growing season (instead of March through August). The coefficient on the two degree days variables remain rather unchanged. Panel C summarizes the predicted decrease in total production from the observed 2012 weather outcomes, which is 18.5 percent in column (1), that is, larger in magnitude than what we had observed for the bigger sample in column (1a) of table 2.2.

Columns (2a), (2b), (2c), and (2d) allow the effect of extreme heat, which had the largest effect on year-to-year yield variability to vary over the growing season. The columns use $k = 4, 5, 6,$ or 7 spline knots, respectively. The coefficient estimates on the $k - 1$ spline polynomials are difficult to interpret, and hence we plot them over the growing season in figure 2.8. There is considerable heterogeneity over the growing season: the most damaging effects occur during phase 0.3 to 0.4 of the growing season irrespective of how many spline knots we use. The behavior at the boundaries (close to 0 and 1) should be interpreted with caution, as there is little mass at these endpoints as shown in figure 2.6.[7]

Panel B of table 2.3 tests whether the time-varying portion (not the constant effect of degree days above 29°C) are statistically significant, which is always the case. Predicted damages of the 2012 heat wave increase to 21 percent in panel C, which is not surprising as most of the excessive heat happened in July, which is in the 0.3 to 0.4 window when extreme heat is most damaging. The spatial distribution of the predicted impacts for the specification in column (2b) is given in the top graph of figure 2.9.[8] Note that

7. Recall that the largest exposure to degree days above 29°C happens around 0.4 to 0.5 of the growing season; that is, the effect is not simply largest when exposure is highest.

8. Since the state-specific planting dates are only available for some years starting in 1979, weather anomalies are calculated as the difference to the observed weather average in our estimation sample.

Table 2.3 The effect of weather on maize yields using time-varying growing seasons

	(1)	(2a)	(2b)	(2c)	(2d)
	A. Time invariant variables				
Thousand degree days 10–29°C	0.333***	0.322***	0.320***	0.317***	0.322***
	(0.091)	(0.087)	(0.085)	(0.086)	(0.083)
Hundred degree days above 29°C	−0.591***				
	(0.086)				
Precipitation (m)	0.649***	0.622**	0.608**	0.589**	0.648***
	(0.211)	(0.217)	(0.230)	(0.216)	(0.222)
Precipitation (m) squared	−0.439**	−0.392**	−0.384**	−0.373**	−0.409**
	(0.166)	(0.166)	(0.173)	(0.166)	(0.170)
	B. Joint sig. of time-varying variable				
$F_{\text{Degree Days Above 29°C}}$		80.49	70.59	64.54	51.75
$p_{\text{Degree Days Above 29°C}}$		1.27e–10	9.43e–11	7.36e–11	2.21e–10
	C. Impact of 2012 weather outcome				
Total production impact (%)	−18.54	−20.89	−20.68	−20.80	−21.68
	D. Prediction error for 2012				
RMSE–2012 county prediction	0.3688	0.3320	0.3333	0.3332	0.3321
Pred. error total prod. 2012 (%)	8.00	4.20	4.48	4.61	3.55
R^2	0.5151	0.5366	0.5364	0.5369	0.5422
Observations	43,249	43,249	43,249	43,249	43,249
Counties	1,659	1,659	1,659	1,659	1,659
Spline knots (time-varying var.)		4	5	6	7

Notes: Table regresses log maize yields for counties east of the 100-degree meridian where state-level plating dates are available in 1979 to 2011. Counties are shown in figure 2.5. Column (1) uses the same specification as column (1a) in table 2.2 except that it only uses counties and years for which planting dates are available and averages the weather variables over the actual growing season (instead of March through August). The remaining columns (2a) to (2d) allow the effect of degree days above 29°C to vary over the growing season. Columns differ by the number of spline knots used in the estimation of the seasonality, varying from 4 to 7 knots. The spline polynomials are shown in figure 2.8. Panel B of the table gives the F-statistics as well as the p-value for the joint significance of the *time-varying* components (not including the constant marginal effect). Panel C gives the predicted production shortfall below trend from the 2012 weather outcomes in percentage points. Panel D compares prediction for 2012 to actual observed yields. The first row shows the root mean squared prediction error of all county-level log yields, while the second row gives the prediction error of total production for all counties combined. Errors are clustered at the state level.

***Significant at the 1 percent level.
**Significant at the 5 percent level.
*Significant at the 10 percent level.

broadly comparable spatial pattern to the results we got when we fixed the growing season to March through August and forced the weather variables to have the same impact for all days of the growing season in figure 2.7, but the magnitude of the impacts is larger.

Panel D again compares predicted log yields and total production to the observed outcomes in 2012. While the prediction error decreases from col-

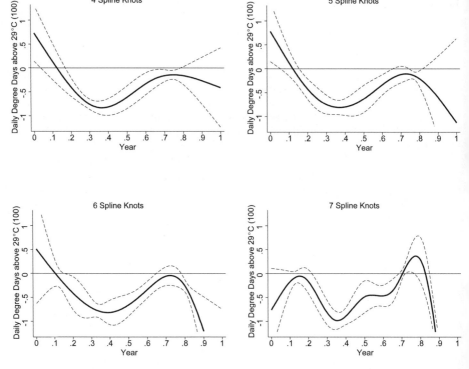

Fig. 2.8   Effect of degree days above 29°C as it varies over the growing season

Notes: Panels show the marginal effect of 100 degree days above 29°C. A reference model that fixes the effect to be the same across the growing season gave an estimate of –0.59 in column (1) of table 2.3.

umns (1) to (2d) as the models become more flexible, it is comparable in column (2d) of table 2.3 to column (1a) of table 2.2. The longer time series of the more simplistic model in table 2.2 gives a better prediction of the trend, which is counterbalanced by more accurately predicted production shortfall in table 2.3.

A lot of media coverage focused on the concurrence of extremely hot temperatures and drought conditions. Table 2.4, therefore, also includes an interaction term between daily degree days above 29°C and daily precipitation levels. The precipitation variables are different from the measures we used until now: we previously measured *growing season total* precipitation and its square. Since we are now interested how the effect varies over the growing season, we use *daily* precipitation and daily precipitation squared, which are then aggregated over the season.

The interaction is not significant in column (2), and the inclusion has almost no effect on the predicted impact of the 2012 weather outcomes in panel C. Columns (3) through (6) consecutively relax the assumption that

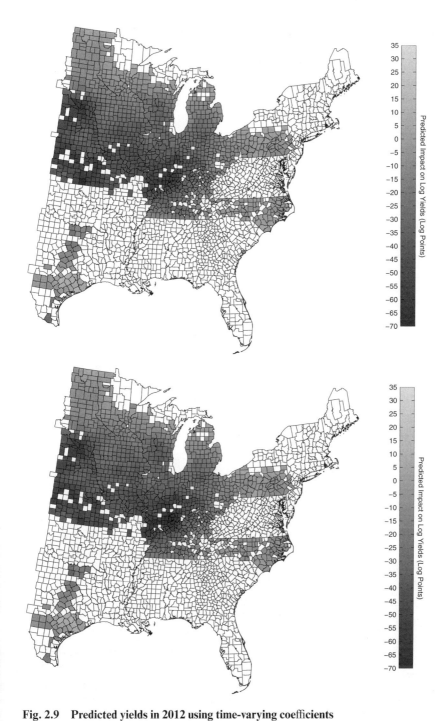

Fig. 2.9   Predicted yields in 2012 using time-varying coefficients

Notes: Both panels show changes in predicted yields in log points. The top panel uses the regression specification in column (2b) of table 2.3, while the bottom panel uses the specification in column (6) of table 2.4.

Table 2.4 **The effect of weather on maize yields using time-varying growing seasons and precipitation interactions**

	(1)	(2)	(3)	(4)	(5)	(6)
	A. Time invariant variables					
Thousand degree days 10–29°C	0.333*** (0.091)	0.354*** (0.075)	0.334*** (0.074)	0.336*** (0.072)	0.313*** (0.074)	
Hundred degree days above 29°C	−0.591*** (0.086)	−0.562*** (0.107)				
Days above 29°C × precipitation		−32.435 (31.586)	−19.560 (25.565)			
Precipitation (m)	0.649*** (0.211)	0.708*** (0.207)	0.650** (0.231)	0.654** (0.237)		
Precipitation (m) squared	−0.439** (0.166)	−0.473*** (0.160)	−0.409** (0.170)	−0.415** (0.173)		
	B. Joint significance of time-varying variable					
$P_{\text{Degree Days Above 29°C}}$			7.88e–10	4.88e–09	2.22e–07	4.00e–09
$P_{\text{Degree Days Above 29°C} \times \text{Precipitation}}$				0.0000619	0.00213	0.0157
$P_{\text{Precipitation}}$					0.00453	0.00426
$P_{\text{Precipitation Squared}}$					0.000857	0.00186
$P_{\text{Degree Days 10–29°C}}$						0.0352
	C. Impact of 2012 weather outcome					
Total production impact (%)	−18.54	−18.78	−20.79	−20.73	−22.19	−22.80
	D. Prediction error for 2012					
RMSE—2012 county prediction	0.3688	0.3672	0.3329	0.3285	0.3328	0.3271
Pred. error total prod. 2012 (%)	8.00	8.09	4.55	4.67	2.96	1.69
R^2	0.5151	0.5167	0.5370	0.5407	0.5524	0.5540
Observations	43,249	43,249	43,249	43,249	43,249	43,249
Counties	1,659	1,659	1,659	1,659	1,659	1,659
Spline knots (time-varying var.)			5	5	5	5

Notes: Table regresses log maize yields for counties east of the 100-degree meridian where state-level plating dates are available in 1979 to 2011. Counties are shown in figure 2.5. Column (1) is the same as column (1) in table 2.3. Column (2) adds an interaction term between daily extreme heat and precipitation. Column (3) allows the effect of extreme heat to vary over the growing season (similar to column [2b] in table 2.3). Columns (4) to (6) allow the effect of other variables to vary over the season: respectively, the effect of the interaction between extreme heat and precipitation, the effect of precipitation and precipitation squared, and the effect of moderate degree days 10°C–29°C. Panel B of the table gives the *p*-values for the joint significance of the *time-varying* components (not including the constant marginal effect). Panel C gives the predicted production shortfall below trend from the 2012 weather outcomes in percentage points. Panel D compares the prediction for 2012 to actual observed yields. The first row shows the root mean squared prediction error of all county-level log yields, while the second row gives the prediction error of total production for all counties combined. Errors are clustered at the state level.
***Significant at the 1 percent level.
**Significant at the 5 percent level.
*Significant at the 10 percent level.

various weather variables are constant over the growing season (we use state-specific restricted cubic splines with 3 spline knots to capture time trends and restricted cubic splines with 5 knots to capture seasonality components of the effects of weather variables for all specifications). While the time-variant portions of all weather variables are significant as shown in panel B (p-values are generally less than 0.05), the predicted weather impacts for 2012 in panel C are comparable to a model where we only allow the effect of degree days above 29°C to vary over the growing season. The spatial distribution of impacts under the most flexible model (column [6]) is shown in the bottom graph of figure 2.9. The pattern is remarkably similar to the top graph that only allows the effect of degree days above 29°C to vary over the growing season.

The model that is most flexible in all weather variables (column [6]) has the lowest prediction error for 2012 as shown in panel D of table 2.4, suggesting that flexibility in the seasonal effects of the weather variables improves the prediction. In summary, switching from a fixed growing season (March through August) to a time-varying growing season gave larger prediction errors, but allowing the effect of the weather variables to vary over the growing season reduced it again. Both the time invariant baseline model as well as the model using time-varying parameters predicted the effects of 2012 fairly accurately.

2.4   Discussion

The 2012 heat wave resulted in significant production shortfalls. A baseline model that holds the growing season as well as the effect of the weather variables over the growing season constant gives predicted declines of 14.4 percent. If we instead average the weather measures over the actual growing season, the impacts increase to 19 percent, and if we allow the effect of extreme heat to vary over the growing season, the predicted damages increase further in magnitude up to 23 percent as the heat wave hit when it is most damaging.

For comparison, a comparable model to our baseline model in Schlenker and Roberts (2009) predicted decreases of slightly more than 20 percent under the Hadley III climate change model by midcentury (2020 to 2049). The predicted impacts from 2012 are hence predicted to become more frequent pretty soon if the climate forecasts turn out to be accurate.

Hansen, Sato, and Ruedy (2012) look at the frequency of extreme temperatures around the world and argue that it is predicted to increase significantly with climate change. The chapter finds that the United States is one of the few areas that has been "lucky" so far, in the sense that it has not seen a significant increase in observed extremes. The year of 2012 might soon be the new normal.

2.5   Conclusion

We model the impact of the 2012 heat wave/drought with two models. A baseline model keeps the growing season as well the effect of various weather measures over the growing season constant. In a new extension, we then obtain the actual growing season on a state level and allow the effect of weather to vary over the growing season. We find that the time-varying components are highly statistically significant.

The baseline model predicts overall production declines in our sample of 14.4 percent. While some areas are severely hit, others actually have above-normal yields. Once we use the actual growing season (instead of the artificially fixed one), the production decline goes up in magnitude to 19 percent. If the effect of extreme heat is allowed to vary over the growing season, the predicted damage increases further to 23 percent as the heat wave hit during a time when it is most damaging. Production shortfalls of around 20 percent in an area that accounts for 40 percent of global production will have strong effects on prices. Recall that historic global corn production shocks (deviations from a trend) ranged from −13 percent to +7 percent in 1961 to 2010.

If climate forecasts turn out to accurate, we will experience increased variability in degree days above 29°C even if the variance of temperatures remains constant. The reason behind this behavior is that degree days above 29°C are a truncated temperature variable. An upward shift in the mean of the variable that leaves the variance constant will increase year-to-year variability of degree days above 29°C as the bound of 29°C binds less frequently. Temperature fluctuations below 29°C have no effect on degree days above 29°C, while temperature fluctuations above the threshold do. An upward shift in temperatures hence shifts more mass of the probability distribution to a region where it translates into fluctuations of damaging degree days. Climate change has the potential to not only decrease average production, but also to make it more volatile. As a response, food price volatility will likely increase, even though some of the increased volatility will be buffered through higher storage levels.

References

Boone, Christopher, Wolfram Schlenker, and Juha Siikamäki. 2013. "Ground-Level Ozone Pollution and Corn Yields in the United States." Working Paper.
Hansen, James, Makiko Sato, and Reto Ruedy. 2012. "Perception of Climate Change." *Proceedings of the National Academy of Sciences* 109 (37): E2415–E2423.
Ortiz-Bobea, Ariel, and Richard E. Just. 2013. "Modeling the Structure of Adaptation in Climate Change Impact Assessment." *American Journal of Agricultural Economics* 95 (2): 244–51.
Roberts, Michael J., and Wolfram Schlenker. 2013. "Identifying Supply and Demand

Elasticities of Agricultural Commodities: Implications for the US Ethanol Mandate." *American Economic Review* 103 (6): 2265–95.

Roberts, Michael J., Wolfram Schlenker, and Jonathan Eyer. 2013. "Agronomic Weather Measures in Econometric Models of Crop Yield with Implications for Climate Change." *American Journal of Agricultural Economics* 95 (2): 236–43.

Schlenker, Wolfram, and Michael J. Roberts. 2009. "Nonlinear Temperature Effects Indicate Severe Damages to US Crop Yields under Climate Change." *Proceedings of the National Academy of Sciences of the United States* 106 (37): 15594–8.

Snyder, R. L. 1985. "Hand Calculating Degree Days." *Agricultural and Forest Meterology* 35 (1–4): 353–8.

Comment   Derek Headey

Overview of the Chapter

In this chapter Berry, Roberts, and Schlenker extend some of their earlier work on the effects of weather shocks on US maize production. A key motivation for their chapter—and the link to the broader theme of this book—is that the United States is a major producer and exporter of maize, such that production shocks in the United States are a potential driver of maize price volatility, which may have important ramifications for the world's poor.[1] The main technical innovations of this chapter are that they now allow the effect of various weather measures to evolve over the growing season, and that the growing season is made more location specific. This new and improved model is then applied to the 2012 growing season, when large parts of the US maize belt experienced a severe heat wave and drought. Strikingly, their improved model predicts yield declines of up to 24 percent. In their concluding remarks they note that some climate change models predict that these kinds of heat spells/droughts may well be the new normal in the US maize belt.

My comments will be confined to four areas: a few technical issues, a quick look at whether their predictions came true, some discussion and exploratory analysis of the impact of US maize production on international prices, and some policy and programmatic implications of their model and results.

Some Technical Issues

Technically, the chapter is strong. The authors build on much simpler attempts to model weather with production outcomes, with a particular

Derek Headey is a research fellow of the International Food Policy Research Institute (IFPRI).

For acknowledgments, sources of research support, and disclosure of the author's material financial relationships, if any, please see http://www.nber.org/chapters/c12807.ack.

1. Maize is the most important staple food in Africa, and a major crop in Latin America.

focus on hot days, defined as those exceeding 29 degrees Celsius. Nevertheless, I have a few concerns with the empirics of the chapter.

First, while the authors do show that the explanatory variables of the model have highly significant marginal effects, there is not much discussion of goodness of fit or predictive capacity of the model. But an obvious use of this kind of model—and one which I discuss below—is that it might serve as an early warning device, or as a gauge of the likely impact of climate change.

Second, the authors refer to the agronomic literature without ever actually citing it. More details would be welcome, particularly those related to heat stress, and particularly given that they make a point of noting that their model looks largely consistent with agronomic evidence. Such evidence should be cited.

Third, on a related note, while the authors engage in quite a few sensitivity analyses, they never vary the 29 degree Celsius threshold. Perhaps they, or others, have done so in earlier work, but the use of a threshold always makes readers wonder whether the choice of threshold is robust.

Fourth, while the authors attempt to model interactions between heat days and precipitation, they do not find any significant interactions. It seems rather unintuitive that heat and moisture (broadly defined, rather than just precipitation) would not interact in some way. One would not expect heat in excess of 29 degrees in very cloudy and humid conditions to have the same effects as very dry heat, particularly prolonged dry heat. Clearly, weather is a highly nonlinear phenomenon in terms of the existence of thresholds and likely interaction effects. However, modeling these nonlinearities— particularly interaction effects—is always very challenging. In this case they interact hot days with precipitation, but precipitation itself seems to have a quadratic relationship with production, which potentially presents an additional challenge to finding a significant interaction effect between precipitation and hot days. While the authors make a sensible attempt to find such a significant interaction, I would urge them to keep testing and experimenting with different specifications and methods.

Predictive Capabilities of the Model

Turning to my second set of comments, the data in this study extend up to August 31, 2012. As such, the authors have a good set of data to make predictions about the summer harvest of 2012, although writing in May of 2013 I now have access to the United States Department of Agriculture (USDA)'s estimates of actual maize production in 2012, which I report in table 2C.1. Specifically, I report yields, production and area, as well as stocks and exports as a share of production. The key number in table 2C.1 is the −16.2 percent drop in maize yields in 2012. This falls in the range of estimates presented by Berry et al. (−15 to –24 percent), but is toward the lower end of that range, particularly the number derived by their unimproved base-

Table 2C.1   **Did their predictions come true? Trends in the US maize sector, 2010–2013**

	Yields (tons)	Production (1000s mt)	Area (1000s ha)	Stocks (% of production)	Exports (% of production)
Levels					
2010	9.59	316,165	32,960	32.4	14.3
2011	9.24	313,949	33,989	31.7	12.2
2012	7.74	273,832	35,360	39.1	7.1
2013[a]	9.92	359,173	36,220	29.6	9.2
Year-on-year growth rates					
2011	–3.7%	–0.7%	3.1%	–2.4	–14.5
2012	–16.2%	–12.8%	4.0%	23.4	–41.8
2013[a]	28.1%	31.2%	2.4%	–24.4	29.0

Source: USDA (2013).

[a]2013 numbers are presumably USDA projections, since the data were downloaded in May 2013.

line model (–15 percent). Nevertheless, the discrepancy between this –16.2 percent estimate and the –24 percent estimate of their most favored model could be explained by different spatial coverage (Berry et al.'s sample pertains to those counties east of the 100 degree meridian, rather than the whole country), and even by some measurement error in the USDA numbers. On the whole, though, their modeling approach shows substantial predictive capacity for 2012. Nevertheless, it would be useful for the authors to retrospectively revisit the predict capacity of their model for the 2012 season after updating their data set. The authors could then explore ways of tweaking the model to improve their predictions, including my suggestion for more extensive testing of nonlinear specifications.

The Links between Climatic Shocks and Food Price Volatility

One weakness of the chapter, albeit from a purely thematic standpoint, is that the authors do not empirically link their analysis to food price volatility. Obviously, the impact of weather shocks on food price volatility is a key motivation for their chapter. The authors note, for example, that the United States accounts for around 40 percent of global maize production, for example. They might also note that the United States accounts for between 50 to 60 percent of global trade (depending on the year), suggesting that the impact of US policies, macroeconomic shocks, and weather shocks might be as large—if not larger—than the impact of policies in the entire rest of the world! Many discussions of the 2008 food price spike also viewed weather shocks as a significant factor, particularly as these shocks acted as a catalyst for trade restrictions and precautionary imports, which further exacerbated price volatility (Dollive 2008; Headey 2010; Headey and Fan 2010).

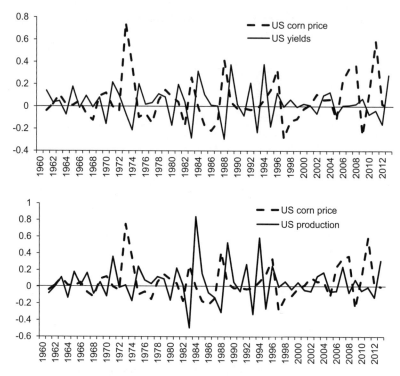

Fig. 2C.1   US production and yield shocks and maize prices
Source: USDA (2013).

But while the links between weather shocks in the United States and global food prices seem intuitive, the issue is not straightforward, particularly because of the potentially dampening effects of grain stocks/reserves. Even if weather shocks become more frequent and severe in the future, food price volatility could well be mitigated by more prudential stocking policies.[2]

Since the 2008 crisis a large number of econometric studies have emerged that try to explain food price dynamics, but I cannot recall a specific paper looking at the impacts of US production shocks on food price dynamics. I have little scope to delve into the issue in any detail here, but in figure 2C.1 and table 2C.2 I take a preliminary look at the relationship between these variables. Figure 2C.1 shows the relationship between maize prices and maize yields in the top panel, and maize prices and maize production in the bottom panel. Yields are presumably strongly driven by weather events in the US context of relatively stable farm policies, but production is partly a

2. At the same time, one issue in the analysis of the 2008 crisis was that low stocks were arguably overemphasized, since weather shocks and strong demand actually drove down private stocks. So to some extent low stocks were a symptom of the crisis, rather than a cause.

Table 2C.2   VAR regressions linking prices, production, stocks, exports for the United States (-A) and the rest of the world (-W)

		Prices equation	Production-A equation	Stocks-W equation	Exports-W equation
Variable	Lag	Elasticity	Elasticity	Elasticity	Elasticity
Prices	L1.	0.10	-0.30	0.15	0.20
	L2.	-0.14	0.13	0.00	-0.32
Stocks-A	L1.	-0.27***	-0.21**	-0.09^a	-0.13
	L2.	0.09	-0.11	0.08	-0.10
Production-A	L1.	0.38*	-0.47*	0.18	0.32
	L2.	0.13	-0.11	0.06	0.17
Exports-A	L1.	0.21	0.05	0.06	-0.21
	L2.	0.22^a	0.16	0.10	-0.02
Stocks-W	L1.	0.16	0.07	0.56***	-0.34
	L2.	-0.49*	0.11	-0.28^a	0.30
Production-W	L1.	-0.66	0.94	-1.13**	1.56
	L2.	0.72	0.14	0.25	0.73
Exports-W	L1.	-0.02	0.19	-0.09	-0.51**
	L2.	0.09	0.30	0.03	-0.30

(continued)

Table 2C.2 (continued)

		Prices equation	Production-A equation	Stocks-W equation	Exports-W equation
	Lag	Elasticity	Elasticity	Elasticity	
Prices	L1.	−0.32	−0.63**	0.04	
	L2.	0.31	0.30	0.02	
Stocks-A	L1.	−0.51**	0.18[a]	−0.05**	
	L2.	0.22	−0.07	−0.01	
Production-A	L1.	0.68	−0.94***	0.08	
	L2.	−0.40	0.01	0.12**	
Exports-A	L1.	−0.65	0.08	0.04	
	L2.	0.33	0.34[a]	0.01	
Stocks-W	L1.	0.08	0.31	0.07	
	L2.	0.54	−0.13	−0.20***	
Production-W	L1.	3.46*	−0.03	−0.67***	
	L2.	0.34	−0.05	0.13	
Exports-W	L1.	0.44	0.00	−0.05	
	L2.	0.52	0.27	0.04	

Exports-W equation (summary statistics):

Equation	rmse	R-sq
Prices	0.14	0.54
Stocks-A	0.43	0.45
Production-A	0.17	0.55
Exports-A	0.22	0.40
Stocks-W	0.10	0.43
Production-W	0.04	0.64
Exports-W	0.23	0.37

Sources: All data, except prices, are derived from USDA (2013). Prices are from FAO (2013).

Notes: Regressions are VAR with seven equations, two lag lengths, with all variables specified as the log of first differences. Regressions used annual data covering the years 1963 to 2013.

***Significant at the 1 percent level.

**Significant at the 5 percent level.

*Significant at the 10 percent level.

[a]Denotes marginal insignificance at the 10 percent level.

function of planting decisions, which are endogenous with respect to prices. When eyeballing the data, one can certainly see some instances in which both production and yields move in opposite directions, and in which a yield/production shock precedes or coincides with a price shock: 1983, 1988, 1995 are strong instances and pertain to price spikes mentioned in the literature. However, if anything, the relationship breaks down after 1995. For example, for yields the correlation with maize prices is –0.35 prior to 1996, but just –0.05 afterward. For production, the correlation is –0.18 prior to 1996 and +0.10 afterward. From this we can infer that many other factors have been driving food prices in recent times. Indeed, even the tremendous 16 percent drop in yields in 2012 does not appear to have had any sizeable impact on international prices.

In table 2C.2 I conduct a very preliminary and exploratory vector autoregression (VAR) analysis of some of these relationships for both US production (denoted –A) and rest of the world production (denoted –W). Specifically, I examine the differences of the log of prices, production, stocks, and exports for both the United States and the rest of the world, implying a VAR system with seven endogenous variables. I make no pretensions that this analysis is sufficiently rigorous to draw strong inferences, since caveats abound: data quality for the rest of the world are pretty questionable, and I have made no theoretical attempt to address the complex role of stocks and little effort to empirically test other specification issues such as structural breaks, interaction effects, threshold effects, and so on (with one exception noted below). Also note that I use US production shocks rather than yield shocks, since it is presumably production that is the direct determinant of a supply shock, rather than yields (even so, the correlation between the two is a very high 0.90). The VAR approach has the advantage of treating all these variables as endogenous, but it could also be criticized as being quite atheoretical. I therefore limit my inferences to highlighting some apparent stylized facts that warrant a more rigorous analysis in the future.

With these caveats in mind, what does table 2C.2 suggest about the role of US production and stocking behavior in determining food prices? In the top left quadrant we see that changes in prices are indeed significantly associated with the first lag of production, with a reasonably large (but moderately significant) elasticity of 0.38. However, we also observe that the first lag of US stocks and the second lag of world stocks are significant, with respective elasticities of –0.27 (significant at the 1 percent level) and –0.49 (significant at the 10 percent level). As expected, this points to a potentially causal effect of stock changes on prices. One might also expect important interaction effects: production shocks may not matter much if existing stocks are high. I find some evidence of that through an ordinary least squares (OLS) regression (with two AR terms not reported), which interacts the lagged change in production with the lagged stocks-to-use ratio for the United States:

$$\Delta \ln price = -0.39 * \Delta \ln prod_{t-1} + 0.01 * \Delta \ln prod_{t-1} * stocks_{t-1}.$$

The regression suggests that the impact of a −10 percent production shock will result in a 0.9 percent price increase when stocks are high (e.g., 30 percent of use), but a 2.9 percent price increase when stocks are low (e.g., 10 percent of use). Again, there are plenty of caveats in a regression such as this, but the finding is nevertheless intuitive.

Another finding of potential importance pertains to the price impacts of US exports. In table 2C.2 the first and second lags of US exports are reasonably large (0.21 and 0.22) but not quite significant at the 10 percent level. However, more parsimonious specifications that drop the mostly insignificant rest of the world variables suggest that the first lag of US exports has an elasticity of 0.22 that *is* significant at the 10 percent level.[3] US exports represents foreign demand for US maize, which previous studies have shown to be quite volatile and highly correlated with international prices (Headey 2010).

There are some other findings of potential significance in table 2C.2: (a) lagged US stocks negatively affect US production (presumably through planting decisions); (b) increases in US production and prices reduce exports to the rest of the world; and (c) several of the rest of the world results mirror the result for US production, stocking, and trade relationships.

In summary, table 2C.2, and the additional regressions referred to above, suggest that:

1. US production shocks do have a reasonably strong impact on US prices (which are conventionally taken as international prices);

2. the effect of production shocks is conditioned by US stock levels; and

3. foreign demand may well be another important factor in explaining price dynamics.

Policy Implications

The linkage between US production shocks and world prices does indeed provide an important motivation for developing econometric models that can successfully predict US production shocks. One can imagine that the model developed by Berry et al. (or future variants thereof) might therefore be very useful for at least three areas of application.

Short-Term "Early Warning" Models

Currently the USDA and similar institutions around the world do give weather forecasts in the hope of improving production and stocking decisions, and in some cases such institutions also give yield and production

---

3. Specifically, that model for US variables only yields the following results in the prices equation: $\Delta \ln price = -0.26 * \Delta \ln stocks_{t-1} + 0.39 * \Delta \ln prod_{t-1} + 0.22 * \Delta \ln exports_{t-1}$.

The first coefficient is significant at the 1 percent level and the last two coefficients are significant at the 10 percent level.

forecasts (presumably based on models bearing some similarity to those in Berry et al.). Thus it may be advisable for the authors to engage with the USDA and other institutions for the purposes of producing improved weather-based yield and production forecasts. One point of note is that the predictive capacity of traditional weather forecasts is another interesting phenomenon often subject to thresholds (i.e., in some contexts, weather forecasts only become accurate relatively late in the season). Thus the authors could consider in future work when in the growing season their model might actually give useful predictions of harvest outcomes.

Long-Term Climate Change Modeling

As global and US climate models improve, particularly with regard to their capacity to predict the altered frequency of weather shocks, a model linking weather shocks to production outcomes would be useful for quantifying the agricultural impacts of climate change. Being climate change researchers, among other things, the authors will no doubt pursue this kind of research in the future.

Policy Modeling

The intuitive theory and evidence linking production shocks to stock levels—and possibly to other shock-mitigation institutions, such as futures markets, virtual reserves, and so on—suggests that this weather model could conceivably fit neatly into a larger economic model (e.g., dynamic computable general equilibrium [CGE] models) linking production, stocking behavior, financial market behavior, and trade behavior. As I and my coauthors had noted in previous work, the predictive models used prior to the 2008 food crisis very much focused on the medium to long term, and had very limited capacity to understand short-term price dynamics (Headey, Fan, and Malaiyandi 2010). Indeed, almost every cited cause of the 2008 crisis is extremely difficult to model convincingly. Headey (2010) shows the volatile and complex nature of international trade behavior, including export restrictions, but also precautionary purchases by major importers. Many authors have looked at the complexity of futures markets (see also Aulerich, Irwin, and Garcia, chapter 6, this volume), with little consensus as to their importance for price behavior. And the issue of stocking behavior is perhaps most complex of all, mixing together the endogenous behavior of private agents, some degree of public intervention, and important interactions with other factors (as we saw above). The work of Berry et al. makes a potentially important contribution by filling in one of those knowledge gaps, namely the links between weather and production shocks. But as climate change seems likely to affect the volatility of the weather (IPCC 2012), and not just secular trends, the incorporation of weather shocks into broader economic models will surely be an important area for future research. The ongoing work in this area by Berry et al. could therefore make a substantial contribution to the broader efforts to understand the causal mechanisms of food price volatility.

References

Dollive, K. 2008. "The Impact of Export Restraints on Rising Grain Prices." Office of Economics Working Paper no. 2008-08-A, US International Trade Commission, Washington, DC.

Food and Agriculture Organization (FAO). 2013. FAO Food Price Index Database. Rome: Food and Agriculture Organization. Accessed March 4. www.fao.org/worldfoodsituation/FoodPricesIndex/en/.

Headey, D. 2010. "Rethinking the Global Food Crisis: The Role of Trade Shocks." IFPRI Discussion Paper no. 831. Washington, DC: International Food Policy Research Institute.

Headey, D., and S. Fan. 2010. *Reflections on the Global Food Crisis: How Did It Happen? How Has It Hurt? And How Can We Prevent The Next One?* Washington, DC: International Food Policy Research Institute (IFPRI).

Headey, D., S. Fan, and S. Malaiyandi. 2010. "Navigating the Perfect Storm: Reflections on the Food, Energy, and Financial Crises." *Agricultural Economics* 41 (S1): 217–28.

Intergovernmental Panel on Climate Change (IPCC). 2012. *Managing the Risks of Extreme Events and Disasters to Advance Climate Change Adaptation.* New York: Cambridge University Press.

United States Department of Agriculture (USDA). 2013. PS&D online database. Accessed March 4. http://www.fas.usda.gov/psdonline/psdQuery.aspx.

Biofuels, Binding Constraints, and Agricultural Commodity Price Volatility

Philip Abbott

3.1 Introduction

The share of US corn production used to produce ethanol increased from 12.4 percent in the 2004 to 2005 crop year to over 38.5 percent in the 2010 to 2011 crop year, and remained at that high level in 2011 and 2012 (ERS 2012). Even after accounting for return of by-products to the feed market,[1] this is a large and persistent new demand for corn that surely has changed price dynamics (Wright 2011; Abbott, Hurt, and Tyner 2008, 2011). Moreover, policy measures to encourage biofuels production, including the Renewable Fuels Standard (RFS) mandates, subsidies to ethanol, regulations on gasoline chemistry, and import tariffs have contributed to incentives to create the capacity to produce ethanol and to use corn for fuel rather than food (Tyner 2008, 2010).

The role of biofuels in determining high agricultural commodity prices in both 2007 to 2008 and 2011 (as well as in drought-affected 2012) remains controversial, nevertheless (National Academy of Sciences 2011). Some have argued since the 2007 to 2008 food crisis that increased biofuels demand has been a key factor for both the level and volatility of commodity prices (Mitchell 2008; Collins 2008; Abbott, Hurt, and Tyner 2008, 2011). Others assert that

Philip Abbott is professor of agricultural economics at Purdue University.

The author would like to thank Wally Tyner, Chris Hurt, Tom Hertel, Brian Wright, an anonymous referee, and participants at the NBER conference for sharing their insights on the issues discussed in this chapter. The views expressed and any errors or omissions are the sole responsibility of the author. For acknowledgments, sources of research support, and disclosure of the author's material financial relationships, if any, please see http://www.nber.org/chapters /c12808.ack.

1. The Renewable Fuels Association (RFA 2012) and others (e.g., Abbott, Hurt, and Tyner 2011) assert the net demand for corn is closer to 28 percent, as distiller's dry grain, a by-product of ethanol production, provides feed to replace about one-third of the corn used for ethanol.

biofuels shocks should mostly affect corn, and that common factors across commodities are more important in explaining price increases (Gilbert 2010; Baffes and Haniotis 2010). The link between energy and corn prices, according to their logic, is the result of speculation and/or macroeconomic factors, not biofuels. Others have argued that these common factors are less important (Irwin and Sanders 2011; Ai, Chatrath, and Song 2006). A Texas A&M study in 2008 (Agricultural Food and Policy Center 2008) also argued for a link from input costs, especially fertilizer and fuel, to agricultural production, but a history of short-run losses by farmers when commodity prices have been low relative to input prices argues this factor may be influential only in the longer run. Time series econometric investigations have been inconclusive (Heady and Fan 2010), with some identifying structural change just before the 2007 to 2008 food crisis (Enders and Holt 2012; Harri, Nalley, and Hudson 2009), but offering little economic insight into the changes found. McPhail (2011) has even argued that causality runs from ethanol demand to crude oil prices, not in the other direction. Calibrated simulation models have also struggled to reproduce plausible effects from biofuels on agricultural prices (Babcock and Fabiosa 2011; Hertel and Beckman 2011). Many studies have, as a result, been vague in assigning the relative significance of factors behind high agricultural commodity prices (e.g., Trostle 2009).

The notion that commodity prices had become not only higher but also more volatile emerged early in the debate on the energy-biofuels-agricultural commodity price relationships (Delgado 2009). Numerous studies have investigated commodity price variability, using both time series econometrics (Balcombe 2009; Cha and Bae 2011; Gilbert 2010) and calibrated simulations (e.g., Hertel and Beckman 2011; Gohin and Treguer 2010; Diffen-baugh et al. 2012). Even the notion that agricultural commodity prices are now more volatile has faced some controversy, however. Whether volatility is measured by variances, coefficients of variation, or deviations from a short-run trend matters, as does the interdependence of factors influencing conditional volatility (Balcombe 2009). The role of policy incentives and constraints has emerged as a key factor in this debate, especially Environmental Protection Agency (EPA) regulations.

It has been argued that this new demand for corn is highly inelastic, contributing to greater corn price volatility, if it is the result of meeting a policy-set minimum—the RFS mandate (Tyner, Taheripour, and Perkis 2010; de Gorter and Just 2009; Hertel, Tyner, and Birur 2010) . Others have noted that a "blend wall"—a limitation on the percentage of ethanol that may be used with gasoline regulated by the EPA—may establish maximum ethanol use, and that this maximum was by 2011 not far from the minimum set by the RFS for corn-based ethanol (Tyner and Viteri 2010). Recent models have at times used a combination of mandated ethanol use with blend wall limitations to capture effects on agricultural commodity prices (McPhail and Babcock 2012; Tyner 2010). But in 2011 exports of ethanol increased dramatically (Wisner 2012; Cooper 2011), suggesting capacity constraints rather than the RFS mandate or blend wall may determine ethanol production and so industrial demand for corn, at least in the short run. Capacity constraints have been important to varying degrees throughout the evolution of corn/ethanol demand, as capacity has been increased to stay ahead of the RFS mandate and in response to market and policy determined incentives.

During this period of increased use of corn for ethanol, several regimes can be identified based on which constraint on ethanol demand is binding. In 2005 to 2006, low corn prices and high crude oil prices, hence high gasoline prices, likely led to rents to binding ethanol capacity constraints as incentives to increase that capacity. Only in late 2008 and early 2009 has there been a significant, nonzero price for ethanol renewable identification numbers (RINs) (the instrument to insure the RFS mandate is met and to allow sale of "quota rights" under the mandate), indicating that this minimum seldom binds (Thompson, Meyer, and Westhoff 2010; OPIS 2012; Paulson 2012). In 2011 the blend wall may have limited domestic demand, but exports brought ethanol production near plant capacity. In 2012, subsidies ended, exports declined, production fell below capacity, and the blend wall became more limiting. In early 2008 it may have been the case that high oil prices drove demands for ethanol and corn that were above mandates but below capacity or blending constraints, so variations in the crude oil price were transmitted to corn prices. As we shall see below, when capacity constraints bind, the direct link between corn and energy prices through biofuels is weaker.

Which constraint is binding, if any, determines relationships between corn, ethanol, gasoline, and crude oil prices. It also determines whether industrial demand for corn is essentially perfectly inelastic or is adjusting in response to relative corn and/or energy prices. When demand is more inelastic, hence when a constraint is binding, corn prices will be more volatile, and that will likely spill over onto other crops. It is likely that there have been several different regimes between 2005 and 2011, based on variations in which constraint binds, explaining structural shifts observed in econometric estimation of price relationships.

Evidence on what is determining ethanol and corn pricing and demand should be seen in both supply-utilization balances relative to capacity, the mandate and the blend wall, and in margins between relevant prices. A careful examination of detailed short-term data on corn, ethanol, and gasoline market performance is one approach that has been noticeably absent in the debate on biofuels and volatility. Therefore, a simple theory will be developed here that incorporates these constraints on ethanol demand, and predictions of that theory under alternative regimes will be compared to actual price and quantity data. Empirical application of that theory may be used to compare predicted versus actual price volatility that varies over critical periods, and will also show how the benefits of subsidies and mandates are shared between farmers, ethanol producers, blenders, and gasoline refiners as the regime changes. The underlying incentives for exports—either mandates elsewhere or profitable substitution for gasoline—will also be explored to gauge whether and how they will influence future increases in ethanol production capacity.

In summary, energy policy favoring biofuels has helped to create a new, large, and persistent demand for corn. Various aspects of implementing that policy suggest very inelastic industrial demand for corn, contributing to both higher prices and greater price volatility. But turbulence in recent economic events has caused the mechanisms through which biofuels demands influence corn and other agricultural commodity prices to vary over time in ways that should be observable in data. Price volatility and "subsidy incidence" depend on which regime is in place. A simple theory along with data on supply, use, and pricing can be used to identify when and to what extent each regime matters.

In the next section, trends and apparent volatility in the relationship between corn and crude oil prices are presented to justify the origins of this debate on volatility and to gauge the relative importance and extent of short-run versus long-run volatility. Details on the policy determined constraints that impact ethanol and corn are then briefly elaborated and a timeline is developed showing when each constraint is most likely to have mattered. A theory related to decisions by gasoline blenders and ethanol producers under these constraints is then developed, followed by the links these create from ethanol to the US corn market. Supply and use balances in the corn market are considered in light of this theory. Special attention is then given to ethanol trade and its implications for market outcomes and modeling. Both quantity and price outcomes are then investigated using monthly data for crude oil, gasoline, corn, and ethanol as well as the timeline of policy set constraints and external economic shocks. Short- and long-run volatility is also examined across these "watershed" periods. Conclusions emphasize how important biofuels have been in determining agricultural market outcomes, and how binding constraints have shaped the evolution of agricultural commodity prices.

3.2 Apparent Volatility

Figure 3.1 presents monthly corn and crude oil prices from 1960 to 2012. Over this longer time horizon these series exhibit imperfectly long periods of relative stability interrupted by short-lived spikes that are sometimes noted in the literature (reviewed in Abbott 2010). The spikes appear more frequently for corn, and trends appear to last longer for crude oil. While some longer-term correlation may be seen between these series, there also appear to be periods when these prices are less well connected. The upward trend of these prices is largely due to inflation, as similar graphs of these series when deflated would exhibit variations around downward trends from the

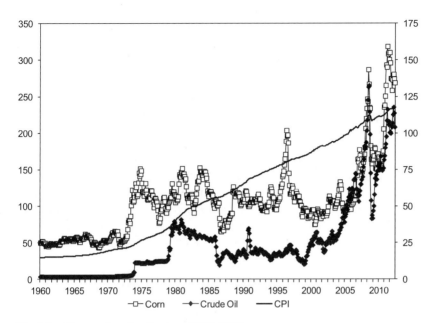

Fig. 3.1   Corn and crude oil prices, 1960–2012
Source: Commodity Price Statistics, IMF (2012).

early 1970s onward. The US Consumer Price Index (CPI) is also shown on figure 3.1 to demonstrate this effect.

Three questions related to these series are investigated here: How is variability properly measured? Does it differ for short-run versus long-run perspectives on the data (e.g., annual versus daily observation)? Has the variability (and correlation) of these series changed over time? To answer these questions, means, standard deviations, coefficients of variation, and correlation coefficients are calculated from the data in figure 3.1 as well as from daily and annual observations of similar prices for the entire period and subperiods from 1960 to 2012. The effects of short-run trends in apparent volatility are also considered. The subperiods considered here are the stable period of 1998 to 2005, the current period from 2006 to 2012, and the two "food crisis/commodity boom" periods of 2007 to 2008 and 2010 to 2012. Those results are shown in table 3.1. (Later we will explore these measures for periods between 2005 and 2012 according to regimes defined by energy policy constraints and corn stockholding.)

Longer-run mean prices are heavily weighted by lower nominal prices in the early years, and are comparable to prices realized from 1998 to 2005. Much higher nominal prices prevail for both corn and crude oil after 2005. Correlation coefficients are similar, above 0.85 for annual and monthly measures, except for the period 1998 to 2005. During that period, when prices are quite low, correlations are lower and decline as the frequency of observation

Table 3.1   Crude oil and corn price volatility, 1960–2012

		1960–2012	1998–2005	2006–2012	2007–2008	2010–2012
Means						
Crude oil	$/barrel	24.27	28.57	81.59	84.08	94.89
Corn	$/mt	106.52	98.06	197.32	193.25	**245.17**
Standard deviations						
Crude oil	Annual	26.24	13.21	18.59	—	—
	Monthly	**25.58**	**12.26**	**21.97**	25.35	14.81
	Daily	—	13.04	20.44	26.03	10.97
Corn	Annual	51.24	8.30	62.46	—	—
	Monthly	**49.46**	**11.15**	**61.25**	41.55	57.13
	Daily	—	10.63	59.13	42.89	54.66
Coefficients of variation						
Crude oil	Annual	1.08	0.46	0.23	—	—
	Monthly	**1.05**	**0.43**	**0.27**	0.30	0.16
	Daily	—	0.46	0.25	0.31	0.12
Corn	Annual	0.48	**0.08**	0.32	—	—
	Monthly	0.46	**0.11**	**0.31**	0.22	0.23
	Daily	—	0.11	**0.30**	0.22	0.22
Correlations						
Crude oil—corn	Annual	0.88	**0.30**	0.87	—	—
	Monthly	0.85	**0.13**	0.81	**0.89**	**0.89**
	Daily	—	–0.06	0.71	**0.86**	**0.77**

Sources: Annual and monthly prices are "world prices" (cash, fob) from IMF commodity price statistics. Daily prices are nearby futures prices from Datastream (Thomson Reuters 2012).

increases. Annual corn and oil prices are correlated at 0.3, whereas the daily price correlation is negative in 1998 to 2005.

The frequency of observation in cases other than the daily correlation between corn and crude oil appears not to matter much to these measures of prices and their volatility. For recent prices the daily correlation is slightly lower, and since 2010 the daily standard deviation of crude oil prices is somewhat lower. Otherwise, daily, monthly, and annual measures are of similar magnitudes. Since the original intent of this chapter was to focus on short-run volatility, we will subsequently focus on monthly measures.

The period of observations is far more important than frequency according to these results, and particularly for volatility. Standard deviations are often higher for longer periods, with some exceptions. These are strongly influenced by the means of subperiods, which differ significantly. The reason to choose a coefficient of variations is that it corrects for differing means that could be due to nothing more than inflation raising the level of nominal prices.[2] While some in recent literature use standard deviations to measure

2. For these series, differing means over time are due to more than inflation. Coefficients of variation calculated for monthly data on prices deflated by the US CPI from 1960 to 2012 are lower for crude oil, falling from 1.05 to 0.68, but are nearly identical for corn, at 0.45. It is evident from figure 3.1 that real prices have varied significantly over this long time period.

variability,[3] the coefficient of variation will be the focus here, as it corrects that problem. For the coefficients of variation for crude oil and corn, it is almost always the case that shorter periods exhibit lower volatility. The two exceptions are the 1998 to 2005 period for corn, which exhibited extreme stability relative to other periods, and crude oil in 2007 to 2008. Not only have means also varied by period, so have correlations. Once again, 1998 to 2005 is the exceptional case.

An alternative measure of volatility would take into account effects of short-run trends that give rise to large coefficients of variation, not due to random fluctuations around that trend. Standard errors around estimated short-run trends were also calculated for these series to gauge this affect. For shorter periods this approach is sensitive to how well the established periods match turning points in the series. For the 2007 to 2008 food crisis period the very strong coincident trends give rise to larger measures of apparent volatility based on coefficients of variation. For other periods this approach makes less difference. This approach does suggest that trends may have been mistaken for increased volatility in some cases.

One hypothesis, then, is that the apparent price volatility is influenced by trends and by regime changes.[4] The trend of rising crude oil prices from 2003 to mid-2008 is what gives rise to higher-measured volatility over that period. For corn, the first (1973 to 1974), second (1995) and third (2007 to 2008) food crises, trends, and regime switching led to much higher prices. This shows up in annual measures and is what makes longer-run volatility seem so high. Volatility does appear to change over comparably long subperiods, however. The volatility of corn prices for 1998 to 2005 was exceptionally low, as is crude oil volatility in 2010 to 2012. As before, these are strongly influenced by change in mean prices—crude oil standard deviations are similar in 2010 to 12 and 1998 to 2005, but mean prices were much lower in 1998 to 2005.

From figure 3.1 it is apparent that both stability and low prices of 1998 to 2005 were not unprecedented. Similar outcomes are observed in the 1960s and early 1990s. But judging the level and volatility of crude oil and corn prices can be distorted if short memories exclude years before 1998. Whether mechanisms determining prices before 1998 and after 2005 are similar is another matter—while the food versus fuel debate had been raised in the

3. Some use variances, which are essentially standard deviations squared. The standard deviation is preferred here because it is in units of measure comparable to the mean price, and squaring this measure would distort the perception of the extent of variability. Coefficients of variation divide standard deviations by corresponding means, to normalize the measure of variability, to facilitate comparisons across series with differing means, and to correct for the fact that as a nominal price increases, its standard deviation is likely to increase in the same proportion—and that does not correspond with the notion of increased variability.

4. Regime changes correspond with changes in the mechanisms that are most important in determining market prices—which could be policies or real external shocks. For example, a binding RFS mandate and a binding "blend wall" are different regimes. Similarly, periods of low corn stocks (food crisis) and of abundant corn stocks (ethanol gold rush) give rise to different regimes.

1980s (Brown 1980), the emergence of ethanol production as a large user of corn is a new phenomenon.

From here forward we will focus entirely on the period after 2005, when biofuels emerged as important to corn and energy markets. After identifying relevant subperiods, defined by the policy constraints that bind gasoline blenders and ethanol producers, we will find similar behaviors. Mean prices will vary across subperiods, and so will volatility and correlations. For shorter periods volatility is lower, and regime switching that changes mean prices will lead to observed higher volatility. These will show up imperfectly in annual data, since crop years and calendar years used for EPA regulations do not coincide, and dates that legislation is passed or takes effect can influence when regimes switch (with anticipation by market participants).

3.3   Ethanol Supply Chain Constraints

Ethanol production, its use in reformulated gasoline, and the subsequent demand for corn as a feedstock, are subject to constraints along the supply chain. Some constraints have arisen due to energy legislation (RFS mandates) and EPA regulation (blend wall, methyl tertiary-butyl ether [MTBE] substitution). Capacity constraints on production also matter to market performance, and investment in capacity is influenced by policy constraints. An important distinction is that some constraints are applied cumulatively on an annual basis—the RFS mandate applies on a calendar year basis (with some flexibility across years), not on monthly production, while others apply over the short run, such as capacity and the blend wall. Constraints that apply annually will be referred to as "stock" constraints, and among these are the condition that annual corn carryout stocks cannot fall below zero, as anticipation of potential stockouts can raise corn prices well ahead of when those stocks might actually fall to zero. Anticipation that other stock constraints may bind will influence pricing, production, stock holding, and investment in capacity. Constraints that apply instantaneously will be referred to as "flow" constraints, and include capacity constraints on gasoline as well as ethanol. This distinction is not necessarily apparent in an annual model, but matters to which constraint may actually appear to bind, and hence determine the regime under which short-term prices are set. Stock constraints considered here include RFS mandates and carryout stocks for corn. Flow constraints include capacity constraints, MTBE substitution (gasoline chemistry), and the blend wall. Flow constraints are more likely to impact production (quantities), whereas stock constraints influence expectations, hence, prices.

The history of constraints on gasoline blending and ethanol production, particularly as a result of energy legislation and EPA regulations, have been extensively documented in literature cited earlier (e.g., Tyner 2008; Carter,

Rausser, and Smith 2012). Only the critical elements determining relevant constraints during 2005 to 2012 are discussed below.

3.3.1   RFS Mandates

Legislation favoring ethanol production from corn has been debated and in place since the late 1970s (Tyner 2008). In 2005, significant changes in legislation governing ethanol production and use were enacted. The Renewable Fuels Standard (RFS), which mandated minimum production levels for future years for ethanol, was enacted then (US Congress 2005). That legislation also included continued subsidization of ethanol production, then through a tax credit to gasoline blenders of $0.51 per gallon (referred to as the volumetric ethanol excise tax credit [VEETC]), and a tariff on imported ethanol, ostensibly to insure foreign producers did not get the subsidy of $0.45 per gallon plus 2.5percent of imported value. The Energy Policy Act of 2007 (US Congress 2007) substantially increased RFS mandated minimum ethanol production levels for the future. The VEETC was reduced to $0.45 during the 2007 to 2008 food crisis, and was eliminated on December 31, 2011. The tariff on imported ethanol for fuel use was also cut in 2012. Numerous other federal and state policy measures influence the profitability of ethanol production, but the tax credit (subsidy), tariff, and mandates were the most significant measures among those impacting the corn market. That legislation also affects ethanol produced from feed stocks other than corn— second generation biofuels. A limit is placed on the amount of ethanol from corn that can be used to meet the various RFS mandates. Renewable identification numbers (RINs) are created along with ethanol production and are used to allow firm-specific quotas imposed on gasoline blenders, which implement the RFS mandate, to be traded (McPhail, Westcott, and Lutman 2011).[5] In principle, the market values for RINs will reflect the extent to which the RFS mandate binds as a constraint on ethanol production. Important features of this policy were the minimums on annual ethanol production from corn that went from four billion gallons in 2006 to fifteen billion gallons in 2015, and subsidies that affect profit margins for either gasoline blenders, ethanol producers, consumers, or farmers—depending on how the supply chain functions.

3.3.2   Blend Wall

EPA regulations limit the amount of ethanol that may be used in reformulated gasoline produced and sold by blenders. Ethanol is corrosive and may do harm in older engines, or engines not designed to tolerate high concentra-

---

5. Blenders are allowed to decide whether RINs acquired in a given year are applied in that year or an adjacent year, so the mandate does not strictly limit production in a given calendar year. That mechanism allows RINs to be traded across years as well as across firms. Paulson (2012) argues that this has contributed to very low observed values for RINs for corn ethanol.

tions of ethanol. While modern flex-fuel vehicles can use blends including up to 85percent ethanol, many vehicles can tolerate no more than 10 to 20 percent without damage. While the science on this may not be exact, the EPA had set a limit at 10 percent (E10) for gasoline not explicitly marketed as E85, and recently permitted 15 percent ethanol (E15) for newer vehicles. There is debate as to whether the allowed concentration can be raised without harming many existing engines, thus changing the effective limit on ethanol use. Logistical and legal issues have meant gasoline stations have been reluctant to switch toward selling E15 or even E85, so for the moment use of ethanol in gasoline is still limited to 10 percent. Tyner and Viteri (2010) describe how this affects ethanol and gasoline markets, and refer to this limitation as the "blend wall." Moreover, they argue that additional logistical and other regional constraints effectively limited ethanol use to about 9 percent of gasoline demand, noting that this may creep upward a bit (toward 10 percent) when the RFS mandate exceeds the apparent blend wall, as it did in 2012. Like the RFS mandate, this constraint is imposed on gasoline blenders, but its effects are then felt all along the ethanol supply chain. A maximum is imposed on ethanol demand for fuel use in the United States that is proportional to gasoline demand, but ethanol production may be affected by ethanol trade, as well.

3.3.3   MTBE/Oxygenate Substitution

Reformulated gasoline sold by blenders mixes "pure" gasoline bought from crude oil refiners with various additives including ethanol and MTBE. Since the early 1990s, the Clean Air Act has required additives to reduce carbon monoxide emissions by including an oxygenate—commonly either MTBE or ethanol (Carter, Rausser, and Smith 2012).[6] Additives such as ethanol are an alternative source of energy to pure gas and may also improve the chemistry of reformulated gasoline, for example, by increasing octane or making the gas burn cleaner. Specifications of reformulated gasoline depend on both performance characteristics of additives and on EPA regulations. At lower concentrations ethanol may serve as an additive, improving gasoline chemistry, and accruing a premium, while at higher concentrations it may simply serve as an energy substitute for pure gas. Since ethanol has fewer British thermal units ([BTUs], less energy) per gallon than gasoline, a gallon of reformulated gasoline yields lower mileage in vehicles the larger is the ethanol concentration. If ethanol serves as an energy substitute, its pricing should reflect this difference in energy content. If ethanol serves as an additive to improve gasoline chemistry, its price may be above the energy equivalent price.

6. The EPA no longer uses a specific oxygenate requirement, but continues to regulate carbon monoxide emissions. Both MTBE and ethanol are used to reduce those emissions in gasoline blending.

In the 1990s it was recognized that MTBE, an inexpensive by-product of crude oil refining, was toxic in groundwater (EIA 2000). By 2006, twenty-five states had banned the use of MTBE in gasoline. Gasoline blenders sought waivers from liability due to MTBE, since they were using it to meet clean air regulations. By mid-2006 it was clear that such waivers would not be granted, as MTBE liability waivers had not been part of the 2005 Energy Act, and subsequent related legislation failed to provide this waiver. This has encouraged blenders to use more expensive ethanol rather than face potential liability costs from MTBE use. These decisions occurred at about the same time as the RFS mandate was established, and so MTBE substitution was another factor contributing to rapid expansion of ethanol production after 2005 (Hertel and Beckman 2011). According to the EIA (2000), reformulated gasoline meets oxygenate requirements at a 5.8 percent ethanol concentration, so this may serve as a rough minimum requirement for ethanol until that concentration is exceeded. Thus, in 2006 this may have been a serious constraint on blenders, giving rise to premiums on ethanol relative to pure gas, but by 2008 enough ethanol was produced nationally to exceed this concentration.

3.3.4   Ethanol Production Capacity Constraints

The various policy measures discussed above created incentives for greater ethanol production and use as fuel. In 2005 the capacity to produce ethanol matched the small demand at that time. As demand for ethanol grew, new production capacity has been built. This occurred at a very rapid pace shortly after both the 2005 and 2007 Energy Acts. High crude oil prices relative to corn and subsidies (VEETC) insured new plants would be profitable, while the RFS mandate guaranteed a market for the output of those plants. Plant construction has stayed ahead of the RFS mandate, but the combination of the limit on corn ethanol to satisfy the mandate and the blend wall have discouraged further increases in capacity, which for corn ethanol is now at the fifteen billion gallon maximum set for 2015 and beyond in the RFS. Hence, new capacity construction is now quite small (RFA 2012). Over the period 2005 to 2012, our results will show that plant capacity has been the determining factor behind ethanol production and short-run pricing, except for a couple of periods—briefly in late 2008 and now that the RFS mandate exceeds the blend wall. The RFS mandate and blend wall were influential over the long run in shaping this investment, but were not binding constraints on short-run market performance for most of this period.

3.3.5   Corn Stocks

Corn is produced/harvested once a year but is consumed continuously over the year. Stocks allow consumption not only to be spread over a crop year, but also to be carried into the next crop year if prices are low and good production had yielded surpluses. Annual carryout stocks cannot fall below zero, however, and in practice cannot fall below some higher pipeline level—in the case of corn this may be near 5 percent of use. The demand for these carryout stocks is understood to be relatively elastic when there are surpluses, but becomes quite inelastic as expected annual carryout stocks become tight. A nonlinear relationship between stocks-to-use ratios and both cash and futures market prices therefore informs expectations and behaviors in agricultural commodity markets. Stocks positions have been seen as important in determining price outcomes, especially around periods of food crisis (Trostle 2009; Wright 2011; Carter, Smith, and Rausser 2012). In the early period when ethanol production was expanding, corn prices remained low due to abundant stocks and surpluses, but prices increased once those stocks were drawn down. In the 2011 to 2012 crop year, low supplies led to expectations of extremely low carryout stocks and high prices, which futures markets had indicated could fall dramatically once a good new crop is harvested. While corn prices were low in May 2012, as the 2012 to 2013 crop year progressed a shortfall due to drought became evident. Corn prices reached historic highs again, and stocks are unlikely to be rebuilt.

Understanding the impact of increased demand for corn to produce ethanol on corn prices requires understanding the expected stocks positions when those changes in demand occur, and its impact on that position. As Abbott, Hurt, and Tyner (2011) argue, impacts of any given factor, such as biofuels demands, interact with other factors such that two shocks can have a bigger impact than each shock might individually, especially if the two shocks together push the market into a low-stocks position. If demand increases when expected stocks are high, overall demand is elastic and increased demands can be accommodated by stocks releases. When stocks are low, the corn market is much less elastic, and price increases will be higher. Persistently higher demand also eventually drove down stocks, as happened from 2005 to 2008. One way of thinking about this relationship between annual carryout stocks and corn prices is as if zero (or pipeline) stocks are an annual "stock" type constraint. The pricing mechanism for corn changes when stocks bind at zero versus when they do not.

3.4   Timeline of "Watershed" Periods and Related Legislation

Table 3.2 presents a timeline for the events shaping development of the corn-ethanol business from 2005 to 2012. It defines "watershed periods" over which constraints shaping market outcomes may have changed. For example the first period, from July 2005 to July 2007, is referred to as the "ethanol gold rush" when high crude oil prices, low corn prices, RFS mandates, and MTBE substitution all encouraged rapid construction of ethanol plant capacity. The second period, from August 2007 to July 2008, is when corn prices then increased, in what is now called the "food crisis." The Great Recession brought an end to the commodity boom, for both crude oil and

Table 3.2   Watershed periods for ethanol-related constraints

Beginning date	End date	Period and related legislation	World price events
July 2005	July 2007	**Ethanol gold rush**	High oil prices
July 2005		Energy Act of 2005—RFS1	Low corn prices
June 2006		MTBE liability issue "resolved"	
August 2007	July 2008	**Food crisis**	Rising corn prices
December 2007		Energy Act of 2007—RFS2	
August 2008	May 2009	**Great Recession**	Commodity prices collapse
January 2009		VEETC reduced to $0.45	Gasoline demand drops
June 2009	December 2009	**Commodity boom restarted**	Rising oil and corn prices
January 2010	**August 2010**	**Blend wall imminent**	**Commodity boom stalls**
September 2010	**December-11**	**Export relief**	**Sugar prices high**
January 2012		**Subsidies ended**	**Ethanol exports and prices fall**
January 2012		VEETC and ethanol tariffs eliminated	Blend wall binding

corn, starting by August 2008, and coinciding more closely with financial crisis than with the beginning of recession in the United States. The NBER dates the end of the Great Recession as June 2009, when another commodity boom had already restarted. By January 2010, the effects of a binding blend wall began to be apparent, but exports relieved pressure on ethanol production starting about September 2010. In 2012, after the subsidies to ethanol ended, exports slowed as well.

These watershed period distinctions are admittedly inexact. They are informed by when legislation was enacted, as indicated in table 3.2, and when prices, production, and trade behavior changed. Since they are informed by institutional factors such as legislation, they do not always coincide with turning points of short-run trends. Figure 3.2 shows a graph that presents US prices for corn, crude oil, gasoline, and ethanol from 2005 to 2012, with the watershed periods indicated by horizontal lines at their beginning/end. Table 3.2 notes the changes in price trends that can be seen in figure 3.2. These period definitions were also informed by the experience of observing these events and trying to understand the underlying economic forces as they occurred, as well as by the results presented later in this chapter. Clear differences in mean prices as well as variances can be seen across these periods, as well as the effects of quantity adjustments due to the constraints discussed above. Those outcomes will be reported below after a theory is developed to help interpret those outcomes.

Setting the month when watershed periods begin or end presents difficulties due to anticipation of both market events and policy changes by firms. For example, the Energy Acts were discussed and subsequently passed in several steps, and then enacted provisions did not all apply immediately. It is also likely that firms anticipated the removal of subsidies at the end of 2011, since that was known well in advance. Firms may make operational

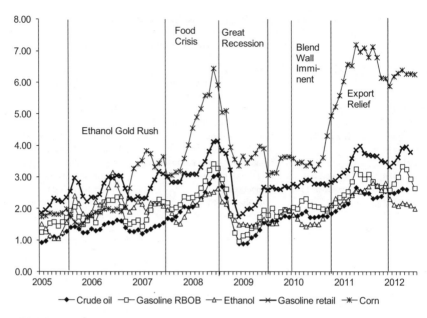

Fig. 3.2   Energy and corn prices, 2005–2012
Sources: EIA (2012) and Hofstrand (2012).

changes ahead of when requirements are imposed. This results in some seemingly gradual transitions as conditions change. Similarly, commodity markets anticipated the end of the Great Recession, so crude oil and corn prices started increasing ahead of the NBER-declared end of the recession. Nevertheless, observing differences in quantities and prices in gasoline, ethanol, and corn markets across these watershed periods is informative in understanding how market regimes, and so outcomes, may have changed.

3.5   Theory on Firm/Plant Constraints

The RFS mandates and blend wall apply directly to gasoline blenders, but effects can spill over onto ethanol producers as well as farmers. Simple theory based on profit maximization by gasoline blenders and ethanol refiners subject to constraints can inform how these constraints impact use and pricing. First, ethanol refiners and then gasoline blenders are modeled here as competitive profit-maximizing actors. Results will be used to understand interactions with the corn market and to interpret short-term market data. Theory presented here also considers extensions to imperfectly competitive markets, but market conditions suggest the competitive models are more likely to be relevant.

3.5.1   Ethanol Refiners

Ethanol refining involves the purchase of corn and natural gas to distill alcohol from the corn. Costs are mostly from the feedstock and energy, and in this model by-products will be subsumed into net other production costs for simplification. For firm or plant i, profit maximization subject to constraints can be represented as:

$$\text{maximize} \quad \pi_e^i = P_e q_e^i - P_c q_{ce}^i - Cost_e^i(q_e^i) \text{ profit}$$

$$\text{subject to} \quad q_e^i \leq K_e^i \text{ capacity constraint}$$

$$q_{ce}^i = \gamma_{ce}^i q_e^i \quad \text{Leontief intermediate requirements for corn,}$$

where π_e^i is profit realized by ethanol firm/plant i,

P_e is the market price of ethanol,
q_e^i is ethanol production of plant i,
P_c is the market price of corn,
q_{ce}^i is the derived demand for corn by plant i,
$Cost_e^i$ is total additional cost (beyond corn cost) to produce ethanol by plant i,
K_e^i is capacity of ethanol firm/plant i, and
γ_{ce}^i is the quantity of corn required to produce one unit of ethanol.

Market aggregations over the $i = 1, \ldots, N$ firms gives:

$$Q_e = \sum_i q_e^i, \ Q_{ce} = \sum_i q_{ce}^i, \ K_e = \sum_i k_e^i$$

where Q_e is market production of ethanol,

Q_{ce} is market derived industrial demand for corn to produce ethanol, and K_e is market capacity for ethanol production.

A competitive outcome with identical firms[7] yields complementary slackness conditions on capacity and rent to that capacity:

$\lambda_e = P_e - \gamma_{ce}^i P_c - (\partial Cost_e^i / \partial q_e^i)$ rent to ethanol capacity,
$Q_e \leq K_e$ market capacity constraint,
$\lambda_e > 0$ if $Q_e = K_e$ complementary slackness, capacity binding, and
$\lambda_e = 0$ if $Q_e < K_e$ marginal cost determines ethanol supply.

We shall assume for the moment that gasoline demand is large relative to ethanol demand, and that the gasoline price effectively determines the ethanol price. If capacity constraints bind, variations in the price of gasoline

---

7. From this point forward we will work at the market level. Issues related to heterogeneous firms will be left for future research.

relative to the price of corn show up as variations in the rent to capacity (λ_e). If capacity constraints do not bind, if marginal "additional" cost is approximately average "additional cost" cost for ethanol production, and if ethanol production is large relative to the corn market, then variations in the gasoline price drive variations in the corn price. These are the fundamental relationships that will govern any linkage between corn and energy prices through biofuels.

The rents to capacity (λ_e) offer incentives for new plant construction, hence investment in expansion of ethanol production. Those rents depend on the price of ethanol (hence gasoline), the cost of corn, and other costs or revenues of plants. Policy also influences expectations that matter to investment decisions (Kesam, Ohyama, and Yang 2011).

Oligopolistic firms in either ethanol (upstream) or corn (downstream) markets would require relaxing the small actor assumptions invoked above, so that:

$$\lambda_e = P_e - \gamma_{ce}^i P_c - \frac{\partial Cost_e^i}{\partial q_e^i} + q_e^i \frac{\partial P_e}{\partial q_e^i} - \gamma_{ce}^i q_e^i \frac{\partial P_c}{\partial q_{ce}^i}.$$

Rents depend on market capacity utilization (especially if firms are heterogeneous, and plant i is typical and not necessarily the least efficient operating firm). They may also depend on corn and ethanol market conditions captured by the conjecture on ethanol price effects ($\partial P_e / \partial q_e^i$) and the conjecture on corn price effects ($\partial P_c / \partial q_{ce}^i$)—hence on factors related to corn market elasticity (e.g., stocks) and demand for ethanol, and so the gasoline price. If plants face binding capacity constraints, and that determines the market outcome (Q_e and q_e^i), conjecture terms are theoretically irrelevant as firms cannot adjust q_e^i to influence prices.

The coefficient Q_e may be determined by blender demand constraints (e.g., the MTBE/oxygenate requirement) that supersede capacity constraints. If ethanol is simply to provide an oxygenate, its demand by blenders is a fixed concentration that still prevents q_e^i from varying to maximize profit. In that case, ethanol refiners face perfectly inelastic demand. Those constraints should look like capacity constraints when they limit ethanol production, and may lead to positive rents, λ_e. On the other hand, the blend wall minimum would lower P_e offered by blenders, and with fixed quantity could give rise to negative λ_e, or losses to ethanol, since corn demand is also fixed by the blender constraint. Understanding how blender demand relates to ethanol production requires specifying the gasoline blender's profit maximization problem.

3.5.2   Gasoline Blenders

In order to understand linkages between gasoline and ethanol and to see how policy constraints may spill over, it is useful to consider reformulated gasoline blending. After all, the EPA enforces mandates and regulations on gasoline blenders, not ethanol refiners. Gasoline supply by profit-maximizing blenders may be modeled as follows, assuming identical blenders aggregated to reflect market outcomes:

maximize $\pi_r = P_r Q_r - (P_e - \tau_e)Q_e - P_g Q_g - \text{Cost}_r(Q_r, Q_{mbte})$ profit

subject to $Q_r \leq K_r$ gasoline/blending capacity constraints

$Q_r = Q_g + \gamma_{ge} Q_e$ blending ethanol and pure gas based on energy

$Q_e \geq \gamma_{go} Q_r - \gamma_{gm} Q_{mtb}$ oxygenate/octane (chemistry) constraint

$\sum_t Q_e \geq \text{RFS}$ RFS—annual minimum ethanol production

$Q_e \leq \gamma_{bw} Q_r$ blend wall maximum on ethanol in gas,

where π_r is profit realized by reformulated gasoline blenders,

P_r is the market price of reformulated gasoline,
Q_r is market production of reformulated gasoline (energy basis),
τ_e is the tax credit given to blenders for use of ethanol in reformulated gasoline (VEETC),
P_g is the market price of gasoline bought by blenders (pure gas ex-refiner),
Q_g is demand for reformulated gasoline from blenders,
Q_{mtbe} is the quantity of MTBE used to fulfill oxygenate requirements,
Cost$_g$ is total additional cost (beyond ethanol and pure gasoline cost) to produce reformulated gasoline, including taxes on sales of gasoline and penalties for MTBE use,
K_r is gasoline/refining/blending capacity,
γ_{ge} is the relative energy content of ethanol (as compared to pure gas),
γ_{go} is the blending requirement for ethanol to meet oxygenate or octane requirements,
γ_{gm} is the contribution of MTBE to meet those requirements, and
γ_{bw} is the EPA-set maximum ethanol concentration for reformulated gasoline.

This model applies on a monthly basis, but the RFS constraint applies annually. A dynamic model with this behavior repeated over the course of a year, and with any linkages across months, would need to be built to properly capture the RFS constraint. For now we simply assume each month's production is added and that sum must exceed the annual RFS mandate.

Reformulated gasoline market demand is given by:

$$Q_r = Qd_r(P_r, \text{other variables}).$$

Competitive blenders take P_r as given at the equilibrium market price for reformulated gasoline. Competitive refiners offer gasoline at P_g, determined by the world price of oil and the cost of crude oil refining. We shall for now assume gasoline demand is inelastic but small relative to world energy markets, making P_g exogenous. Binding refining constraints or oligopoly would drive a wedge between gasoline and crude oil prices. If ethanol use is small relative to gasoline demand, the price of gasoline may still be exogenous to blenders.

Some outcomes may be determined when P_g is fixed, the competitive case. If no constraints bind, and gas refining as well as blending are competitive, ethanol should be priced at its energy equivalent to gasoline, plus the tax credit. In this case, the VEETC is fully passed down to ethanol refiners:

$$P_e - \tau_e = \gamma_{ge} P_g = \gamma_{ge}\left(P_r - \frac{\partial Cost_r^i}{\partial Q_r}\right).$$

Blending capacity constraints would raise P_r relative to P_g, so:

$$P_e - \tau_e = \gamma_{ge} P_g = \gamma_{ge}\left(P_r \frac{\partial Cost_r^i}{\partial Q_r} + \lambda_r\right),$$

where λ_r is the rent to capacity for blenders. In addition to this capacity rent, constraints related to ethanol use in blending may affect the difference between P_g and P_r. Coefficient P_r will reflect any premiums or discounts accruing to ethanol relative to its energy value, and any impacts on blending costs, such as avoiding costs due to MTBE usage or liability.

If the oxygenate or octane (chemistry) constraint binds:

$$P_e - \tau_e = \gamma_{ge} P_g + \lambda_o,$$

where λ_o is the marginal value to ethanol, beyond its energy contribution, due to the blending chemistry benefits it brings. If ethanol raises octane in reformulated gasoline, a premium should accrue to ethanol from this effect. Similarly, if ethanol meets oxygenate requirements for gasoline in lieu of MTBE, this will also contribute a premium to ethanol relative to its energy content. That premium will reflect any costs associated with continuing to use MTBE as an oxygenate, subsumed here in the additional cost function. The extent of ethanol use in gasoline will cause these premiums to vary over time. If the price of gasoline is high, and if these constraints do not bind, λ_o may approach zero.

The RFS-mandated minimum could also generate a premium for ethanol over its energy equivalent price:

$$P_e - \tau_e = \gamma_{ge} P_g + \lambda_{rfs}.$$

Like the corn stockout condition, this constraint applies over a year (calendar year, not crop year). Hence, this premium likely would depend on expectations that the RFS may eventually bind. This premium should give rise to a positive price for corn ethanol RINs, the tradable instrument that implements this constraint for blenders.

It is likely in a strict math program that either the oxygenate/octane or

RFS constraint binds, but not both, since both are minimums on ethanol use in blending, and their being equal would be an unlikely coincidence. But the chemistry constraints are flow constraints that bind at each instant, whereas the RFS mandate is a stock constraint that binds on an annual basis. In an uncertain world, both could influence expectations, and so, short-run ethanol prices. The RFS constraint in practice is further complicated by the possibility that RINs, hence ethanol production, may be used to satisfy the RFS constraint in the year used or in an adjacent year, as chosen by the blender subject to restrictions (Paulson 2012). It is not in practice the strict inequality posited above.

A binding blend wall constraint puts pressure on the ethanol price in the other direction, leading to discounts on ethanol so that a maximum usage restriction is not exceeded:

$$P_e - \tau_e = \gamma_{ge} P_g - \lambda_{bw},$$

where λ_{bw} is the discount on the ethanol constraint due to a binding blend wall. Once again, it is unlikely that a blend wall minimum and RFS or oxygenate maximum would bind simultaneously, though in recent years these constraints have moved quite close together. Moreover, if the blend wall is lower than the RFS minimum, the solution to this problem is infeasible in the absence of ethanol trade.

Key results include that ethanol prices will follow gasoline prices and so crude oil prices if blenders are competitive and chemistry or blending capacity constraints do not bind. Ethanol prices will be passed on to corn prices only if ethanol production capacity constraints do not bind. When those capacity constraints bind ethanol generates a perfectly inelastic demand for corn, and rents absorb corn versus crude oil price variations.

3.6 Corn Market Implications

In order to determine linkages between energy markets and corn, a simple model of the US corn market will be developed here. That model is then used to interpret implications of the above results for corn prices, demand and volatility, as well as to assess data on prices and quantities for corn, ethanol, and gasoline.

3.6.1 Modeling US Corn

Equilibrium in the corn market equates supply with various demand components, including feed use, food use, derived industrial demand for corn to produce ethanol, and export demand:

$$Q_c(P_c) = Q_{cf}(P_c) + Q_{cs}(P_c) + Q_{cx}(P_c) + Q_{ce},$$

where Q_c is corn supply that is fixed in the very short run and responds to price over the longer run, including beginning stocks.

Q_{cf} is feed, food, seed, and residual demand for corn (everything in domestic use but ethanol), which is presumably relatively price inelastic, with elasticity mostly coming from feed use.

Q_{cs} is carryout stocks demand, which would be very elastic in periods of abundant supply (surplus) and quite inelastic in periods of short supply. Stockout conditions could be thought of as a constraint on corn demand that sometimes binds, affecting the overall elasticity of corn demand. Stockouts are an annual phenomenon, occurring just before next year's harvest, so in the short run expectations on this future outcome should influence the corn price. This is captured by specifying a nonlinear carryout stocks demand function as described above.

Q_{cx} is net export demand for corn, which would be price elastic for a small country trader, but is likely inelastic for the United States, since it accounts for over half of world corn trade in most recent years.

Q_{ce} is the derived demand for corn by the ethanol market. If capacity constraints are binding this is perfectly inelastic at $\gamma_{ce}^i K_e$, and if capacity constraints do not bind this demand may be perfectly elastic at a price determined by the price of gasoline, $P_c = [P_e - (\partial Cost_e^i / \partial q_e^i)] / \gamma_{ce}^i$). Alternatively, Q_e and therefore $Q_{ce} = \gamma_{ce}^i Q_e$ may be determined by gasoline blending requirements, such as the RFS mandate or oxygenate rules. In those cases industrial corn demand is perfectly inelastic, as well.

Figure 3.3 graphically depicts this model in a two-panel diagram framework commonly used for trade analysis. In it the demand components are summed to arrive at the kinked overall demand function for corn, similar to that found in Tyner (2010) and McPhail and Babcock (2012). The demand for corn to produce ethanol includes two horizontal portions determined by the RFS mandate (minimum) and either the blend wall or capacity constraints (maximum). The novel feature here is that it is capacity constraints in the short run, not the RFS or blend wall, which will bind, determining prices. The flat portion of that demand curve, also for the overall domestic demand curve, occurs when ethanol production falls between its upper and lower bounds, and will be higher or lower depending on crude oil/gasoline prices, as given by the ethanol pricing relationship derived above when capacity rents are zero. Hence, there is a region where corn and gasoline prices may be directly linked, but given current constraints that is over a quite small range.

This graph is based on a simple Excel model implementing the above theory, and calibrated to fit the 2005 to 2006 crop year using elasticities that are on the low side of those found in the literature. The shift in demand for ethanol from 2005 to 2009 is represented here as an exogenous shift to the right of corn demand for ethanol corresponding with the actual increase over that period.

Equilibrium is found here in the right-hand panel that depicts foreign

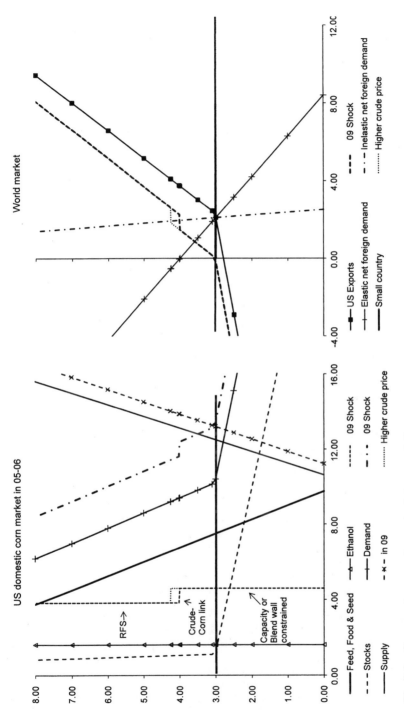

Fig. 3.3 Corn supply, use and exports: A two-panel diagram

trade in corn.[8] That is done to highlight the nature and uncertainty of foreign demand. Several cases can be seen in that graph. If the United States were a small country in the world market, taking the world price as given, corn exports fall to zero as the US net export supply of corn shifts leftward as a result of the domestic demand increase. If corn export demand is relatively elastic, exports fall substantially with a small increase in the United States and so world corn price. If export demand is quite inelastic, a larger price increase follows from a smaller export decline. The result for inelastic export demand is close to several results from some more complex calibrated modeling exercises (e.g., McPhail and Babcock 2012), with ethanol raising corn prices by about 33 percent, hence from $3.00 per bushel in 2005 to about $4.00 in 2009. The net export demand elasticity facing the US corn market has been the subject of controversy over time, with some insisting that export demand over the time frame modeled in figure 3.3 (four years) should be relatively elastic. An early study (Elobeid et al. 2007) forecasting the implications of biofuels demands found assuming relatively elastic foreign demand the implausible result that the United States would import corn while the world price need not rise above $4.00 per bushel to accommodate ethanol production at more than twice levels seen in 2011 and 2012. Modeling results depend critically on the corn export demand elasticity as well as domestic behavioral parameters. To get bigger price impacts than are found here in the short run, very low elasticities need to be assumed—or some other driving factors need to be invoked.

3.6.2 Prices, Subsidies, and Volatility

Implications for price volatility can be found from the above theory. Key relationships governing the corn market include an equilibrium condition that includes derived demand for corn based on ethanol production—that in many circumstances is exogenous:

$$Q_c(P_c) = Q_{cf}(P_c) + Q_{cs}(P_c) + Q_{cx}(P_c) + \gamma_{ce}^i Q_e \quad \text{Corn market equilibrium}$$

and the relationship between corn and ethanol prices, that includes rents to capacity in addition to the net marginal cost of ethanol production:

$$\lambda_e = P_e - \gamma_{ce}^i P_c - \frac{\partial Cost_e^i}{\partial q_e^i} \quad \text{Ethanol rents}$$

Several cases may be identified depending on which constraint binds. For ethanol producers these include capacity constraints and the blend wall:

Case e1: $\lambda_e = 0$, $P_c = \left(P_e - \dfrac{\partial Cost_e^i}{\partial q_e^i} \right) / \gamma_{ce}^i)$ Elastic ethanol demand

Case e2: $Q_e = K_e$, $Q_e = \gamma_{go} Q_r$, or $Q_e = \text{RFS/T}$ Binding production constraints

---

8. Net export supply from the United States in the right panel of figure 3.3 represents the difference between supply and overall demand in the left panel. Overall demand is the sum of the separate domestic demand components—feed, food, seed, and industrial uses. Equilibrium equates net export supply by the United States with net foreign demand for corn.

Case e3: $\lambda_e = F(Q_e/K_e, \partial P_e/\partial q_e^i, \partial P_c/\partial q_{ce}^i)$ Oligopolistic markups
Case e4: $\lambda_e < 0$ and $Q_e = \gamma_{bw} Q_r$ Blend wall binding

Case e1 corresponds with a competitively determined price for ethanol linked directly to the price of corn, or the flat part of overall corn demand in figure 3.3. In that case, ethanol demand is perfectly elastic at a price driven by the price of gasoline and the cost to produce ethanol, so corn and energy prices are strongly related, the volume of ethanol production varies with those prices, and subsidies and other factors influencing the ethanol price are transmitted to the corn market. Figure 3.3 showed that this held over a narrow range, and more often a constraint would bind. Case e2 corresponds with capacity constraints (maximum) binding for ethanol production. It may also represent cases where ethanol production is set by capacity constraints on gasoline blending or the RFS mandate. Ethanol production is fixed by those constraints, so it is exogenous to the corn market. In that case the rent to capacity absorbs variations in corn and ethanol prices, which move independently. Subsidies would not be passed to the corn market, and the effect of ethanol on corn is entirely the consequence of adding a fixed, large demand. Case e3 shows that the rents to capacity could also be nonzero in an oligopolistic market, but quantities of ethanol produced would need to be managed (reduced) to generate these oligopolistic rents. Since there are now over 200 plants, and if ethanol production is essentially at capacity, this case is unlikely to be relevant. Case e4 occurs when the blend wall binds, at levels below capacity. Ethanol production is fixed here by the maximum on ethanol demand by blenders, and rents can be negative in this case, reflecting the limitation on demand rather than supply. Subsequent data investigations will suggest case e2 is the case most often encountered from 2005 to 2011, with a brief period when case e1 applied. In 2011 and 2012 the blend wall appears to bind (case e4), but exports of ethanol allowed production between the blend wall and capacity. The nature and consequences of ethanol trade will be discussed later.

To investigate constraints on gasoline blenders we also need their pricing relationship:

$$P_e - \tau_e = \gamma_{ge} P_g + \lambda_x \quad \text{Blender pricing}$$

Once again, several cases can be identified, based on which constraint binds:

Case b1: $\lambda_x = 0$ Energy equivalent pricing
Case b2: $\lambda_x > 0$ and $Q_e = Q_e$ RFS, oxygenate or octane premiums
Case b3: $\lambda_x < 0$ and $Q_e = \gamma_{bw} Q_r$ Blend wall binding

In the competitive case with no binding constraints (b1) ethanol would be priced at its energy equivalent value, so the price of ethanol should follow the price of gasoline. If blending chemistry, such as premiums to ethanol as an oxygenate or octane booster are relevant or if the RFS mandate is binding, ethanol is purchased by blenders at a premium relative to its energy value, and demand for ethanol by blenders is determined by the relevant constraint. If the blend wall limits purchases of ethanol it will sell at a discount. In each case ethanol demand, hence production, is fixed by a constraint. In the competitive case any subsidy (τ_e) is transmitted from blenders to the ethanol price, and some of it may be absorbed by rents to blenders (λ_x) in constrained cases.

Volatility of the corn price in most cases is the consequence of a fixed, non-price-responsive demand having been added to the market. Only when the two competitive cases apply (e1 and b1) will variability in crude oil prices be passed to the corn market directly via the biofuels channel. Examining market performance recently for corn will illustrate that the fixed demand cases have dominated, except during brief periods. Ethanol prices follow gasoline, subject to premiums or discounts due to constraints on blenders, largely independent of the corn price. The one factor through which ethanol most affects volatility would be that the increased demand for corn moves the market away from surplus, characterized by large carryout stocks, and into a period in which stocks are low so that component of corn demand becomes inelastic. If corn production catches up with demand, both lower prices and lower variability should return.

3.6.3   Corn Market Performance

Figure 3.4 shows quarterly supply and use data for corn taken from the feed grains database of ERS (2012). Production is shown as a diamond at the beginning of each crop year and carryout stocks are shown at the end. Both show substantial variability over 2005 to 2012. Demand is divided into demand to produce ethanol (alcohol for fuel), all other domestic demand components (feed, food, seed, and other industrial uses), and exports. Both seasonality and substantially variability are seen for domestic uses excluding ethanol, and export demand is now smaller than both domestic uses, showing somewhat more variability recently. The "other use" category shows the most volatility, and has absorbed much of the increased biofuels demand, as production has not yet grown sufficiently to meet 2005 feed usage. Export demand fell from its 2007 to 2008 peak, but is similar to 2005 levels. Demand for ethanol use is growing over this period, but at a very steady rate. Little variation around trend is seen in the derived demand for ethanol, corresponding with demand levels fixed by growing capacity to meet the RFS mandate and the earlier oxygenate requirements. That demand exhibits a flat period around the Great Recession (2008 to 2009), and its trajectory slows as the RFS is nearly met and the blend wall starts to bind. This path is consistent with the notion that ethanol demand is determined in energy markets and by policy, largely independent of events in the corn market. But

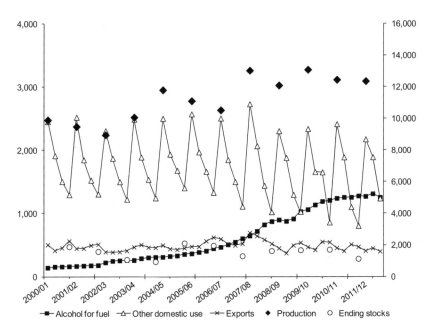

Fig. 3.4   Quarterly corn supply-use balances, including ethanol demand
Source: ERS (2012).

it is also apparent that ethanol demand has grown to be a large component of corn use.

3.7   International Trade of Ethanol

While there have been both imports and exports of small quantities of ethanol at least over the last decade (and before), trade became large enough to matter in 2006, when ethanol imports reached 15 percent of US domestic production. Neither its share nor volume later reached the levels during this "ethanol gold rush" period when both MTBE substitution and the RFS mandate created a demand well in excess of capacity. As production capacity increased in 2007 net imports fell to 6.7 percent of production, and by 2009 that share was only 2 percent. The year 2010 saw a rise in ethanol exports and substantial two-way trade, with net exports reaching 7.6 percent of production in 2011, in spite of imports at levels comparable to those in 2007. High corn prices due to drought and elimination of the subsidy caused exports to fall in 2012. Figure 3.5 plots imports and exports of ethanol against production, highlighting their small shares, apparent seasonality of trade, and the relation between price changes and trade flows. High prices in 2006, 2008, and 2009 appear to have pulled in imports later in each year, but the price

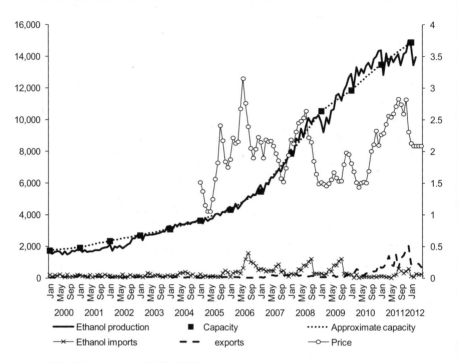

Fig. 3.5 Ethanol trade, 2000–2012
Sources: RFA (2012), ITC (2012), and Hofstrand (2012).

increases (and then falls) after 2009 appear more closely related to export demand.

Figure 3.6 presents ethanol prices, trade unit values, and margins between those prices.[9] It should first be observed that margins between domestic and border prices are quite volatile. While transportation costs matter for ethanol, they are unlikely to vary to that extent. Import unit values follow domestic prices at least somewhat until 2009. The Great Recession and collapse of trade and the strengthening dollar caused import unit values to fall much more than domestic prices, but cheap imports did not elicit much trade. Export unit values were remarkably stable, suggesting this was a specialty, differentiated product until 2010, when export unit values begin to closely follow US domestic prices. This switch corresponds with the switch in direction of trade at about the same time.

Explaining the two-way trade, and imports at a high cost in 2011, requires another differentiated product story. Ethanol imports in 2011, from Brazil

9. Unit values, equal to the value of imports or exports divided by the corresponding quantity of imports or exports, are a commonly used but imperfect proxy for border prices. If ethanol is a relatively homogeneous product then these should be a reasonable approximation, but there is some diversity in the quality of products traded.

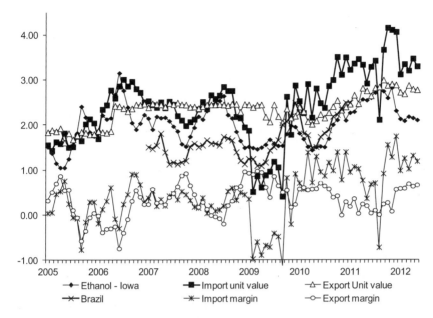

Fig. 3.6   Ethanol Iowa and border prices, 2005–2012
Sources: Hofstrand (2012), ITC (2012), and Newman (2011).

and made from sugar cane, were used to satisfy second generation biofuels mandates and regional regulations that could not include corn-based ethanol. They commanded a premium large enough to bring a small volume of imports from Brazil when price relatives had the United States exporting ethanol to Brazil as well (RFA 2010; Cooper 2011; Wisner 2012). It is policy constraints that created this differentiation, not product quality.

The relationship to Brazil's ethanol industry also helps to explain the shift in trade to US ethanol exports, as well. Brazil's ethanol industry is advanced, and has for a long period provided an alternative there to crude oil imports for gasoline (Valdes 2011). Ethanol produced from sugar cane has historically been more cost-effective than from US corn, yielding a price in Brazil below US prices. Figure 3.6 also shows a short price series for Brazil (Newman 2011) that captures this low price from the series' start in 2007 to 2009, and shows that prices in Brazil reached and then tracked US prices after mid-2009—when net trade reversed direction. During this period there have been major increases in world sugar prices and a shortfall in Brazilian sugar production, inciting a switch from ethanol to cane sugar production there. In Brazil switching from ethanol to sugar is relatively easy, and occurs when prices dictate the switch (Valdes 2011). Brazil's ethanol regime is also strongly conditioned by its own policy. For example, mandates there to use ethanol were reduced over this recent period. Changes in the exchange rate between the Brazilian real and the dollar have also significantly influenced these relative prices. A strong real in 2011 made imports of ethanol from Brazil more expensive, and US exports to Brazil cheaper. A strong dollar contributed to the low US ethanol import unit values in early 2009. A better Brazilian sugar crop in the future, a change in the value of the real, and lower world sugar prices could change the incentives now dictating the direction and magnitude of ethanol trade at the US border. In 2012, some of these effects were already evident as Brazilian ethanol imports fell significantly.

Policy influenced trade in export markets in which the United States replaced Brazil in 2011, as well. For example, imports by the European Union are influenced by policy constraints there (Hertel, Tyner, and Birur 2010). Newman (2011) argued that the European Union took advantage of subsidies and loopholes in trade classifications that gave rise to increasing ethanol imports until 2012. Those imports were under 20 percent of small US exports until 2010, but over one-quarter of the dramatically larger US exports in 2010 and 2011. Higher corn prices, removal of the subsidy, and tighter trade regulations led to EU ethanol imports falling over 40 percent in 2012. In 2011, EU imports were two-thirds of Brazilian imports, and only 2.1 percent of US ethanol production when exports peaked.

Imports into the United States have also benefited from provisions of the Caribbean Basin Initiative that allowed duty-free ethanol imports under a tariff rate quota. The quota under that agreement has never been reached, however (Newman 2011).

Ethanol exports in 2011 appear to have benefited from the VEETC, so production approached capacity, domestic demand remained at the blend wall, and exports made up the difference. In 2012, after the subsidy was eliminated, export margins increased and ethanol prices fell. Production appears to have fallen near the RFS mandate while exports make up the difference between that lower production level and the blend wall.

One trade-related question concerns whether the subsidy to ethanol use (VEETC) is also paid to foreigners. The tariff on ethanol was intended to prevent (actually counteract) the subsidy from being paid to foreigners, and some have argued that it was more than sufficient to accomplish that when ethanol was primarily imported. No such provisions prevent exports from receiving the subsidy, so long as the ethanol passes through blenders and contains a small amount of gasoline. While the RFA has argued that exports do not receive a subsidy as blended products are not exported, industry analysts have argued otherwise, and trade data are not sufficiently differentiated to tell. The small margin between the domestic price of ethanol and export unit values, that increased once the subsidy was removed, also suggests exports have received at least some of the subsidy, consistent with the theory presented above so long as exporters buy ethanol from blenders, not ethanol refiners.

Another question is, What modeling approach should be used to capture ethanol trade, and should that be used to revise the theory elaborated above? The volatility of margins suggests any short-term model relying on the law of one price (i.e., standard trade price linkages) is bound to fail. That theory gave rise to the prediction of the United States importing corn due to ethanol (Elobeid et al. 2007). Armington approaches based on domestic-international differentials will also miss much of the detail of trade, such as the change in direction of trade, two-way trade in 2011, and the emergence of newly large trade flows in 2006. Armington specifications will hold trade near the status quo. Elobeid and Tokgoz's (2008) trade model that incorporates both imperfect transmission of prices and an Armington-like net demand function misses the switch from imports to exports by construction. It has been argued that ethanol programs were created to meet domestic policy goals, and trade levels are a residual response to shortages or surpluses arising from those programs (Newman 2011). An example is US exports in 2011, necessitated by a binding blend wall and the need to meet a larger RFS mandate, or constrained by capacity. This suggests old "vent-for-surplus" trade models. Trade flows have also arisen to capture profits from loopholes in policy regimes, such as differing tariff definitions and opportunities to benefit from subsidies (as in trade with the EU). While trade flows have emerged in response to international price signals, the resulting flows have been just too small to fully arbitrage large price differentials. It is therefore likely that it is necessary to examine effects of trade on ethanol pricing separately under different trade regimes. What worked for the period of high imports will be likely to fail in the period of high exports. The magnitudes of trade flows remain relatively small compared to domestic markets. Domestic events in trading partner economies are also important to explaining those trade flows, especially in Brazil.

3.8   Evidence over Watershed Periods

Monthly quantity and price data for ethanol are examined over the "watershed periods" between 2005 and 2012 as defined in table 3.2. Quantity data is compared to capacity, RFS mandate, blend wall, and MTBE substitution constraints. Price data is used to determine profit margins for ethanol refiners and gasoline blenders as well as to examine price volatility and correlations over these subperiods.

3.8.1   Quantities—Ethanol Production

Figure 3.7 plots monthly ethanol production expressed as an annual flow. Capacity data in that graph are approximated from observations reported by RFA (2012) in January of each year and by assuming a linear trend between each year's observation on capacity. The RFS mandate applies on a cumulative annual basis, with bars on the graph showing the target level

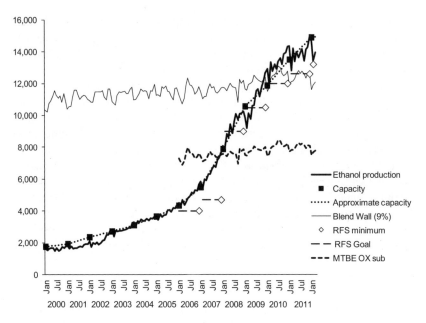

Fig. 3.7   Ethanol production, capacity and policy constraints, 2000–2012
Sources: EIA (2012) and RFA (2012).

over the course of the year, and diamonds indicating the year-end-mandated minimum use. The blend wall is approximated here at 9 percent of gasoline production (from Tyner and Viteri [2010]—and as they suggest, the binding blend wall may now be closer to 10 percent). The MTBE/oxygenate substitution requirement is at 5.8 percent of gasoline production based on the reformulated gasoline specification (EIA 2000). Each of these is an approximation to the actual restrictions on gasoline blenders.

It is apparent from figure 3.7 that capacity constraints bind most often, and appear to determine production in most months. The ethanol production line lies on top of the capacity approximation except for a couple of brief but notable periods. While capacity in 2005 was below the RFS mandate for 2006, during the ethanol gold rush period capacity was increased to stay above the mandated minimum. Except in 2008, following the dramatic increase in the RFS mandate in the 2007 Energy Act, capacity exceeded the mandate by January of the year to which it would apply. In 2008 it took four months to get ahead of the RFS, and then the collapse of oil, gasoline, and corn prices after recession and financial crisis in mid-2008 brought ethanol production below capacity. Ethanol profitability fell to its lowest level during this one period when production was obviously below capacity. In mid-2009 production had risen to capacity and was sufficient to meet the RFS mandate, and over 2010 production was slightly above capacity. Industry analysts argue that optimization of plant operations now (and in 2010) allows them to operate above nameplate capacity—the figure reported by RFA—for sustained periods, and this data is consistent with that claim.[10] In 2011, when the blend wall was imminent, and then when exports allowed production above the blend wall, production flows at or slightly below reported capacity are probably below actual capacity. It is apparent from this data that the RFS mandate may have shaped investment in capacity, but it only threatened to constrain production in early 2009, and this is the one period when RINs were not effectively zero. Moreover, from 2000 to 2011 production has been essentially at capacity, except during that period in early 2009, and fell below capacity again in 2012. This smooth, constrained growth in production generated similarly smooth growth in demand for corn as a feedstock to ethanol production.

The MTBE/oxygenate substitution requirement was not met by ethanol production until late 2007. The need to meet that requirement surely helped to spur investment during the gold rush period, but was no longer binding as the food crisis set in and afterward. The blend wall maximum on usage began to bind in early 2010, but production exceeded this constraint soon afterward. Trade data show that from mid-2010 onward ethanol production could remain above the blend wall as surpluses were exported. The effects of these two constraints are more apparent in prices and profitability margins than they are in quantities.

During the initial gold rush watershed period, the RFS mandate and MTBE substitution both shaped investment in capacity, which in turn dictated production. During the food crisis period, MTBE substitution was no longer binding, and the increased RFS mandate evoked large increases in capacity, which once again determined production. The Great Recession and collapse of commodity prices brought production briefly below capacity. Recovery and a renewed commodity boom brought production back to capacity until the blend wall and drought threatened to limit production. But in 2010 onward exports have allowed production to exceed the blend wall at a level near capacity. Changes in circumstances in Brazil and the end of subsidies captured by exporters limited export demand for ethanol and made simultaneously meeting the blend wall (at E10) and the RFS mandate infeasible without exports. One can see evidence of that in 2012. As conditions in world sugar markets changed and Brazil realized a better sugar crop, US ethanol exports have declined, leading to idled capacity and a more severely limiting blend wall.

3.8.2   Prices, Margins, and Profits

Prices for ethanol, corn, gasoline, and crude oil shown in figure 3.2 are averaged over the watershed periods in table 3.3. That figure shows etha-

10. The EIA now reports both "nameplate" and "sustainable" capacity. Sustainable capacity is about 4 percent higher. Nameplate capacity used here is as reported by the RFA.

Table 3.3   **Energy and corn prices by watershed period**

	Crude oil	Gasoline RBOB	Ethanol	Gasoline retail	Corn
2005–2012	1.77	2.15	2.00	2.90	3.93
Early 2005	1.07	1.45	1.23	2.12	1.82
Ethanol gold rush	1.39	1.88	2.16	2.64	2.43
Food crisis	2.23	2.56	2.10	3.29	4.48
Great Recession	1.45	1.64	1.70	2.52	3.95
Commodity boom	1.63	1.90	1.72	2.63	3.53
Blend wall imminent	1.79	2.11	1.59	2.81	3.46
Export relief	2.29	2.65	2.45	3.40	6.22
Subsidies ended	2.57	3.00	2.11	3.75	6.29

nol prices peaking during the gold rush period, remaining high during the food crisis, and then falling until export demand and high energy prices caused ethanol prices to peak again in 2011. Crude oil and gasoline prices rose through the food crisis, fell rapidly during the Great Recession period, and have been generally rising for each period afterward. Corn prices are somewhat less regular. They were low until the food crisis period, when they trended upward rapidly, then fell rapidly during the early part of the Great Recession period. They remained at levels that were low relative to the food crisis, but higher than pre-crisis levels until the export relief period saw high corn prices—precisely when one might have expected those higher corn prices and hence higher ethanol costs to discourage production and exports.

It is useful to compute profit and trade margins from the gasoline and corn prices discussed above in order to see the incentives to ethanol production. Moreover, these margins reflect the constraints that define each period. Figure 3.8 presents profit margins for ethanol refiners over variable costs as calculated by Hofstrand (2012) using ethanol and corn prices for representative plants in Iowa. It also presents margins for gasoline blenders buying ethanol, relative to strict energy-based pricing, adjusted for the VEETC subsidy. These margin as well as the trade margins shown in figure 3.6 are averaged over the watershed periods in table 3.4.

Ethanol production margins over variable cost (rents $- \lambda_e$) are positive in every period, but lowest once the subsidies ended in 2012. These margins were highest during the early gold rush period, when both the RFS mandate and MTBE substitution called for greater capacity. They were lower as corn prices increased during the food crisis, and lower still during the Great Recession period, when production briefly fell below capacity. Figure 3.7 shows that these margins were quite low in late 2008, but never went negative and subsequently showed seasonal peaks late in each subsequent year. Rising gasoline prices raised margins in the restarted commodity boom, but pressure from the imminent blend wall then lowered these margins. In late 2011 and early 2012, the export relief period, high crude oil and gaso-

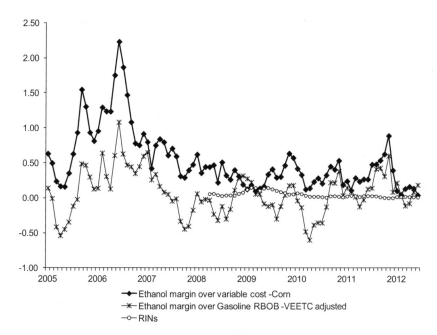

Fig. 3.8   Ethanol margins relative to corn and gasoline, 2005–2012
Sources: EIA (2012), Hofstrand (2012), and OPIS (2012).

Table 3.4   **Ethanol margins by watershed period**

	Production margin over variable cost	Margin over gasoline RBOB, VEETC adjusted	RINs	Import margin	Export margin
2005–2012	0.54	0.07		0.43	0.34
Early 2005	0.34	–0.27		0.36	0.59
Ethanol gold rush	1.08	0.36		0.24	0.01
Food crisis	0.45	–0.16	0.05	0.27	0.33
Great Recession	0.23	0.10	0.09	0.04	0.72
Commodity boom	0.40	–0.03	0.10	–0.12	0.51
Blend wall imminent	0.26	–0.31	0.03	0.96	0.61
Export relief	0.40	0.20	0.02	0.93	0.22
Subsidies ended	0.11	0.06	0.02	1.16	0.64

Sources: EIA (2012), Hofstrand (2012), OPIS (2012), ITC (2012), and author's calculations.

line prices counteracted the higher corn prices, yielding positive margins to ethanol production. When drought in 2012 brought even higher corn prices, margins fell.

Prior to the gold rush period, ethanol was priced below its energy value, but the need to use ethanol as an MTBE substitute led to the largest observed blending margins in 2006 to 2007. During the food crisis this margin (λ_x)

turned negative again as MTBE substitution requirements were exceeded, in spite of the subsidy, and became quite negative as the blend wall constraint approached. As export demand and high oil prices caused the demand for ethanol to increase, these margins turned positive, but fell once the subsidy was removed. Changes in these data crudely suggest only $0.15 of the $0.45 subsidy was found in margins to blenders, with the remainder passed through to the ethanol price. Margins relative to energy cost are always smaller than the margins accruing to ethanol refiners, consistent with ethanol prices more often following gasoline prices than corn prices. The RINs are even smaller, and only above $0.03 during the food crisis and Great Recession, when production briefly fell below capacity. This again was likely driven by greater variations over this period in crude oil and so gasoline prices, with corn prices sustaining a higher level after the Great Recession than before the food crisis.

What is notable about trade margins is that they are driven by switches in the predominant direction of trade flows and by product differentiation. The differential between exports and domestic prices fell to its lowest level when exports became significant, and an outlet for domestic surpluses, during the export relief period (excluding an anomaly in the gold rush period). Export prices had become close to, and related to, domestic ethanol prices only during this export relief period. When subsidies ended in 2012, export margins increased nearly $0.37 (ITC 2012), suggesting exports received only a portion of the subsidy, smaller than the portion accruing to blenders. In the case of imports, the margin in the later periods reflects the premiums accruing to imports that meet the second generation RFS mandate, not the corn ethanol mandate.

3.8.3   Volatility and Correlation

Data on price volatility and correlations across watershed periods further highlight the importance of mechanisms related to constraints on ethanol refiners and gasoline blenders. Table 3.5 reports coefficients of variation

Table 3.5	Price volatility by watershed period				
	Crude oil	Gasoline RBOB	Ethanol	Gasoline retail	Corn
1960–2012	1.05				0.46
2005–2012	0.31	0.27	0.22	0.20	0.43
Early 2005	0.09	0.10	0.15	0.08	0.03
Ethanol gold rush	0.09	0.16	0.16	0.12	0.34
Food crisis	0.22	0.19	0.18	0.14	0.27
Great Recession	0.47	0.42	0.18	0.33	0.17
Commodity boom	0.09	0.06	0.10	0.05	0.09
Blend wall imminent	0.04	0.06	0.08	0.02	0.04
Export relief	0.12	0.14	0.11	0.11	0.14
mid-2009–2012	0.19	0.20	0.21	0.15	0.30

Table 3.6   **Price correlations by watershed period**

	Crude oil/corn	Ethanol/ corn	Ethanol/ gasoline	Crude oil/gasoline	Margins-corn/ gasoline
1960–2012	0.85				
2005–2012	0.83	0.52	0.67	0.95	0.70
Ethanol gold rush	–0.13	–0.08	0.62	0.90	0.70
Food crisis	0.94	0.92	0.89	0.99	0.71
Great Recession	0.96	0.95	0.96	0.98	–0.29
Commodity boom	–0.12	0.39	0.52	0.73	0.81
Blend wall imminent	0.04	0.71	–0.69	0.78	0.94
Export relief	0.83	0.77	0.73	0.90	0.85

Sources: Author's calculations from EIA (2012) and Hofstrand (2012).

computed from monthly price data for the watershed periods of 2005 to 2012. Table 3.6 reports correlation coefficients for prices over these subperiods.[11]

Over the entire 2005 to 2012 period, volatility as measured by coefficients of variation was much lower for crude oil but comparable for corn, relative to volatility from 1960 to 2012. Once again, shorter subperiods yield lower volatility. Trends during subperiods generate much of observed volatility, and differences in price levels are explained by differing circumstances during each of the watershed periods. Remarkably low coefficients of variation are found for watershed periods, especially after the end of the Great Recession. Corn is an excellent example. In each subperiod after the Great Recession the coefficient of variation is less than 0.15, while it was above 0.4 for both 1960 to 2012 and 2005 to 2012. Volatility is also lower for gasoline prices than for crude oil or corn prices, and that carries over to ethanol prices. The food crisis and Great Recession exhibited the greatest volatility for all prices, characterized by strong upward coincident trends during the food crisis and rapid collapse of prices shortly afterward. This led to a misperception that volatility had increased. These data are also not consistent with the notion that the high price volatility observed from 2007 to 2009 has persisted in more recent years. That there are several subperiods since 2009 contributes to these low subperiod volatility measures. Had we measured volatility without trying to understand the changing economic mechanisms (see measures for mid-2009 to 2012 in table 3.5), we would have found higher volatility, comparable to what is found during the food crisis period. But changes in means and short-run trends explainable by economic conditions led to this apparent volatility, and these measures remain generally smaller than those found for the longer periods, 1960 to 2012 and 2005 to 2012.

11. Monthly price series include too few observations to determine volatility and correlations after ethanol subsidies ended in 2012.

Similar to volatility, correlations of corn and energy prices are higher over longer periods of time than they are over subperiods. Also, correlations vary across subperiods in ways that are broadly consistent with changing economic mechanisms as explained above, with some anomalies. For example, the correlation between ethanol and corn prices should be lower when capacity constraints bind (case e2) than during periods when capacity rents are low and these prices are linked by refiner pricing decisions (case e1). Ethanol and corn prices over 2005 to 2012 are correlated only at a coefficient of 0.53, and this measure was lower during the gold rush and restarted commodity boom periods. As the blend wall became imminent and then exports relieved the blend wall constraint, as expected, correlations when capacity may not bind are higher, above 0.7. The anomaly to this logic is the food crisis and Great Recession periods that are characterized by strongly rising and then falling trends. The high correlations, over 0.9 for these periods, may reflect other forces that drove the trends, rather than these biofuels mechanisms. Capacity constraints were nonbinding only briefly over these periods.

The ethanol-gasoline price correlation exhibits similar patterns. It is higher over the entire period than over several subperiods. When the blend wall became imminent, and the rent to that constraint increased, this correlation actually turned negative. This correlation was also much higher during the food crisis and Great Recession than for other periods, again reflecting the strong trends. The correlations of the margin between gasoline and ethanol prices are also highly correlated with the profit margin of ethanol refiners in periods when the blend wall binds.

A somewhat surprising aspect is that correlations between crude oil and corn prices are higher for the overall period and for several subperiods than are the correlations directly related to the biofuels mechanism. This also suggests other factors beyond biofuels contribute to this correlation. But the lowest correlations between crude oil and corn do occur in recent subperiods when the correlation between gasoline and crude oil prices is weaker.

3.9 Conclusions

Increasing ethanol production since 2005 has led to a large, persistent, new demand for corn that has contributed to higher corn prices and sometimes tighter links between energy and agricultural prices. Constraints that arose from energy legislation and EPA regulations have shaped the trajectory of the derived demand for corn to produce ethanol, and determined mechanisms dictating the short-run relationships across prices. The influence of specific regulations has varied over time—substitution of ethanol in place of MTBE was an early factor in 2006, while the blend wall limit on concentration of ethanol in gasoline is now more important. While each of these factors has surely mattered to the evolution of ethanol and corn markets, it is constraints on production capacity that have determined corn demand

and pricing relationships over the short to medium run during most of the period from 2005 to 2012.

Capacity constraints are what have generally bound, determining ethanol production and hence derived demand for corn, except briefly in late 2008 to 2009 and again in 2012. Energy policy (RFS, MTBE, and blend wall) influenced capacity increments, shaping incentives to invest, but have not strictly bound ethanol refiner behavior to date. Capacity has always remained somewhat ahead of the RFS mandate, and investment slowed as the mandate maximum on corn ethanol approached and the blend wall was reached. Exports relieved pressure from the blend wall in 2011 and allowed a solution to meeting the infeasible problem of satisfying an RFS-mandated minimum above the blend wall determined maximum. How we get around the blend wall is important to the future—with the corn-based RFS mandate met, some second generation mandates were waived, and the blend wall was binding, so new construction of corn ethanol plants has slowed dramatically. Large exports were possible due to circumstances in Brazil. High world sugar prices, a sugar production shortfall, and a strong currency caused Brazil to shift from a large exporter to an importer of ethanol, but those circumstances are unlikely to persist over the longer term. Lower exports were already evident in 2012.

Two mechanisms stand out as key in this analysis as a consequence of binding capacity constraints. Rents to capacity allow independent variation of gasoline (hence ethanol) and corn prices. Smoothly trending capacity has in most months determined demand for corn, leading to a perfectly inelastic demand component to satisfy biofuels needs.

When capacity constraints bind, corn and crude oil prices can live independent lives. Ethanol profit margins vary as these prices vary, and have yielded positive profits except during subperiods when capacity constraints do not bind. Except during those subperiods, crude oil price volatility is not passed directly to the corn market via the biofuels mechanism. When we are between constraints, in theory corn and crude prices are directly linked. But that is a small window that opened only in late 2008 to early 2009, and recently. Data on price variability, correlations, and profit margins are largely consistent with this theory over the short term.

With ethanol capacity constraints binding, industrial demand for corn to produce alcohol is inelastic but not highly variable around its increasing trend. Its effect on corn markets is through the increased, persistent, but stable demand. Corn stocks and the capacity to produce enough corn to meet that demand determine the corn price regime, hence variability. Ethanol contributes a large, inelastic demand component, and drove us to a low-stocks state when corn production was unable to catch up with demand.

Now the combination of the blend wall and RFS are infeasible without trade or use of RINs. Exports have relieved pressure from the blend wall, but with plants now operating below capacity, profit margins for ethanol are lower. Subsidized exports in 2011 were the difference between production near capacity and the blend wall. That exports have not vanished with high corn prices reflects the importance of the blend wall now. Once subsidies were removed, export margins increased, ethanol prices fell, export demand declined, and production fell to nearer the RFS mandate. Prices of corn and ethanol are more strongly linked under this circumstance.

Flow constraints, such as capacity and the blend wall, directly impact quantities and determine production, whereas the effects of stocks constraints, such as the RFS mandate and corn carryout stocks, have had noticeable effects on prices, even if they did not strictly bind. Stocks constraints have worked through expectations, which in turn influenced pricing.

Volatility has varied as the regime determining corn prices has changed. Short-term volatility has been small, and regime changes or trends lead to larger apparent long-run volatility as seen in annual data. Strong, coincident short-run trends, particularly in 2007 to 2008, led to a misperception that volatility had permanently increased. It is the big moves, not noise around long-run equilibrium, which gave rise to observed volatility. From this perspective, it is high prices, not greater volatility, which defines the current era.

While the expanding biofuels demand has surely mattered to the high prices for corn and other agricultural commodities, the simple longer-term model here yields effects comparable to many other factors found in the literature. While that demand may have raised corn prices by about 33 percent from 2005 to 2009, to get both price and volatility results required that this effect be combined with others that moved the corn market to a position of low stocks. Such price effects can seldom be judged in isolation. For example, if/when production catches up to this demand, lower corn prices, and so lower biofuels demand impacts, are expected. To get the high short-term prices observed for agricultural markets recently, either much lower short-term elasticities must be assumed, or other factors contributed to market outcomes.

In the future, modifications to energy policy, trade adjustments, and capacity investment will determine the role biofuels play in shaping agricultural commodity prices. Expansion from the corn mandate is finished and progress on second generation biofuels is not evident. But reliance on trade to get around the blend wall is a strategy likely to contribute to lower prices in the future.

References

Abbott, P. 2010. "Stabilization Policies in Developing Countries after the 2007–08 Food Crisis." OECD Working Paper TAD/CA/APM/WP(2010)44, Organisation for Economic Co-operation and Development, Paris.

Abbott, P., C. Hurt, and W. Tyner. 2008. "What's Driving Food Prices?" Farm Foundation Issue Report. http://www.farmfoundation.org/webcontent/Farm-Foundation -Issue-Report-Whats-Driving-Food-Prices-404.aspx.

———. 2011. "What's Driving Food Prices in 2011?" Oak Brook, IL: Farm Foundation.

Agricultural Food and Policy Center. 2008. "The Effects of Ethanol on Texas Food and Feed." College Station: Texas A&M University.

Ai, C., A. Chatrath, and F. Song. 2006. "On the Comovement of Commodity Prices." *American Journal of Agricultural Economics* 88:574–88.

Babcock, B. A., and J. F. Fabiosa. 2011. "The Impact of Ethanol and Ethanol Subsidies on Corn Prices: Revisiting History." Ames, IA: Center for Agricultural and Rural Development (CARD).

Baffes, J., and T. Haniotis. 2010. "Placing the 2006/08 Commodity Price Boom into Perspective." Washington, DC: World Bank.

Balcombe, K. 2009. "The Nature and Determinants of Volatility in Agricultural Prices: An Empirical Study from 1962–2008." Workshop on Institutions and Policies to Manage Global Market Risks and Price Spikes in Basic Food Commodities. Rome: Food and Agriculture Organization of the United Nations (FAO). http://www.fao.org/economic/est/publications/publications/en/.

Brown, L. R. 1980. "Food or Fuel: New Competition for the World's Cropland." Washington, DC: Worldwatch Institute.

Carter, C., G. Rausser, and A. Smith. 2012. "The Effect of the US Ethanol Mandate on Corn Prices." Giannini Foundation Working Paper, University of California, Davis.

Cha, K. S., and J. H. Bae. 2011. "Dynamic Impacts of High Oil Prices on the Bioethanol and Feedstock Markets." *Energy Policy* 39:753–60.

Collins, K. 2008. "The Role of Biofuels and Other Factors in Increasing Farm and Food Prices." Chicago: Kraft Global Foods.

Cooper, G. 2011. "The Ethanol Shuffle." *The E-Exchange.* Washington, DC: Renewable Fuels Association.

de Gorter, H. D., and D. R. Just. 2009. "The Economics of a Blend Mandate for Biofuels." *American Journal of Agricultural Economics* 91:738–50.

Delgado, C. 2009. "Driven by Increased Price Volatility, the Global Food Crisis is Not Over." In *Policy Dialogue on High Food Prices: Outlook and Donor Mid-term Responses*, February 12–13. Paris: Organisation for Economic Co-operation and Development (OECD).

Diffenbaugh, N. S., T. W. Hertel, M. Scherer, and M. Verma. 2012. "Response of Corn Markets to Climate Volatility under Alternative Energy Futures." *Nature Climate Change,* advance online publication. http://www.nature.com/nclimate/journal /v2/n7/full/nclimate1491.html.

Economic Research Service (ERS) 2012. Feed Grain Database. Washington, DC: United States Department of Agriculture. http://www.ers.usda.gov/data-products /feed-grains-database.aspx#.Uu5qGfb5Gw8.

Energy Information Administration (EIA). 2000. "MTBE, Oxygenates, and Motor Gasoline." Washington, DC: Department of Energy.

———. 2012. "Monthly Energy Review." Washington, DC: Department of Energy.

Elobeid, A., and S. Tokgoz. 2008. "Removing Distortions in the US Ethanol Market: What Does It Imply for the United States and Brazil?" *American Journal of Agricultural Economics* 90:918–32.

Elobeid, A., S. Tokgoz, D. J. Hayes, B. A. Babcock, and C. E. Hart. 2007. "The Long-Run Impact of Corn-Based Ethanol on the Grain, Oilseed, and Livestock Sectors with Implications for Biotech Crops." *AgBioForum* 10:11–8.

Enders, W., and M. T. Holt. 2012. "Sharp Breaks or Smooth Shifts? An Investigation of the Evolution of Primary Commodity Prices." *American Journal of Agricultural Economics* 94:659–73.

Gilbert, C. L. 2010. "How to Understand High Food Prices." *Journal of Agricultural Economics* 61:398–425.

Gohin, A., and D. Tréguer. 2010. "On the (De)Stabilization Effects of Biofuels: Relative Contributions of Policy Instruments and Market Forces." *Journal of Agricultural and Resource Economics* 35:72–86.

Harri, A., L. Nalley, and D. Hudson. 2009. "The Relationship between Oil, Exchange Rates, and Commodity Prices." *Journal of Agricultural and Applied Economics* 41:501–10.

Headey, D., and S. Fan. 2010. *Reflections on the Global Food Crisis.* Washington, DC: International Food Policy Research Institute (IFPRI).

Hertel, T. W., and J. Beckman. 2011. "Commodity Price Volatility in the Biofuel Era: An Examination of the Linkage between Energy and Agricultural Markets." NBER Working Paper no. 16824, Cambridge, MA.

Hertel, T. W., W. E. Tyner, and D. Birur. 2010. "The Global Impacts of Multi-national Biofuels Mandates." *Energy Journal* 31 (1): 75–100.

Hofstrand, D. 2012. "Ethanol Supply Chain Profitability." AgMRC Renewable Energy Newsletter. Ames, Iowa: Agricultural Marketing Resource Center, Iowa State University.

International Monetary Fund (IMF). 2012. "International Commodity Prices." Washington, DC: International Monetary Fund. http://www.imfstatistics.org /imf/.

International Trade Commission (ITC) 2012. Trade Dataweb. Washington, DC: International Trade Commission, Department of Commerce.

Irwin, S. H., and D. R. Sanders. 2011. "Index Funds, Financialization, and Commodity Futures Markets." *Applied Economic Perspectives and Policy* 33:1–31.

Kesam, J. P., A. Ohyama, and H. S.Yang. 2011. "An Economic Evaluation of the Renewable Fuel Standard (RFS) Biofuel Program: An Industrial Policy Approach." University of Illinois and Economics Research Paper no. LE09-035. Urbana-Champaign: University of Illinois.

McPhail, L. L. 2011. "Assessing the Impact of US Ethanol on Fossil Fuel Markets: A Structural VAR Approach." *Energy Economics* 33:1177–85.

McPhail, L. L., and B. A. Babcock. 2012. "Impact of US Biofuel Policy on US Corn and Gasoline Price Variability." *Energy* 37:505–13.

McPhail, L., P. Westcott, and H. Lutman. 2011. "The Renewable Identification Number System and US Biofuel Mandates." Washington, DC: Economic Research Service, United States Department of Agriculture.

Mitchell, D. 2008. "A Note on Rising Food Prices." Policy Research Working Paper no. WPS 4682, World Bank, Washington, DC.

National Academy of Sciences. 2011. *Renewable Fuel Standard: Potential Economic and Environmental Effects of U.S. Biofuel Policy.* Washington, DC: National Academies Press.

Newman, D. 2011. "US Ethanol Policy and Trade." Industries Analysis Seminar Series. Washington, DC: US International Trade Commission. http://www.usitc .gov/research_and_analysis/seminars_industry.htm.

Oil Price Information Service (OPIS). 2012. "Ethanol RINs." Gaithersburg, MD: Oil Price Information Service.

Paulson, N. 2012. "Is the Ethanol Mandate Truly a Mandate? An Estimate of Banked RINs Stocks." *Farmdoc Daily.* Illinois Farm Business Farm Management Association and Department of Agricultural and Consumer Economics, University of Illinois.

Renewable Fuels Association (RFA). 2010. "The Paradox of Rising US Ethanol Exports: Increased Market Opportunities and the Expense of Enhanced National Security?" Washington, DC: Renewable Fuels Association. http://www.ethanol rfa.org/news/entry/us-ethanol-exports-new-markets-missed-opportunities/.

———. 2012. "Ethanol Industry Statistics." Washington, DC: Renewable Fuels Association. http://www.ethanolrfa.org/pages/statistics.

Thompson, W., S. Meyer, and P. Westhoff. 2010. "The New Markets for Renewable Identification Numbers." *Applied Economic Perspectives and Policy* 32:588–603.

Thomson Reuters. 2012. Datastream. Thomson Reuters. http://thomsonreuters.com /datastream-professional/.

Trostle, R. 2009. "Fluctuating Food Commodity Prices: A Complex Issue With No Easy Answers." *Amber Waves* 6:11–7.

Tyner, W. E. 2008. "The US Ethanol and Biofuels Boom: Its Origins, Current Status, and Future Prospects." *BioScience* 58:646–53.

———. 2010. "The Integration of Energy and Agricultural Markets." *Agricultural Economics* 41:193–201.

Tyner, W. E., F. Taheripour, and D. Perkis. 2010. "Comparison of Fixed versus Variable Biofuels Incentives." *Energy Policy* 38:5530–40.

Tyner, W. E., and D. Viteri. 2010. "Implications of Blending Limits on the US Ethanol and Biofuels Markets." *Biofuels* 1:251–3.

United States Congress. 2005. Energy Policy Act of 2005, Pub. L. no. 109-58. Washington, DC.

———. 2007. Energy Independence and Security Act of 2007. H.R. 6, 110th Cong.

Valdes, C. 2011. "Brazil's Ethanol Industry: Looking Forward." Washington, DC: Economic Research Service, United States Department of Agriculture. http:// www.ers.usda.gov/publications/bio-bioenergy/bio-02.aspx#.Uu55Efb5Gw8.

Wisner, R. 2012. "Ethanol Exports: A Way to Scale the Blend Wall?" Renewable Energy and Climate Change Newsletter. Ames, IA: Agricultural Marketing Resource Center.

Wright, B. D. 2011. "The Economics of Grain Price Volatility." *Applied Economic Perspectives and Policy* 33:32–58.

Comment   Brian D. Wright

The huge diversion of corn in the United States for use in biofuels, beginning in 2005, is an unprecedented phenomenon that has transformed the economic outlook for farmers and animal feeders in the United States, and for consumers globally dependent on grains as a staple food. In the seven years since then, the rationales for this expansion have changed frequently. Initially, the driver was the sudden need for a substitute after a fuel oxygenate

Brian D. Wright is professor of agricultural and resource economics at the University of California, Berkeley.

For acknowledgments, sources of research support, and disclosure of the author's material financial relationships, if any, please see http://www.nber.org/chapters/c12809.ack.

was reported to pollute groundwater and have carcinogenic properties. Then scientists, environmentalists, and farmers supported further expansion as a gasoline substitute that reduced the emission of carbon dioxide. Serious scientific concerns regarding climatic effects of induced land-use changes have recently broken this consensus, but agricultural sector support and energy security arguments have kept the main policies in place.

In his chapter for this conference, Abbott focuses appropriately on the effects of biofuels policy on price volatility, as distinct from the effects on price levels. As Abbott notes, much has been written on this controversial issue, but his review shows how confused and confusing the literature on this politically sensitive topic has been. Given the very rapid expansion of the grain ethanol industry, the continuing changes in its drivers, and the complexity of the regulatory environment, this confusion is understandable.

Abbott's contribution is to make a serious and informative effort to characterize the rapidly evolving policy environment and relate it to the evolution of prices of corn, ethanol, gasoline, and crude oil, and of margins for blenders and ethanol producers. He carefully discusses constraints in the supply chain, including Renewable Fuel Standard (RFS) yearly mandates, the "blend wall" constraining domestic use in reformulated gasoline, MTBE oxygenate substitution, ethanol production capacity constraints, and corn stock constraints. As in Abbott, Hurt, and Tyner (2011), he rightly recognizes the nonlinear interactions of these constraints, and the key role played by corn stocks in the response of corn prices to short-run shocks in demand or supply.

Starting in 2005, he identifies (table 3.2) seven distinct "watershed periods" for ethanol-related constraints: ethanol gold rush, food crisis, Great Recession, commodity boom restarted, blend wall imminent, export relief, and subsidies ended. In assessing price volatility, he first considers daily, monthly, and annual observations, but concludes that the interval of observation is "far more important than frequency." The standard deviations tend to be higher for longer periods, and "strongly influenced by the means of subperiods" (96). He settles on monthly data for later discussion. His analysis is understandability limited by the lack of a dynamic model for the effects of corn stocks and RINs on monthly volatility.

Abbott briefly recognizes that apparent volatility might be influenced by trends, but does not follow up with any attempt to separate trends from variation around those trends. Given the large price changes over the period, this issue deserves more attention. To take an extreme case, crude oil price is constant until 1973, so the volatility from 1960 to 2012 (tables 3.2 and 3.5), likely dominated by trend, is not informative about crude oil price variation in his data, which was zero from 1960 to 1973 (figure 3.1).

Abbott shows how correlations between prices of crude oil, gasoline, ethanol, and corn differ between watershed periods. It is striking how they differ between regimes. For example, the crude oil/corn price correlation varies from –0.12 in the commodity boom to 0.96 in the Great Recession. But again, the trends in each series deserve more attention. To again take the extreme example, the high crude oil/corn price correlation of 0.85 for 1960 to 2012 might well reflect long-run moves in both series, but might well be a spurious measure of their economic relationship.

The accuracy and interpretation of price correlation measures is important. Abbott argues that ethanol plant capacity constraints were binding over most of the period since 2005, contrary to conclusions of other writers. His policy review and the evidence he presents on margins for ethanol production, and on the price of RINs, are highly informative and align with his conclusion. However in the excellent discussion in his conclusion, he notes that:

> When capacity constraints bind, corn and crude oil prices can live independent lives. Ethanol profit margins vary as these prices vary, and have yielded positive profits except during brief subperiods when capacity constraints do not bind. Except during those subperiods, crude oil price volatility is not passed directly to the corn market via the biofuels mechanism. (127)

Given this discussion, the high correlation of crude oil and corn prices of 0.83 for 2005 to 2012 is not what one might expect, and not obviously consistent with the dominance of capacity constraints. Abbott implies at the end of his abstract that he believes trends in both series distort these correlations. If he can further clarify this issue his analysis will be more ultimately persuasive.

If Abbott is correct, we are now in a new regime where trade has declined in importance and the RFS and the blend wall are more prominent as key constraints in the ethanol market. If the blend wall is continually shifted outward, capacity constraints could bind for many years.

Abbott deserves credit for taking the meandering policy path seriously and showing how policy changes affect the relations between prices of crude oil, ethanol, and corn. (Given the rapidity of regime changes, he might be more careful to emphasize that some correlations relate less to annual than to monthly volatility.) Some observers have argued that the exposure to the more elastic crude oil market demand will actually stabilize the corn market. Others believe that corn ethanol policy has introduced crude oil price fluctuations as a new source of demand-side instability into the grain market. Abbott's careful work will help us analyze corn market volatility and its relation to biofuels policy, as that policy further evolves.

Reference

Abbott, P., C. Hurt, and W. Tyner. 2011. "What's Driving Food Prices in 2011?" Oak Brook, IL: Farm Foundation.

4

The Evolving Relationships between Agricultural and Energy Commodity Prices
A Shifting-Mean Vector Autoregressive Analysis

Walter Enders and Matthew T. Holt

4.1 Introduction

That primary commodity prices have, in recent years, steadily moved higher into uncharted territory is unassailable. As illustrated by the plot of the World Bank's nominal monthly food price index shown in figure 4.1, there was nearly an exponential increase in the overall price of food from the late 1990s through late 2008. Despite the so-called Great Recession, between 1960 and 2011 the absolute high for the food price index was 223.56 in February 2011, indicating that food prices at this point were 224 percent higher than in 2005. Prices for other primary commodities, including those for many other field crops, many livestock and livestock products, as well as various energy products, have followed similar patterns in recent years.

Considering the above, two basic questions are this: What are behind these recent price moves? And might we expect similar patterns to continue into the not-too-distant future? Generally speaking, the goal of this chapter is to address the former question, and to do so for a select yet important subset of commodity prices—the later question, while intrinsically interesting to policymakers, market analysts, producers, consumers, and economists alike, is beyond the scope of the present study, and remains as an important topic

Walter Enders is professor and the Bidgood Chair of Economics and Finance at the University of Alabama. Matthew T. Holt is professor and the Dwight Harrigan Endowed Faculty Fellow in Natural Resources Economics at the University of Alabama.

The authors acknowledge support for this project from USDA-ERS Cooperative Agreement no. 58-3000-0-0061. We thank an anonymous reviewer and Lutz Kilian for detailed comments on earlier drafts, as well as participants in the NBER conference "The Economics of Food Price Volatility," in Seattle, Washington, August 15–16, 2012, for helpful comments and suggestions. For acknowledgments, sources of research support, and disclosure of the authors' material financial relationships, if any, please see http://www.nber.org/chapters/c12810.ack.

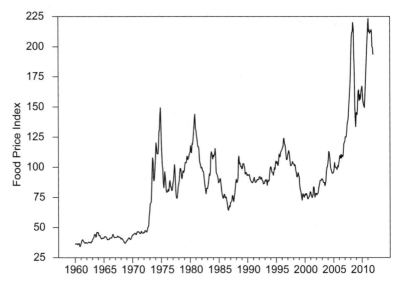

Fig. 4.1   Monthly World Bank food price index, 1960–2011
Note: 2005 = 100.

for future research. More specifically, we attempt to address the first question here by building on recent work by Enders and Holt (2012) wherein the recent movements of primary commodity prices are investigated by using univariate time-series methods. In this earlier study, methods outlined by Perron (1989), Bai and Perron (1998, 2003), Becker, Enders, and Hurn (2004, 2006), and González and Teräsvirta (2008) were used to examine the timing and nature of shifts (breaks) for a suite of real commodity prices. Left unaddressed in this analysis, however, was the potential interactions among some of these key variables. We know, for example, that energy is an important input in the production, transport, and processing of many primary commodities (see, e.g., Pimentel 2003;Hill et al. 2006). Moreover, the relationship between energy and, say, maize has likely undergone changes in recent years with the rise of the production and use of corn-based ethanol in the United States.

The potential for new and interesting interactions between the prices for energy and those for basic food/feed stuffs have not gone unnoticed in the literature. For example, Balcombe and Rapsomanikis (2008) examined linkages between sugar, ethanol, and oil prices for Brazil by using weekly data for the period July 2000 through May 2006. Likewise, Serra et al. (2011) examined the interactions among monthly nominal prices for maize, ethanol, oil, and gasoline over the January 1990 through December 2008 period. Both of these studies focused on potential interactions among the variables considered by using a classical vector error correction model (VECM) framework suitably modified to allow for possible nonlinearities in speeds of adjustment back to equilibrium. In a study that used a similar framework, although without focusing directly on nonlinearities in the mean equations, Zhang et al. (2009) examined linkages among weekly US prices for maize, soybeans, ethanol, gasoline, and oil by using a VECM modified to allow for multivariate generalized autoregressive heteroskedasticity.

While each of the aforementioned studies have provided useful insights into the linkages between energy and field crop commodity prices, the methodological framework employed warrants further discussion. Specifically, the VECM approach is predicated on the notion that the relevant variables in the system behave in a manner consistent with having an autoregressive unit root. Furthermore, the variables are said to be cointegrated if they share at least one common stochastic trend.[1] This methodological approach stands in contrast to that of the frameworks presented by Perron (1989), Bai and Perron (1998, 2003), Becker, Enders, and Hurn (2004, 2006), and González and Teräsvirta (2008), among others, wherein it is assumed that the variables in question have a stable autoregressive process around some otherwise shifting or breaking mean. Indeed, this notion is what underlies the previous work by Enders and Holt (2012). In this instance shocks (shifts) are not permanent, and are therefore not part of the underlying data-generating mechanism, as they surely must be in the VECM framework, but are instead effectively exogenous to the data-generating process.

In many instances it seems reasonable to believe that commodity prices do, in fact, fundamentally behave in a manner consistent with possessing stable dynamics around a shifting or breaking mean. The option to store current production for future consumption, for example, links the prices of storable commodities through time in a manner consistent with an autoregressive process with mean-reverting behavior, albeit perhaps in a manner consistent with nonlinear adjustments. See, for example, Williams and Wright (1991) and Deaton and Laroque (1995). Moreover, these results apparently hold for heterogeneous expectations regimes, including forward- as well as backward-looking expectations (Chavas 2000). As discussed by Wang and Tomek (2007), these and other results on the theory of commodity price formation call into question the basic notion of the unit root hypothesis when applied to many commodity prices.

Considering price behavior for extractable, nonrenewable resources, and most notably for oil, there is not common agreement in the literature regarding the underlying properties of the data. As already noted, Perron (1989) argues that oil prices move in a manner consistent with autoregressive stationarity around a breaking, deterministic mean. Berck and Roberts (1996) analyze a long time series of nonrenewable commodity prices and conclude

---

1. It is possible, of course, for one or more of the variables in question to have a stable autoregressive process (i.e., to not possess a unit root), in which case the variable in question will be identified with one unique contegrating relationship of its own. See Enders (2010) for additional details.

that the unit root hypothesis holds.[2] Pindyck (1999), who analyzes 127 years of energy price data, concluded, alternatively, that trend stationarity provides the more relevant description of the data. By using a newer set of tests that allows for multiple breaks under the alternative, Lee, List, and Strazicich (2006) reach conclusions similar to Pindyck's (1999). Alternatively, Maslyuk and Smyth (2008) conclude that stochastic trends are appropriate for oil prices, while Ghoshray and Johnson (2010) find that energy prices seemingly fluctuate around breaking trends. Finally, both Dvir and Rogoff (2009), by using annual data, and Alquist, Kilian, and Vigfusson (2013), by using monthly and quarterly data, identified a highly significant structural break in the price of oil in 1973, which casts further doubt on the unit root hypothesis for the real price of oil, at least when considering long epochs.

From an economic perspective, much of the debate regarding the properties of oil prices apparently hinges on whether or not the world has achieved "peak oil," as noted by Geman (2007). From an econometric perspective, the results appear to be sensitive to the overall sample size, the time period being analyzed, and the frequency with which the data are sampled (e.g., weekly versus monthly versus annual). In the very least there is scope to consider the possibility that energy (i.e., oil) prices behave in a mean-reverting manner, with the underlying mean itself possibly including several breaks or shifts.

How might we proceed when considering a set of variables that are likely stationary around shifting (breaking) means? There is a small but relevant literature on this topic. Ng and Vogelsang (2002), for example, explored the specification and estimation of vector autoregressions (VARs) with one or more discrete structural breaks in the equations involved. Similarly, Holt and Teräsvirta (2012) outline an approach to examine coshifting in a multivariate setting in a manner consistent with the univariate time-varying autoregressive (TVAR) model of Lin and Teräsvirta (1994) and the Quick-Shift procedures developed by González and Teräsvirta (2008).

Before proceeding, a reasonable question is, How do nonstructural VAR models that perhaps include occasional breaks or shifts in mean correspond with the more structural approach to commodity price modeling; that is, an approach wherein supply, demand, and storage behaviors are explicitly accounted for (see, e.g., Williams and Wright 1991)? In earlier work, Deaton and Laroque (1992, 1995) found that a competitive storage model combined with *iid* supply shocks produced too little serial correlation relative to observed behavior. More recently, however, Cafiero et al. (2011) show, by using a much finer grid to approximate the equilibrium price function, that structural storage models can generate levels of serial correlation consistent with that observed in commodity prices, even when supply shocks are *iid*. Moreover, the models considered by Cafiero et al. (2011) are capable of producing infrequent booms and busts due to occasional stock outs or near

2. They did not, however, analyze the behavior of oil prices per se.

stock outs. The vector autoregressive framework wherein occasional mean shifts or breaks are incorporated, presumably to account for occasional booms or busts, seems to be an entirely consistent albeit reduced form way of modeling commodity price movements.

Considering the above, the overall goal of this chapter is to identify the key factors responsible for the general run-up of US grain prices. We do so by building on Enders and Holt's (2012) analysis of the recent run-up of sixteen commodity prices using univariate time-series methods. Instead, we use a time-varying multiple equation model to focus on interactions among the prices for oil, maize, soybeans, ethanol, and ocean freight rates over the 1985 to 2011 period. In section 4.2, we review some of the arguments that have been put forth to explain the recent price boom. We also discuss some of the modeling strategies that have been employed to examine the proposed explanations. In section 4.3 we discuss our data set and the rationale for selecting the variables to include in the analysis. Given that cobreaking is in its infancy, we utilize two different methodologies to measure the effects of shifts in the underlying causal variables on grain prices. In section 4.4 we use a simple unrestricted vector autoregression (VAR) to estimate some of the key relationships between grain prices and a number of macroeconomic variables. The nature of the model is such that mean shifts in any one variable are allowed to change the means of all other variables. Given some of the limitations of VAR analysis, in section 4.5 we discuss some of the issues involved in estimating nonlinear models of shifting means. In order to determine whether the variables are stationary, in section 4.6 we report results of nonlinear unit root tests. In particular, we perform unit root and stationarity tests of all of the variables by employing a new testing procedure developed by Enders and Lee (2012). The advantage of their approach is that we can readily test for a unit root in the slowly evolving mean. In section 4.7, we go on to develop a parametric model of structural change in the spirit of the shifting-mean vector autoregressive framework similar to that considered by Ng and Vogelsang (2002), but modified in a manner consistent with Holt and Teräsvirta (2012) to allow for the possibility of gradual or smooth shifts (as opposed to discrete breaks). The results are assessed by, among other things, decomposing the effects of the shifts of, in particular, oil prices on the prices for other commodities. The final section concludes.

4.2   The Recent Commodity Price Boom: A Brief Review

As detailed in Kilian (2008), Hamilton (2009), Wright (2011), Carter, Rausser, and Smith (2011), and Enders and Holt (2012), there are likely a variety of reasons underlying the recently observed boom-bust-boom pattern for many primary commodity prices. Clearly, the first decade of the twenty-first century has generally been a period of significant income growth in many developing countries, and most notably in China, India, and parts

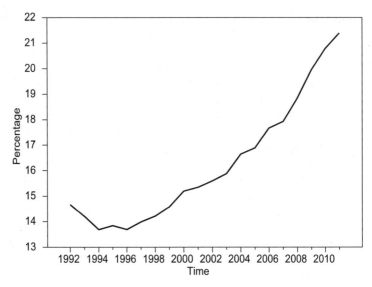

Fig. 4.2   Percent of total global oil consumption by Brazil, China, India, and Russia, 1992–2011

Source: US Energy Information Administration (www.eia.gov/).

of South America including Brazil. Zhang and Law (2010) show that this income growth has led the BRIC countries to incorporate larger quantities of grains, meat, and other proteins in their diets.[3]

The second notable effect of increased purchasing power in developing countries has been a sharp increase in the demand for energy, and most notably for petroleum. Hamilton (2009) reviews many of the details surrounding recent shifts in energy consumption and, specifically, discusses the role of the BRICs. Likewise, Kilian and Hicks (2013) provide empirical evidence that strong growth in a number of emerging markets helped fuel the energy price boom between 2003 and 2008. The recent situation is summarized in figure 4.2, which shows the percent of total world oil consumption from 1992 to 2011 by the BRIC nations. As illustrated there, in the mid-1990s BRIC consumption was stable at about 14 percent of global consumption. Beginning in the late 1990s and early in the first decade of the twenty-first century, however, these countries' share of total world consumption rose steadily to just slightly over 21 percent by 2011.

Of more than passing interest is that the prices for many coarse grains (and sugar) and crude oil are increasingly tied in new and evolving ways. Specifically, the rise of ethanol production and use in the United States

3. BRIC is an acronym that stands for the emerging economies of Brazil, India, China, and Russia.

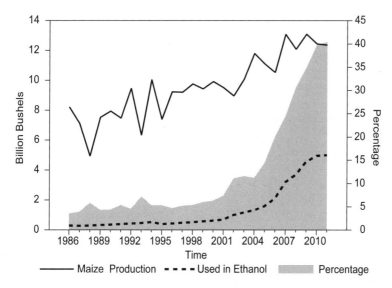

Fig. 4.3   US maize production, maize used in ethanol, and percent of US maize production used in ethanol production, 1986–2011
Source: US Department of Energy (www.afdc.energy.gov/afdc/data/).

and elsewhere has had a large impact on land use, commodity prices, and the relationship between prices for energy and nonenergy commodities (Abbott, Hurt, and Tyner 2008). In the United States ethanol production was first encouraged by the tax incentives included in the 1978 Energy Tax Act, providing for federal excise tax exemptions for gasoline blended with 10 percent ethanol. Over time other federal- and state-level subsidies were also created. As well, import tariffs were incorporated to limit the amount of ethanol coming into the United States from abroad. Furthermore, a so-called Renewable Fuel Standard, which dictates that gasoline sold in the United States contains a certain volume of renewable fuels, was established as part of the Energy Policy Act of 2005. Of equal if not greater importance for the rise of ethanol were the state bans on methyl tertiary-butyl ether (MTBE), as noted by Zhang, Vedenov, and Wetzstein (2007) and Serra et al. (2011). MTBE is a widely used oxygenate in the gasoline production process, and is a known contaminant of water supplies. Ethanol is a reasonable substitute for MTBE in the refining process, with the switch from MTBE to ethanol gaining considerable traction in early 2006 (Serra et al. 2011).

Perhaps nowhere has the impact of increased ethanol use been more profound than in the market for maize, as illustrated in figure 4.3. As the figure shows, between 1986 and 2001 the total amount of maize used for ethanol in the United States never exceeded 10 percent of total maize production. A notable uptick in this pattern occurred in the early twenty-first century, with dramatic increases being observed starting in 2006. The result is that by 2011 over 40 percent of the total annual maize crop was being utilized in ethanol production. Because in the United States maize and soy in particular can be produced on much of the same land base, much of the increased maize acreage apparently came at the expense of area planted to soy.

Other factors have undoubtedly played a role in the most recent surge in commodity prices. Carter, Rausser, and Smith (2011), Wright (2011), and Kilian and Murphy (forthcoming), for example, discuss the importance of stockholding behavior, both for storable field crops as well as for non-renewable energy resources, in price determination. For example, shortfalls in crop production will result in inventories being drawn down. Moreover, even seemingly small production shocks are capable, given the generally inelastic nature of short-run consumption demands, of causing rather large price swings (see, e.g., Roberts and Schlenker 2010). Certainly there is considerable evidence of weather shocks during much of the period in question in various producing regions of the world. Wright (2011) argues that much of the recent increase in nominal prices for major field crops can be explained by a standard model of supply and demand with storage. Specifically, Wright (2011) notes that during much of the mid and late years of the first decade of the twenty-first century stock-to-use ratios for major grains were, on a global level, at or near the levels observed during the previous commodity price boom in the mid-1970s.

It is also likely that general macroeconomic conditions have had an impact on commodity price behavior in recent times. As Frankel (2008) discusses, there is evidence of linkages via monetary policy between real interest rates, exchange rates, and the prices for agricultural and mineral commodities.[4] For example, declines in the real value of the dollar have made US grains relatively less expensive to foreigners. There is ample evidence that low interest rates and a weak dollar were at work in the most recent commodity price boom. For example, Chen et al. (2010) apply a factor model to prices for fifty-one traded commodities. They show that not only does the first, highly persistent component, mimic (nominal) exchange rate movements to a high degree, but the factor model also provides substantially improved forecasts of exchange rates relative to a random walk model. These macroeconomic factors, perhaps exacerbated by relatively loose monetary policy in the United States and elsewhere during the middle of the first decade of the twenty-first century, likely played a significant role in the recent commodity price boom. Hamilton (2010), for example, has argued that the second round of quantitative easing (i.e., undertaken by the Federal Reserve in 2010) likely

---

4. Even so, subsequent results presented by Frankel and Rose (2010) seemingly contradict some of the earlier findings reported by Frankel (2008).

helped boost commodity prices in 2010 and 2011 even after their steep but temporary declines following the financial crises in 2008 and 2009.[5]

What is clear is that a variety of conditions likely contributed to the recent commodity price boom. The evolving and changing relationship between energy and food, and most notably, between energy and coarse grains, is likely a contributing factor. So, too, are the likely effects of macroeconomic conditions tied to real interest rates and, relatedly, real exchange rates. As well, inventory behavior in the face of increasing consumption demand and supply shocks also likely played a role. Identifying and isolating each of these effects in a comprehensive structural model, while perhaps desirable, is likely not feasible. For these reasons we follow Carter, Rausser, and Smith (2011), Serra et al. (2011), Enders and Holt (2012), and others, and focus here on a set of reduced-form time-series models. Specifically, we are interested in seeing how the time and nature of structural shifts or breaks in sets of variables identified in some sense as being "causal" for commodity prices (including commodity prices themselves) affected commodity price behavior. While Enders and Holt (2012) examined issues of this sort in a univariate setting, a central innovation of this chapter is to extend their analyses to a multivariate framework.

4.3   Data

Given the large number of factors that have been identified with the recent run-up in commodity prices, we focus on two estimation strategies, each with its own set of causal variables. The first uses an unrestricted vector autoregression (VAR) to analyze the relationship between grain prices and a number of macroeconomic variables including real exchange rates, interest rates, and energy prices. The second uses a shifting-mean vector autoregression (SM-VAR) that focuses on a larger set of agricultural commodities and variables more directly influencing commodity prices such as ocean freight rates and climate conditions. In both analyses, all commodity prices are converted to real terms by deflating by the producer price index (PPI). We then further transform the data by converting it to natural logarithmic form.

4.3.1   Data Used in the VAR

In the broad overview analysis, a standard VAR analysis is performed by focusing on relationships among real grain prices, real energy prices, the

---

5. Gilbert (2010), for example, argues that a driving force behind the recent run-up in commodity prices is speculation, either through physically holding (and withholding) stocks or indirectly by the influence of index-based investment funds on futures prices. We do not consider the role of speculation as a factor in the longer-term movements in grain prices as Irwin and Sanders (2011) provide rather convincing evidence that there are no obvious empirical links between index fund trading and commodity futures price movements.

real exchange rate, and a measure of the real interest rate. The grain price measure is an index constructed by the World Bank as a composite of representative world prices for rice (weight of 30.2 percent), wheat (weight of 25.3 percent), maize and sorghum (weight of 40.8 percent), and barley (weight of 3.7 percent).[6] The energy price index is also constructed by the World Bank; it is a composite of the prices for coal (weight of 4.7 percent), crude oil (weight of 84.6 percent), and natural gas (weight of 10.8 percent). Both indices are normalized to average to 100 during 2005. The real exchange rate is the so-called broad exchange trade-weighted exchange rate, which in turn is a weighted average of the foreign exchange values of the US dollar against the currencies of a large group of major US trading partners converted to real terms. The real exchange rate is constructed and reported by the board of governors of the Federal Reserve System.[7] Finally, the interest rate is the three-month Treasury bill secondary market rate adjusted for inflation. The inflation rate, in turn, is constructed as:

$$infl_t = 400[(CCPI_t/CCPI_{t-3}) - 1],$$

where *CCPI* denotes the core consumer price index; that is, the consumer price index (CPI) adjusted by deleting prices for food and energy. The real interest rate measure is constructed then by subtracting the inflation rate from the nominal three-month Treasury bill rate.[8]

Time-series plots for these four monthly series, 1974 to 2011, are presented in figure 4.4. There we see that the real grain price index declined from 1974 through the mid-1980s, leveled off until the mid-1990s, declined again until about until about 2000, and since then has generally increased. The real energy price index was generally stable from the mid-1980s through the mid to late 1990s, then declined sharply in 1999, and has since tended to increase rather steadily. The real exchange rate shows sharp increases in the early to mid-1980s and again in the late 1990s and early years of the twenty-first century, with a generally steep decline starting in about 2002. As expected, the real Treasury bill rate peaked in the early 1980s, and has generally declined since then, although several plateau periods have also been observed.

4.3.2   Data Used in the SM-VAR

Turning to the data used in the SM-VAR analysis, we focus on interactions among a select set of specific commodity prices. Specifically, we focus on interactions among monthly prices for maize, soy, crude oil (or more simply,

---

6. A time-series compilation of World Bank commodity price data may be downloaded from the url: http://blogs.worldbank.org/prospects/category/tags/historical-commodity-prices.

7. The data may be obtained from the url: http://www.federalreserve.gov/releases/h10/summary/default.htm.

8. Data for core CPI and the three-month Treasury bill rate were obtained from the St. Louis Federal Reserve's FRED database.

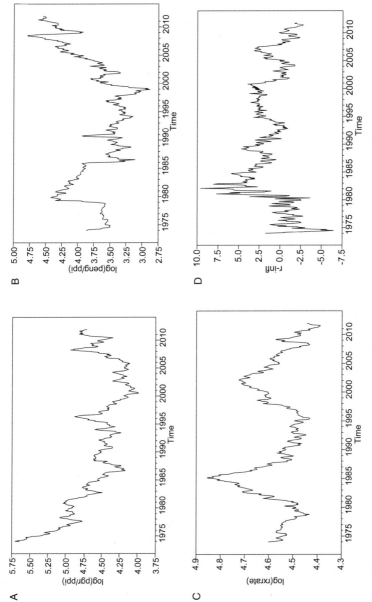

Fig. 4.4 Monthly data used in preliminary VAR analysis, 1974–2011: *A*, log of real grain price index; *B*, log of real energy price index; *C*, log of real exchange rate; *D*, real three-month treasury bill rate.

oil), a measure of ocean freight rates, and the price of ethanol. Because the production and transport of agricultural commodities are subject to the vagaries of weather, we also consider a climate extremes index. The maize, soy, and oil prices used in this analysis are reported by the World Bank. Maize prices are recorded in dollars per metric ton (dollars/mt), and represent US number 2 yellow, free on board (FOB), Gulf prices. Likewise, soy prices are also reported in dollars per metric ton, and are US, cost, insurance, and freight (CIF), Rotterdam prices. The crude oil price is recorded in dollars per barrel (dollars/bbl), and represents an average of spot market prices for Brent, Dubai, and West Texas intermediate crude; crude oil prices are equally weighted in constructing the World Bank composite oil price measure. Additional details regarding these variables are reported in the technical appendix that accompanies Enders and Holt (2012).

Freight rates are a major factor in world trade of primary commodities. Moreover, because in the short run the fleet of transport vessels is essentially fixed, Kilian (2009) argues that variations in ocean freight rates can be viewed as an observable real activity variable, which in turn help identify flow demand shifts. The data were constructed by Lutz Kilian, and represent an average of dry bulk shipping freight rates for cargoes consisting of grain, oilseeds, coal, iron ore, fertilizer, and scrap metal as reported by *Drewry's Shipping Monthly*. A composite index is then constructed in a manner described in more detail in Kilian (2009). In the index the value for January 1968 is normalized to one. These data were obtained directly from Lutz Kilian by private correspondence. Importantly, unlike the data used in Kilian's (2009) paper and reported on his website, the data we use for the dry bulk shipping freight rates have not been detrended.[9]

Because markets for energy have evolved rapidly in recent years with the rise of ethanol production, there is reason to believe that prices for major field crops (and most notably, maize) and energy are now linked in new and more complex ways (Abbott, Hurt, and Tyner 2008). In an attempt to examine these linkages in more detail, we also include a measure of ethanol price. Specifically, the ethanol price used here is the FOB Omaha rack price, quoted in dollars per gallon, and collected and reported by the Nebraska state government.[10] Ethanol price data are only available beginning in January 1982.

A final measure of interest relates to climate anomalies that might affect the production, marketing, and transport of agricultural commodities. Although several alternatives are available, we use the National Oceanic and Atmospheric Administration's (NOAA) National Climatic Data Center's

9. In the analysis reported in Kilian (2009), the dry bulk shipping freight rates were detrended to account for declining real unit costs of shipping over time.

10. The data were obtained from the url: http://www.neo.ne.gov/statshtml/66.html. Similar data for ethanol were employed by, for example, Serra et al. (2011).

climate extreme index (CEI) for the Upper Midwest climate region.[11] The index, developed by Karl et al. (1996) and Gleason et al. (2008), incorporates information on monthly maximum and minimum temperature, daily precipitation, and the monthly Palmer Drought Severity Index (PDSI) measures.

Time-series plots, 1974 to 2011, of the data used in the SM-VAR model are reported in figure 4.5. For our purposes, it is important to note that the real prices for maize and soy generally declined until the early years of the twenty-first century, at which point they started to trend upward. A somewhat similar pattern is evident for the price of crude oil, although the upturn since the early twenty-first century has been more pronounced. The real price of ocean freight generally trended down from the early 1970s through the early twenty-first century, and experienced a notable upturn until the most recent recession beginning in late 2007. Since then real ocean freight rates have generally remained low relative to historical norms. The real price of ethanol also tended to trend downward from 1982 through the early years of the twenty-first century, and then trended upward rather sharply, again, until the onset of the most recent recession. Finally, the climate extreme index is apparently rather volatile, although without any discernable trend. Even so, it may contain a cyclical component.

4.4 A VAR Analysis

In this section we employ a vector-autoregression to analyze the dynamic interrelationships between real grain prices and the key macroeconomic variables that have been identified as affecting the agricultural sector. As indicated in Ng and Vogelsang (2002), a VAR containing variables with structural breaks is misspecified unless the breaks are properly modeled and included in the estimated VAR. Nevertheless, the cobreaking literature is still in its early stages and, as we explain in more detail in following sections, it is not always clear how to estimate a system with cobreaking (shifting) variables. Moreover, given that we are working with the variables shown in figure 4.4, a number of potential breaks are likely to be smooth so that the number of breaks, the functional form of the breaks, and the break dates are unknown. As such, in this section, we utilize the results from a VAR without incorporating an explicit parametric model for breaks (shifts). The benefit of our VAR analysis is that we can measure the extent to which shifts in the macroeconomic variables are transmitted to real grain prices without having to impose any particular structural assumptions on the data. We rely on Sims (1980) and Sims, Stock, and Watson (1990) who indicate how

11. For example, Fox, Fishback, and Rhode (2011) explored the impacts of a well-known drought measure, the Palmer Drought Severity Index (PDSI), along with other measures, on the price of maize, 1895 to 1932. Likewise, Schmitz (1997) examined the role of the PDSI in explaining US beef cow breeding herd inventory adjustments.

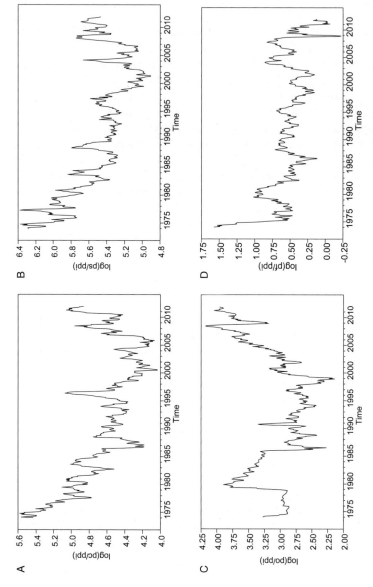

Fig. 4.5 Monthly data used in SM-NVAR analysis, 1974–2011: *A,* log of real maize price; *B,* log of real soy price; *C,* log of real oil price; *D,* log of real ocean freight index; *E,* log of real ethanol price; *F,* climate extreme index, upper midwest.

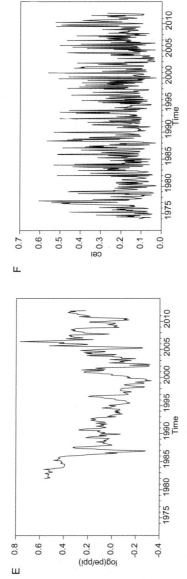

Fig. 4.5 (cont.)

to conduct inference in a regression (or a VAR) combining stationary and nonstationary variables. Subsequently, we develop a more disaggregated model in which we explicitly estimate the structural breaks and their transmission across sectors.

Since an unrestricted VAR is atheoretic, we need only select the relevant variables to include in the model, determine the lag length, and decide on an orthogonalization of the regression residuals. In addition to the real price of grain, we began with a block of three variables that have often been credited with influencing real agricultural prices: the real price of energy, the real interest rate, and the real multilateral exchange rate. When we used the sample period running from January 1974 to December 2011, the multivariate Akaike information criterion (AIC) selected a lag length of seven months for our basic four-variable VAR. As shown by Sims, Stock, and Watson (1990), it is generally not appropriate to apply Granger causality tests to nonstationary variables. Hence, we performed the standard block exogeneity test described in Enders (2010, 318–19) but we let the AIC suggest which other variables we might want to add to the four-variable VAR. Even though the AIC is quite generous in this regard, we maintained the four-variable model as none of the following variables reduced the AIC: real ocean freight rates, the climate index, and various measures of real US output including the cyclical portion of Hodrick-Prescott (HP)-filtered US real disposable income.

In order to avoid performing our innovation accounting using an ad hoc Choleski decomposition, we used the following strategy to decompose the regression residuals into pure orthogonal shocks. Let the subscripts $i = 1, 2, 3,$ and 4 denote real energy prices, the real exchange rate, the real T-bill rate, and the real grain price, respectively. Also, for each period t, let e_{it} denote the regression residual from the i–th equation of the VAR and let ε_{it} denote the pure orthogonal innovation (i.e., the "own" shock) to variable i. In every period t, the relationship between the regression errors and the orthogonal innovations is:

$$
(1) \quad
\begin{bmatrix} e_{1t} \\ e_{2t} \\ e_{3t} \\ e_{4t} \end{bmatrix}
=
\begin{bmatrix}
g_{11} & g_{12} & g_{13} & g_{14} \\
g_{21} & g_{22} & g_{23} & g_{24} \\
g_{31} & g_{32} & g_{33} & g_{34} \\
g_{41} & g_{42} & g_{43} & g_{44}
\end{bmatrix}
\begin{bmatrix} \varepsilon_{1t} \\ \varepsilon_{2t} \\ \varepsilon_{3t} \\ \varepsilon_{4t} \end{bmatrix},
$$

so that in matrix form: $e_t = G\varepsilon_t$ where the g_{ij} are parameters such that the covariance matrix of the regression residuals, Ee_te_t', is $GE(\varepsilon_t\varepsilon_t')G'$ and G is the (4×4) matrix of the g_{ij}.

As it stands, equation (1) indicates that each variable is contemporaneously affected by the innovations in every other variable. However, it is far more likely that some variables are causally prior to others in the sense that they are affected by others only with a lag. For example, since a grain price shock is unlikely to have a contemporaneous effect on the macroeconomic variables, the macroeconomic block should be causally prior to real grain prices. Moreover, without imposing some structural restrictions on the G matrix, the ε_{it} shocks are unidentified. As described by Enders (2010, 325–9), exact identification of the orthogonal innovations from the covariance matrix requires six restrictions. The assumption that the 3×3 block of macroeconomic variables is causally prior to each other requires nine restrictions—$g_{ij} = 0$ ($i \neq j$ for $i < 4$)—whereas the exact identification requires only six restrictions. However, imposing these nine restrictions (so that the system is overidentified) results in a sample value of χ^2 equal to 11.88; with three degrees of freedom, the prob−value for the restriction is 0.0078. The reason for the rejection of the restriction is that the contemporaneous correlation between the residuals of the real exchange rate and real T-bill equations (i.e., e_{2t} and e_{3t}) is 0.55. However, when we do not force $g_{23} = 0$, the following set of eight restrictions results in a χ^2 value of 0.975, which is insignificant at any conventional level:

$$
(2) \quad
\begin{bmatrix} e_{1t} \\ e_{2t} \\ e_{3t} \\ e_{4t} \end{bmatrix}
=
\begin{bmatrix}
g_{11} & 0 & 0 & 0 \\
0 & g_{22} & g_{23} & 0 \\
0 & 0 & g_{33} & 0 \\
g_{41} & g_{42} & g_{43} & g_{44}
\end{bmatrix}
\begin{bmatrix} \varepsilon_{1t} \\ \varepsilon_{2t} \\ \varepsilon_{3t} \\ \varepsilon_{4t} \end{bmatrix}.
$$

As such, our decomposition allows real energy, real exchange rate, and real T-bill shocks to contemporaneously affect grain prices and allows real interest rate shocks to contemporaneously affect the real exchange rate. Otherwise, the contemporaneous innovations in each variable are due to "own" shocks.

Figure 4.6 shows the impulse responses of grain to a +1-standard deviation shock in each of the innovations given the set of shocks identified by equation (2). In order to make the comparisons meaningful, the magnitudes of the responses have been normalized by the standard deviation of the grain shock. Interestingly, the initial effect of a grain price innovation continues to build for three periods and, although it begins to decay, is quite persistent. A positive energy price shock has a positive effect on grain prices; by month 5, a +1-standard deviation shock in energy prices induces a 0.5 standard deviation increase in the real price of grain. Not surprisingly, higher interest rates and a stronger dollar both act to decrease the real price of grain. After all, higher interest rates increase grain-holding costs and a stronger dollar increases the price of US grain to importers. Note that after six months, +1-standard deviation shocks to the real exchange rate and the real interest rate depress real grain prices by about 0.50 and 0.35 standard deviations, respectively.

The variance decompositions suggest a modest degree of interaction among the macroeconomic variables and real grain prices. As shown in

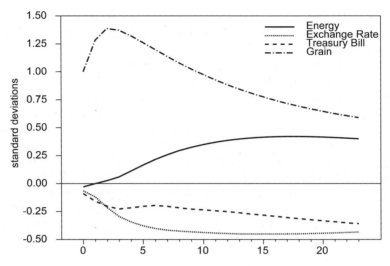

Fig. 4.6 Impulse response functions for grain with respect to energy price, the real exchange rate, the real Treasury bill rate, and own grain price

Note: All impulse response functions are normalized by the standard deviation of grain.

Table 4.1		Percentage of the forecast error variance for grain			
Steps ahead	Std. error	Energy	Exchange rate	T-bill	Grains
1	0.035	0.00	0.36	1.25	98.39
6	0.114	1.42	3.60	2.30	92.68
12	0.152	5.64	9.20	3.87	81.30
18	0.179	7.35	12.15	4.81	75.69
24	0.198	8.87	14.51	5.93	70.69

table 4.1, almost all of the six-month ahead forecast error variance of the real price of grain is due to its own innovations (92.68 percent). However, after one year, real energy prices, the real exchange rate, and the real T-bill rate account for 5.64 percent, 9.20 percent, and 3.87 percent of the forecast error variance, respectively. After two years, these percentages grow to 8.87 percent, 14.51 percent, and 5.93 percent, respectively.

Nevertheless, these percentages can be misleading since there are subperiods during which the influence of the macroeconomic variables on grain prices was substantial. In order to show this, we decomposed the actual movements in real grain prices into the portions contributed by each of the four innovations. If we abstract from the deterministic portion of the VAR, each of the four variables can be written in the form:

$$(3) \quad y_{iT+j} = A_{i1}(L)\varepsilon_{1T+j} + A_{i2}(L)\varepsilon_{2T+j} + A_{i3}(L)\varepsilon_{3T+j} + A_{i4}(L)\varepsilon_{4T+j} + y_{iT},$$

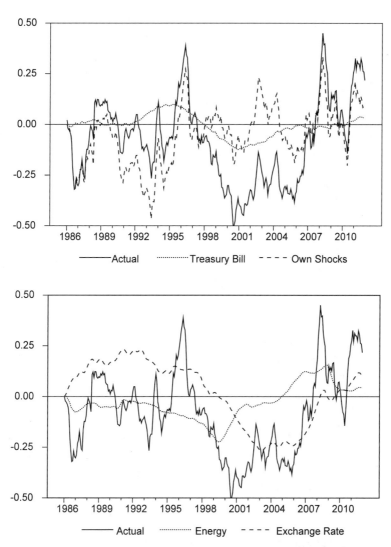

Fig. 4.7 Historical decompositions of real grain prices with respect to the real Treasury bill rate and own shocks (top panel) and real energy price and real exchange rate (bottom panel)

where the $A_{ik}(k = 1,2,3,4)$ are j–th order polynomials in the lag operator L. As such, the $A_{ik}(L)\varepsilon_{kT+j}$ are the part of variable i attributable to innovations in variable k over the period $T + 1$ to $T + j$. As such, a time-series plot of $A_{4k}(L)\varepsilon_{kT+j}$ shows how movements in variable k affected the real price of grain. In essence, the plots show the counterfactual analysis of how real grain prices would have evolved had there been only k-type shocks.

The top portion of figure 4.7 shows how real interest rate and real grain price innovations (i.e., "own" innovations) affected the real price of grain. The solid line in the figure shows the actual movement in grain prices so that it is possible to see the influence of each of the two variables on actual grain price movements. As can be seen by the short-dotted line in the figure, real interest rate movements have a small positive effect in the mid-1990s and a small negative effect from 1998 through most of the remaining sample period. Nevertheless, the downward movement in real interest rates (see panel D of figure 4.4) has caused the absolute value of this negative effect to steadily diminish. As such, it can be argued that the decline of real interest rates has exerted pressure for grain prices to rise relative to pre-early-twenty-first century levels. Notice how shocks to the price of grain accounted for the sharp movements in real grain prices in 1987 and 1988, 1995, and 2007 to 2009.[12]

The lower portion of figure 4.7 shows the effects of energy and exchange rate innovations on the price of grain over the 1986:1 to 2011:12 period. It appears that the effects of energy prices and the real exchange rate on the real price of grain were generally offsetting. From 1986 through 1997, the real exchange rate acted to boost the price of grain. After all, during the period when the dollar was relatively weak, the foreign demand for US grains is anticipated to be relatively high. Since the prices are in logarithms, it should be clear that in the early 1990s the exchange rate acted to increase real grain prices by as much as 25 percent. As the weak dollar stimulated the foreign demand for US grain, the dollar price of grain was bolstered. Subsequently, the steady appreciation of the real value of the dollar from 1995 through 2002 induced a decline in real grain prices. By 1996, the overall effect of exchange rate movements on grain prices was negative. In contrast, high energy prices had a depressing effect on real grain prices through 1999. However, the run-up in energy prices beginning in 1999 acted to increase grain prices—by mid-2000, the overall effect of energy price innovations on grains became positive. By 2006, the effect was to increase grain prices by almost 20 percent.

4.5   Modeling Time-Series Variables with Shifting Means

Although the VAR results are informative, it is useful to develop a complementary parametric model that allows us to explicitly estimate the shifting means. To begin, consider a stationary series $y_t, t = 1,\ldots,T$, that in the present case represents a particular commodity price. A simple shifting-mean (SM) autoregressive model of order p for y_t, that is, an SM-AR(p), is given by:

$$(4) \qquad\qquad y_t = \tilde{\delta}(t) + \sum_{j=1}^{p} \theta_j y_{t-j} + \varepsilon_t,$$

12. Note that the term "own" shocks for grain can be misleading since all excluded variables actually affecting grain prices influence ε_{4t}.

where $\varepsilon_t \sim$ iid$(0, \sigma^2)$, and where under stationarity all roots of the lag polynomial $1 - \sum_{j=1}^{p}\theta_j L^j$ lie outside the unit circle. In equation (4) $\tilde{\delta}(t)$ is the deterministic, nonlinear shift function. As usual in a Dickey-Fuller test, it is standard to assume that $\tilde{\delta}(t)$ contains a time-invariant intercept and, perhaps, a deterministic linear trend (or quadratic trend) term. In this case y_t would be said to be "trend stationary."

In recent years economists have focused on more detailed specifications for the time-varying intercept, $\tilde{\delta}(t)$. For example, one approach, popularized by Bai and Perron (1998, 2003), is to assume that shifts over time in the intercept happen in a discrete manner. That is, we may write $\tilde{\delta}(t)$ as:

$$(5) \qquad \tilde{\delta}(t) = \delta_0 + \sum_{i=1}^{k}\delta_i \mathrm{l}(t > \tau_i),$$

where $\mathrm{l}(\cdot)$ is a Heaviside indicator function such that $\mathrm{l}(\cdot) = 1$ for $t > \tau_i$ and is zero otherwise. In equation (5) τ_i, $i = 1,...,k$, denotes the discrete break dates. For our purposes, there are several problems with the specification in equation (5). First, the number of breaks or the timing of breaks are unknown a priori, and therefore these additional parameters must also be estimated as part of the modeling process. More importantly, the nature of the breaks in equation (5) is assumed to be sharp in that each break fully manifests itself at the date τ_i. However, suppose there is at least one relatively long, gradual shift in the evolution of y_t, which in turn must be accounted for by $\tilde{\delta}(t)$. In this instance it is likely that the Bai-Perron procedure would require multiple "breaks" in order to accurately account for what is otherwise one gradual shift. As an alternative to equation (5), then, Lin and Teräsvirta (1994) and González and Teräsvirta (2008) proposed the following nonlinear specification:

$$(6) \qquad \tilde{\delta}(t) = \delta_0 + \sum_{i=1}^{k}\delta_i G(t^*;\eta_i,c_i),$$

where $G(\cdot)$ is the so-called transition function and $t^* = t/Tq$. For example, $G(\cdot)$ is often given by:

$$(7) \qquad G(t^*;\eta_i,c_i) = [1 + \exp\{-\exp(\eta_i)(t^* - c_i)/\sigma_{t^*}\}]^{-1},$$

where σ_{t^*} denotes the standard deviation of t^*.[13] In other words, equation (7) is a standard two-parameter logistic function in the rescaled time trend index, t^*, where by construction $G(\cdot)$ is strictly bounded on the unit interval. The speed with which the logistic function transitions from zero to one is determined by the magnitude of $\gamma = \exp(\eta_i)$. For large values of γ, that is, as $\gamma \to \infty$, it follows that $G(\cdot)$ will effectively become a step function with properties identical to those of the Heaviside indicator functions in equation (5), where the switch date or break date is associated with $t^* = c_i$. Alterna-

---

13. Normalizing $\exp(\eta_i)$ by σ_{t^*} effectively renders this parameter unit free, which in turn is desirable for numerical reasons during estimation.

tively, for considerably smaller values of γ the transition from zero to unity will be smooth or gradual, and in the extreme as $\gamma \rightarrow 0$ the shift effectively disappears. Lin and Teräsvirta (1994) refer to the combination of equations (4), (6), and (7) as the time-varying autoregressive model, or TVAR.[14] The TVAR model represents a generalization of the methods considered by Bai and Perrron (1998, 2003) in that both smooth shifts and sharp breaks are accommodated.

Of course, equation (7) is not the only transition function that might be considered. Others include the quadratic logistic function (see, e.g., van Dijk, Teräsvirta, and Franses 2002) and the generalized exponential introduced by Goodwin, Holt, and Prestemon (2011). Considering the later, the transition function may be defined as:

$$(8) \quad G(t^*; \eta_i, c_i, \kappa_i) = 1 - \exp\{-\exp(\eta_i)[(t^* - c_i)/\sigma_{t^*}]^{2\kappa_i}\}, \kappa_i = 1, 2, \ldots, \kappa_{max}.$$

In equation (8) when $\kappa_i = 1$ the standard two-parameter exponential transition function obtains, which results in something analogous to a V-shaped transition function that is symmetric around the centrality parameter, c_i. When $\kappa_i \geq 2$ in equation (8) the generalized exponential function obtains, which generates a U-shaped time-path for the transition function, also symmetric around c_i. Indeed, as k_i becomes large, say, typically, 4 or 5, the generalized exponential function approximates a pair of Heaviside indicator functions that are offsetting.[15] Depending on the underlying properties of the data, combinations of logistic functions and/or the generalized exponential function provide considerable flexibility when modeling a combination of smooth shifts and discrete breaks in a univariate series.

Estimation of the SM-AR can be done by using nonlinear least squares (van Dijk, Teräsvirta, and Franses 2002) or by using a grid search (Enders and Holt 2012). Additional details regarding estimation of SM-AR models are provided by Teräsvirta, Tjøstheim, and Granger (2010).

A third alternative to modeling the intercept term, $\tilde{\delta}(t)$, in equation (4) was introduced by Becker, Enders, and Hurn (2004). Specifically, they propose approximating the time-varying intercept in equation (4) by using low-frequency terms from a Fourier approximation of $\tilde{\delta}(t)$ in t. For example,

$$(9) \quad \tilde{\delta}(t) = \delta_0 + \delta_1 t + \sum_{k=1}^{n} \{\alpha_k \sin(2\pi kt/T) + \beta_k \cos(2\pi kt/T)\}, n \leq T/2.$$

As illustrated by Enders and Lee (2012), the combination of equation (9) with equation (4) provides considerable flexibility in modeling a wide array of smoothly shifting intercepts in univariate autoregressive models.

14. More generally, Lin and Teräsvirta (1994) consider a situation where all parameters in equation (1) can change in a manner defined by the transition function, $G(\cdot)$. As in González and Teräsvirta (2008) and Enders and Holt (2012), we restrict attention here to the case where only the intercept term varies over time.

15. A pair of logistic functions could also be used to approximate either V-shaped or U-shaped shifts, albeit at the expense of estimating more (nonlinear and correlated) parameters.

Irrespective of the method used to model the time-varying intercept in equation (4), the unconditional (shifting) mean of the series, y_t, may be obtained by taking the unconditional expectation of equation (4) and solving, to obtain:

$$(10) \qquad E_t y_t = \left(\sum_{j=1}^{p} \theta_j L^j \right)^{-1} \tilde{\delta}(t) = \sum_{j=0}^{\infty} \varphi_j \tilde{\delta}(t - j),$$

where $\varphi_0 = 1$. According to equation (10) the shifting mean of y_t will depend on the precise way for which $\tilde{\delta}(t)$ is specified, as well as the model's autoregressive parameters.

4.5.1   Shifting Means: Multivariate Methods

In principle the above specifications can be extended to a multivariate setting in a straightforward manner. For example, let $i = 1,\ldots,n$, index the particular commodity prices considered in the system. We may therefore define $y_t = (y_{1t},\ldots,y_{nt})'$ as an $(n \times 1)$ vector of observations on commodity prices at time t.[16] The multivariate counterpart to equation (4), that is, the shifting-mean vector autoregression (SM-VAR), is given by:

$$(11) \qquad \mathbf{y}_t = \tilde{\boldsymbol{\delta}}(t) + \sum_{j=1}^{p} \boldsymbol{\Theta}_j \mathbf{y}_{t-j} + \boldsymbol{\varepsilon}_t,$$

where $\boldsymbol{\Theta}_j$ is a $(n \times n)$ parameter matrix, $j = 1,\ldots,p$, and where $\boldsymbol{\varepsilon}_t \sim$ iid$(\mathbf{0}, \boldsymbol{\Sigma})$, where $E(\boldsymbol{\varepsilon}_t) = \mathbf{0}$, and where $\boldsymbol{\Sigma}$ is a $(n \times n)$ positive definite covariance matrix. Assuming the vector autoregressive structure of the system is dynamically stable, the roots of $|\mathbf{I} - \sum_{j=1}^{p} \boldsymbol{\Theta}_j L^j|$ are assumed to lie outside the unit circle. In equation (11) $\tilde{\boldsymbol{\delta}}(t) = (\delta_1(t^*),\ldots,\delta_n(t^*))'$ is a $(n \times 1)$ time-varying intercept vector, where a typical element might be given by:

$$(12) \qquad \tilde{\delta}_l(t) = \delta_{0l} + \sum_{i=1}^{k_l} \delta_{li} G(t^*; \eta_{li}, c_{li}), l = 1,\ldots,n.$$

In equation (12) the $G(\cdot)$ transition functions could, as in the univariate case, be given by some combination of equations (7) and/or (8). In a manner analogous to the univariate case, the system in equation (11) may be written as:

$$(13) \qquad \left(\mathbf{I} - \sum_{j=1}^{p} \boldsymbol{\Theta}_j L^j \right) \mathbf{y}_t = \tilde{\boldsymbol{\delta}}(t) + \boldsymbol{\varepsilon}_t,$$

so as in equation (10), the vector-valued shifting-mean for y_t can be generalized such that:

$$(14) \qquad E_t y_t = \left(\mathbf{I} - \sum_{j=1}^{p} \boldsymbol{\Theta}_j L^j \right)^{-1} \tilde{\boldsymbol{\delta}}(t) = \sum_{j=0}^{\infty} \boldsymbol{\Theta}_j \tilde{\boldsymbol{\delta}}(t - j),$$

---

16. Henceforth, bolded variables are used to denote appropriately defined vectors or arrays.

where $\Phi_0 = I$, an $(n \times n)$ identity matrix. Note that equation (13) implies that a shift in the series for, say, y_{it}, will necessarily cause a shift in, say, y_{jt} (Ng and Vogelsang 2002). Indeed, the only way this is not true is either if (a) the coefficients on lagged y_{jt} in the equation for y_{it} sum to zero or, alternatively, (b) if prior observations on y_{jt} do not Granger cause y_{it}.

4.5.2   Shifting Means: A Testing Framework

An automatic question is, How might the presence of shifting means be tested for, especially in a multivariate framework? And how many shifts might be required for each equation? Prior research has focused almost exclusively on testing in a univariate autoregressive (AR) context. We review the general univariate testing approach and then discuss how such tests can be adapted for use in a SM-VAR setting. We focus on the shifting-mean model where either the logistic function in equation (7) or the generalized exponential function in equation (8) are used to characterize mean shifts.

Univariate Models

Consider the following univariate AR model or order p, that is, an AR(p):

$$(15) \qquad y_t = \delta_0 + \alpha' z_t + \varepsilon_t,$$

where $z_t = (y_{t-1}, \ldots, y_{t-p})'$ is a $(p \times 1)$ vector, and where $\alpha = (\alpha_1, \ldots, \alpha_p)'$, a $(p \times 1)$ parameter vector. Of course equation (15) is just a special case of the SM-AR where, in particular, no mean (intercept) shifts occur. The alternative to equation (12) might simply be

$$(16) \qquad y_t = \delta_0 + \delta_1 G(t^*; \eta_1, c_1) + \alpha' z_t + \varepsilon_t,$$

where $G(t^*; \eta_1, c_1)$ is the transition function, presumably associated with either the logistic function in equation (7) or the generalized exponential function in equation (8). At this point it would seem that equation (15) could be estimated and the results used to simply test the hypothesis $H_0 : \delta_1 = 0$. Such an approach would be invalid, however, in that equation (15) can be obtained from equation (16) either by restricting $\delta_1 = 0$ or by setting $\eta_1 = 0$ (so that the logistic function degenerates into a constant). The point is, when $\delta_1 = 0$ there are unidentified nuisance parameters under the null, namely, η_1 and c_1. The result is that the estimator for δ_1 (and likewise, for η_1) will be associated with a nonstandard distribution, even as $T \to \infty$. This general result is due to a series of papers by Davies (1977, 1987), and is typically referred to simply as the "Davies problem" in the literature. To circumvent the problem, Lukkonen, Saikkonen, and Teräsvirta (1988) proposed that the $G(\cdot)$ function in equation (16) could be replaced with a reasonable Taylor series approximation, taken at the limiting value $\exp(\eta_1) = 0$. For example, if a third-order Taylor approximation is used, equation (16) may be rewritten as:

(17) $$y_t = \beta_0 + \beta_1 t^* + \beta_2 t^{*2} + \beta_3 t^{*3} + \pi' z_t + \xi_t,$$

where π is a $(p \times 1)$ parameter vector, and where ξ_t equals the original error term, ε_t, plus approximation error. The Lagrange multiplier (LM) test for a constant mean can be conducted by regressing the residuals from equation (15) on the regressors in equation (17) and using the standard sample F-statistic for the null hypothesis:

(18) $$H_0 = \beta_1 = \beta_2 = \beta_3 = 0.$$

Assuming that the null hypothesis of a constant mean in equation (18) is rejected, Lin and Teräsvirta (1994) go on to describe a sequence of tests that may be used in an attempt to identify the nature of the mean shift; that is, whether it is more likely to be of the logistic function or generalized exponential function variety. Specifically, if equation (18) is rejected we may take equation (17) as the maintained model, and then test:

(19) $$H_{03} : \beta_3 = 0,$$

$$H_{02} : \beta_2 = 0|\beta_3 = 0,$$

$$H_{01} : \beta_1 = 0|\beta_2 = \beta_3 = 0.$$

The idea is that if either H_{03} or H_{01} is associated with the smallest p–value that the corresponding mean-shift is more likely a logisitic function. And of course in this case the possibility of a sharp break in the model's intercept is not precluded. Alternatively, if H_{02} has the smallest p–value, then the mean-shift is more likely to have occurred in a manner consistent with the generalized exponential function in equation (8).

Escribano and Jordà (1999) consider a modification to the testing sequence outlined above. Specifically, they extend the testing equation in (17) to include a fourth-order term, t^{*4}. That is, the testing equation they propose is:

(20) $$y_t = \beta_0 + \beta_1 t^* + \beta_2 t^{*2} + \beta_3 t^{*3} + \beta_4 t^{*4} + \alpha' z_t + \xi_t.$$

The LM test for the null hypothesis of no mean shifts in equation (20) is the sample F-value for the restriction:

(21) $$H_0' = \beta_1 = \beta_2 = \beta_3 = \beta_4 = 0.$$

Escribano and Jordà (1999) propose the following testing sequence:

(22) $$H_{0E} : \beta_2 = \beta_4 = 0,$$

$$H_{0L} : \beta_1 = \beta_3 = 0,$$

as an aid in identifying the form of the underlying shift (transition) function. Specifically, if H_{0E} has the smallest p–value, then the underlying mean-shift is most likely of the generalized exponential form in equation (8). Otherwise, if H_{0L} is associated with the smallest p–value, then the underlying mean shift is likely associated with the logistic transition function in equation (7).

After completion of the testing sequence, a provisional SM-AR model may be specified as:

$$y_t = \delta_0 + \delta_1 G_1(t^*; \eta_1, c_1) + \sum_{j=1}^{p} \theta_j y_{t-j} + \varepsilon_t,$$

where $G_1(\cdot)$ is given by either equations (7) or (8). And once the parameters of the provisional SM-AR model have been estimated, it is desirable to perform additional diagnostic tests or checks. For example, it is useful to know if there is any evidence of remaining autocorrelation or, most importantly, if there is evidence of remaining intercept shifts. As described by Eitrheim and Teräsvirta (1996), the provisional SM-AR model may be used to perform a series of LM tests designed to address these questions. Specifically, define the skeleton of the SM-VAR as:

$$F(\mathbf{x}_t, \boldsymbol{\psi}) = \delta_0 + \delta_1 G_1(t^*; \boldsymbol{\theta}) + \boldsymbol{\alpha}' \mathbf{z}_t,$$

where $\mathbf{x}_t = (1, z_t)'$ and $\boldsymbol{\psi} = (\delta_0, \delta_1, \boldsymbol{\alpha}', \boldsymbol{\theta})$, where $\boldsymbol{\theta} = (\eta_1, c_1)$. Let $\hat{\varepsilon}_t$ denote the residuals from the estimated SM-AR. And let $\nabla F(\mathbf{x}_t, \boldsymbol{\psi})$ denote the gradient of the skeleton of the SM-AR with respect to its parameters, that is, define $\nabla F(\mathbf{x}_t, \hat{\boldsymbol{\psi}}) = \partial F(\cdot) / \partial \boldsymbol{\psi}|_{\psi = \hat{\psi}}$.

In order to test for remaining autocorrelation, an auxiliary regression of the form:

$$(23) \qquad \hat{\varepsilon}_t = \boldsymbol{\omega}' \nabla F(\mathbf{x}_t, \hat{\boldsymbol{\psi}})' + \sum_{j=1}^{q} q_j \hat{\varepsilon}_{t-j} + \xi_t$$

may be performed as an LM-type F-test of the null hypothesis $H_0 : q_1 = \ldots = q_q = 0$. Doing so constitutes a test for remaining serial correlation at lag q. To test for remaining mean shifts the auxiliary regression from equation (21) may be modified as follows:

$$(24) \qquad \hat{\varepsilon}_t = \boldsymbol{\omega}' \nabla F(\mathbf{x}_t, \hat{\boldsymbol{\psi}})' + \sum_{j=1}^{\tau_{max}} \vartheta_j t^{*j} + \xi_t,$$

where τ_{max} typically equals either three or four. The null hypothesis of no remaining intercept shifts is $H_0 : \vartheta_1 = \ldots \vartheta_{\tau_{max}} = 0$. Again, this LM test for remaining intercept (mean) shifts may be performed as an F-test as previously described. If necessary, the testing sequence in either equations (19) or (22) may also be used to help identify the nature of the underlying transition function for any remaining mean shifts.

Multivariate Models

To date, relatively limited research has been conducted on the general topic of SM-VAR models or, similarly, shifting-mean near vector autoregressive (SM-NVAR) models. Unlike the approaches of Anderson and Vahid (1998), Rothman, van Dijk, and Franses (2001), and Camacho (2004), we use the scaled time variable $t^* = t/T, t = 1, \ldots, T$, and do not wish to impose a priori the same transition function across equations. Furthermore, we want to consider the possibility that a mix of logistic and generalized exponential transition functions might be used in the modeling exercise. Conducting systems tests in cases like this can quickly become unwieldy, especially when n, the number of equations in the system, is large. For these reasons we follow Holt and Teräsvirta (2012) and proceed by employing univariate tests on an equation-by-equation basis. Provisional models for each equation may be estimated by using nonlinear least squares, and model assessments performed. Once provisional models have been satisfactorily estimated, it is then possible to use these as starting values to jointly estimate the parameters in a SM-VAR or SM-NVAR.

A final caveat is in order. Specifically, it is not desirable to use univariate methods to identify shifting means if additional explanatory variables should be included in the regression. Specifically, using equation (15) where $\mathbf{z}_t = (y_{t-1}, \ldots, y_{t-p})'$ will generally not yield the correct number of shifts if, in fact, additional explanatory variables should be included in the model. Fortunately, the solution in this case is relatively straightforward. Suppose, for example, that the focus is on modeling y_{it} and, moreover, that y_{jt} apparently Granger causes y_{it}. In this case $\mathbf{z}_t$ can be redefined as $\mathbf{z}_t = (y_{it-1}, \ldots, y_{it-p}, y_{jt-1}, \ldots, y_{jt-p})'$, in which case the models in equations (15), (16), and (17) directly apply. In other words, by including appropriate conditioning variables in $\mathbf{z}_t$ the univariate testing and evaluation procedures defined previously may be readily applied. Simulation results reported in an earlier version of Holt and Teräsvirta (2012) indicate this approach tends to pick the correct number of shifts, k_i, with reasonable accuracy. Moreover, this basic framework is exactly that described originally by Lin and Teräsvirta (1994) when considering the specification and estimation of TVAR models.

4.6   Unit Root Tests with Shifting-Mean Alternatives

Before beginning to estimate our SM-VAR or SM-NVAR, it is necessary to determine whether or not the variables used in the analysis contain unit roots. As demonstrated by Perron (1989, 1997), in the presence of neglected structural change, standard unit root tests are misspecified and suffer from serious size distortions. If the breaks are sharp, it is possible to use dummy variables to construct a modified unit root test with good size and reasonable power. Nevertheless, as shown by Prodan (2008), if there are offsetting or U-shaped breaks, the dummy variable approach performs poorly when estimating the number of breaks and the break dates. Moreover, Becker, Enders, and Hurn (2004) show that the dummy variable approach loses power in the presence of the types of smooth shifts displayed by real commodity prices. In essence, to mimic a gradual structural break, it is necessary to combine a number of dummy variables into a single step-function.

In order to control for smooth structural change, Enders and Lee (2012) augment the standard Dickey-Fuller test with a Fourier approximation for the deterministic terms. Consider:

$$(25) \qquad \Delta y_t = a_0 + \gamma t + d(t) + \rho y_{t-1} + \sum_{i=1}^{p} \beta_i \Delta y_{t-1} + \varepsilon_t,$$

where the structural breaks are approximated by the deterministic Fourier expression $d(t)$,

$$(26) \qquad d(t) = \sum_{k=1}^{n} \alpha_k \sin(2\pi kt/T) + \sum_{k=1}^{n} \beta_k \cos(2\pi kt/T) + e(n).$$

In equation (26), n is the number of frequencies used in the approximation, the α_k and β_k are parameters, and $e(n)$ is approximation error. The notation is designed to highlight the fact that $e(n)$ is a decreasing function of n such that $e(n) = 0$ when $n = T/2$. In the absence of structural change, $d(t) = 0$, so that the linear model is nested in equations (25) and (26).

Note that the specification in equation (26) has a number of desirable econometric properties. Unlike a Taylor series approximation in the powers of t (i.e., $t, t^2, t^3, \ldots$), the trigonometric components are all bounded. Moreover, since a Fourier approximation is an orthogonal basis, hypothesis testing is facilitated in that each term in the approximation is orthogonal to every other term. Perhaps most important, unlike a Taylor series expansion, a Fourier approximation is a global (not a local) approximation that need not be evaluated at a particular point in the sample space. Least squares and maximum likelihood estimation methods force the evaluation of a Taylor series expansion to occur at the mean of the series. However, this is undesirable in a model of structural change because the behavior of a series near its midpoint can be quite different from that elsewhere in the sample.

In order to avoid overfitting and to preserve degrees of freedom, Enders and Lee (2012) recommend using only a few low frequency components in the estimation. Since structural breaks shift the spectral density function toward zero, they are able to demonstrate that the low frequency components of a Fourier approximation can often capture the behavior of a series containing multiple structural breaks. Although the approximation works best with smooth breaks, it is also the case that the approximation with only a few low frequency components is able to detect and control for many types of sharp breaks.

The critical values for the null hypothesis of a unit root (i.e., $\rho = 0$) depend on whether t is included as a regressor in equation (25) and on the value of n used in equation (26). The value of n can be prespecified or selected by using a standard model selection criterion such as the AIC or Schwarz-Bayesian criterion (SBC).

Instead of using cumulative frequencies, it is possible to reduce the number of parameters estimated by performing a grid search over the low-order frequencies ($k = 1, 2, 3, \ldots$) and then conducting the unit root test using the single best-fitting frequency, k^*. Another variant of the test relies on the well-known fact that the trend coefficient in equation (22) is poorly estimated in highly persistent data. In order to produce a test with enhanced power, Enders and Lee (2012) develop a testing procedure based on the Lagrange multiplier (LM) methodology. The idea is to estimate the coefficients of the deterministic terms using first-differences and then to detrend the series using these coefficients. The third variant is Becker, Enders, and Lee's (2006) introduction of Fourier terms into the Kwiatkowski et al. (1992) stationary test. As such, it is possible to test the null of a stationary series fluctuating around a slowly changing mean against the alternative of a unit root. Since all unit root tests suffer from low power, it often makes sense to confirm unit root tests with a procedure using the null of stationarity.

Table 4.2 reports the results of the standard Dickey-Fuller test and the four different Fourier tests applied to the seven series used in our analysis. Notice that the start of the sample period is 1974:01 for all variables save ethanol. For each series, the first row of the table shows the estimated value of ρ assuming linearity (i.e., setting $d(t) = 0$) and the second row shows the associated t-statistic for the null hypothesis $\rho = 0$. Given that the time trend is insignificant in each equation, the 5 percent critical value for the null hypothesis is -2.87. Notice that it is possible to reject the null hypothesis of a unit root for maize, soybeans, ocean freight, and the climate index, but not for oil, ethanol, and the real exchange rate.

The next three rows of the table show the results when we augment equation (26) with cumulative frequencies and use the AIC to select the value of n from the subset of possibilities: $n = 1, 2,$ or 3. For example, for oil, the AIC selects a value of $n = 3$ and the estimate of ρ (called $\rho(n)$, to denote the use of cumulative frequencies) is -0.096. The t-statistic for the null hypothesis $\rho(n) = 0$ is equal to -5.50 whereas the 5 percent critical value is -5.03. Notice that the Fourier unit root suggests that every series, except the real exchange rate, is stationary around a slowly evolving mean. We reach the same conclusion with the variant of the test using the single best-fitting frequency k^* and with the LM version of the test. However, when we use the Fourier-augmented Kwiatkowski, Phillips, Schmidt, and Shin (KPSS) test at conventional significance levels, we cannot reject the null hypothesis of stationarity for any of the series. Nevertheless, given the preponderance of the evidence, we proceed assuming that only the real exchange rate is nonstationary. As such, it is excluded from our SM-NVAR. Moreover, we exclude the real interest rate as our unrestricted VAR indicated that it has only limited effects on real grain prices.

4.7 Empirical Results: SM-NVAR Model

The discussion in previous sections serves as an important guide to determining which variables to include in the SM-VAR analysis of linkages among

Table 4.2   **Unit root test results**

	Maize	Soybeans	Oil	Freight	Rexrate	Climate	Ethanol
ρ	−0.022	−0.037	−0.015	−0.048	−0.010	−0.605	−0.040
	(−2.92)	(−3.54)	(−1.88)	(**−4.27**)	(−1.70)	(**−8.22**)	(−0.901)
n	3	3	3	3	3	1	1
$\rho(n)$	−0.092	−0.099	−0.096	−0.074	−0.038	−0.610	−0.120
	(**−5.43**)	(**−5.77**)	(**−5.50**)	(**−5.28**)	(−3.491)	(**−8.24**)	(**−4.86**)
k^*	1	1	2	3	2	3	1
$\rho(k^*)$	−0.053	−0.071	−0.060	−0.073	−0.029	−0.626	−0.119
	(**−4.14**)	(**−4.93**)	(**−4.18**)	(**−5.17**)	(−3.15)	(**−8.36**)	(**−4.86**)
τ_{LM}	−0.088	−0.099	−0.095	−0.079	−0.047	−0.589	−0.125
	(**−5.30**)	(**−5.74**)	(**−5.34**)	(**−4.66**)	(−3.79)	(**−8.07**)	(**−4.97**)
τ_{KPSS}	0.0106	0.0122	0.0140	0.0127	0.0302	0.028	0.0085
Lags	2	2	4	3	3	4	3
Start	1974:01	1974:01	1974:01	1974:01	1974:01	1974:01	1983:01

Notes: No series contains a deterministic trend: the null that the coefficient on a trend term equals zero could never be rejected at conventional significance levels. ρ is the estimated parameter for the augmented Dickey-Fuller test. The critical value is −2.87 at the 5 percent level. Bold figures are significant at the 5 percent level. The n is the number of cumulative frequencies used in the estimation of the Fourier version of the ADF test and ρ^* is the coefficient on the lagged level term. The 5 percent critical value is −3.76 for $n = 1$, −4.45 for $n = 2$, and −5.03 for $n = 3$. Bold figures are significant at the 5 percent level. The k^* is the best-fitting frequency and $\rho(k^*)$ is the coefficient on the lagged level term. The 5 percent critical values are −3.76, −3.26, and −3.06, for $k^* = 1, 2$, and 3, respectively. Bold figures are significant at the 5 percent level. τ_{LM} is the sample value of τ test for the LM version of the Fourier unit root test. The value of n is the same as that for the DF version of the test. The critical values for $n = 1, 2$, and 3 are −4.05, −4.79, and −5.42, respectively. τ_{KPSS} is the sample of the variance ratios for the stationary version of the Fourier test. Hence, the null hypothesis is that the series is stationary. The 5 percent critical values are 0.169, 0.102, and 0.072, for $n = 1, 2$, and 3, respectively. The null of stationarity cannot be rejected for any of the series. For the Climate series, the value of n selected by the Fourier KPSS test was 1. Lags denote the number of lags in the model; lags −1 is the number of lags used in the ADF versions of the Dickey-Fuller type tests. Start is the starting date of the estimation (accounting for lags).

the (real) prices for: (a) maize, $\ln(pc_t/ppi_t)$; (b) soy, $\ln(ps_t/ppi_t)$; (c) crude oil, $\ln(po_t/ppi_t)$; (d) ocean freight rates, $\ln(pf_t/ppi_t)$; and (e) ethanol, $\ln(pe_t/ppi_t)$.[17] Because of the role that weather conditions and climate shocks play in the production and transportation of maize and soy, we also consider the climate extreme index, *cei*. Due to data limitations for ethanol, the period we investigate, after reserving the first thirteen months for lag-length tests, runs from February 1985 through December 2011, a total of 323 observations.

17. More specifically, prior to estimation all real prices are normalized to a unit value for January 1996 and then multiplied by 100. The natural logarithm is then applied to this transformed series.

Table 4.3   Structure of individual equations in the shifting-mean near VAR

Commodity	Lag length	Maize (y_{1t})	Soybeans (y_{2t})	Oil (y_{3t})	Ocean freight (y_{4t})	Ethanol (y_{5t})	Climate extreme (y_{6t})
Maize (y_{1t})	2	✓	✓	✓	✓		✓
Soybeans (y_{2t})	2		✓		✓		
Oil (y_{3t})	2			✓			
Ocean freight (y_{4t})	3			✓	✓		
Ethanol (y_{5t})	3	✓		✓		✓	
Climate extreme (y_{6t})	1						3

Note: Lag length is determined by using the Hannan-Quinn (HQC) criterion. A ✓ indicates that lags of the variable in the associated column are included in the respective equation.

4.7.1   Basic Model Specification

The testing and estimation frameworks described above for univariate shifting-mean models are used here to investigate intercept shifts (breaks) in a select group of commodity prices. The approach requires that we first fit a separate transfer-type function (without shifts) to each variable considered. Following Zhang (2008), the lag length for each equation is determined by using the Hannan-Quinn (1979) criterion (HQC), which in turn is something of a compromise between the more liberal Akaike information criterion (AIC) and the more conservative Schwarz-Bayesian criterion. A series of Granger noncausality tests are performed in order to determine which variables should be included in each transfer function (equation). The variables included in each equation, also with optimal lag lengths, are reported in table 4.3.

As indicated in table 4.3, the base (i.e., linear model with no shifts) model for maize contains two lags of its own price, as well as the prices for soy, oil, and ocean freight. In addition, two lags of the climate extreme index are included. Preliminary results indicate that ethanol price does not Granger-cause maize price, a result that, moreover, was confirmed by using similar data by Elmarzougui and Larue (2011). Rapsomanikis and Hallam (2006) and Balcombe and Raspomanikis (2008) reached a similar conclusion regarding the relationship between ethanol and sugar prices in Brazil. As indicated in table 4.3, the base model for soy prices contains two lags of its own price as well as two lags of the ocean freight rate. Of interest is that corn prices apparently do not Granger-cause soy prices. Preliminary results indicated that oil price is apparently strongly exogenous; the linear model for oil includes only two lags of its own price. Again, similar results were reported by Rapsomanikis and Hallam (2006), Balcombe and Raspomanikis (2008), and Elmarzougui and Larue (2011). Over a somewhat different time period Kilian (2009) did, however, find evidence of the ocean freight rate, as a measure of real economic activity, having significant feedbacks to oil prices. The ocean freight index is associated with three lags of its own values and the price of oil. Likewise, ethanol price is also specified with three lags, and is a function of its own lagged values, the lagged price of maize, and the lagged price of oil. This result is also consistent with prior findings. Lastly, the climate extreme index is determined to be best explained by only one lag of its own value.

4.7.2   Intercept Nonconstancy Test Results

As explained in the methodology section, the LM testing framework for shifting intercepts may be applied to each equation. Specifically, the base (linear, no-shift) model specifications outlined in table 4.3 are used to examine the presence of intercept shifts, and hence, shifting means. The results of these tests, obtained by using both third- and fourth-order Taylor approximations in time under the alternative, are summarized in table 4.4.

The result of testing intercept constancy for maize with a third-order approximation, that is, a test of H_0 in equation (18), indicates that the null of no intercept shifts cannot be rejected at the 5 percent significance level, but can be rejected at the 10 percent level. The results of the test based on a fourth-order approximation, that is, a test of H_0' in equation (19) are more conclusive, with the null in this case being rejected at the 5 percent level. The results of the testing sequence in this case, that is, tests of H_{0E} and H_{0L} in equation (22), provide support for an intercept shift in the maize price equation that is U-shaped; that is, a shift that belongs to the family of generalized exponential transition functions in equation (8). Results in table 4.4 also suggest the presence of an intercept shift for soy. In this case, however, the testing sequence applied to the fourth-order approximation is indeterminate. Alternatively, when the testing sequence in equation (19) is applied to the soy equation, the evidence points toward an intercept shift consistent with the logistic transition function in equation (7).

Test results for a shifting intercept in the oil price equation strongly reject the null of no shift when either the third- or fourth-order approximations are used. Even so, the testing sequence in equation (19) based on the third-order approximation points to a U-shaped intercept shift, while the testing sequence in equation (20) points to an intercept shift consistent with a logistic function specification. In the case of oil, the correct specification will be determined by fitting both versions and then comparing results for overall explanatory power as well as model diagnostic test results.

Turning to the model for the ocean freight index, results in table 4.4 indicate no evidence of an intercept shift when a third-order approximation is used. Alternatively, the null of no intercept shifts is clearly rejected when a fourth-order approximation is used. Moreover, the testing sequence in equation (22) suggests that the shift may be consistent with a generalized exponential transition function, although the evidence in favor of a logistic-type shift is also strong.

Table 4.4   Results of intercept constancy tests for select commodity prices

Commodity	H_0	H_{03}	H_{02}	H_{01}	H_0'	H_{0E}	H_{0L}	Shift type
Maize	0.056	0.006	0.835	0.995	**0.030**	0.008	0.050	Exponential
Soybeans	**0.021**	0.029	0.030	0.644	**0.045**	0.206	0.807	Logistic
Oil	**1.60×10^{-4}**	0.328	1.63×10^{-3}	2.33×10^{-3}	**1.08×10^{-4}**	0.047	0.024	Undetermined
Freight	0.792	0.332	0.764	0.955	**0.027**	**4.89×10^{-3}**	6.81×10^{-3}	Exponential
Ethanol	**1.25×10^{-3}**	0.369	0.176	2.82×10^{-4}	**3.10×10^{-3}**	0.781	0.718	Logistic
Climate index	0.196	0.648	0.037	0.734	0.319	0.987	0.805	—

Notes: The column headed H_0 includes approximate p-values for a test of the null hypothesis in equation (15) obtained by including third-order terms in the trend variable in testing equation (14). Columns headed H_{03}, H_{02}, and H_{03} record p-values for the testing sequence in equation (17), as proposed by Lin and Teräsvirta (1994). Similarly, the column headed H_0' includes approximate p-values for a test of the null hypothesis in equation (19) obtained by including fourth-order terms in the trend variable in testing equation (14). Columns headed H_{0E} and H_{0L} report p-values for the testing sequence in equation (21), as proposed by Lin and Teräsvirta (1994) and Escribano and Jordà (1999). Bolded numbers in the H_0 and H_0' indicate that the null hypothesis of no intercept shifts is rejected at the 0.05 significance level. Underlined numbers in the columns headed H_{03}, H_{02}, and H_{03} and, likewise, H_{0E} and H_{0L}, indicate the minimal p-value in the testing sequence. The final column indicates the likely nature of the intercept shift as determined from the testing sequences.

Ethanol is similar to soy in that the null hypothesis of no intercept shifts is resoundingly rejected irrespective of whether a third-order or fourth-order approximation is used. Even so, the testing sequence in equation (22) applied to the fourth-order approximation is noninformative. Alternatively, the testing sequence in equation (19) applied to the third-order approximation strongly suggests that the intercept break in the price of ethanol is consistent with a logistic function shift.

Finally, and perhaps not surprisingly given a visual inspection of the data plot in figure 4.5, there was no evidence of an intercept shift, and hence no evidence of a shifting mean, for the climate extreme index. Alternatively, Gleason et al. (2008) report notable trends in regional US climate extreme indices during the summer and warm seasons since the mid-1970s. To further investigate this possibility, we employed the bootstrap testing framework based on a Fourier approximation to the shifting mean as outlined by Becker, Enders, and Hurn (2004). Applying this test we obtain an empirical p-value of 0.20, further confirming the results for the climate extremes index reported in table 4.4.[18]

4.7.3   Single-Equation Shifting-Mean Results

The pretests for intercept constancy test results are used as a guide to fit a provisional univariate shifting-mean model for each equation. In the case where a shifting mean consistent with the generalized exponential transition function is called for, a simple grid search over plausible values for the κ parameter is employed, namely, $\kappa = 1,\ldots 8$. The diagnostic testing framework outlined in the methodology section, that is, testing for remaining autocorrelation and for remaining intercept shifts, is also applied. Summary results for the preferred univariate shifting-mean models are summarized in table 4.5.

As reported in table 4.5, with the exception of soy, a single transition function (shift function) adequately captures the corresponding intercept shifts; in the case of soy, two logistic transition functions are required to summarize its idiosyncratic shifts. Of course, these results do not necessarily imply that only one or two mean shifts in the relevant price occurs. For example, maize has one idiosyncratic intercept shift, but in turn is a function of lagged prices for soy, ocean freight, oil, and climate extremes. By virtue of the algebraic result in equation (14), the shifting mean for maize will necessarily be a function of any (all) mean shifts in the right-hand-side variables as well. Alternatively, oil price, which is a function only of its own lagged values, will necessarily be identified as having one and only one mean shift.[19]

18. Indeed, the sample employed here, that is, effectively from 1985 to 2011, may be too short to identify any meaningful shifts in climate extremes.

19. With respect to oil, both a logistic function shift and a generalized exponential function shift were fitted to the data. All model fit and diagnostic test results pointed toward the model with a single logistic function shift.

Table 4.5   Single-equation model assessment and diagnostic test results

Measure	Maize	Soybeans	Oil	Freight	Ethanol
No. shifts	1	2	1	1	1
Shift type	GEXP	LOGIT	LOGIT	GEXP	LOGIT
$\hat{\kappa}$	4	–	–	2	–
R^2	0.943	0.944	0.970	0.920	0.885
$\hat{\sigma}_\varepsilon$	0.054	0.046	0.079	0.054	0.067
$\hat{\sigma}_{\varepsilon,NL}/\hat{\sigma}_{\varepsilon,L}$	0.993	0.991	0.967	0.977	0.968
AIC	−2.960	−3.299	−2.224	−2.973	−2.528
HQC	−2.895	−3.248	−2.197	−2.926	−2.468
AR(4)	0.714	0.595	0.568	0.753	0.388
AR(6)	0.780	0.458	0.142	0.870	0.638
AR(12)	0.333	0.590	0.076	0.056	0.797
ARCH(6)	0.959	0.458	0.142	0.000	5.45×10^{-4}
ARCH(12)	0.845	0.590	0.001	0.000	4.55×10^{-5}
H_0	0.132	0.799	0.515	0.083	0.168
H_0'	0.073	0.469	0.675	0.078	0.251
LJB	105.46	121.20	181.53	324.07	16.75

Notes: The effective sample size, T, is 323 observations. No. of shifts indicates the number of intrinsic intercept shifts estimated for each equation. Shift type indicates whether the intercept shift is of the generalized exponential (GEXP) or logistic (LOGIT) form. $\hat{\kappa}$ indicates the estimated value for the κ parameter in the generalized exponential shift function, determined by simple grid search. R^2 is the unadjusted R^2, and $\hat{\sigma}_\varepsilon$ is the residual standard error. $\hat{\sigma}_{\varepsilon,NL}/\hat{\sigma}_{\varepsilon,L}$ is the ratio of the respective standard error from the shifting-mean model relative to the constant intercept model. AIC is the Akaike information criterion, and HQC is the Hannan-Quinn criterion. AR(j), $j = 4, 6, 12$, is the p-value from an F-version of the LM test for remaining autocorrelation up to lag j. Entries for ARCH(j), $j = 6,12$ are similarly defined for ARCH errors up to lag j. Entries for H_0 are p–values from an F-version of an LM test for remaining intercept shifts based on using third-order terms in t^*. Likewise, values for H_0' are p-values from an F-version of an LM test for remaining intercept shifts based on using fourth-order terms in t^*. LJB is the Lomnicki-Jarque-Bera test of normality of the residuals (critical value from the $\chi^2(2)$ distribution is 13.82 at the 0.001 significance level).

Returning to the results in table 4.5, there is no strong evidence of remaining residual autocorrelation in any of the provisional shifting-mean models. Also, tests for remaining intercept shifts indicate in all cases that the null hypothesis cannot be rejected at conventional significance levels.

Additional diagnostic test results for the provisional shifting-mean models are reported in table 4.6. Specifically, p–values for LM tests for omitted variables in each equation are reported in the table. The results of these tests effectively confirm the basic model structure for each equation in the SM-NVAR outlined in table 4.3. Taken as a whole, the results reported in tables 4.5 and 4.6 suggest that the provisional shifting-mean models are

Table 4.6   Single-equation Lagrange multiplier test results for excluded variables

Null hypothesis	p-value
No lagged ethanol price effects in maize price eqn.	0.073
No lagged maize price effects in soy in maize price eqn.	0.178
No lagged oil price effects in soy price eqn.	0.165
No lagged ethanol price effects in soy price eqn.	0.096
No lagged climate extreme effects in soy price eqn.	0.832
No lagged maize price effects in oil price eqn.	0.608
No lagged soy price effects in oil price eqn.	0.858
No lagged ocean freight rate effects in oil price eqn.	0.490
No lagged ethanol price effects in oil price eqn.	0.724
No lagged climate extreme effects in oil price eqn.	0.160
No lagged maize price effects in ocean freight rate eqn.	0.409
No lagged soy price effects in ocean freight rate eqn.	0.072
No lagged ethanol price effects in ocean freight rate eqn.	0.074
No lagged climate extreme effects in ocean freight rate eqn.	0.070
No lagged soy price effects in ethanol price eqn.	0.960
No lagged climate extreme effects in ethanol price eqn.	0.250

Notes: In all instances the null hypothesis is that lagged values of the variable indicated should be excluded from the equation indicated. Entries in the column headed p-values are approximate p-values from an F-version of an LM test of the indicated null hypothesis. All tests were performed in a manner consistent with the diagnostic testing framework for smooth transition models outlined by Eitrheim and Teräsvirta (1996).

legitimate for further investigation in the form of a shifting-mean near vector autoregressive model. We now turn to these results.

4.7.4   Shifting-Mean Near Vector Autoregression Results

As described by Holt and Teräsvirta (2012), the parameter estimates for the single-equation shifting-mean models described previously may be used as starting values to estimate the parameters of an SM-NVAR by using full information maximum likelihood (FIML) methods. Also, following van Dijk, Strikholm, and Teräsvirta (2003) and Teräsvirta, Tjøstheim, and Granger (2010), we constrain the speed-of-adjustment parameters that is, the η_i's, in the respective transition functions when performing the FMIL estimations. Specifically, we constrain each η_i so that $\exp(\eta_i) \in [0.75, 50]$. We follow Enders and Holt (2012) and restrict the values for c_i in each transition function so that $c_i \in [0.05, 0.95]$, which in turn is akin to the so called "trimming condition" typically applied in the estimation of threshold models. Employing these restrictions helps alleviate numerical problems within the iterations of the FIML estimation framework.

Results for the estimated equations in the SM-NVAR are reported in table 4.7, while summary statistics, including the estimated error correlation matrix, are presented in table 4.8. Estimated transition functions along

Table 4.7 **SM-VAR estimation results**

A. Maize price, $y_{1t} = \ln(pc_t/ppi_t)$

$$y_{1t} = \left(-\underset{(0.519)}{0.201} + \underset{(0.075)}{0.293}\, G_1(t^*; \hat{\eta}_1, \hat{c}_1)\right)\underset{(0.008)}{0.085} + \underset{(0.053)}{1.081}\, y_{1t-1} + \left(1 - \underset{(0.053)}{1.081} - \underset{(0.008)}{0.085}\right)y_{1t-2}$$

$$+ \underset{(0.006)}{0.210}\, y_{2t-1} - \underset{(0.005)}{0.182}\, y_{2t-2} - \underset{(0.005)}{0.042}\, y_{3t-1} + \underset{(0.004)}{0.070}\, y_{3t-2} + \underset{(0.008)}{0.092}\, y_{4t-1} - \underset{(0.004)}{0.072}\, y_{4t-2}$$

$$+ \underset{(0.016)}{0.047}\, y_{6t-1} - \underset{(0.014)}{0.018}\, y_{6t-1} + \hat{\varepsilon}_{1t},\; G_1(t^*; \hat{\eta}_1, \hat{c}_1)$$

$$= 1 - \exp\left\{-\exp\left(\underset{(-)}{3.912}\right)\left[\left(t^* - \underset{(0.037)}{0.770}\right)\Big/\hat{\sigma}_{t^*}\right]^8\right\},\, R^2 = 0.942$$

B. Soybean price, $y_{2t} = \ln(ps_t/ppi_t)$

$$y_{2t} = \left(-\underset{(0.399)}{2.944} + \underset{(0.144)}{0.582}\, G_2(t^*; \hat{\eta}_2, \hat{c}_2) - \underset{(0.228)}{0.982}\, G_3(t^*; \hat{\eta}_3, \hat{c}_3)\right)\underset{(0.020)}{0.090} + \underset{(0.097)}{1.150}\, y_{2t-1}$$

$$+ \left(1 - \underset{(0.097)}{1.150} - \underset{(0.020)}{0.090}\right)y_{2t-2} + \underset{(0.012)}{0.086}\, y_{4t-1} - \underset{(0.013)}{0.052}\, y_{4t-2} + \hat{\varepsilon}_{2t},$$

$$G_2(t^*; \hat{\eta}_2, \hat{c}_2) = \left[1 + \exp\left\{-\exp\left(\underset{(-)}{3.912}\right)\left(t^* - \underset{(0.003)}{0.824}\right)\Big/\hat{\sigma}_{t^*}\right\}\right]^{-1},$$

$$G_3(t^*; \hat{\eta}_3, \hat{c}_3) = \left[1 + \exp\left\{-\exp\left(\underset{(-)}{-0.288}\right)\left(t^* - \underset{(0.003)}{0.874}\right)\Big/\hat{\sigma}_{t^*}\right\}\right]^{-1},\, R^2 = 0.944$$

C. Oil price, $y_{3t} = \ln(po_t/ppi_t)$

$$y_{3t} = \left(\underset{(0.075)}{0.292} + \underset{(0.115)}{1.170}\, G_4(t^*; \eta_4, c_4)\right)\underset{(0.025)}{0.105} + \underset{(0.072)}{1.193}\, y_{3t-1} + \left(1 - \underset{(0.072)}{1.193} - \underset{(0.025)}{0.105}\right)y_{3t-2} + \hat{\varepsilon}_{3t},$$

$$G_4(t^*; \eta_4, c_4) = \left[1 + \exp\left\{-\exp\left(\underset{(0.380)}{1.490}\right)\left(t^* - \underset{(0.037)}{0.770}\right)\Big/\hat{\sigma}_{t^*}\right\}\right]^{-1},$$

$$R^2 = 0.972$$

D. Ocean freight rate, $y_{4t} = \ln(pf_t/ppi_t)$

$$y_{4t} = \left(\underset{(0.181)}{6.131} - \underset{(0.110)}{0.383}\, G_5(t^*; \hat{\eta}_5, \hat{c}_5)\right)\underset{(0.030)}{0.086} + \underset{(0.002)}{0.111}\, y_{3t-1} - \underset{(0.002)}{0.138}\, y_{3t-2} + \underset{(0.003)}{0.005}\, y_{3t-3}$$

$$+ \underset{(0.099)}{1.312}\, y_{4t-1} - \underset{(0.138)}{0.595}\, y_{4t-2}\left(1 - \underset{(0.099)}{1.312} + \underset{(0.138)}{0.595} - \underset{(0.030)}{0.086}\right)y_{4t-3} + \hat{\varepsilon}_{4t},$$

$$G_5(t^*; \hat{\eta}_5, \hat{c}_5) = 1 - \exp\left\{-\exp\left(\underset{(1.874)}{3.900}\right)\left[\left(t^* - \underset{(0.045)}{0.768}\right)\Big/\hat{\sigma}_{t^*}\right]^4\right\},$$

$$R^2 = 0.920$$

(continued)

Table 4.7   (continued)

E. Ethanol, $y_{5t} = \ln(pe_t/ppi_t)$

$$y_{5t} = \left(\underset{(0.114)}{1.889} - \underset{(0.102)}{1.029}\, G_6\left(t^*; \hat{\eta}_6, \hat{c}_6\right)\right)\underset{(0.027)}{0.206} + \underset{(0.004)}{0.120}\, y_{1t-1} + \underset{(0.004)}{0.057}\, y_{1t-2}$$

$$+ \underset{(0.003)}{0.162}\, y_{1t-3} - \underset{(0.006)}{0.150}\, y_{3t-1} - \underset{(0.005)}{0.115}\, y_{3t-2} + \underset{(0.004)}{0.076}\, y_{3t-3} + \underset{(0.099)}{1.120}\, y_{5t-1}$$

$$- \underset{(0.070)}{0.451}\, y_{5t-2} + \left(1 - \underset{(0.099)}{1.120} + \underset{(0.070)}{0.451} - \underset{(0.027)}{0.206}\right)y_{5t-3} + \hat{\varepsilon}_{5t},$$

$$G_6(t^*; \hat{\eta}_6, \hat{c}_6) = \left[1 + \exp\left\{-\exp\left(\underset{(0.278)}{0.290}\right)\left(t^* - \underset{(-)}{0.950}\right)\Big/\hat{\sigma}_{t^*}\right\}\right]^{-1},$$

$$R^2 = 0.885$$

F. Climate extreme index, $y_{6t} = cei_t$

$$y_{6t} = \left(\underset{(0.014)}{0.201}\right)\underset{(0.064)}{0.823} + \left(1 - \underset{(0.064)}{0.823}\right)y_{6t-1} + \hat{\varepsilon}_{6t}, R^2 = 0.029$$

Note: Asymptotic heteroskedasticity robust standard errors are given below parameter estimates in parentheses, R^2 is the squared correlation between actual and fitted values for each equation, and $\hat{\varepsilon}_{jt}$ denotes the j'th equation's residual at time t, $j = 1, \ldots, 6$.

with the implied shifting means for each variable in the system are shown in figure 4.8.

As indicated in tables 4.7 and 4.8, the estimated SM-NVAR fits the data reasonably well, and it results in an improvement in fit relative to the standard NVAR—the system AIC and HQC measures for the SM-NVAR are lower than their counterparts for the corresponding NVAR that does not include mean shifts. Based on the system R^2 advocated by Magee (1990), the SM-NVAR with intercept shifts apparently results in a substantial improvement in explanatory power relative to the NVAR without shifts. Finally, as reported in table 4.8, estimated residual correlations are generally small with two exceptions: (a) between maize and soy (0.527), and (b) between oil and ethanol (0.305). There is also modest correlation between the residuals for oil and ocean freight (0.119).

Of interest here are the estimated mean-shift (transition) functions for each price equation. Results in table 4.7 indicate that the idiosyncratic intercept shift for maize, a generalized exponential transition function, is centered around October 2005, with the shift starting in late 1999 and ending in 2011. The two idiosyncratic intercept shifts for soy are fitted as logistic functions, with the first one being rather sharp, and centered at March 2007. In contrast the second shift for soy is evolving rather slowly (i.e., is close to linear), and is centered around August 2008. The single logistic function intercept shift for crude oil is quite smooth, and is centered around March 2004, with 10 percent of the adjustment taking place by June 2006 and 90

Table 4.8   **SM-VAR summary statistics**

$$\ln L_{SM-VAR} = 2606.598,$$

$$\text{AIC}_{SM-VAR} = -32.690, \text{AIC}_{VAR} = -32.560,$$

$$\text{HQC}_{SM-VAR} = -32.331, \text{HQC}_{VAR} = -32.284$$

$$\tilde{R}^2 = 0.999, \tilde{R}^{*2} = 0.121$$

System covariance matrix:

$$\hat{\Sigma} = \mathbf{Y P Y}, \text{ where}$$

$$
\begin{array}{ccccccc}
 & y_{1t} & y_{2t} & y_{3t} & y_{4t} & y_{5t} & y_{6t}
\end{array}
$$

$$
P = \{\rho_{ij}\} =
\begin{array}{c}
y_{1t} \\ y_{2t} \\ y_{3t} \\ y_{4t} \\ y_{5t} \\ y_{6t}
\end{array}
\begin{pmatrix}
1 & 0.527 & -0.054 & -0.024 & -0.012 & -0.038 \\
 & 1 & -0.002 & 0.094 & -0.011 & -0.067 \\
 & & 1 & 0.119 & 0.305 & -0.010 \\
 & & & 1 & -0.003 & -0.018 \\
 & & & & 1 & -0.021 \\
 & & & & & 1
\end{pmatrix}
$$

$$Y = \text{diag}\{\hat{\sigma}_1, ..., \hat{\sigma}_6\} = \text{diag}\{0.053, 0.045, 0.078, 0.053, 0.066, 0.122\}$$

Notes: AIC is the system Akaike information criterion and HQC denotes the system Hannan-Quinn criterion. A subscripted SM-VAR refers to the model estimated as a shifting-mean vector autoregression and a subscripted VAR refers to a standard VAR model without intercept shifts. $\tilde{R}^2$ denotes the likelihood system R^2 defined by Magee (1990), while $\tilde{R}^{*2}$ indicates the relative contribution to $\tilde{R}^2$ of the intercept shifts. **P** indicates the estimated correlation matrix, and $\mathbf{Y}$ is a diagonal matrix with the square root of each equation's estimated error variance on the main diagonal. $i = 1 = \ln(pc_t/ppi_t)$, $i = 2 = \ln(ps_t/ppi_t)$, $i = 3 = \ln(po_t/ppi_t)$, $i = 4 = \ln(pf_t/ppi_t)$, $i = 5 = \ln(pe_t/ppi_t)$, $i = 6 = cei_t$, $i = j = 1, ..., 6$.

percent of the adjustment occurring by December 2007. Regarding ocean freight rates, the estimated idiosyncratic intercept shift also belongs to the family of generalized exponential functions. This shift is centered around September 2005, which very nearly coincides with the center of the idiosyncratic shift for maize. The shift for ocean freight begins in 2002, and is complete by late 2010. Finally, the idiosyncratic shift for ethanol is also of the logistic function variety, and is centered around August 2010. As with soy, this shift is also rather gradual throughout the sample period.

4.7.5   Shifting Means

As already noted, the algebraic solution for the SM-NVAR shifting means in equation (14) will, in principle, incorporate the intercept shifts of several, and perhaps all, equations in the system. In the present case it is possible to solve for the reduced form for these intercept shifts and, moreover, to obtain their approximate standard errors by using a standard delta method

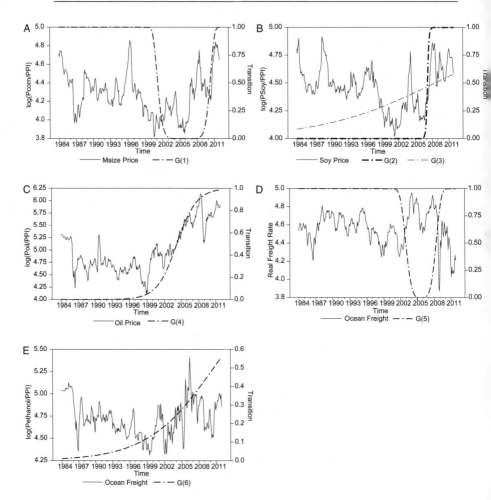

Fig. 4.8   Data and estimated transition function, 1984–2011: *A,* **log real price of maize;** *B,* **log real price of soy;** *C,* **real log price of oil;** *D,* **log real ocean freight rate index;** *E,* **log real ethanol price.**

approximation. The estimated shifting means for each commodity price, including their constituent shifts and approximate standard errors, are reported in table 4.9.[20]

Turning first to the shifting mean for maize, with the exception of the shifts for soy, that is, those for $G_2(\cdot)$ and $G_3(\cdot)$, the estimated mean shifts are

---

20. Standard errors for the shift parameters are approximate for all of the usual reasons that standard errors derived by using the delta method are approximate. In addition, the Davies (1977, 1987) problem applies equally here as well, which only further contributes to the approximate nature of these measures.

Table 4.9   SM-VAR shifting means for maize, soy, oil, ocean freight, and ethanol

Maize:

$$E_t y_{1t} = \underset{(0.130)}{4.172} + \underset{(0.110)}{0.299} G_1(t^*; \hat{\eta}_1, \hat{c}_1) + \underset{(0.171)}{0.180} G_2(t^*; \hat{\eta}_2, \hat{c}_2) - \underset{(0.269)}{0.310} G_3(t^*; \hat{\eta}_3, \hat{c}_3)$$

$$+ \underset{(0.162)}{0.279} G_4(t^*; \hat{\eta}_4, \hat{c}_4) - \underset{(0.078)}{0.149} G_5(t^*; \hat{\eta}_5, \hat{c}_5)$$

Soy:

$$E_t y_{2t} = \underset{(0.095)}{4.798} + \underset{(0.133)}{0.584} G_2(t^*; \hat{\eta}_2, \hat{c}_2) + \underset{(0.306)}{1.008} G_3(t^*; \hat{\eta}_3, \hat{c}_3) - \underset{(0.134)}{0.113} G_4(t^*; \hat{\eta}_4, \hat{c}_4)$$

$$- \underset{(0.120)}{0.149} G_5(t^*; \hat{\eta}_5, \hat{c}_5)$$

Oil:

$$E_t y_{3t} = \underset{(0.079)}{4.678} + \underset{(0.255)}{1.157} G_4(t^*; \hat{\eta}_4, \hat{c}_4)$$

Freight:

$$E_t y_{4t} = \underset{(0.206)}{4.959} - \underset{(0.300)}{0.303} G_4(t^*; \hat{\eta}_4, \hat{c}_4) - \underset{(0.234)}{0.400} G_5(t^*; \hat{\eta}_5, \hat{c}_5)$$

Ethanol:

$$E_t y_{5t} = \underset{(0.086)}{4.705} + \underset{(0.031)}{0.022} G_1(t^*; \hat{\eta}_1, \hat{c}_1) + \underset{(0.018)}{0.013} G_2(t^*; \hat{\eta}_2, \hat{c}_2) - \underset{(0.030)}{0.023} G_3(t^*; \hat{\eta}_3, \hat{c}_3)$$

$$+ \underset{(0.146)}{0.647} G_4(t^*; \hat{\eta}_4, \hat{c}_4) - \underset{(0.017)}{0.011} G_5(t^*; \hat{\eta}_5, \hat{c}_5) - \underset{(0.188)}{1.039} G_6(t^*; \hat{\eta}_6, \hat{c}_6)$$

Notes: Approximate standard errors obtained by using the delta method are given below parameter estimates in parentheses. $G_1(\cdot)$ is the idiosyncratic transition function for maize; $G_2(\cdot)$ and $G_3(\cdot)$ are similarly defined for soy; $G_4(\cdot)$ is the idiosyncratic shift for oil; $G_5(\cdot)$ is likewise defined for the ocean freight index; and $G_6(\cdot)$ is the idiosyncratic shift for ethanol. Specifications for the transition functions along with their estimated parameters are reported in table 4.7.

apparently statistically significant at usual levels. The effect of the idiosyncratic shift for maize on its own mean price is positive. But recall that $G_1(\cdot)$ is U-shaped, assuming unit values only between 1985 and 2000, and again starting in 2011. The shift in crude oil price had a positive effect on the unconditional mean for maize and, moreover, was nearly equal in magnitude to the idiosyncratic shift for maize. The shift in ocean freight has a negative effect on the mean for maize, but recall this shift is also U-shaped. In other words, during the period when $G_5(\cdot)$ was less than one, approximately between 2002 and 2010, the effect of the ocean freight shift on maize was mitigated. What is clear is the idiosyncratic shift in oil, occurring approximately between 2004 and 2007, had a direct effect on the unconditional mean for maize. Of course, this does not mean that a structural shift in the real price of oil "caused" a corresponding shift in the real price of maize. In other words, the possibility that a common but otherwise excluded third factor could be the underlying driver cannot be ruled out. For example, expansionary monetary policy and, correspondingly, a devaluation of the US dollar relative to other major currencies could be the underlying causal factor in this instance. Even so, whatever the reason, it seems that structural shifts in real prices for maize and oil during the 2004 to 2007 period coincided.

Turning next to the shifting mean for soy, results in table 4.9 reveal that only the idiosyncratic shifts for soy had any statistically significant effect on the unconditional mean for soy price. Specifically, the shifts in both crude oil price and ocean freight rates appear to have only a negligible (and insignificant) impact on the shifting mean for soy. In this sense, while movements in oil price and ocean freight rates apparently contributed to short- and intermediate-run movements in soy prices, their respective shifts had no lasting effect on the long-run mean price for soy.

The results in table 4.9 indicate that the effect of the shift in crude oil price on ocean freight rates, while negative, was not statistically significant. It therefore seems for all practical purposes that the shifting mean for ocean freight rates, like those for crude oil and soy prices, really depends only on its own idiosyncratic shift. Finally, turning to the shifting mean for ethanol, results in table 4.4 suggest that, in addition to the idiosyncratic shift in ethanol price, the only other factor that has a statistically significant effect on ethanol's underlying mean is the price of oil. Of interest is that ethanol's own shift, $G_6(\cdot)$, is: (a) slowly evolving, and (b) has a negative effect on ethanol's underlying shifting mean. Even so, the effect of the shift in the price of oil on the unconditional mean for ethanol is quantitatively and qualitatively large, and from approximately the year 2000 on, more than offsets the otherwise negative shift in the price of ethanol. The effect of the shift in crude oil price on the mean price of ethanol becomes qualitatively large starting in 2003, with the effect peaking in late 2008 with the onset of the financial crises. As already noted, a number of policy changes occurred during this period of time, including the US renewable fuel standard put into place in 2005 and the phasing out of MTBE in gasoline production in 2006. Even so, it is likely that without the underlying recent shift in crude oil price that ethanol price (and presumably production) would be nowhere near the levels observed in recent years.

As a final exercise, it is also possible to use the delta approximation method to obtain point-wise approximate standard errors, and therefore 90 percent confidence intervals, for the shifting means themselves. The results of this exercise for each commodity price in the estimated SM-NVAR are reported in figure 4.9. As illustrated in panel A of the figure, the shifting mean for real maize price generally drifted down from the mid-1980s through about the year 2000, at which point it dipped significantly between early 2000 and the middle of 2002. This trend then reversed from 2002 until the fall of 2006. From late 2006 through late 2007 the upward trend was even more accelerated. From early 2008 through the middle of 2009, that is, during a period coinciding largely with the financial crises, the shifting mean for maize then reverses direction, drifting somewhat lower. Beginning in the middle of 2009 the upward trend in the mean real price for maize resumes. Aside from these general patterns, it is also interesting to note that beginning in early 2000, the approximate 90 percent confidence band for maize price began to widen.

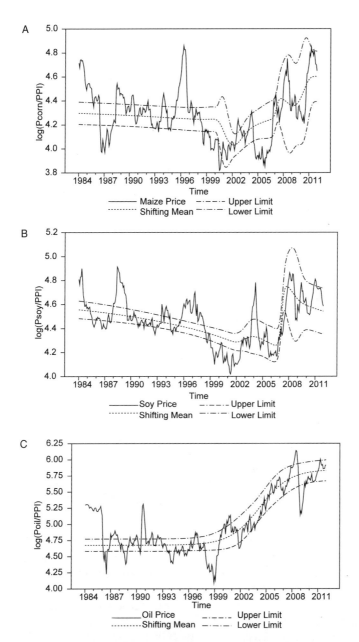

Fig. 4.9 Observed log real prices, shifting means, and 90 percent confidence intervals: *A*, log real price of maize, shifting means, and 90 percent confidence bands; *B*, log real price of soy, shifting means, and 90 percent confidence bands; *C*, log real price of oil, shifting means, and 90 percent confidence bands; *D*, log real ocean freight rate, shifting means, and 90 percent confidence bands; *E*, log real price of ethanol, shifting means, and 90 percent confidence bands.

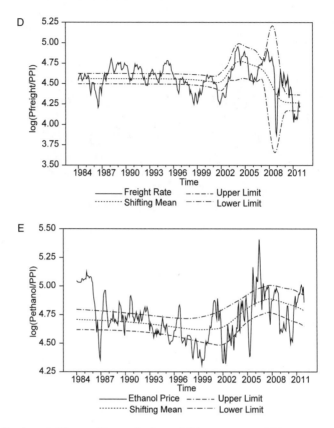

Fig. 4.9   (cont.) Observed log real prices, shifting means, and 90 percent confidence intervals: *A*, log real price of maize, shifting means, and 90 percent confidence bands; *B*, log real price of soy, shifting means, and 90 percent confidence bands; *C*, log real price of oil, shifting means, and 90 percent confidence bands; *D*, log real ocean freight rate, shifting means, and 90 percent confidence bands; *E*, log real price of ethanol, shifting means, and 90 percent confidence bands.

Moreover, the widening of this band accelerated dramatically starting in late 2006. The implication is that the recent shifts in the underlying unconditional mean for maize, while notable for both their direction and magnitude, were also associated with greater uncertainty.

Panel B in figure 4.9 illustrates comparable results for soy. As illustrated there, the shifting mean for soy prices generally drifted lower from the mid-1980s until late 2006. From the fall of 2006 through late 2007, the shifting mean for real soy prices increased dramatically. According to model results, the general downward trend in the mean for soy prices resumed at that time. But again, it is noteworthy that the approximate 90 percent confidence bands for soy's shifting mean started to widen in 2002, and widened dramatically starting in late 2008. Again, while the shifts in the underlying mean for real soy prices have been dramatic in recent years, they have apparently also been associated with a greater degree of overall uncertainty.

Regarding the shifting mean for the price of crude oil, the plots in panel C of figure 4.9 reveal nothing surprising—the shifting mean started to move steadily upward in early 2000, rose rather dramatically from 2001 through 2008, and has increased at a decreasing rate since then. The width of the 90 percent confidence bands also remained rather stable, although they widened slightly in the early years of the twenty-first century and again since 2008.

Regarding the shifting mean for the ocean freight index, the plot in panel D of figure 4.9 shows that no discernable shifts occurred from the mid-1980s through the early years of the twenty-first century. Beginning in early 2002 the mean for ocean freight started to move higher, and continued to do so through the middle of 2004. At that point the trend in ocean freight's mean started to edge lower, with the downward trend accelerating between early 2007 and late 2009. In the last several years in the sample it seems that the shifting mean for ocean freight rates has leveled off at a new, somewhat lower level. Of almost greater interest are the corresponding shifts in the 90 percent confidence bands for ocean freight's shifting mean. The confidence bands widened somewhat between early 2003 and late 2007, and then increased dramatically in magnitude between late 2007 and late 2009, a period that almost exactly coincides with the National Bureau of Economic Research (NBER) dates for the most recent economic downturn (i.e., December 2007 through June 2009).

The shifting mean for real ethanol price is plotted in panel E of figure 4.9. As indicated there, the underlying mean for real ethanol price drifted lower from the mid-1980s through late 2001. At that point ethanol's mean started moving higher, peaking in late 2007. Since that time the underlying mean for real ethanol price has resumed a gradual downward trend. Also, while there was some widening in the confidence bands for this mean starting early in the twenty-first century, the increase has not been dramatic.

4.7.6   Effects of Shifts on Agricultural Prices

In figures 4.10, 4.11, and 4.12, we perform a counterfactual analysis to ascertain the effects of the various shifts on the mean prices of maize, soy, and ethanol. Similar to our VAR results, we plot the estimated means of the various commodity prices along with the hypothetical paths obtained by zeroing out each estimated shift. By comparing the two paths (and recalling that the variables are in logarithms), it is possible to directly show the influence of each shift. Regarding maize, it is not surprising to note that panel A of figure 4.10 shows that the idiosyncratic, or own, shift was especially important. Had the shift not occurred, the estimated mean price of maize by the end of 2011 would have been about 30 percent less than the actual mean estimate. This is similar in magnitude to the results from the VAR analysis

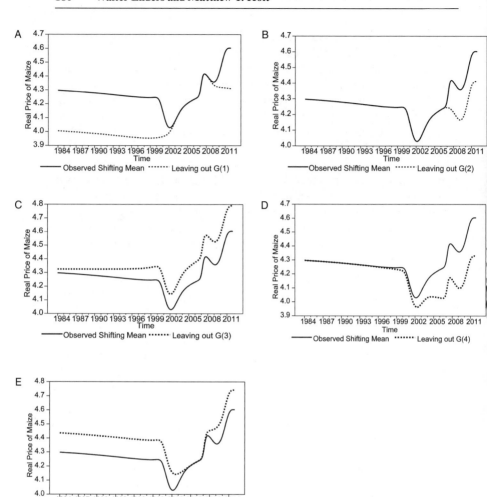

Fig. 4.10   Comparative dynamics of the shifting mean for real maize price with excluded shifts, 1984–2011: *A,* effect on maize of leaving out own-shift for maize; *B,* effect on maize of leaving out first shift for soy; *C,* effect on maize of leaving out second shift for soy; *D,* effect on maize of leaving out shift for oil; *E,* effect on maize of leaving out shift for ocean freight.

that was shown in the top panel of figure 4.7. Recall that the estimated own shift in maize can include shifts resulting from the real exchange rate and interest rate changes analyzed in the VAR portion of our analysis. The effects of the independent shifts in soy are mixed: the first mean shift for soy acted to increase the price of maize whereas the second acted to lower the price. What is clear (see panel D) is that the recent run-up in oil prices has served to increase the price of maize by more than 20 percent. Moreover, as shown

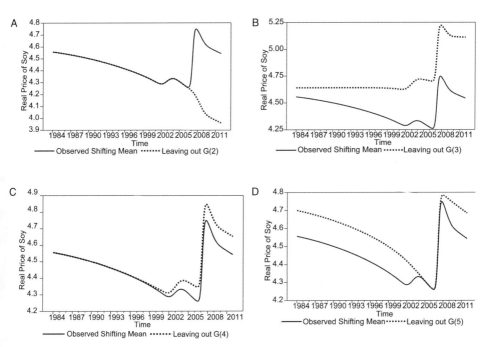

Fig. 4.11   **Comparative dynamics of the shifting mean for real soy price with excluded shifts, 1984–2011:** *A*, effect on soy of leaving out first own-shift for soy; *B*, effect on soy of leaving out second own-shift for soy; *C*, effect on soy of leaving out shift for oil; *D*, effect on soy of leaving out shift for ocean freight.

in panel E of the figure, the effect of the recent decline in the mean of ocean freight rates has had a depressing effect on maize prices of approximately 12 percent.

Figure 4.11 illustrates that own shifts for soy were of primary importance in determining the time path for its unconditional mean. As with maize, the decline in ocean freight rates has acted to keep the mean price of soy about 11 percent lower than otherwise. The effect of the run-up in oil prices had a small but negative effect on soy prices. As shown in panel C of figure 4.11, the estimated mean price of soy would have been about 10 percent higher had the mean price of oil not shifted. Even so, recall from table 4.4 that the oil shift is not statistically significant in the soy price equation.

Panel F of figure 4.12 indicates that ethanol's own shift had a large effect on its own mean price path. By the end of the sample, the magnitude of the effect was approximately 70 percent. Note that the shift in maize and the two shifts in soy had only minor effects on ethanol prices. The key result, shown in panel D of the figure, is that the run-up in oil prices had a pronounced effect on ethanol prices. We estimate than the mean price of ethanol would have actually declined had the mean shift in the price of oil not occurred.

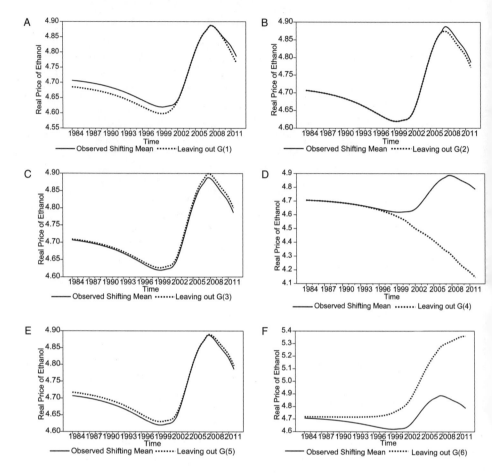

Fig. 4.12 Comparative dynamics of the shifting mean for real soy price with ex-cluded shifts, 1984–2011: *A*, effect on ethanol of leaving out shift for maize; *B*, effect on ethanol of leaving out first shift for soy; *C*, effect on ethanol of leaving out second shift for soy; *D*, effect on ethanol of leaving out shift for oil; *E*, effect on ethanol of leaving out shift for ocean freight; *F*, effect on ethanol of leaving out own-shift for ethanol.

Instead, the run-up in oil prices added approximately 60 percent to the mean price of ethanol; instead of falling by almost 50 percent, the mean of ethanol prices rose by approximately 10 percent.

4.8   Conclusions

Increases in energy prices, income growth in China, Brazil, and India, new uses for ethanol, the renewable fuel standard adopted in 2005, changes in storage costs, and macroeconomic factors such as exchange rate and interest rate changes have all been identified as being causal factors for the recent and unprecedented high levels for grain prices. Since the cobreaking (coshifting) literature is still in its relative infancy, we use several methodologically distinct approaches in order to gain deeper insights into the role of some of these factors in the run-up of grain prices. A simple VAR indicates that mean shifts in real energy prices, exchange rates, and interest rates have all contributed to recent spikes in grain prices. Idiosyncratic shocks have also played an important role. The second methodology extends Enders and Holt's (2012) univariate analysis to a time-varying multiple equation setting that allows for the possibility of smoothly evolving mean shifts. In addition to the general rise in real energy prices, the introduction of ethanol as an important fuel source is found to be a causal factor in the run-up of grain prices, although identifying such an effect per se is not easily accomplished in our analysis given the coincidence between the rise in ethanol demand (and prices) and the rise in oil price. Furthermore, while the mean path for ocean freight rates experienced a substantive shift between approximately 2004 and 2007, this shift did not by itself contribute to the observed mean shifts for maize and soy prices during this period. What is clear, however, is that the general decline in the mean path for real ocean freight rates beginning in late 2008 did coincide with a downturn in the mean paths for grain prices. Finally, the results also reveal that the confidence bands around the shifting means for maize and soy prices as well as ocean freight rates increased substantially beginning in the 2007 to 2008 period. Among other things, these results suggest that grain prices have in recent times likely experienced more intrinsic volatility.

References

Abbott, Philip, Christopher Hurt, and Wallace E. Tyner. 2008. "What's Driving Food Prices?" Technical Report, Farm Foundation Issue Report, July 11. Oak Brook. http://www.farmfoundation.org/webcontent/Farm-Foundation-Issue-Report -Whats-Driving-Food-Prices-404.aspx.

Alquist, Ron, Lutz Kilian, and Robert J. Vigfusson. 2013. *Handbook of Economic Forecasting*, vol. 2. Amsterdam: North Holland.

Anderson, Heather M., and Farshid Vahid. 1998. "Testing Multiple Equation Systems for Common Nonlinear Components." *Journal of Econometrics* 84 (1): 1–36.

Bai, Jushan, and Pierre Perron. 1998. "Estimating and Testing Linear Models with Multiple Structural Changes." *Econometrica* 66 (1): 47–78.

———. 2003. "Computation and Analysis of Multiple Structural Change Models." *Journal of Applied Econometrics* 18 (1): 1–22.

Balcombe, Kelvin, and George Rapsomanikis. 2008. "Bayesian Estimation and Selection of Nonlinear Vector Error Correction Models: The Case of the Sugar-EthanolOil Nexus in Brazil." *American Journal of Agricultural Economics* 90 (3): 658–68.

Becker, Ralf, Walter Enders, and Stan Hurn. 2004. "A General Test for Time Dependence in Parameters." *Journal of Applied Econometrics* 19 (7): 899–906.

———. 2006. "Modeling Inflation and Money Demand Using a Fourier Series Approximation." In *Nonlinear Time Series Analysis of Business Cycles*, edited by Philip Rothman, Costas Milas, and Dick van Dijk, 221–44. Amsterdam: Elsevier.

Becker, Ralf, Walter Enders, and Junsoo Lee. 2006. "A Stationarity Test in the Presence of an Unknown Number of Smooth Breaks." *Journal of Time Series Analysis* 27 (3): 381–409.

Berck, Peter, and Michael Roberts. 1996. "Natural Resource Prices: Will They Ever Turn Up?" *Journal of Environmental Economics and Management* 31 (1): 65–78.

Cafiero, Carlo, Eugenio S. A. Bobenrieth H., Juan R. A. Bobenrieth H., and Brian D. Wright. 2011. "The Empirical Relevance of the Competitive Storage Model." *Journal of Econometrics* 162 (1): 44–54.

Camacho, Maximo. 2004. "Vector Smooth Transition Regression Models for US GDP and the Composite Index of Leading Indicators." *Journal of Forecasting* 23 (3): 173–96.

Carter, Colin A., Gordon C. Rausser, and Aaron Smith. 2011. "Commodity Booms and Busts." *Annual Review of Resource Economics* 3 (1): 87–118.

Chavas, Jean-Paul. 2000. "On Information and Market Dynamics: The Case of the US Beef Market." *Journal of Economic Dynamics and Control* 24 (5–7): 833–53.

Chen, Shu-Ling, John Douglas Jackson, Hyeongwoo Kim, and Pramesti Resiandini. 2010. "What Drives Commodity Prices?" Auburn Economics Working Paper Series auwp2010-05, Department of Economics, Auburn University.

Davies, Robert B. 1977. "Hypothesis Testing When A Nuisance Parameter is Present Only Under the Alternative." *Biometrika* 64 (2): 247–54.

———. 1987. "Hypothesis Testing When A Nuisance Parameter is Present Only Under the Alternative." *Biometrika* 74 (1): 33–43.

Deaton, Angus, and Guy Laroque. 1992. "On the Behaviour of Commodity Prices." *Review of Economic Studies* 59 (1): 1–23.

———. 1995. "Estimating a Nonlinear Rational Expectations Commodity Price Model with Unobservable State Variables." *Journal of Applied Econometrics* 10 (S): 89–40.

Dvir, Eyal, and Kenneth S. Rogoff. 2009. "Three Epochs of Oil." NBER Working Paper no. 14927, Cambridge, MA.

Eitrheim, Øyvind, and Timo Teräsvirta. 1996. "Testing the Adequacy of Smooth Transition Autoregressive Models." *Journal of Econometrics* 74 (1): 59–75.

Elmarzougui, Eskandar, and Bruno Larue. 2011. "On the Evolving Relationship between Corn and Oil Prices." *Cahiers de recherche* CREATE Working Paper no. 2011-3, Center for Research on the Economics of the Environment, Agrifood, Transports, and Energy.

Enders, Walter. 2010. *Applied Econometric Time Series*, 3rd ed. Hoboken, NJ: Wiley.

Enders, Walter, and Matthew T. Holt. 2012. "Sharp Breaks or Smooth Shifts? An Investigation of the Evolution of Primary Commodity Prices." *American Journal of Agricultural Economics* 94 (3): 659–73.

Enders, Walter, and Junsoo Lee. 2012. "A Unit Root Test Using a Fourier Series to Approximate Smooth Breaks." *Oxford Bulletin of Economics and Statistics* 74 (4): 574–99.

Escribano, Alvaro, and Oscar Jorda. 1999. "Improved Testing and Specification of Smooth Transition Regression Models." In *Nonlinear Time Series Analysis of Economic and Financial Data*, edited by Phillip Rothman, 289–319. Dordrecht, the Netherlands: Kluwer Academic.

Fox, Jonathan F., Price V. Fishback, and Paul W. Rhode. 2011. "The Effects of

Weather Shocks on Crop Prices in Unfettered Markets: The United States Prior to the Farm Programs, 1895–1932." In *The Economics of Climate Change: Adaptations Past and Present*, edited by Gary D. Libecap and Richard H. Steckel, 99–130. Chicago: University of Chicago Press.

Frankel, Jeffrey A. 2008. "The Effect of Monetary Policy on Real Commodity Prices." In *Asset Prices and Monetary Policy*, edited by John Y. Campbell, 291–333. Chicago: University of Chicago Press.

Frankel, Jeffrey A., and Andrew K. Rose. 2010. "Determinants of Agricultural and Mineral Commodity Prices." In *Inflation in an Era of Relative Price Shocks*, edited by Renee Fry, Callum Jones, and Christopher Kent. RBA Annual Conference Volume, Reserve Bank of Australia, February.

Geman, Helyette. 2007. "Mean Reversion versus Random Walk in Oil and Natural Gas Prices." In *Advances in Mathematical Finance, Applied and Numerical Harmonic Analysis*, edited by Michael Fu, Robert Jarrow, Ju-Yi Yen, and Robert Elliott, 219–28. Boston: Birkhauser Boston.

Ghoshray, Atanu, and Ben Johnson. 2010. "Trends in World Energy Prices." *Energy Economics* 32 (5): 1147–56.

Gilbert, Christopher L. 2010. "How to Understand High Food Prices." *Journal of Agricultural Economics* 61 (2): 398–425.

Gleason, Karin L., Jay H. Lawrimore, David H. Levinson, Thomas R. Karl, and David J. Karoly. 2008. "A Revised US Climate Extremes Index." *Journal of Climate* 21:2124–37.

González, Andres and Timo Teräsvirta. 2008. "Modelling Autoregressive Processes with a Shifting Mean." *Studies in Nonlinear Dynamics & Econometrics* 12 (1): 1–21.

Goodwin, Barry K., Matthew T. Holt, and Jeffrey P. Prestemon. 2011. "North American Oriented Strand Board Markets, Arbitrage Activity, and Market Price Dynamics: A Smooth Transition Approach." *American Journal of Agricultural Economics* 93 (4): 993–1014.

Hamilton, James D. 2009. "Causes and Consequences of the Oil Shock of 2007–08." *Brookings Papers on Economic Activity* 2009 (Spring): 215–59.

———. 2010. "Commodity Inflation." Econbrowser: Analysis of Current Economic Conditions and Policy, November 10. http:/www.econbrowser.com/archives /2010/11/commodity_infla_2.html.

Hannan, E. J., and B. G. Quinn. 1979. "The Determination of the Order of an Autoregression." *Journal of the Royal Statistical Society Series B (Methodological)* 41 (2): 190–5.

Hill, Jason, Erik Nelson, David Tilman, Stephen Polasky, and Douglas Tiffany. 2006. "Environmental, Economic, and Energetic Costs and Benefits of Biodiesel and Ethanol Biofuels." *Proceedings of the National Academy of Science* 103:11206–10.

Holt, Matthew T., and Timo Teräsvirta. 2012. "Global Hemispheric Temperature Trends and Co-Trending: A Shifting Mean Vector Autoregressive Analysis." April. Unpublished Manuscript, Department of Economics, Finance & Legal Studies, University of Alabama.

Irwin, Scott H., and Dwight R. Sanders. 2011. "Index Funds, Financialization, and Commodity Futures Markets." *Applied Economic Perspectives and Policy* 33 (1): 1–31.

Karl, Thomas R., Richard W. Knight, David R. Easterling, and Robert G. Quayle. 1996. "Indices of Climate Change for the United States." *Bulletin of the American Meteorological Society* 77:279–92.

Kilian, Lutz. 2008. "The Economic Effects of Energy Price Shocks." *Journal of Economic Literature* 46 (4): 871–909.

———. 2009. "Not All Oil Price Shocks Are Alike: Disentangling Demand

and Supply Shocks in the Crude Oil Market." *American Economic Review* 99: 1053–69.

Kilian, Lutz, and Bruce Hicks. 2013. "Did Unexpectedly Strong Economic Growth Cause the Oil Price Shock of 2003–2008?" *Journal of Forecasting* 32 (5): 385–94.

Kilian, Lutz, and Daniel P. Murphy. Forthcoming. "The Role of Inventories and Speculative Trading in the Global Market for Crude Oil." *Journal of Applied Econometrics.*

Kwiatkowski, Denis, Peter C. B. Phillips, Peter Schmidt, and Yongcheol Shin. 1992. "Testing the Null Hypothesis of Stationarity against the Alternative of a Unit Root: How Sure Are We That Economic Time Series Have a Unit Root?" *Journal of Econometrics* 54 (1–3): 159–78.

Lee, Junsoo, John A. List, and Mark C. Strazicich. 2006. "Non-Renewable Resource Prices: Deterministic or Stochastic Trends?" *Journal of Environmental Economics and Management* 51 (3): 354–70.

Lin, Chien-Fu Jeff, and Timo Teräsvirta. 1994. "Testing the Constancy of Regression Parameters against Continuous Structural Change." *Journal of Econometrics* 62 (2): 211–28.

Lukkonen, Ritva, Pentti Saikkonen, and Timo Teräsvirta. 1988. "Testing Linearity against Smooth Transition Autoregressive Models." *Biometrika* 75 (3): 491–9.

Magee, Lonnie. 1990. "R^2 Measures Based on Wald and Likelihood Ratio Joint Significance Tests." *American Statistician* 44 (3): 250–3.

Maslyuk, Svetlana, and Russell Smyth. 2008. "Unit Root Properties of Crude Oil Spot and Futures Prices." *Energy Policy* 96 (7): 2591–600.

Ng, Serena, and Timothy Vogelsang. 2002. "Analysis of Vector Autoregressions in the Presence of Shifts in Mean." *Econometric Reviews* 21 (3): 353–81.

Perron, Pierre. 1989. "The Great Crash, the Oil Price Shock, and the Unit Root Hypothesis." *Econometrica* 57 (6): 1361–401.

———. 1997. "Further Evidence on Breaking Trend Functions in Macroeconomic Variables." *Journal of Econometrics* 80 (2): 355–85.

Pimentel, David. 2003. "Ethanol Fuels: Energy Balance, Economics, and Environmental Impacts are Negative." *Natural Resources Research* 12 (2): 127–34.

Pindyck, Robert S. 1999. "The Long-Run Evolutions of Energy Prices." *Energy Journal* 20 (2): 1–28.

Prodan, Ruxandra. 2008. "Potential Pitfalls in Determining Multiple Structural Changes with an Application to Purchasing Power Parity." *Journal of Business and Economic Statistics* 26:50–65.

Rapsomanikis, George, and David Hallam. 2006. "Threshold Cointegration in the Sugar-Ethanol-Oil Price System in Brazil: Evidence from Nonlinear Vector Error Correction Models." FAO Commodity and Trade Policy Research Papers 22, September. Rome: Food and Agriculture Organization of the United Nations. http://www.fao.org/esfescfen/41470/41522/.

Roberts, Michael J., and Wolfram Schlenker. 2010. "Identifying Supply and Demand Elasticities of Agricultural Commodities: Implications for the US Ethanol Mandate." NBER Working Paper no. 15921, Cambridge, MA.

Rothman, Philip, Dick van Dijk, and Philip Hans Franses. 2001. "Multivariate Star Analysis of Money Output Relationship." *Macroeconomic Dynamics* 5 (04): 506–32.

Schmitz, John D. 1997. "Dynamics of Beef Cow Herd Size: An Inventory Approach." *American Journal of Agricultural Economics* 19 (2): 532–42.

Serra, Teresa, David Zilberman, Jose M. Gil, and Barry K. Goodwin. 2011. "Nonlinearities in the US Corn-Ethanol-Oil-Gasoline Price System." *Agricultural Economics* 42 (1): 35–45.

Sims, Christopher A. 1980. "Macroeconomics and Reality." *Econometrica* 48 (1): 1–48.

Sims, Christopher A., James H. Stock, and Mark W. Watson. 1990. "Inference in Linear Time Series Models with Some Unit Roots." *Econometrica* 58 (1): 113–44.

Teräsvirta, Timo, Dag Tjøstheim, and Clive W. J. Granger. 2010. *Modelling Non-Linear Economic Time Series.* Oxford: Oxford University Press.

van Dijk, Dick, Birgit Strikholm, and Timo Teräsvirta. 2003. "The Effects of Institutional and Technological Change and Business Cycle Fluctuations on Seasonal Patterns in Quarterly Industrial Production Series." *Econometrics Journal* 6 (1): 79–98.

van Dijk, Dick, Timo Teräsvirta, and Philip Hans Franses. 2002. "Smooth Transition Autoregressive Models—A Survey of Recent Developments." *Econometric Reviews* 21 (1): 1–47.

Wang, Dabin, and William G. Tomek. 2007. "Commodity Prices and Unit Root Tests." *American Journal of Agricultural Economics* 89 (4): 873–89.

Williams, Jeffrey C., and Brian D. Wright. 1991. *Storage and Commodity Markets.* Cambridge: Cambridge University Press.

Wright, Brian D. 2011. "The Economics of Grain Price Volatility." *Applied Economic Perspectives and Policy* 33 (1): 32–58.

Zhang, Ming. 2008. *Artificial Higher Order Neural Networks for Economics and Business.* Hershey, PA: IGI Publishing.

Zhang, Wenlang, and Daniel Law. 2010. "What Drives China's Food-Price Inflation and How Does It Affect the Aggregate Inflation?" Working Paper no. 1006, Hong Kong Monetary Authority, July.

Zhang, Zibin, Luanne Lohr, Cesar Escalante, and Michael Wetzstein. 2009. "Ethanol, Corn, and Soybean Price Relations in a Volatile Vehicle-Fuels Market." *Energies* 2 (2): 320–39.

Zhang, Zibin, Dmitry Vedenov, and Michael Wetzstein. 2007. "Can The US Ethanol Industry Compete in the Alternative Fuels Market?" *Agricultural Economics* 37 (1): 105–12.

Comment   Barry K. Goodwin

I am pleased to have this opportunity to comment on the excellent chapter of Enders and Holt. As is typical of the work of these two researchers, the chapter represents the "leading edge" in time-series analysis of important commodity price relationships. In this case, it is the linkages among energy and agricultural commodity markets that are the focus of the analysis. The relationships among these markets has become a critical issue in applied price analysis, particularly since 2007, when the Energy Independence and Security Act of 2007 (Pub.L. 110-140) was passed. Among other important changes, this legislation significantly increased the mandated amount of

Barry K. Goodwin is the William Neal Reynolds Distinguished Professor in the Departments of Economics and Agricultural and Resource Economics at North Carolina State University.

For acknowledgments, sources of research support, and disclosure of the author's material financial relationships, if any, please see http://www.nber.org/chapters/c12811.ack.

biofuels that must be added to gasoline (i.e., the Renewable Fuels Standard) from 4.7 billion gallons in 2007 to 36 billion gallons by 2022. This legislative change, taken together with significant increases in worldwide demand for fuel, has brought about unprecedented volatility and high prices for agricultural commodities. The authors acknowledge the important impact of the biofuels policy as well as significant income growth in the "BRIC" countries of Brazil, Russia, India, and China, which served to stimulate the demand for fuels worldwide. The analysis is very competently executed and the results are compelling. I have little to offer in the way of critical comments but rather intend for my comments to serve as a catalyst for further inquiry.

The analysis of Enders and Holt consists of two nonstructural time-series models. The models are not as tightly linked as one might prefer. The first model consists of a standard vector autoregressive (VAR) model containing composite indexes of grain and energy prices, along with real exchange rates and the real rate of interest. The real rate of interest is calculated using changes in the US consumer price index (CPI) while prices are deflated using the US producer price index (PPI). This transformation of the data to place values in real terms raises two important questions. First, it is not clear why two different price indexes—indexes that tend to be very different from one another—are used in a single model to adjust for inflation. This raises a related question about which index is appropriate for deflating agricultural and energy prices. This is a fundamental question for which a precise answer that all can agree on is elusive. Agricultural prices have shown a long-run downward trend, reflecting significant structural changes in both supply and demand. Deflating such trending prices presents challenges since it often results in historical prices being inflated to unreasonably high levels. This is especially true of the CPI, which has risen much faster than has been the case for many basic commodities, including agricultural products. Thus, a second important question pertains to whether it is most appropriate to deflate prices. The real prices are utilized in a logarithmic form in the VAR models and thus deflation is somewhat analogous to including the deflator as a regressor in the model, albeit with a restricted coefficient. While it is true that the inclusion of interest rates and exchange rates complicates this straightforward interpretation, a more flexible approach would be to simply include the appropriate deflator as a regressor in the VAR model and work with nominal prices.

Inferences are drawn from the VAR estimates by applying a specific Choleski decomposition that imposes a set Granger causality structure on the relationships. Although the ordering is supported by specification tests, one may raise questions about some of the restrictions that are imposed. For example, the specification only allows for contemporaneous impacts of real energy, real exchange rate, and real T-bill shocks on grain prices and real interest rate shocks on real exchange rates. One may wonder why, for example, energy prices are not contemporaneously impacted by exchange rate and interest rate shocks. The VAR models serve to highlight important dynamic relationships among agricultural and energy prices and serve as an introduction to a more detailed VAR model with structural breaks.

The more substantial part of the analysis comes from a shifting-mean or SM-VAR analysis. The analysis models the mean values of the variables as a flexible function of t by including multiple mean-shifting functions $g(t)$. A different set of variables is included in this segment of the analysis— maize, soy, and crude oil prices, a measure of ocean freight transport costs, and the price of ethanol. Again, the variables are deflated using the PPI and the aforementioned suggestion of simply including the PPI as a regressor in the model seems particularly appropriate here. Likewise, the link between the two different empirical models is tenuous since such different variables are included in the models. The measure of ocean freight rates is intended to be an indicator of overall global economic activity and has been used within this context before (see, for example, Kilian 2009). Ethanol has played a major role in the ongoing biofuels debate, with approximately 40 percent of US corn now going toward ethanol production. Corn prices and acreage have reached all-time highs and many attribute these structural shifts in the corn market directly to the biofuels mandate. The model also includes a measure of weather shocks that is derived from the National Climatic Data Center's climate extreme index (CEI) for the Upper Midwest climate region.

That weather shocks have important impacts on agricultural markets is beyond debate. However, one must question this specific measure of weather impacts on prices for goods heavily traded in the global economy. The climate index applies to a particularly narrow region of the overall area of production of corn and competing crops and it is thus not surprising that the measure turns out to have little significant relationship with commodity prices. Although the impacts of weather on crop yields and thus prices tends to be systemic, a more global measure of weather-related yield shocks may be more appropriate.

A central goal of the analysis is to identify and characterize structural shifts among these commodities. To this end, the authors employ a rich and flexible approach to including multiple mean-shifting functions in the VAR models. This approach follows a long progression of the development of time-series methods for identifying and capturing the effects of structural changes in empirical models. The basic approach is familiar to any undergraduate econometrics student. For known break points, the data are divided at the discrete break and the fit of the model is compared to one without any such break. The familiar "Chow" (Chow 1960) test allows standard inferential techniques to be applied in order to determine the significance of any such structural break. This approach works well when knowledge of the institutional setting underlying the empirical model suggests a particular break. However, the problem becomes more problematic when the timing and number of break points is unknown. A common approach long applied in the empirical literature is to search over numerous break points and then to select the most significant Chow test statistics in order to identify the timing of the discrete break. However, as Andrews (1993) and Hansen (1992) have noted, such an approach leads to nonstandard inferential problems of the sort identified by Davies (1977). Because the test statistic is a supremum and because parameters associated with alternative regimes are unobserved under the null hypothesis of no break, it does not have a standard F or χ^2 distribution. Andrews (1993) and Hansen (1992) have developed alternative test statistics that overcome this problem, either through the use of limiting distributions or simulated critical values of the test statistics. Other approaches to testing for structural breaks with unknown join points have been developed within the context of cumulative sums or sums of squares (CUSUM) tests by Brown, Durbin, and Evans (1975) and Ploberger and Krämer (1992). These approaches have been generalized to the case of multiple discrete breaks with unknown join points by Bai and Perron (1998).

In contrast to discrete breaks, structural change often occurs at a gradual pace. To accommodate such graduate changes, specifications and inferential procedures that utilize gradual shifting means have been developed. For example, Lin and Teräsvirta (1994) have developed "transition functions" that specify a function of t that is allowed to shift gradually. Thus, a time-shifting mean may be written as $g(t) = g_0 * G(\eta, \tau) + (1 - G(\eta, \tau)) * g_1$, where $G(\cdot)$ is a function that is bounded between $(0,1)$ and η and τ are parameters that identify the timing and speed of adjustment between regimes. Popular choices for $G(\cdot)$ include exponential and logistic functions. Depending on the specification of the transition function, a change may be transitory (either symmetric or asymmetric) or permanent. Multiple transition functions may be included in the regression model so as to allow for considerable flexibility that includes multiple, overlapping structural shifts. This is the approach that Enders and Holt adopt and I believe it offers a strong method of representing structural breaks that is conceptually sound. One feature that I find particularly appealing is the manner in which mean shifts, which contemporaneously impact only the equation in which they appear, are allowed to impact other variables in the system through lags. Enders and Holt pursue a very innovative approach to isolating the effects of each mean shift in the system. Their graphical analysis provides important insights into the dynamics of each individual mean shift across the system.

I believe that this literature, from simple Chow tests of known break points to more sophisticated models with multiple, gradual structural shifts, represents a natural progression of the science of modeling structural breaks. Each successive specification allows for greater flexibility in representing structural change, albeit at the cost of additional parameters to be estimated and greater complexity in the nonlinearities of the estimation problem. Two observations seem relevant. First, we do in fact know the timing of many of the events thought to coincide with the structural changes being modeled. For example, we have strong prior suspicions that the Energy Independence Act of 2007 played a major causal role in bringing about structural changes in the underlying economic relationships characterizing agricultural and energy markets. To the extent that such information may be used in specifying the tests, greater statistical efficiency and a more precise evaluation of the specific event in question—the energy legislation—may be possible. Knowing the timing of the suspected change a priori also circumvents many of the complications associated with nonstandard approaches to testing.

A second thought pertains to taking this natural progression of flexible specifications to its natural end—a fully nonparametric representation of a shifting mean. Recent advances in semiparametric modeling have included methods for additive models that consist of a mixture of parametric and nonparametric components. An example can be found in the "generalized additive models" of Hastie and Tibshirani (1986) and Linton (2000). Backfitting and integration algorithms are available for estimating such models. Such methods can be amended to impose specific conditions such as monotonicity and concavity. Though technical hurdles may exist, this seems to be a promising avenue for future research in this area and represents a natural next step in specifying more flexible models.

Finally, a few minor suggestions that may be relevant for future work in this area are appropriate. A key variable in modeling price dynamics, particularly since 2007, is the ratio of stocks to use. Stocks have reached historically low levels and there may be some merit in including stocks in the VAR model. Likewise, corn, soy, and energy prices all have strongly seasonal deterministic components. The omission of these components may confound identification of the structural breaks that are the focus of the chapter.

Perhaps my biggest quibble with the chapter, though one that I am entirely sympathetic to, lies in the assertion made in the first line of the abstract that "we identify the key factors responsible for the general run-up of US grain prices." I would argue that in strict terms, this is not really the case. Rather, the models identify the timing and speed of adjustment but not the structural factors responsible for the changes. As a result, inferences that attempt to identify the causal relationships driving structural changes are more anecdotal in nature and generally involve an informal assessment (i.e., by "eyeballing" the results) of the structural factors that actually underlie the changes that are identified. In spite of such limitations, the results provide valuable insights into the timing and characteristics of structural shifts that can be weighed against the observable shifts that coincided with the changes. As I note, I am certainly sympathetic to this approach to modeling and such a criticism is rather banal as it goes with the territory of nonstructural time-series modeling—an approach that I often adopt and thus any such criticisms are also applicable to my own research. That said, the structural versus nonstructural debate will continue and one must always be sensitive to the strengths and shortcomings of both.

In summary, this is an outstanding chapter by two leading applied time-series econometricians. The focus on biofuels and energy impacts on commodity markets is timely and the results contribute significantly to our understanding of structural shifts in the markets that have been impacted by the policies and by other exogenous factors. As always, their work is meticulous and is exceptionally well executed. While I have identified modest suggestions for additional research, I believe this chapter makes important contributions to knowledge—both in terms of the innovative methods applied and in the empirical results that emerge from the analysis.

References

Andrews, D. W. K. 1993. "Tests for Parameter Instability and Structural Change with Unknown Change." *Econometrica* 61:821–56.

Bai, J., and P. Perron. 1998. "Estimating and Testing Linear Models with Multiple Structural Changes." *Econometrica* 66:47–78.

Brown R. L., J. Durbin, and J. M. Evans. 1975. "Techniques for Testing the Constancy of Regression Relationships over Time." *Journal of the Royal Statistical Society B* 37:149–63.

Chow, Gregory C. 1960. "Tests of Equality between Sets of Coefficients in Two Linear Regressions." *Econometrica* 28:591–605.

Davies, R. B. 1977. "Hypothesis Testing When a Nuisance Parameter is Present Only under the Alternative." *Biometrika* 64:247–54.

Hansen, B. 1992. "Test for Parameter Instability in Regressions with I(1) Processes." *Journal of Business and Economic Statistics* 10:321–35.

Hastie, T., and R. Tibshirani. 1986. "Generalized Additive Models (with Discussion)." *Statistical Science* 1:297–318.

Kilian, L. 2009. "Not All Oil Price Shocks Are Alike: Disentangling Demand and Supply Shocks in the Crude Oil Market." *American Economic Review* 99:1053–69.

Lin, C.-F. J., and T. Teräsvirta. 1994. "Testing the Constancy of Regression Parameters against Continuous Structural Change." *Journal of Econometrics* 62:211–28.

Linton, O. 2000. "Efficient Estimation of Generalized Additive Nonparametric Regression Models." *Econometric Theory* 16:502–23.

Ploberger, W., and W. Krämer. 1992. "The CUSUM Test with OLS Residuals." *Econometrica* 60:271–85.

5

Bubble Troubles? Rational Storage, Mean Reversion, and Runs in Commodity Prices

Eugenio S. A. Bobenrieth, Juan R. A. Bobenrieth, and Brian D. Wright

5.1 Introduction

Recent volatility of prices of major grains has revealed new interest in understanding the price behavior of storable commodities such as grains. A well-grounded model of a market for a storable staple product subject to random shocks to excess supply has been available since Gustafson (1958). Its basic logic of intertemporal arbitrage is widely accepted, and it can generate price series that have large "spikes" and "runs" of the type that attract the concern of consumers and policymakers. However, models of this type have been little used in recent analyses of commodity price fluctuations.

There are two key reasons. One is the absence of empirical support. For more than three decades the model could not be seriously tested, due to lack of both appropriate data and a satisfactory estimation procedure. When a version of the Gustafson model was eventually tested (Deaton and Laroque 1992, 1995, 1996), it was roundly rejected due to failure to replicate the high levels of serial correlation observed in commodity price data. Cafiero et al.

Eugenio S. A. Bobenrieth is professor at Departamento de Economía Agraria and Instituto de Economía, Pontificia Universidad Católica de Chile, and a research fellow at Finance UC. Juan R. A. Bobenrieth is associate professor at Departamento de Matemática, Universidad del Bío-Bío. Brian D. Wright is professor of agricultural and resource economics at the University of California, Berkeley.

Work on this chapter was supported by the Energy Biosciences Institute and by CONICYT/ Fondo Nacional de Desarrollo Científico y Tecnológico (FONDECYT) Projects 1090017 and 1130257. Eugenio Bobenrieth's research for this chapter was done partially when he was a professor at Universidad de Concepción, Chile. Eugenio Bobenrieth acknowledges partial financial support from Grupo Security through Finance UC, and from Project NS 100046 of the Iniciativa Científica Milenio of the Ministerio de Economía, Fomento y Turismo, Chile. For acknowledgments, sources of research support, and disclosure of the authors' material financial relationships, if any, please see http://www.nber.org/chapters/c12812.ack.

(2011), after solving a problem of numerical accuracy in the Deaton and Laroque estimation procedure, derived estimates for several commodities consistent with the observed price correlations.

A second reason is the common impression that commodity prices can occasionally exhibit bubble-like behavior in which conditional price expectations rise without bound, and that the storage model cannot satisfactorily replicate such behavior. Recent tests have, in some cases, detected price "exuberance" in observations of sporadic runs of prices of securities rising faster than the rate of interest. Some authors (for example, Phillips, Wu, and Yu 2011) have related such price behavior to former United States Federal Reserve Bank chairman Greenspan's remark in December 1996 regarding "irrational exuberance" of asset prices. Researchers including Gilbert (2010) and Gutierrez (2012) have looked for similar behavior in commodity markets. Others believe that the existence of bubbles in recent grain price data is obvious only after they "crash." (Timmer 2009).

In models in the tradition of Gustafson (1958), (including Samuelson 1971; Gardner 1979; Newbery and Stiglitz 1981; Wright and Williams 1982), the conditional expectation of price at far horizons is bounded. In their pioneering model of commodity price behavior with responsive supply, Scheinkman and Schechtman (1983, 433) presented a model in which, if price at zero harvest is infinite, and zero harvest has positive probability, then the long run conditional expectation of price is unbounded. They inferred that in this case "the model is exactly like an exhaustible resource model. Since stocks are always held, discounted expected prices must exceed today's prices by the marginal cost of storage. This seems a very unrealistic behavior for the price of a producible commodity and thus it must be true that in fact $x(\bar{z}) = 0$ for some $\bar{z} > 0$." Hence they decided to restrict attention to models in which stocks carried to the next period can fall to zero. Since continuously increasing price is something not observed in commodity markets (in contrast to price spikes, or price runs that eventually crash), their decision to restrict attention to models in which stocks carried to the next period can be zero, so that "mean reversion" occurs when available supply is below some strictly positive level, is understandable.

Several studies have identified mean reversion, variously defined, in commodity prices, adding empirical support to the informal inference of Scheinkman and Schechtman (1983) that the standard model of storage must have occasional "stockouts." (i.e., periods with zero discretionary stocks).

After a brief review of the issues regarding consistency of the standard version of the model with observed time series of prices, we focus on the questions regarding the capacity of the model to replicate bubble behavior and mean reversion. We draw on Scheinkman and Schechtman (1983) and Bobenrieth, Bobenrieth, and Wright (2002) to derive new implications for price behavior, and simulate a sample of price realizations in which the conditional expectation of price goes to infinity. We then establish some empirical implications for sample averages of returns from time series of prices, and relate these to findings of mean reversion.

5.2   The Model

In this chapter we use a stylized model of a market for a storable commodity such as a food grain to reconsider the capacity of storage arbitrage to replicate key features of commodity price behavior identified in empirical studies. We model a competitive market for a single storable consumption commodity such as a food grain in which time is discrete and all agents have rational expectations, in which the price process has an invariant distribution similar to that of Scheinkman and Schechtman (1983) and Bobenrieth, Bobenrieth, and Wright (2002). The distribution of the harvest disturbance can have an atom at its minimum value, here normalized at zero, and price at zero consumption is infinite.

Production is subject in each period to a common exogenous independent and identically distributed (i.i.d.) disturbance $\omega \in [0,\bar{\omega}]$, $0 < \bar{\omega} < \infty$. The distribution of ω is of the form $\alpha L_d + (1 - \alpha)L_c$, where $\alpha \in [0,1]$, L_d is a discrete distribution with a unique atom at 0, and L_c is an absolutely continuous distribution, with continuous derivative when restricted to its support $[0,\bar{\omega}]$.

Assume that there is a continuum of identical producers, a continuum of identical storers, and a continuum of identical consumers; each of the three has total measure one. There is a one-period lag between the producers' choice of effort $\lambda \geq 0$ and output of the commodity $\omega'\lambda$, where ω' is next period's harvest shock. Cost of effort is given by a function $g : \mathbb{R}_+ \to \mathbb{R}_+$, with $g(0) = 0$, $g'(0) = 0$, and $g'(\lambda) > 0$, $g''(\lambda) > 0$ for all $\lambda > 0$. Storers can hold any nonnegative amount of available supply from one year to the next, and then these stocks are all available for consumption or for further storage.

We replace the key assumption of Scheinkman and Schechtman (1983) that the physical storage cost function is strictly convex and its derivative appears additively in the Euler equation with the assumption that the physical storage cost function is zero; the sole cost of storage is the cost of capital invested. Given storage x and effort λ, the next period total available supply is $z' \equiv x + w'\lambda$. Producers and storers are risk neutral and have a common constant discount factor $\delta \equiv 1/(1 + r)$, where $r > 0$ is the discount rate.

The utility function of the representative consumer $U : \mathbb{R}_+ \to \mathbb{R}_+$ is continuous, once continuously differentiable, strictly increasing, and strictly concave. It satisfies $U(0) = 0$, $U'(0) = \infty$.[1] The inverse consumption demand

---

1. Unbounded marginal utility implies no substitution at the margin, an assumption which is more plausible for aggregate rather than for individual food commodities.

curve, with zero income elasticity, is then $f = U'$.[2] We assume U has a finite upper bound, and thus total revenue $cf(c)$ is also bounded, and that the expectation of f with respect to L_c is finite.[3] The perfectly competitive market yields the same solution as the surplus maximization problem. The Bellman equation for the surplus problem is:

$$v(z) = \max_{x,\lambda}\{U(z - x) - g(\lambda) + \delta E[v(z')]\}, \quad \text{subject to}$$

$$z' = x + \omega'\lambda,$$

$$x \geq 0, \ z - x \geq 0, \ \lambda \geq 0,$$

where $E[\cdot]$ denotes the expectation with respect to next period's productivity shock ω'.

By standard results (see, for example, Stokey and Lucas with Prescott [1989]), v is continuous, strictly increasing, strictly concave, and the optimal storage and effort functions $x(z)$ and $\lambda(z)$ are single valued and continuous.

Consumption and price are given by the functions $c(z) \equiv z - x(z)$, $p(z) \equiv f(z - x(z))$.

The storage and effort functions x and λ satisfy the Euler conditions:

(1) $f(z - x(z)) \geq \delta E[v'(x(z) + \omega'\lambda(z))]$,   with equality if $x(z) > 0$,

(2) $g'(\lambda(z)) \geq \delta E[\omega'v'(x(z) + \omega'\lambda(z))]$,   with equality if $\lambda(z) > 0$,

and the envelope condition $v'(z) = f(z - x(z))$.

Given initial available supply, $z > 0$, if the probability of zero productivity shock, α, is strictly positive, condition (1) implies that $z' > 0$ and $x(z') > 0$, and this arbitrage condition holds with equality in the current period and for the indefinite future. When positive, storage $x(z)$ is strictly increasing with z, and effort $\lambda(z)$ is decreasing with z. Note that $p(0) = f(0) = \infty$.

Define available supply at time t as z_t. Given arbitrary fixed $z_0 > 0$, the function that yields the supremum of the support of z_{t+1} is $\hat{z}(z_t) \equiv x(z_t) + \lambda(z_t)\overline{\omega}$. From the fact that there exists a unique fixed point z^* of $\hat{z}$ such that $\hat{z}(z) < z$ for all $z > z^*$, we conclude that $z_t \leq \overline{z} \equiv \max\{z_0, \max\{\hat{z}(z) : 0 \leq z \leq z^*\}\}$, for all $t \geq 0$. Then a suitable state space is $S \equiv [0,\overline{z}]$. Storage takes values in the set $[0,\overline{x}]$, where $\overline{x} \equiv x(\overline{z})$.

5.3   Empirical Relevance Revisited

5.3.1   Failure to Match Observed High Price Correlations

Deaton and Laroque (1992, 1995, 1996) presented empirical tests of the Gustafson model (1958) using, first, simulations of the model, and then

---

2. As discussed in footnote 1 of Scheinkman and Schechtman 1983, specification of a quasi-linear utility function is one way to incorporate income in the setting of general equilibrium models that generate the same set of equilibria as this partial equilibrium specification.

3. This guarantees that for a model with harvest disturbances with distribution L_c there is a finite threshold price above which discretionary stocks are zero.

econometric estimates based on the short available annual time series of prices of a number of commodities. Deaton (2014, 96) summarizes their overall conclusion:

> We have a long-established theory—whose insights are deep enough that *some* part of them *must* be correct—which is at odds with the evidence and where it is far from obvious what is wrong.

Cafiero et al. (2011) show, first, that a version of the Gustafson model with lower consumption demand elasticity can generate the high levels of serial correlation observed in commodity prices. Second, they show that application of Deaton and Laroque's (1995, 1996) econometric approach, modified to improve its numerical accuracy, using the same data set, yields empirical results that are consistent with observed levels of price variation and autocorrelation for seven major commodities. In a subsequent paper, Cafiero et al. (forthcoming) derive maximum likelihood estimates that impose no more assumptions than the previous pseudomaximum likelihood estimates for the global sugar market, and obtain even better results.

Thus we are now in a position to consider the relevance of the Gustafson model for interpreting and testing recent claims regarding the behavior of commodity prices. In particular, we address in this chapter claims that grain markets display mean reversion, or that they have recently been disrupted by bubbles (Gilbert 2010; Piesse and Thirtle 2009; Timmer 2009, 2010; Gutierrez 2012), or by exuberant behavior (Phillips, Wu, and Yu 2011), and the popular notion that such claims can be resolved, at least in principle, from observed price behavior.

The model tested by Deaton and Laroque (1992, 1995, 1996) and Cafiero et al. (2011, forthcoming) assumes linear demand, implying that stocks go to zero at a finite price. To address questions about mean reversion, speculative runs and related phenomena, we have adopted a demand specification that, if $\alpha > 0$, does not impose mean reversion at high prices, and allows for unbounded price expectations.[4] Thus our model is capable of producing behavior that includes conditional expectations of prices that go to infinity as the horizon recedes, as observed by Scheinkman and Schechtman (1983). Is this extension of the model of any empirical relevance to actual price behavior in commodities such as grains?

5.3.2   Behavior of the Model with Unbounded Conditional Price Expectations

Scheinkman and Schechtman (1983) stated that price behavior when $\alpha > 0$ and price at zero consumption is infinite is very unrealistic for a producible commodity, because then the model "is exactly like an exhaustible resource model. Since stocks are always held, discounted expected prices

---

4. As for the linear case, questions have been raised about the realism of the behavior of prices in that model.

must exceed today's prices by the marginal cost of storage" (433). Thus we start by considering a case of the model, that is in fact a natural resource model.

The Deterministic Finite Natural Resource Model

If $\alpha = 1$ then our model, which has no storage cost, is the deterministic Hotelling model of consumption of a finite resource with unbounded price. Standard results are that price rises monotonically at the rate of interest, so that discounted future prices equal the current price. Such price behavior is indeed inconsistent with actual stochastic evolution of prices for commodities such as food grains. Does this price behavior generalize to the case in which $0 < \alpha < 1$?

The Stochastic Model with Unbounded Price Expectations

Intertemporal storage arbitrage implies that, in the model with $0 < \alpha < 1$, $\{\delta^t p_{m+t}\}_{t \geq 0}$ is a martingale and $\{E_m[\delta^t p_{m+t}] : t \geq 0\} = p_m$, where $E_m[\cdot]$ denotes the expectation conditional on the price p_m at time m. Indeed the conditional expectation of price behaves exactly as the price in the deterministic natural resources model discussed above. But in this stochastic model the price path does not follow its expectation, contrary to the inference of Scheinkman and Schechtman (1983). Nor does the statement of Bessembinder et al. (1995, 362) that the path of conditional expectations at different horizons "describes several points on the path that investors expect the spot price will take" hold for this model. To the contrary, as the horizon recedes, the path of realized prices eventually drifts down and away from the rising profile of conditional expectations, any fraction of which becomes an upper bound on that realized path.

The sequence of probability measures of prices conditional on any initial price p_m converges to a unique invariant measure, uniformly in p_m, and consequently the sequence of discounted prices converges in probability to zero, uniformly in p_m.[5]

More precisely:

THEOREM 1: *Let* $\alpha < 1$. *Given* $\beta > 0$ *and* $\varepsilon > 0$, *there exists* $T \in \mathbb{N}$ *such that for any price realization* p_m,

---

5. If $0 \leq \alpha < 1$, the sequence of probability measures of z_t, $\{\gamma_t\}_{t=0}^{\infty}$ converges in the total variation norm to a unique invariant probability γ_*, regardless of the value of z_0. The idea of the proof for the case, $0 \leq \alpha < 1$ can be found in Bobenrieth, Bobenrieth, and Wright (2002). It follows immediately that the sequence of probability measures of prices $\{\gamma_t c^{-1} f^{-1}\}_{t=0}^{\infty}$ converges in the total variation norm to the unique invariant probability measure $\gamma_* c^{-1} f^{-1}$. Note that $\text{Prob}[p_t \geq y] = (\gamma_t c^{-1} f^{-1})([y, \infty])$, where $p_t = f(c(z_t))$ is the price at time t. $H_t(y) \equiv \text{Prob}[p_t \geq y]$ converges uniformly to a unique invariant upper c.d.f. H_*, with $\lim_{p \to \infty} H_*(p) = 0$. If $0 \leq \alpha < 1$, then the support of the invariant distribution of prices is an interval $[\underline{p}, \infty]$ with $0 < \underline{p} < \infty$.

$$\text{Prob}[\delta^t p_{m+t} < \beta \mid p_m] \geq 1 - \varepsilon, \ \forall \, t \geq T.$$

Theorem 1 implies that for any sample size $N \in \mathbb{N}$, given any finite sequence of realized initial prices $\{p_m, p_{m+1}, \cdots, p_{m+N-1}\}$, we have the following bound on the joint probability of the gross discounted relative price changes from each initial price in the sample, beyond a finite T', where T' is independent of the finite sequence of initial price realizations:

$$\text{Prob}\left[\frac{\delta^t p_{m+t}}{p_m} < \beta, \frac{\delta^t p_{m+1+t}}{p_{m+1}} < \beta, \cdots, \frac{\delta^t p_{m+N-1+t}}{p_{m+N-1}} < \beta \mid p_{m+N-1} \right] \geq 1 - \varepsilon,$$

for all $t \geq T'$.[6]

The existence of a unique invariant distribution, which is a global attractor, implies for this price process that, with probability one, the sequence of price realizations is dense on the support $[\underline{p}, \infty]$ of the invariant distribution. The infinite sequence of price realizations visits every neighborhood of every price in the support, no matter how high, infinitely often, almost surely. Given this fact, the following proposition regarding discounted prices might not be surprising:

PROPOSITION 1: *Let* $\alpha < 1$. *For any given price realization* p_m, *for arbitrary positive real number D, there exists a horizon* $d \in \mathbb{N}$, *such that:*

$$\text{Prob}[\delta^t p_{m+t} > D \mid p_m] > 0, \ \forall \, t \geq d.$$

For the case $0 < \alpha < 1$, the maximum of the support of the conditional distribution of discounted price goes to infinity as the horizon increases, in contrast to the case for the standard Gustafson model with bounded price, where the maximum goes to zero. To prove Proposition 1, we need Proposition 2, which might seem counterintuitive given Proposition 1.

For the discussion that follows, given a price realization p_m, let $E_m[\cdot]$ denote the expectation conditional on p_m.

PROPOSITION 2: *Let* $\alpha < 1$. *Given any price realization* p_m, *the sequence of discounted prices,* $\{\delta^t p_{m+t}\}_{t \geq 0}$, *goes to zero, almost surely (as* $t \to \infty$*).*

PROOF OF PROPOSITION 2: The Euler condition for storage arbitrage (1) implies that, if $\alpha > 0$, $\{\delta^t p_{m+t}\}_{t \geq 0}$ is a martingale and $\sup\{E_m[\delta^t p_{m+t}] : t \geq 0\} = p_m < \infty$. In the case $\alpha = 0$, $\{\delta^t p_{m+t}\}_{t \geq 0}$ is a supermartingale and $\sup\{E_m[\delta^t p_{m+t}] : t \geq 0\} = p^* < \infty$. In both cases, by the Martingale Convergence Theorem (due to Doob) we conclude that $\delta^t p_{m+t} \to Y$ a.s. (as $t \to \infty$), where Y is a real random variable. By Theorem 1, $\delta^t p_{m+t} \to 0$ in probability (as $t \to \infty$), and hence $Y = 0$ almost surely. Q.E.D.

---

6. In the proof presented in the appendix, we use the facts that the Markov operator is stable and quasicompact, and that given any initial price, any neighborhood of infinity, and any integer k, the price process visits that neighborhood in a time that is some multiple of k, with positive probability.

PROOF OF PROPOSITION 1: For the nontrivial case $0 < \alpha < 1$, we prove the result by contradiction. If not, there exists a price realization p_m, a real number $D > 0$ and a sequence of natural numbers $\{t_k\}_{k \in \mathbb{N}} \uparrow \infty$ with $\text{Prob}[\delta^{t_k} p_{m+t_k} > D \,|\, p_m] = 0$, for all t_k. Therefore $\delta^{t_k} p_{m+t_k} \leq D$ a.s., for all t_k. Then the Lebesgue dominated convergence theorem and the fact that $\lim_{t_k \to \infty} \delta^{t_k} p_{m+t_k} = 0$ a.s. imply that $\lim_{t_k \to \infty} E_m[\delta^{t_k} p_{m+t_k}] = 0$, a contradiction to $E_m[\delta^{t_k} p_{m+t_k}] = p_m > 0$, for all t_k. $\hspace{2cm}$ Q.E.D.

If $0 < \alpha < 1$, we have that $E_m[\delta^t p_{m+t}] = p_m$, $\forall\, t \geq 0$. Nevertheless, Proposition 2 states $\{\delta^t p_{m+t}\}_{t \geq 0}$, converges to zero almost surely, implying that $\{E_m[\delta^t p_{m+t}]\}_{t \geq 0}$ does not converge to the expectation of the almost sure limit of $\{\delta^t p_{m+t}\}_{t \geq 0}$. As a consequence, the sequence of discounted prices is not uniformly integrable.

Proposition 2 is easy to understand in a model with $\alpha = 0$, but if $0 < \alpha < 1$, how can the discounted price be going to zero, almost surely, if there is positive probability that discounted price exceeds D at any sufficiently far horizon? The explanation hinges on the distinction drawn above between a profile of expectations conditional on a price realization and the path of realizations. By Proposition 2, with probability one, for any given path of discounted price realizations there is a time beyond which that path is permanently below D. But by Proposition 1, there is no finite horizon beyond which all paths possible from date m are below D. In fact, at any finite horizon, with positive probability price rises at a rate greater than the discount rate r, continuously within that horizon. Although any path of discounted price realizations eventually remains permanently below D, before it does so, it can exceed any given arbitrary high finite bound. It is recognition of such a possibility that keeps $E_m[\delta^t p_{m+t}]$ equal to p_m as the horizon, and the probability that the discounted price will be below D at that horizon, both increase.[7]

Proposition 2 implies that, given a price realization p_m, the sample mean and sample variance of a discounted price sequence go to zero almost surely, that is:

$$N^{-1} \sum_{t=0}^{N-1} \delta^t p_{m+t} \to 0 \text{ a.s. (as } N \to \infty\text{), and}$$

$$N^{-1} \sum_{t=0}^{N-1} \left[\delta^t p_{m+t} - N^{-1} \sum_{j=0}^{N-1} \delta^j p_{m+j} \right]^2 \to 0 \text{ a.s. (as } N \to \infty\text{).}$$

Thus the estimators are consistent with respect to the first two moments of the limiting distribution of discounted price. For the case $0 < \alpha < 1$, the sample average of discounted price realizations starting at any price realization, p_m, is eventually permanently below any arbitrary positive fraction of the profile of expectations, conditional on p_m, of discounted price. Nevertheless the variance of the distribution of discounted price, conditional on p_m, goes to infinity as $t \to \infty$.

7. José Scheinkman has pointed out that similar behavior is discussed in a different model by Martin (2012).

The behavior of the price path is related to the profile of conditional expectations at time m by the following theorem:

THEOREM 2: *Let* $0 < \alpha < 1$. *Given any price realization* p_m, *with probability one, for any* $1 \leq l < \infty$, *there exists a finite time* $\tau(l)$, *which depends on the sequence of price realizations, such that:*

$$\frac{E_m[p_{m+t}]}{l} > p_{m+t}, \; \forall \, t \geq \tau(l),$$

implying that

$$p_{m+t} = o(E_m[p_{m+t}]), \quad \text{a.s.}$$

PROOF OF THEOREM 2: By Proposition 2, $\delta^t p_{m+t} \to 0$ (as $t \to \infty$), with probability one. Therefore, given any $l, 1 \leq l < \infty$, there exists a time $\tau(l)$ that satisfies $\delta^t p_{m+t} \cdot l < p_m = \delta^t E_m[p_{m+t}], \; \forall \, t \geq \tau(l)$.　　　Q.E.D.

Theorem 2 defines a sequence of upper bounds on the path of price realizations. Note that the profile of conditional expectations $E_m[p_{m+t}]$ is itself an upper bound beyond some date $\tau(1)$. Any given fraction of the profile of expectations conditional on initial price is an upper bound on any price realized beyond some fixed horizon, with probability one.

5.4   Price Behavior in this Model: Do We See Bubbles?

The behavior of price expectations and realizations in the model is illustrated in the example in figure 5.1. At time 0 the profile of conditional expectations, $E_0[p_t]$, rises to infinity at the discount rate. A possible sequence of price realizations is illustrated as a grey curve.[8] After period 23, all the realizations of price lie below $E_0[p_t]$. The curve $E_0[p_t]/2$ shows another bound at half the price expectations is effective beginning at date 39. It is obvious that further bounds generated by successively higher values of l would imply that the long-run rate of increase of realized price is strictly lower than the discount rate, 4%, even though the storage arbitrage condition (1) holds, with equality, each period, and that price runs of any finite length, understood as sequences of prices rising faster than the interest rate, recur infinitely often along the path of realizations, almost surely. Figure 5.2 shows the logarithms of the same price series, dramatizing the runs of price increases greater than the rate of interest.

These figures show that runs of prices rising for several years at a rate greater than the rate of interest before crashing, denoted "explosive" by Phillips, Wu, and Yu (2011), and fulfilling the empirical ex post criterion for identification of bubbles in grain prices enunciated by Timmer (2009, 2010), are consistent with our equilibrium model with rational expectations. In this

---

8. Bobenrieth, Bobenrieth, and Wright (2008) offers a foundation for a strategy for numerical solution of marginal values in cases where they are unbounded.

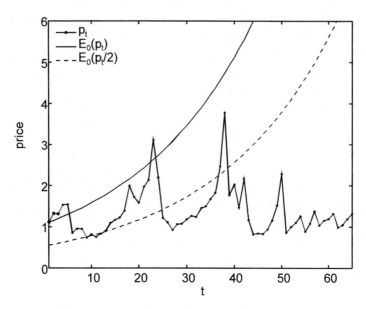

Fig. 5.1 Expectations of prices conditional on price at time 0 and a sample of price realizations

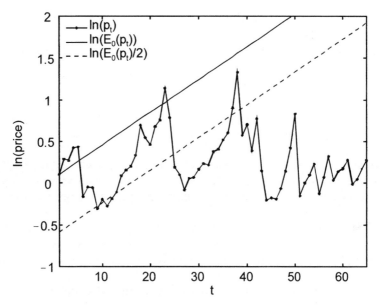

Fig. 5.2 Logarithms of expectations of prices conditional on price at time 0 and logarithms of a sample of price realizations

model, they do not signify the disruptive effects of irrational speculation, but rather the dampening effect of storage that prevents sharper price jumps, but with declining effectiveness if low harvests persist.

Discussions of volatile grain price behavior often raise the issue of price bubbles, frequently without defining the term. Brunnermeier (2008, 578) includes a key feature of most definitions of finance economists when he states, "Bubbles arise if the price exceeds the asset's fundamental value. This can occur if investors hold the asset because they believe that they can sell it at a higher price than some other investor even though the asset's price exceeds its fundamental value." Are price runs characteristic of price behavior in our model, as illustrated in figures 5.1 and 5.2, consistent with this definition? In our model we have assumed no convenience yield, and the law of one price holds. In that setting, when storage is positive, the value of a commodity such as food grain equals its value in consumption, as indicated in the envelope condition after equations (1) and (2) above. Storage is a one-period investment, so its "fundamental" is the market price, which derives its marginal value from its value in consumption. Thus, in our model, bubbles consistent with Brunnermeier's definition cannot occur. In this model, they do not signify the disruptive effects of rational or irrational speculation, but rather the dampening effect of storage that prevents sharper price jumps, but with declining effectiveness, during episodes of repeated low harvests.

5.5 Some Empirical Implications

Implications of the model for the empirical behavior of sample averages of returns on the stocks, held over specific intervals, are summarized in the following theorem:

THEOREM 3: *Let* $0 < \alpha < 1$. *With probability one, for any given path of price realizations* $\{p_t\}_{t \geq 0}$, *for any* $n \in \mathbb{N}$ *and for any* $\beta > 0$, *there exist* $J = J(\{p_t\}_{t \geq 0}, n, \beta) \in \mathbb{N}$, $k = k(\{p_t\}_{t \geq 0}, J, \beta) \in \mathbb{N}$, $k > n$, *and* $K = K(\{p_t\}_{t > 0}, k, \beta) \in \mathbb{N}$, $K > J$, *such that:*

(i)
$$J^{-1}\sum_{t=0}^{J-1}\left[\frac{\delta^n p_{t+n} - p_t}{p_t}\right] \in (-\beta, \beta),$$

(ii)
$$J^{-1}\sum_{t=0}^{J-1}\left[\frac{\delta^k p_{t+k} - p_t}{p_t}\right] \in (-1, -1 + \beta), \quad and$$

(iii)
$$K^{-1}\sum_{t=0}^{K-1}\left[\frac{\delta^k p_{t+k} - p_t}{p_t}\right] \in (-\beta, \beta).$$

PROOF OF THEOREM 3: For $j \in \mathbb{N}$ and for $t \in \mathbb{N} \cup \{0\}$, let $Y_{t+j} \equiv (\delta^j p_{t+j} - p_t)/p_t$. The arbitrage equation for storage (1) implies that there exists $\bar{p} \geq p(x^j(z_t))$, $\bar{p}$ depends on z_t, such that $\delta^j \alpha_1^j \bar{p} = p_t$, where α_1 is the size of the atom at zero of the distribution of ω, and $x^j \equiv x \circ x \circ \cdots \circ x$ (j times). Therefore,

$$-1 \leq Y_{t+j} \leq \delta^j \frac{\bar{p}}{p_t} = \frac{1}{\alpha_1^j}.$$

The arbitrage equation (1) also implies $E_t[Y_{t+j}] = 0$. It follows that the sequence $\{X_t\}_{t \geq 0}$, where $X_t \equiv Y_{t+j}$, is uniformly bounded, and $\sum_{i=1}^{\infty} \sup_t |\mathrm{Cov}(X_t, X_{t-i})| < \infty$. A strong law of large numbers (see Davidson 1994, 297) implies that

(2) $$\lim_{N \to \infty} N^{-1} \sum_{t=0}^{N-1} \left[\frac{\delta^j p_{t+j} - p_t}{p_t} \right] = 0, \quad \text{a.s.}$$

Evaluating (2) for $j = n$ we conclude that there exists $J \in \mathbb{N}$ such that (i) holds. For this J, by Proposition 2,

$$\lim_{k \to \infty} J^{-1} \sum_{t=0}^{J-1} \left[\frac{\delta^k p_{t+k} - p_t}{p_t} \right] = -1, \quad \text{a.s.},$$

establishing expression (ii) for large enough k. Finally, evaluating (2) for $j = k$ we obtain $K, K > J$, satisfying expression (iii). Q.E.D.

Expression (i) of Theorem 3 shows that the average excess rate of return on stocks held over n periods is greater than a given, arbitrary $-\beta$, for a sufficiently large sample size J, as implied by a strong law of large numbers.[9] Expression (ii) states that, with the same sample of initial holding dates, if we increase the holding interval sufficiently to k periods (and increase the sample size by $k - n$ periods to accommodate the extended lead), the average gross discounted return is within an arbitrary β of a total loss. At this sample size, the sample average of expression (ii) could be considered a downward-biased estimator of the expected k – period rate of increase in price, which in this model is constant. Thus for any sample of prices of any given length, one can find a sufficiently far horizon such that the estimated average return can be taken to imply mean reversion, as defined, for example, in Bessembinder et al. (1995) even if the behavior of prices does not exhibit mean reversion, as in the stationary model considered here. Expression (iii) reflects the fact that the sample average for the longer holding period approaches the conditional expectation for that horizon when the sample size is sufficiently increased.

Comparison of results of expressions (i) through (iii) has another inter-

---

9. A similar result is confirmed (on a very different time scale) for daily returns for wheats on the Kansas City and Minneapolis grain exchanges in Bobenrieth (1996).

pretation, more relevant for estimation of the long-run return on storage from any given time zero. As the horizon is increased, the discounted present value of price realizations conditional on any price p_t in the sample of size J in expression (*i*) eventually converges along the path of realizations, to a neighborhood of zero in finite time, as stated in Proposition 2. From this point of view, comparison of expression (*ii*) with expression (*i*) reflects the convergence of the gross discounted value to its almost sure limit of a 100 percent loss over the holding period, as the latter goes to infinity. But expression (*iii*) shows an increase in the average excess rate of return back to an arbitrary neighborhood of the conditional expectation of zero when sufficient observations are added to include some that have high rates of price increase through the fixed horizon. Note that expression (*iii*) does not imply that an initial investment at time zero can be restored to profitability if held for a sufficiently long time.

5.6 Conclusions

The remarkable work of Gustafson (1958) introduced a market model that numerically derives the storage demand given consumer demand, yield distribution, cost of storage and interest rate, and assuming maximization of expected profits. The standard model shows why price distributions tend to be skewed, and why they do not closely reflect production shocks. Recent empirical results confirm that it can, contrary to previous claims, also match the high price correlations seen in annual prices of major commodities. However, the model as presented by Gustafson cannot address the behavior of prices if their profile of conditional expectations are unbounded, as in some models of speculative behavior.

Here we consider an extension of the Gustafson model, introduced in Scheinkman and Schechtman (1983) and addressed by Bobenrieth, Bobenrieth, and Wright (2002), in which price expectations are unbounded, and derived its implications for price time series and empirical tests of price behavior. We present versions of the model that exhibit price behavior that could be characterized as "explosive" or "exuberant" with episodes of price runs that might be identified as "bubbles." In this model, conditional price expectations go to infinity as the horizon recedes, consistent with stationary behavior. This behavior is indistinguishable from that produced by a version of the standard model with bounded conditional price expectations, so a test to establish that price is unbounded is infeasible.

The stationary price process that we have examined reveals the importance of distinguishing any given profile of conditional price expectations from the path of price realizations. The rate of increase of any profile of conditional price expectations in our model is constant at the discount rate, while beyond some future period the path of realized prices lies permanently below the profile of expectations conditional on the current price. Returns on storage are returns consistent with "mean reversion" at sufficiently long holding periods, even though the long-run expectation of price is infinite.

Appendix

PROOF OF THEOREM 1: Consider the probability of the complement,

$$\text{Prob}[\delta^t p_{m+t} \geq \beta | p_m] = \text{Prob}\left[p_{m+t} \geq \frac{\beta}{\delta^t} | p_m\right] = \mu_t\left(\left[\frac{\beta}{\delta^t},\infty\right]\right),$$

where μ_t is the probability measure of the price at time $m + t$, conditional on p_m. Furthermore,

$$\mu_t\left(\left[\frac{\beta}{\delta^t},\infty\right]\right) \leq | \mu_t - \mu_* | + \mu_*\left(\left[\frac{\beta}{\delta^t},\infty\right]\right),$$

where μ_* is the invariant probability measure of the price process and $|\cdot|$ denotes the total variation norm.

The transition probability of the price process satisfies, with respect to the point ∞, what is called in Futia a generalized uniqueness criterion (Futia 1982, 390). In addition, the corresponding Markov operator L is stable and quasicompact (Theorems 4.6 and 4.10 in Futia [1982], 394, 397). Using Theorem 3.6 in Futia (1982, 390), and Theorem 4 in Yosida and Kakutani (1941, 200), we obtain the following conclusion: independent of p_m, there exists constants $M > 0$, $\eta > 0$, such that:

$$\| (L^*)^t - L_1^* \| \leq \frac{M}{(1 + \eta)^t} \qquad \forall \, t \in \mathbb{N},$$

where L^* is the adjoint of the Markov operator L, L_1^* is a continuous linear operator, the image of which consists precisely of the fixed points of L^*, and $\|\cdot\|$ is the operator norm. Therefore, if δ_{p_m} denotes the unit point mass at p_m, then:

$$| \mu_t - \mu_* | = |(L^*)^t(\delta_{p_m}) - L_1^*(\delta_{p_m})| \leq \|(L^*)^t - L_1^*\| \leq \frac{M}{(1 + \eta)^t} \; \forall \, t \in \mathbb{N}.$$

Finally, since μ_* has no atom at infinity, we have that $\lim_{t \to \infty} \mu_*(\beta/\delta^t,\infty) = 0$.
$$\text{Q.E.D.}$$

References

Bessembinder, H., J. F. Coughenour, P. J. Seguin, and M. Smaller. 1995. "Mean Reversion in Equilibrium Asset Prices." *Journal of Finance* 50 (1): 361–75.

Bobenrieth, E. S. A. 1996. "Commodity Prices Under Time-Heterogeneous Shocks Density." PhD diss.,University of California at Berkeley.

Bobenrieth, E. S. A., J. R. A. Bobenrieth, and B. D. Wright. 2002. "A Commodity Price Process with a Unique Continuous Invariant Distribution Having Infinite Mean." *Econometrica* 70:1213–19.

———. 2008. "A Foundation for the Solution of Consumption-Saving Behavior with a Borrowing Constraint and Unbounded Marginal Utility." *Journal of Economic Dynamics & Control* 32:695–708.

Brunnermeier, M. K. 2008. "Bubbles." In *New Palgrave Dictionary of Economics*, 2nd ed. Edited by S. Durlauf and L. Blume. New York: Palgrave Macmillan.

Cafiero, C., E. S. A. Bobenrieth, J. R. A. Bobenrieth, and B. D. Wright. 2011. "The Empirical Relevance of the Competitive Storage Model." *Journal of Econometrics* 162:44–54.

———. Forthcoming. "Maximum Likelihood Estimation of the Standard Commodity Storage Model: Evidence from Sugar Prices." *American Journal of Agricultural Economics*.

Davidson, J. 1994. *Stochastic Limit Theory*. Oxford: Oxford University Press.

Deaton, A. 2014. "Puzzles and Paradoxes: A Life in Applied Economics." In *Eminent Economists II*, edited by Michael Szenberg and Lall Ramrattan. Cambridge: Cambridge University Press.

Deaton, A., and G. Laroque. 1992. "On the Behaviour of Commodity Prices." *Review of Economic Studies* 59:1–23.

———. 1995. "Estimating a Nonlinear Rational Expectations Commodity Price Model with Unobservable State Variables." *Journal of Applied Econometrics* 10: S9–S40.

———. 1996. "Competitive Storage and Commodity Price Dynamics." *Journal of Political Economy* 104:896–923.

Futia, C. A. 1982. "Invariant Distributions and Limiting Behavior of Markovian Economic Models." *Econometrica* 50:377–408.

Gardner, B. L. 1979. *Optimal Stockpiling of Grain*. Lexington, MA: Lexington Books.

Gilbert, C. L. 2010. "Speculative Influences on Commodity Futures Prices 2006–2008." UNCTAD Discussion Paper no 197, United Nations Conference on Trade and Development.

Gustafson, R. L. 1958. "Carryover Levels for Grains." USDA Technical Bulletin no. 1178. Washington, DC: United States Department of Agriculture.

Gutierrez, L. 2012. "Speculative Bubbles in Agricultural Commodity Markets." *European Review of Agricultural Economics*. doi: 10.1093/erae/jbs017.

Martin, I. 2012. "On the Valuation of Long-Rated Assets." *Journal of Political Economy* 120 (2): 346–58.

Newbery, D. M., and J. E. Stiglitz. 1981. *The Theory of Commodity Price Stabilization: A Study in the Economics of Risk*. New York: Oxford University Press.

Phillips, P. C. B., Y. Wu, and J. Yu. 2011. "Explosive Behavior in the 1990s NASDAQ: When Did Exuberance Escalate Asset Values?" *International Economic Review* 162:44–54.

Piesse, J., and C. Thirtle. 2009. "Three Bubbles and a Panic: An Explanatory Review of Recent Food Commodity Price Events." *Food Policy* 34 (2): 119–29.

Samuelson, P. 1971. "Stochastic Speculative Price." *Proceedings of the National Academy of Sciences* 68:335–7.

Scheinkman, J. A., and J. Schechtman. 1983. "A Simple Competitive Model with Production and Storage." *Review of Economic Studies* 50:427–41.

Stokey, N. L., R. E. Lucas, Jr., with E. C. Prescott. 1989. *Recursive Methods in Economic Dynamics.* Cambridge, MA: Harvard University Press.

Timmer, C. P. 2009. "Did Speculation Affect World Rice Prices?" Working Paper prepared for the FAO "Rice Policies in Asia" conference, Chiang Mai, Thailand, February 9–12.

———. 2010. "Reflections on Food Crises Past." *Food Policy* 35 (1): 1–11.

Wright, B. D., and J. C. Williams. 1982. "The Economic Role of Commodity Storage." *Economic Journal* 92:596–614.

Yosida, K., and S. Kakutani. 1941. "Operator-Theoretical Treatment of Markoff's Process and Mean Ergodic Theorem." *Annals of Mathematics* 42:188–228.

Comment   Jock R. Anderson

This meeting has been fascinating for me, bringing together as it has many aspects of risk management that I have struggled with over the decades.[1] It has been long since I ventured into the field of staple grain price volatility per se, so the opportunity to react to this new chapter is welcome indeed.[2]

I have, longer than most because of my advantage of seeing him at work (and play) as an undergraduate, long been a great admirer of Brian Wright's work, and this occasion does not disappoint. This is an elegant, albeit rather mathematical piece, that serves a most useful purpose; to wit, substantiating the relevance of the standard model of storage roles in commodity markets.

Brian (Wright 2011, 37) speaks of "the remarkable work of Gustafson (1958)"; I think we should also acknowledge the remarkable work of Brian Davern Wright, who has taken the Gustafson conceptualization of storage and its economics to enviable heights. In the present and related work, Brian has been perspicacious in teaming up with the Chilean fraternity for this intriguing piece.

As best I can tell the mathematics is cogent and correct, albeit thankfully sparse; I leave it to others more able to judge to pronounce on this aspect. The approach is commendable; construct a parsimonious model that cap-

Jock R. Anderson is emeritus professor of agricultural economics at the University of New England, Armidale, Australia.

For acknowledgments, sources of research support, and disclosure of the author's material financial relationships, if any, please see http://www.nber.org/chapters/c12813.ack.

1. My modest efforts have included Anderson, Dillon, and Hardaker (1977), Hardaker, Huirne, and Anderson (1997), and Scandizzo, Hazell, and Anderson (1984) on dealing with agricultural risk management in general, and on unpredictable food price variability (volatility) more specifically in Anderson and Scandizzo (1984), and Anderson and Roumasset (1996).

2. For example, Quiggin and Anderson (1979, 1981), seemingly never cited by Brian Wright, perhaps because we rather dodged storage aspects per se.

tures the key elements of commodity storage decision making, manipulate it instructively, and produce model outcomes that reflect recent but controversial results about the nature of prices in important markets.

The use of rhyming slang in the titular "bubble trouble?" is ingeniously entertaining, although perhaps insufficiently pointed? Perhaps "bubble fuddle!" might more overtly address the misconceptions of those who have flirted with the fragile surface tension of these metaphorical temporary phenomena.

The standard model of storage economics, so insightfully exposited by Williams and Wright (1991), is thus elevated in relevance by this newest contribution of these dynamic programmers. As Wright (2011) observes, there is still much to be learned about the functioning of commodity markets, but this piece will help at the margins to guide those bent on their better understanding, and in this way hopefully better underpinning policy making in this domain. In Brian's case, this may mean he will resort more (a) to his own "atavistic tendency to pillory" (Wright 2011, 33) in exposing those who see speculative bubbles or "irrational exuberance" in price time-series data amenable to more conventional econometric interpretation, as well perhaps (b) to fostering better evidence-based policy in risky markets for food staples (e.g., World Bank [2012]), which seems remarkably aligned to Wright (2012).

To close, the authors have developed a simple and transparent model that yields informative insights to the stochastic characteristics of markets with storage. They have delivered the work in a neat and tidy (if nearly perfect) manner and we can thus be thankful for their job well done.

References

Anderson, J. R., J. L. Dillon, and J. B. Hardaker. 1977. *Agricultural Decision Analysis*. Ames: Iowa State University Press.

Anderson, J. R., and J. A. Roumasset. 1996. "Food Insecurity and Stochastic Aspects of Poverty." *Asian Journal of Agricultural Economics* 2 (1): 53–66.

Anderson, J. R., and P. L. Scandizzo. 1984. "Food Risk and the Poor." *Food Policy* 9 (1): 44–52.

Hardaker, J. B., R. B. M. Huirne, and J. R. Anderson. 1997. *Coping with Risk in Agriculture*. Wallingford, England: CAB International.

Quiggin, J. C., and J. R. Anderson. 1979. "Stabilization and Risk Reduction in Australian Agriculture." *Australian Journal of Agricultural Economics* 23 (3): 191–206.

———. 1981. "Price Bands and Buffer Funds." *Economic Record* 57 (156): 67–73.

Scandizzo, P. L., P. B. R. Hazell, and J. R. Anderson. 1984. *Risky Agricultural Markets: Price Forecasting and the Need for Intervention Policies*. Boulder: Westview.

Williams, J. C., and B. D. Wright. 1991. *Storage and Commodity Markets*. Cambridge: Cambridge University Press.

World Bank. 2012. *Responding to Higher and More Volatile World Food Prices*. Economic And Sector Work Report No. 68420-GLB. Washington, DC: Agriculture and Rural Development Department, IBRD. http://documents.worldbank.org/curated/en/2012/01/16355176/responding-higher-more-volatile-world-food-prices.

Wright, B. D. 2011. "The Economics of Grain Price Volatility." *Applied Economic Perspectives and Policy* 33 (1): 32–58.

———. 2012. "International Grain Reserves and other Instruments to Address Volatility in Grain Markets." *World Bank Research Observer* 27 (2): 222–60. http://www.wds.worldbank.org/servlet/WDSContentServer/WDSP/IB/2009/08/25/000158349_20090825154655/Rendered/PDF/WPS5028.pdf.

6

Bubbles, Food Prices, and Speculation
Evidence from the CFTC's Daily Large Trader Data Files

Nicole M. Aulerich, Scott H. Irwin, and Philip Garcia

The nature and cause of recent spikes in commodity prices is the subject of an acrimonious and worldwide debate. Hedge fund manager Michael W. Masters has led the charge that price spikes were driven in large part by a new type of speculator in commodity futures markets—financial index investors.[1] He has testified numerous times before the US Congress and

Nicole M. Aulerich is an associate at Cornerstone Research. Scott H. Irwin is the Laurence J. Norton Chair of Agricultural Marketing at the University of Illinois at Urbana-Champaign. Philip Garcia is the T. A. Hieronymus Distinguished Chair in Futures Markets at the University of Illinois at Urbana-Champaign.

We gratefully acknowledge the helpful discussions and comments provided by Dwight Sanders and Aaron Smith. We also received helpful comments at the 2009 NCCC-134 "Applied Commodity Price Analysis, Forecasting, and Market Risk Management" conference, the 2012 NBER "Economics of Food Price Volatility" conference, and seminars at the Commodity Futures Trading Commission (CFTC) and University of California, Berkeley. Jeff Harris, formerly chief economist of the CFTC, and Lin Hoffman, of the Economic Research Service of the US Department of Agriculture, provided invaluable assistance in obtaining access to the CFTC large trader data files used in this study. This material is based upon work supported by cooperative agreement with the Economic Research Service of the US Department of Agriculture under project no. 58 3000-8-0063. Any opinions, findings, conclusions, or recommendations expressed in this publication are those of the authors and do not necessarily reflect the view of the US Department of Agriculture or the US Commodity Futures Trading Commission. For acknowledgments, sources of research support, and disclosure of the authors' material financial relationships, if any, please see http://www.nber.org/chapters/c12814.ack.

1. Commodity index investments are packaged in a variety of forms but share a common goal—provide investors with long-only exposure to returns from an index of commodity prices. Investors may enter directly into over-the-counter (OTC) contracts with swap dealers to gain the desired exposure to returns from a particular index of commodity prices. Some firms also offer investment funds whose returns are tied to a commodity index. Exchange-traded funds (ETFs) and exchange-traded structured notes (ETNs) also have been developed that track commodity indexes. See Engelke and Yuen (2008), Stoll and Whaley (2010), and Irwin and Sanders (2011) for further details on commodity index investments.

US Commodity Futures Trading Commission (CFTC) (e.g., Masters 2008, 2009) with variations of the following argument:

> Institutional Investors, with nearly $30 trillion in assets under management, have decided en masse to embrace commodities futures as an investable asset class. In the last five years, they have poured hundreds of billions of dollars into the commodities futures markets, a large fraction of which has gone into energy futures. While individually these Investors are trying to do the right thing for their portfolios (and stakeholders), they are unaware that collectively they are having a massive impact on the futures markets that makes the Hunt brothers pale in comparison. In the last 4 1/2 years, assets allocated to commodity index replication trading strategies have grown from $13 billion in 2003 to $317 billion in July 2008. At the same time, the prices for the 25 commodities that make up these indices have risen by an average of over 200%. Today's commodities futures markets are excessively speculative, and the speculative position limits designed to protect the markets have been raised, or in some cases, eliminated. Congress must act to re-establish hard and fast position limits across all markets. (Masters and White 2008, 1)

In essence, Masters argues that unprecedented buying pressure from index investors created a massive bubble in commodity futures prices, and this bubble was transmitted to spot prices through arbitrage linkages between futures and spot prices. The end result was that commodity prices, crude oil in particular, far exceeded fundamental values. Irwin and Sanders (2012c) use the term "Masters Hypothesis" as a shorthand label for this argument.

Several well-known international organizations (e.g., Robles, Torero, and von Braun 2009; De Schutter 2010; Herman, Kelly, and Nash 2011; UNCTAD 2011) have been among the most ardent supporters of the Masters Hypothesis, arguing that financial index investors were one of the main drivers of spikes in food commodity prices that have occurred since 2007. Because consumers in less-developed countries devote a relatively high proportion of disposable income to food purchases, a sharp increase in the price of food is harmful to the health and well-being of large numbers of people. For example, Robert Zoellick, president of the World Bank Group, stated in February 2011 that, "Global food prices are rising to dangerous levels and threaten tens of millions of poor people around the world. The price hike is already pushing millions of people into poverty, and putting stress on the most vulnerable who spend more than half of their income on food" (WB 2011, n.p.). More directly, the US Senate's Permanent Subcommittee on Investigations (USS/PSI 2009) concluded that financial index investment in wheat, one of the most important food commodities in the world, constituted "excessive speculation" under the US Commodity Exchange Act. Food price spikes have also been recently linked to riots and political unrest (Bellemare 2012). In this environment it is not hard to understand why food prices have become such a high-priority issue in public policy debates (e.g., G20 2011).

   While there has been considerable discussion about the potential conceptual problems of the Masters Hypothesis and contradictory facts (e.g., Irwin, Sanders, and Merrin 2009; Pirrong 2010; Wright 2011; Dwyer, Holloway, and Wright 2012), it should be noted that financial index investment flows may cause market prices to deviate from fundamental values under certain theoretical conditions. Irwin and Sanders (2012c) posit the following conditions: (a) commodity futures markets may not be sufficiently liquid to absorb the large order flow-of-index investors; (b) financial index investors are in effect noise traders who make arbitrage risky, and this opens the possibility of index investors "creating their own space" if their positions are large enough (De Long et al. 1990); and (c) the large order flow-of-index investors on the long side of the market may be seen (erroneously) as a reflection of valuable private information about commodity price prospects, which has the effect of driving the futures price higher as other traders subsequently revise their own demands upward (Grossman 1986). Singleton (2011) notes that learning about economic fundamentals with heterogeneous information may induce excessive price volatility, drift in commodity prices, and a tendency toward booms and busts. He argues that under these conditions the flow of financial index investments into commodity markets may harm price discovery and social welfare.[2]

   A number of recent studies investigate whether an empirical relationship can be detected between financial index positions and price movements in agricultural futures markets.[3] One line of research uses time-series regression tests, such as Granger causality tests. Gilbert (2009) does not find evidence of

2. Several other recent papers develop theoretical models where financial index investment impacts the price of risk, or risk premiums, in commodity futures markets (Acharya, Lochstoer, and Ramadorai 2010; Etula 2010; Brunetti and Reiffen 2011; Hamilton and Wu 2011, 2012; Cheng, Kirilenko, and Xiong 2012). Irwin and Sanders (2012a) argue that it is important to contrast the "rational and beneficial" impact of index investment in these theoretical models, which has the net effect of reducing risk premiums and lowering the cost of hedging for traditional physical market participants, with the "irrational and harmful" impact of index investment under the Masters Hypothesis.

3. Some recent studies provide indirect tests of the relationship between financial index positions and agricultural futures prices. For example, Tang and Xiong (2010) conclude that index investing has an impact on commodity prices (agricultural and nonagricultural) based on a trend toward increasing comovement of futures prices for commodities included in popular investment indexes. In contrast, Buyuksahin and Robe (2011) report that index investment activity is not associated with the increasing correlation between commodity and stock returns. Janzen, Smith, and Carter (2012) find no evidence of increasing comovement between cotton and crude oil or metal prices after accounting for supply, demand, and inventory shocks specific to cotton. Some recent studies test for the existence of price bubbles in agricultural futures markets (Gilbert 2009; Phillips and Yu 2010; Adammer, Bohl, and Stephan 2011; Gutierrez 2011), with mixed results. See Fattouh, Kilian, and Mahadeva (2012) for a comprehensive review of studies on the impact of financial index investors, and speculation in general, in the crude oil market.

a significant time-series relationship between weekly financial index trading and returns in corn, soybeans, and wheat futures markets, but in subsequent work reports evidence of a significant relationship with an index of food price changes (Gilbert 2010) and returns in less liquid agricultural futures markets such as soybean oil, feeder cattle, live cattle, and lean hogs (Gilbert and Pfuderer 2012). Stoll and Whaley (2010) use a variety of tests, including Granger causality tests, and find no evidence that the weekly positions of financial index traders impact prices in twelve agricultural futures markets. Capelle-Blancard and Coulibaly (2011), Sanders and Irwin (2011a, b), and Hamilton and Wu (2012) report similar results for the same twelve agricultural futures markets. Brunetti, Buyuksahin, and Harris (2011) conduct a battery of Granger causality tests and do not find a statistical link between daily index positions and subsequent returns or volatility in the corn futures market.

Motivated by the observation that traditional time-series tests can be criticized for a lack of statistical power due to the large volatility of returns in commodity futures markets (Summers 1986), a second line of research uses cross-sectional regression tests. Sanders and Irwin (2010) find little evidence that the relative size of weekly financial index positions in twelve agricultural futures markets is correlated to subsequent returns across markets. Irwin and Sanders (2012c) conduct similar cross-sectional tests using quarterly data on financial index positions in nineteen agricultural, energy, and metals futures markets and report no evidence of a significant cross-sectional relationship with returns or volatility.

A third line of research investigates whether there is a significant relationship between financial index investor trading and the difference, or spread, between futures prices of different contract maturities. Stoll and Whaley (2010), Hamilton and Wu (2012), and Garcia, Irwin, and Smith (2012) conduct various time-series regression tests and do not find a systematic tendency for spreads in agricultural futures markets to increase or decrease over time as financial index positions increase. Irwin et al. (2011) conduct Granger causality tests and do not find a significant relationship between index positions and spreads in corn, soybean, and wheat futures markets; however, they do find that spreads increase during the narrow window when existing index positions are rolled from one nearby contract to the next, but the increase is temporary as spreads quickly return to the level prevailing before the roll window. Mou (2010) conducts several tests and concludes that the rolling of positions by index investors leads to a substantial expansion in spreads over time in livestock futures markets and a modest expansion in grain futures markets. Brunetti and Reiffen (2011) estimate a generalized autoregressive conditional heteroskedasticity (GARCH) model and report a negative relationship between index investor positions and spreads in corn, soybeans, and wheat futures markets.

The bulk of the studies reviewed above do not support the Masters Hypothesis in agricultural futures markets. Nonetheless, research to date is subject to important data limitations—as proponents of the Masters Hypothesis have duly noted.[4] First, public data on financial index positions in agricultural futures markets are only available weekly. This limitation on sample size likely reduces the power of time-series methods to detect index impacts. Weekly observations may also mask impacts that occur over shorter time intervals. Second, public data on index positions are not available prior to 2006. Previous research suggests financial index positions grew most rapidly during 2004 to 2005 (Sanders, Irwin, and Merrin 2010; Sanders and Irwin 2011b; Brunetti and Reiffen 2011) and excluding this time period may bias tests against finding an impact of index trading. Third, public data on index positions are aggregated across all futures contract maturity months, which does not allow changes in prices and positions to be matched precisely by contract maturity months. This limits the ability to evaluate market impact during the crucial period when index positions are "rolled" from one contract to the next.

The purpose of this chapter is to analyze the market impact of financial index investment in agricultural futures markets using nonpublic data from the Large Trader Reporting System (LTRS) maintained by the US Commodity Futures Trading Commission (CFTC). These data are not subject to the previously noted limitations since the nonpublic CFTC data files include financial index investor positions on a daily basis and positions are disaggregated by contract maturity. Furthermore, the data can be used to reliably estimate index trader positions before 2006 in order to capture the period of their most rapid position growth. Daily data from the LTRS are available for the January 2000 through September 2009 sample period.[5] The twelve agricultural futures markets included in the study are: corn, soybeans, soybean oil, and wheat traded at the Chicago Board of Trade (CBOT); wheat traded at the Kansas City Board of Trade (KCBOT); feeder cattle, lean hogs, and live cattle traded at the Chicago Mercantile Exchange (CME); and cocoa, cotton, coffee, and sugar traded at the Intercontinental Exchange (ICE). This is the first study to use the daily LTRS data files for all twelve agricultural futures markets included in the CFTC's Supplemental Commitments of Traders report.[6]

The empirical analysis considers index investor positions in terms of

---

4. For an example, see the letter "Swaps, Spots, and Bubbles" by Sir Richard Branson, Michael Masters, and David Frenk published in the July 29, 2010, issue of the *Economist* magazine (http://www.economist.com/node/16690679).

5. Data before January 2000 are not considered based on conversations with CFTC staff, who indicated that trader classifications in the LTRS are likely to be less accurate before this date.

6. Brunetti and Reiffen (2011) use daily LTRS data for the corn, soybean, and wheat futures markets and Brunetti, Buyuksahin, and Harris (2011) use daily LTRS data for the corn futures market.

aggregate new net flows into financial index investment and the *rolling of existing* index positions from one contract to another. Analysis based on the aggregate new net flows of index investor positions affords the most direct test of the Masters Hypothesis (i.e., a "wave" of financial index investment artificially inflated prices in agricultural futures markets) because aggregate positions represent the new investment decisions of financial index investors. Analysis based on the rolling of existing financial index positions is also important to consider because the size of index position changes in roll periods is substantially larger than the size of position changes in nonroll periods. Stoll and Whaley (2010) argue that roll-period tests are most likely to exhibit a price pressure effect due to the size of index position changes during these periods.

Bivariate Granger causality tests are used to investigate lead-lag dynamics between aggregate financial index trader positions and daily futures returns (price changes) or volatility in each agricultural futures market. Volatility tests are less directly related to the Masters Hypothesis but are included because some previous studies find that index trader positions and price volatility are negatively related (Sanders and Irwin 2011a; Irwin and Sanders 2012c). Following Capelle-Blancard and Coulibaly (2011) and Sanders and Irwin (2011a), seemingly unrelated regression (SUR) is used to estimate lead-lag dynamics. The SUR approach improves the power of statistical tests by taking into account the contemporaneous correlation of model residuals across markets and allows a test of the overall impact of index investment across markets. In addition, cross-market equality constraints are placed on parameters when appropriate, which should further improve the power of statistical tests. The sample for this analysis is limited to January 2004 to September 2009 since CIT trading activity is much smaller before this time period. A total of 1,147 daily observations are available over this sample period for each market, which should be more than adequate to efficiently estimate the type of time-series regression models considered here.

Bivariate Granger causality tests are also used to investigate lead-lag dynamics when the sample is limited to the roll window of index investors. Since index positions are concentrated in nearby contracts (closest to expiration) they must be "rolled" to the next nearest to expiration contract before the nearby contract expires. Previous studies typically assume that the roll window is the conventional five-day "Goldman roll." The disaggregated LTRS data allows a more accurate data-dependent roll period to be defined. Bivariate Granger causality tests are conducted in an SUR framework for the nearby and next nearby contracts during the defined roll window for each agricultural futures market. This allows estimation of separate price pressure effects as index investors simultaneously roll positions out of the nearby contract and into the next nearby contract. The large variation in positions of index investors during the roll window should make these statistical tests among the most powerful considered in this study.

6.1   CFTC Large Trader Reporting System

The CFTC Large Trader Reporting System (LTRS) is designed for surveillance purposes to detect and deter futures and options market manipulation (Fenton and Martinaitas 2005). Positions must be reported to the CFTC on a daily basis if they meet or exceed reporting levels. For example, the current reporting level in the corn futures contract is 250 contracts, or 1.25 million bushels. The LTRS database contains end-of-day reportable positions for long futures, short futures, long delta-adjusted options, and short delta-adjusted options[7] for each trader ID and contract maturity.[8] In recent years about 70 percent to 90 percent of open interest in commodity futures markets has been reported to the CFTC and included in the LTRS (CFTC 2012b).

A weekly snapshot of the LTRS data is compiled in aggregate form and released to the general public as the Commitment of Traders (COT) report. The COT pools traders into two broad categories (commercial and noncommercial), all contract maturities are aggregated into one open interest figure, and the report is released each Friday with the data as of the end-of-day on the preceding Tuesday (CFTC 2012a). The COT report covers over ninety US commodity markets and two versions are published: (a) the Futures-Only Commitments of Traders report that includes futures market open interest only, and (b) the Futures-and-Options-Combined Commitments of Traders report that includes futures market open interest and delta-weighted options market open interest.

In response to industry concerns regarding financial index positions, the CFTC changed the reporting system in 2007 by creating the Supplemental Commitment of Traders (SCOT) report. This report separates commodity index traders (CITs) from the original commercial and noncommercial COT categories (CFTC 2006).[9] The CFTC staff engaged in a detailed process to identify index traders in the LTRS for inclusion in the new category. The process included screening all traders with large long positions in commodity futures contracts, analyzing futures positions to determine a pattern consistent with index trading, reviewing line of business forms (form 40) to obtain more detailed information on their use of the market, and conducting an expansive series of phone and in-person interviews with traders. The CFTC does not distinguish index and nonindex positions in this process. So, if a trader is identified as an index trader, then all of their positions are counted as index positions. The first weekly SCOT report was published in January

---

7. Delta is the change in option price for a 1 percent change in the price of the underlying futures contract. Adjusting options positions by delta makes options positions comparable to futures positions in terms of price changes.

8. The data do not include positions of day traders or scalpers since these participants seldom carry positions overnight.

9. To be consistent with the terminology used by the CFTC, financial index investors will be referred to as commodity index traders (CITs) in the remainder of the chapter.

2007 and provided aggregate futures and delta-adjusted options positions of CITs in twelve agricultural futures markets: CBOT corn, soybeans, soybean oil, and wheat; KCBOT wheat; CME feeder cattle, lean hogs, and live cattle; and ICE cocoa, cotton, coffee, and sugar. The CIT category was computed retroactively back through 2006 to provide context for the initial release of the data in 2007.

The CFTC acknowledges that the classification procedure used to create the CIT category was imperfect and that, "Some traders assigned to this category are engaged in other futures activity that could not be disaggregated. As a result, the index traders category, which is typically made up of traders with long-only futures positions, will include some short futures positions where traders have multidimensional trading activities, the preponderance of which is index trading." (CFTC 2006, 10) Despite these limitations, Irwin and Sanders (2012c) show that aggregate CIT positions in agricultural futures markets are highly correlated with quarterly benchmark positions available from the CFTC since the end of 2007. This indicates measurement errors associated with aggregate CIT positions are likely rather small and supports the widespread view that CIT data provide valuable information about index trader activity in agricultural futures markets.[10]

As noted, CITs are drawn from the original commercial and noncommercial categories in the LTRS. The CITs from the commercial category are traders whose positions predominantly reflect hedging of OTC transactions associated with financial index investors seeking exposure to commodity prices following a standardized commodity index. The CITs from the noncommercial category are mostly managed funds, pension funds, and other institutional investors also seeking exposure to commodity price movements. Sanders, Irwin, and Merrin (2010) show that approximately 85 percent of index trader positions in the twelve SCOT markets are in fact drawn from the long commercial category, with the other 15 percent from the long noncommercial category. This implies that the bulk of index positions in the twelve SCOT markets are initially established in the OTC market and the underlying position is then transmitted to the futures market by swap dealers hedging OTC exposure.

---

10. The CFTC created another weekly report based on LRTS positions in 2009 called the Disaggregated Commitments of Traders (DCOT) report. Index trader positions in the DCOT report may be found in three of the four categories created for the report: swap dealers, managed money, and other reportables. While there is a moderately high correlation between swap dealer and CIT positions in agricultural futures markets across the DCOT and SCOT reports, Irwin and Sanders (2012c) show that aggregate CIT positions are more highly correlated with quarterly benchmark positions than those found in the DCOT. Irwin and Sanders (2012c) also show that the correlation between aggregate DCOT swap dealer positions and quarterly benchmark positions in energy and metals futures markets is low due to the active long and short nonindex swap trade and consequent internal netting of positions by swap dealers in these markets. This means that aggregate DCOT swap dealer positions in energy and metals futures markets likely mask the true size of index positions, and therefore represent a poor proxy for total index positions in these markets.

6.2   Commodity Index Trader Positions

Data on the positions of CITs are collected from the LTRS for the same twelve markets included in the weekly SCOT report over January 2000 through September 2009. In contrast to the weekly data on CIT positions made public in the SCOT report, CIT positions collected directly from the LTRS are reported on a daily basis, disaggregated by contract maturity month, and indicate if the position is in futures or options. The CIT classifications are applied retroactively from 2000 through 2005 to approximate CIT positions before the official CFTC index trader classifications that began in 2006. This assumes that traders classified as CITs over 2006 to 2009 also were CITs in previous periods. Discussions with CFTC staff indicate that CIT designations have changed little since the classification scheme was first implemented in 2006, which provides support for its retroactive application.[11]

The growth in CIT positions in commodity futures markets is pronounced during the 2000 to 2009 period. Table 6.1 provides a breakdown by year of the average daily net long open interest (long minus short contracts) held by CITs in the twelve markets. Note that CIT futures positions are aggregated across all contract maturities and options positions are excluded. Previous studies (Sanders, Irwin, and Merrin 2010; Sanders and Irwin 2011b; Brunetti and Reiffen 2011) have found that the most rapid period of growth in CIT positions in grain futures markets predated the 2007 to 2008 spike in prices and this general pattern is confirmed in table 6.1. There is a small base of positions in 2000 to 2003, rapid growth during 2004 to 2005, and then a leveling off or more modest growth during 2006 to 2009. For example, the net long position of CITs in CBOT wheat increased from an average of 25,702 contracts in 2003 to 134,408 contracts in 2005, over a fivefold increase. The rapid growth in CIT positions is also apparent in CBOT wheat as a percentage of total open interest (long), which increased from 25 percent to 55 percent over the same time frame. There were some exceptions to this pattern. Growth in CIT positions in feeder cattle, live cattle, coffee, and cocoa was more linear from 2000 to 2009.

While there is some variation in the pattern across markets, the averages in table 6.1 clearly reveal that CITs became large participants in commodity futures markets during a relatively short time frame. By 2009, the lowest

---

11. This assumption does not imply that the number of CIT traders is constant across the sample period. In fact, the number of CIT traders rises over time in parallel with the rise in aggregate CIT positions. For example, the number of CIT traders in corn increases from 7 in 2000 to 31 in 2008. Retroactive application of CIT classifications prior to 2006 could induce two types of misclassification error. First, CITs that traded between 2000 and 2005 but ceased operation sometime before 2006 would be excluded from the CIT category over 2000 to 2005. Second, traders classified as CITs over 2006 to 2008 would be incorrectly categorized as CITs over 2000 to 2006 if they changed their line of business at some point before 2006. Given the stability in CIT classifications over 2006 to 2008, the likelihood of either type of error is minimal.

Table 6.1   Average daily net futures positions of commodity index traders (CITs) in twelve agricultural futures markets, all contracts, 2000–2009

Market	Year									
	2000	2001	2002	2003	2004	2005	2006	2007	2008	2009
					A. Number of contracts					
Cocoa	2,208	1,447	1,892	2,612	11,549	7,483	13,272	17,534	23,612	16,195
Coffee	2,728	1,475	2,867	6,916	21,735	23,114	33,862	42,716	54,434	38,165
Cotton	4,967	4,009	5,579	7,863	16,132	38,696	71,430	87,229	95,249	65,637
Sugar	12,898	10,059	17,659	23,497	61,931	98,672	136,135	230,434	309,598	180,138
Feeder cattle	1	101	1,557	1,933	2,838	4,362	6,562	8,315	8,265	6,210
Lean hogs	7,858	6,479	8,654	10,546	26,801	43,871	76,923	80,275	100,138	56,472
Live cattle	22,360	12,779	12,067	13,941	33,118	52,931	86,152	112,310	128,549	90,465
Corn	28,732	30,217	48,209	53,656	117,364	233,142	393,954	357,482	358,979	289,860
Soybeans	6,509	4,920	9,563	28,279	36,692	76,884	114,591	147,449	143,982	122,437
Soybean oil	−122	1	949	1,402	10,773	38,030	65,801	72,351	68,371	54,855
Wheat CBOT	20,178	18,704	21,439	25,702	56,682	134,408	195,194	185,341	165,968	151,227
Wheat KCBOT	5,591	5,777	7,921	9,543	14,971	18,210	25,480	31,372	26,156	26,178

B. Percent of total open interest

Cocoa	2	1	3	11	6	10	12	16	14
Coffee	6	3	9	23	24	31	28	37	31
Cotton	8	6	10	20	37	45	41	43	52
Sugar	7	7	12	21	24	28	33	37	25
Feeder cattle	0	1	11	17	17	22	29	27	27
Lean hogs	16	15	25	34	43	48	44	47	42
Live cattle	18	11	13	29	35	38	45	48	42
Corn	7	7	13	19	33	32	28	29	34
Soybeans	4	3	12	16	28	31	29	33	32
Soybean oil	0	0	1	7	24	28	25	26	25
Wheat CBOT	15	14	25	37	55	45	46	48	49
Wheat KCBOT	8	8	16	22	20	18	24	26	29

Notes: Data for 2009 end on September 29, 2009. Positions of commodity index traders (CITs) are aggregated across all contract maturity months on a given day and exclude options positions.

CIT percentage of total market open interest was 14 percent (cocoa) and the highest was 52 percent (cotton). The average across all twelve markets in 2009 was 34 percent. Concerns about the price impacts of index funds are more understandable in light of the historic magnitude of this structural change in market participation (Irwin and Sanders 2012a).

Figure 6.1 provides daily detail on the growth of CIT positions for one of the most actively traded markets, the corn futures market.[12] Panel A displays the daily net long open interest in terms of number of contracts held by CIT traders for two categories: (a) nearby and first deferred corn contracts combined, and (b) all other deferred corn contracts combined. Panel B displays the percent of total CIT open interest in all other deferred corn contracts. Separating positions into these two categories highlights any changes in the maturity of futures contracts held by CITs.

Total CIT open interest in corn was at a moderate level, between 25,000 and 50,000 contracts through the end of 2003, and then increased rapidly starting in early 2004, with a peak of more than 425,000 contracts in July 2006. The CIT open interest leveled off and then declined thereafter in early 2009 with a subsequent rebound in late 2009. There is an increase in the importance of other deferred contracts starting in 2007, as reflected by the dark portion of panel A and the line in panel B. For example, about a quarter of CIT positions were held in longer maturity corn futures contracts in 2008. However, the magnitude of the increase in CIT activity for more distant contracts was less pronounced in several markets (soybean oil, feeder cattle, cocoa, coffee, and sugar).

Based on inspection of the data, other characteristics of CIT positions were identified. The CIT traders bypass certain cotton, lean hogs, soybeans, and soybean oil contract maturities, presumably due to trading or liquidity costs considerations. These contracts are excluded in the later statistical analysis of price impacts.[13] It was also determined that CITs do not trade actively in agricultural options markets. The proportion of combined futures and delta-adjusted options positions represented by options has increased modestly over time, but it is unusual for options to make up more than 5 percent of the total. As a result, only futures positions are used in the later statistical analysis. The CIT traders are also interconnected across markets; specifically, this data set contains forty-two unique index traders with thirty-three trading in ten or more markets and none trading in less than five.

---

12. The patterns in the corn market are representative of those identified in other markets except where identified in the text. Similar figures for the other commodities are available from the authors.

13. The CITs generally did not trade in the August and September soybean contracts, August, September, and October soybean oil contract, May lean-hog contract, or October cotton contract.

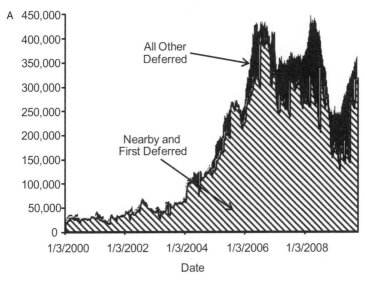

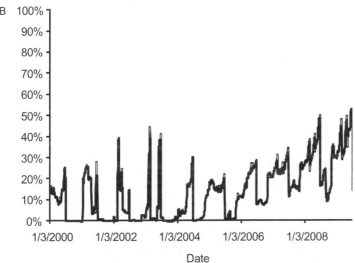

Fig. 6.1   Composition of daily net long open interest of commodity index traders (CITs) in the corn futures market, January 3, 2000–September 29, 2009: *A*, number of contracts; *B*, percent of position in all other deferred contracts.

6.3   Rolling of Commodity Index Trader Positions

Since commodity futures contracts have a limited life, CITs develop strategies to transfer (roll) long positions from an expiring contract to a later contract. The S&P GSCI Index™ is one of the most widely tracked indexes and the roll process for this index is described as follows:

> The rolling forward of the underlying futures contracts in the excess return index portfolio occurs once each month, on the fifth through ninth business days (the roll period). As explained above, some of the underlying commodity contracts expire in the next month and thus need to be rolled forward. The simplest way to think of the process is as rolling from one basket of nearby futures (the first nearby basket) to a basket of futures contracts that are further from expiration (the second nearby basket). The S&P GSCI™ is calculated as though these rolls occur at the end of each day during the roll period at the daily settlement prices.[14]

The implication is that CIT trading ebbs and flows in specific contracts, as positions shift from one maturity to another. The nearby contract carries the majority of the open interest and the deferred contracts constitute the remaining positions.

Figure 6.2 presents an example of this "ebbing and flowing" for the 2007 calendar year in the March, May, July, September, and December corn futures contracts. Each contract expires roughly in the third week of the expiration month. The top solid black line in panel A represents the net long open interest aggregated across all contracts each business day. Total position size of CITs in corn was about 400,000 contracts at the start of the year, quickly declined to about 350,000 contracts, and then varied little from that level over the remainder of 2007. The "hills" below the total line show the composition of CIT positions on each day and clearly illustrate the pattern of rolling positions from one contract to the next. Positions build up rapidly during the period when a contract is the nearest-to-maturity (nearby) and decline equally rapidly as the contract approaches expiration and positions are moved the next contract (first deferred) as shown in panel B. Note that the pattern is somewhat different for the December 2007 "new crop" contract, with positions being held at some level in this contract for almost the entire year. Panel C shows that the changes in the nearby and first deferred series are nearly mirror images.[15] Changes in the nearby are negative as traders exit this contract and changes in the deferred are positive as traders enter the next contract.

While the pattern of rolling positions from one contract maturity to the next is obvious in figure 6.2, the length of time that the roll period ordinarily

---

14. This material can be found at the following website: http://www2.goldmansachs.com /services/securities/products/sp-gsci-commodity-index/roll-period.html.
15. The simple correlation between the two series is −0.94.

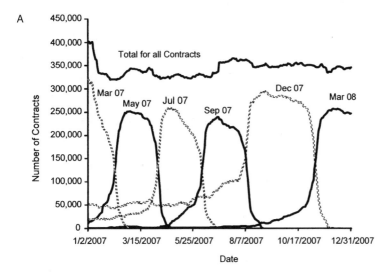

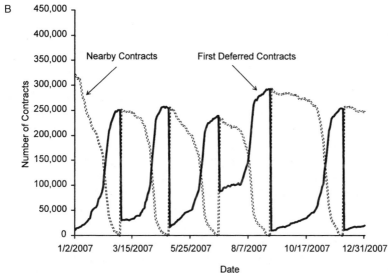

Fig. 6.2   Level and change in daily net long open interest of commodity index traders (CITs) in the corn futures market, January 2, 2007–December 31, 2007: *A*, total and contract-by-contract net long open interest; *B*, nearby and first deferred contract net long open interest; *C*, change in nearby and first deferred net long open interest.

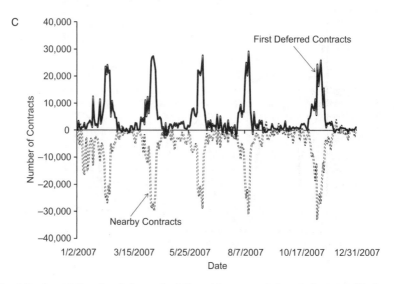

Fig. 6.2 (cont.) **Level and change in daily net long open interest of commodity index traders (CITs) in the corn futures market, January 2, 2007–December 31, 2007: *A*, total and contract-by-contract net long open interest; *B*, nearby and first deferred contract net long open interest; *C*, change in nearby and first deferred net long open interest.**

encompasses is less obvious. Previous studies (Mou 2010; Stoll and Whaley 2010; Irwin et al. 2011; Hamilton and Wu 2012) typically assume the roll window is equivalent to the so-called "Goldman roll" period, which as the previous quote indicates, spans the fifth through ninth business day in the calendar month before contract expiration.[16] The disaggregated LTRS positions allow us to determine if this is a reasonable assumption. As a starting point, figure 6.3 displays CIT positions in the December 2004 and December 2008 corn futures contracts for the twenty-five business days before the Goldman roll period and the ten business days after. The Goldman roll period coincides with the peak of rolling activity by CITs, but there is also substantial rolling of positions that occurs outside of the Goldman roll. In addition, there is a clear increase in the amount of rolling outside of the Goldman window when comparing 2008 to 2004; a pattern that holds for the other agricultural futures markets and is consistent with numerous accounts in the financial press of index traders expanding the time frame in which they roll to mask trades, seek greater liquidity, or capture advantageous spreads (e.g., Meyer and Cui 2009; Kemp 2010).

To determine a roll period that encompasses the bulk of CIT rolling activity, four different roll windows are considered: roll window number one

---

16. The study by Brunetti and Reiffen (2011) is an exception. They consider roll trades to be all position changes of CITs during the period that a contract is in the nearby position.

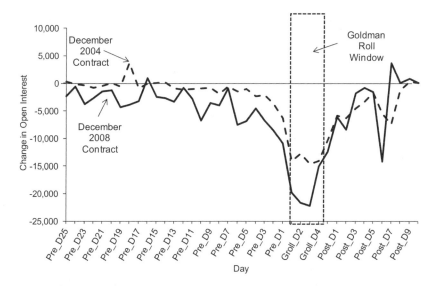

Fig. 6.3   Commodity index trader (CIT) change in open interest for the December 2004 and December 2008 corn futures contracts twenty-five days before and ten days after the Goldman roll window

begins on the first business day of the calendar month that falls two months before the contract expiration month and ends on the tenth business day of the month before expiration; roll window number two begins on the tenth business day of the calendar month that falls two months before the contract expiration month and ends on the tenth business day of the month before expiration; roll window number three begins on the first business day of the calendar month before the contract expiration month and ends on the tenth business day of the same month; and roll window number four begins on the fifth business day of the calendar month before the contract expiration month and ends on the ninth business day of the same month (Goldman roll window). A schematic of the alternative roll windows is presented in figure 6.4.

The percentage of total rolling activity in the four roll windows is presented in figure 6.5 for each year over 2004 to 2009. Total rolling activity is based on the sum of CIT position changes for the two calendar months prior to the expiration month. Note that annual averages for all markets and contracts are shown. Data before 2004 are not presented due to the relatively small amount of rolling activity in these years. The figure shows that roll number one and roll number two contain about 90 percent of total rolling activity with only a small downward trend over time. Roll number three averages about 75 percent and declines modestly across the sample period. Roll number four (the Goldman roll) contains approximately 65 percent of roll activity in 2004 but decreases to only about 50 percent in 2009, which corroborates the trends in figure 6.3. In sum, there is a clear danger of miss-

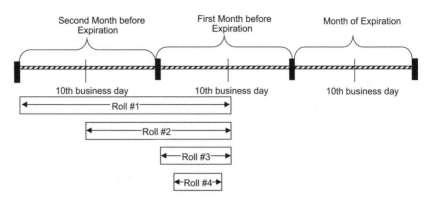

Fig. 6.4   Alternative roll windows for commodity index traders (CITs)

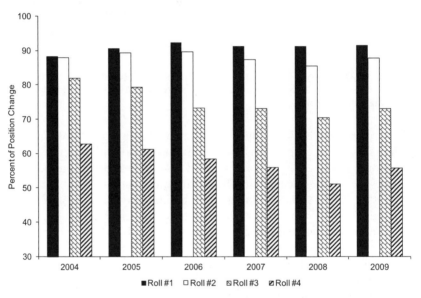

Fig. 6.5   Proportion of commodity index trader (CIT) roll activity in alternative roll windows in twelve agricultural futures markets, annual average across all markets and contracts, 2004–2009

Note: See text and figure 6.4 for definitions of roll windows.

ing a substantial part of CIT rolling activity by restricting attention to the Goldman roll window.

6.4   Granger Causality Tests of Aggregate CIT Positions and Returns or Volatility

Figure 6.2 highlights the relevance of considering CIT positions in terms of both the change in *aggregate new net flows* into index investment and the *rolling of existing* index positions from one contract to another. This follows Stoll and Whaley's (2010) argument that analyzing financial index investment in aggregate and by individual contract maturities is important.

The directional relationship between aggregate CIT positions and agricultural futures prices can be tested two ways. The first and more controversial relationship is the influence of aggregate CIT positions on price movements. This relationship is investigated to determine if the flow of CIT positions systematically precede changes in returns or volatility. This directly tests the Masters Hypothesis; that is, a "wave" of financial index investment artificially inflated prices and volatility in agricultural futures markets. Aggregate CIT investment flows are used to test these relationships because aggregate positions represent the new investment decisions of index traders. The second, and less debated, relationship is just the reverse—the influence of changes in agricultural futures prices on aggregate index positions. Note that both types of tests focus on the January 2004 through September 2009 period since CIT trading activity is limited before 2004.

6.4.1   Econometric Models

Granger causality tests are widely used to assess the relationships between two time series using lead-lag variables. These tests reflect the basic idea that if event x causes event y, then event x should precede event y in time. Several recent studies of index trader impacts in commodity futures markets use similar methods and specify commodity futures returns as a function of lagged returns and lagged measures of index trader participation (e.g., Gilbert 2009; Stoll and Whaley 2010; Brunetti, Buyuksahin, and Harris 2011; Sanders and Irwin 2011a, b; Hamilton and Wu 2012). As is well known, the results of Granger causality tests require careful interpretation. For example, the rejection of the null hypothesis of no Granger causality may not be reflective of a true causal relationship between x and y, but rather the omission of variable z that is the true cause of both x and y (Newbold 1982). Furthermore, the failure to reject the null hypothesis of no Granger causality between x and y is sufficient to imply the absence of "structural causality" only in the case of a linear system (Hoover 2001, 155). Despite these and other related issues, Hamilton (1994) argues that,

> Granger causality tests can be a useful tool for testing hypotheses that can be framed as statements about the predictability of a particular series. On the other hand, one may be skeptical about their utility as a general diagnostic for establishing the direction of causation between two arbitrary series. For this reason, its best to describe these as tests of whether y helps forecast x rather than tests of whether y causes x. The tests may have implications for the latter question, but only in conjunction with other assumptions. (308)

Since agricultural futures prices and CIT positions are not two arbitrary series but instead are posited to have a direct relationship under the Masters Hypothesis, Granger causality tests should be useful in detecting a relationship between the two series if one exists.

Equations (1) and (2) display the specification for Granger causality tests between returns or volatility, respectively, and aggregate CIT positions,

(1) $$R_{t,k} = \alpha_k + \sum_{i=1}^{m} \gamma_{i,k} R_{t-i,k} + \sum_{j=1}^{n} \beta_{j,k} X_{t-j,k} + \varepsilon_{t,k}$$

(2) $$V_{t,k} = \alpha_k + \sum_{i=1}^{m} \gamma_{i,k} V_{t-i,k} + \sum_{j=1}^{n} \beta_{j,k} X_{t-j,k} + M_{t,k} + v_{t,k},$$

where $R_{t,k}$ is the return $[R_{t,k} = (\ln P_{t,k} - \ln P_{t-1,k}) * 100]$ on day t in market k, $X_{t,k}$ is the change in the aggregate net long CIT position (long minus short contracts), $V_{t,k}$ is implied volatility, and $M_{t,k}$ is a set of monthly dummy variables to allow for changing seasonal volatility (these dummy variables are only used if significant). The null hypothesis of no CIT impact is that the slope coefficients, β_j, in equation (1) or equation (2) equal zero. An alternative consistent with a bubble-type impact and the Masters Hypothesis is that the $\beta_j > 0$, such that an increase in CIT positions portends relatively large subsequent returns or volatility.[17]

The nearby series for most futures markets is computed by rolling from the nearby contract to the first deferred contract on the last day of the month prior to the expiration month of the nearby contract, which is the convention in numerous previous studies. For instance, in February the nearest contract for corn is March. On the last business day in February the price series is rolled to May, the next nearest contract. Price and position changes are not calculated across contracts, so changes on a switching date correspond to the contract entering the series. Due to the nature of their contract expiration rules, cocoa, coffee, cotton, and sugar are rolled on the day following the fifteenth day of the month prior to the delivery month. Implied volatility is a widely accepted method of calculating forward-looking volatility (e.g., Hull 2000, 255). It is obtained from barchart.com and computed as the mean implied volatility of the two nearest-the-money calls and the two nearest-the-money puts for nearby contracts using the Black options pricing model.

A total of 1,147 daily observations over January 2004 to September 2009 are available for each of the twelve agricultural futures markets, which should be more than adequate for efficiently estimating the type of time-

---

17. This specification could be extended to include the positions of other types of traders in agricultural futures markets; for example, noncommercial and commercial market participants. Such a multivariate specification could potentially improve the power of the Granger causality tests since the tests would be conditioned on the dynamic interaction of multiple types of traders rather than index traders alone. Two previous studies conduct this type of multivariate analysis (Stoll and Whaley 2010; Brunetti, Buyuksahin, and Harris 2011) and do not find that conditioning on other traders' positions substantially alters Granger causality test results.

series regression models considered. For all variables, an augmented Dickey-Fuller test is used to test for stationarity. In every case, the test including a constant and trend rejects the null hypothesis of nonstationarity.[18] The lag structure, (m,n), for each market is determined by a search procedure over $m = 5$ and $n = 5$ and choosing the model that minimizes the Schwarz criteria to avoid overparmeterization (Enders 1995, 88).

Following Capelle-Blancard and Coulibaly (2011) and Sanders and Irwin (2011a), we increase the power of causality tests by modeling the K markets as a system. Since the error term in equation (1) or equation (2) is contemporaneously correlated across markets, the power of causality tests can be increased by applying Zellner's seemingly unrelated regression (SUR) framework (see Harvey 1991, 69). Efficiency gains over OLS estimates increase with the contemporaneous correlation between errors and with the number of equations. Except for the two studies noted above, previous research on the lead-lag relationship between CIT positions and commodity futures returns conducts tests on a market-by-market basis. This may result in a loss of statistical power because information on the correlation of the error term across markets is ignored.

To further increase statistical power, coefficients are restricted across market equations when appropriate (see Harvey 1991, 69). The strategy for selecting the restricted SUR model follows the sequential testing procedure outlined by Harvey (1991, 186) where the most general model is first estimated (no cross-market parameter restrictions). Then, using a Wald test, the hypothesis of equal parameter estimates is tested across markets. When the null of equal parameter estimates is not rejected, then the restriction is placed on the model. Specifically, all K models are first estimated as an SUR system using the lag structure chosen with the OLS search procedure. Then, for each estimated parameter the null hypothesis that the cross-equation parameters are equivalent is tested (e.g., $\gamma_{1,1} = \gamma_{1,2} = \ldots = \gamma_{1,K}$). If the null hypothesis is not rejected the parameter restriction is imposed resulting in a pooled estimate or single parameter across equations (e.g., γ_1.). By pooling parameters—when we fail to reject that they are equivalent—the number of parameter estimates is decreased and efficiency is further enhanced.

Bivariate causality in a single market, k, is tested under the null hypothesis in equation (1) or equation (2) that CIT positions cannot be used to predict (do not lead) market returns: $H_0 : \beta_{j,k} = 0$ for all j. A rejection of this null hypothesis, using an F-test of the stated restriction, provides direct evidence that CIT positions are indeed useful for forecasting returns or volatility in that market. In order to gauge the aggregate impact of CIT positions in a given market, the null hypothesis that $\sum_{j=1}^{n} \beta_{j,k} = 0$ in each k

---

18. Since nonstationarity tests have low power, Enders (1995) argues that rejection of the null with a constant and trend provides strong evidence that a series is stationary. Detailed results are available from the authors.

market reveals the cumulative directional impact of traders positions on returns or volatility. Clearly, in the event that the lag structure is $n = 1$ then the test of null hypothesis that $\sum_{j=1}^{n}\beta_{j,k} = 0$ is equivalent to a simple test on the parameter restriction that $\beta_{1,k} = 0$. Finally, the SUR estimation allows for the testing of system-wide causality, $H_0 : \beta_{j,k} = 0$ for all j and k, and for the systematic impact across all twelve agricultural futures markets, $\sum_{k=1}^{12}\sum_{j=1}^{n}\beta_{j,k} = 0$. This is an important improvement over a strictly market-by-market OLS approach to causality testing because it allows for broader statements about systematic impacts.[19]

Grosche (2012) and Gilbert and Pfuderer (2012) argue that hypothesis tests such as those outlined above should be viewed through the lens of informational efficiency. Specifically, the efficient-markets hypothesis (EMH) implies that prices reflect all available public information, and therefore, it is impossible at time t to forecast the price for any future period $t + k$ based on the public information set available at t (Fama 1970). Consequently, Grosche and Gilbert and Pfuderer indicate that it would be surprising to find that past CIT positions predict current returns in relatively efficient agricultural futures markets. A problem with applying this argument to the present study is that the disaggregated daily CIT positions from the LTRS are never released to the public. While it is true that an aggregate snapshot of LTRS positions is released in the CFTC's weekly COT report, the data for this report are compiled on Tuesday but not released to the public until the following Friday. Since the CIT positions from the LTRS, in either disaggregated or aggregated form, are not in the public domain on a given date, the informational efficiency issue raised by Grosche and Gilbert and Pfuderer is not applicable to the Granger causality regressions estimated in this study.

6.4.2   Aggregate CIT Positions Do Not Cause Returns or Volatility

Tests of the null hypothesis that aggregate CIT positions do not impact daily returns are reported in table 6.2. The second column presents the minimum BIC lag structure (m, n) and it is $(1, 1)$ for all commodities except live cattle and lean hogs. The cross-market restriction of equal intercept terms is imposed, while the remaining parameters are allowed to vary across markets. The third column presents the p-value for the test of the null hypothesis that aggregate CIT positions do not lead returns in each individual market, $\beta_{j,k} = 0 \,\forall\, j$. The null is rejected in three of the twelve markets (feeder cattle, lean hogs, and KCBOT wheat); however, in each of these cases the fourth column shows that the cumulative estimated impact $\sum_{j=1}^{n}\beta_j$ is negative. The fifth column reports the p-value associated with a test of the null hypothesis that the cumulative impact is zero for each market. When n

---

19. For comparison purposes we estimated equations (1) and (2) using ordinary least squares (OLS) market by market. In addition, we estimated the reverse causality versions of equations (1) and (2) using OLS market by market. The OLS estimation results, which are qualitatively similar to the SUR results presented in following sections, are reported in the appendix.

Table 6.2   **Granger causality test results for the null hypothesis that the change in aggregate commodity index trader (CIT) net position does not cause returns, January 2004 through September 2009**

$$R_{t,k} = \alpha_{t,k} + \sum_{i=1}^{m} \gamma_{i,k} R_{t-i,k} + \sum_{j=1}^{n} \beta_{j,k} X_{t-j,k} + \varepsilon_{t,k} \text{ for each market } k \text{ and time } t$$

Market, k	m, n	p-value $\beta_j = 0, \forall j$	Estimate $\Sigma \beta_j$	p-value $\Sigma \beta_j = 0$	One std. dev. impact
Cocoa	1, 1	0.512	0.00009		0.034
Coffee	1, 1	0.683	0.00005		0.021
Cotton	1, 1	0.563	−0.00004		−0.024
Sugar	1, 1	0.804	−0.00001		−0.023
Feeder cattle	1, 1	0.040*	−0.00029		−0.032
Lean hogs	2, 1	0.000*	−0.00017		−0.127
Live cattle	1, 2	0.890	0.00000	0.92	−0.002
Corn	1, 1	0.259	−0.00001		−0.027
Soybeans	1, 1	0.288	0.00003		0.032
Soybean oil	1, 1	0.258	−0.00004		−0.029
Wheat CBOT	1, 1	0.051	−0.00003		−0.042
Wheat KCBOT	1, 1	0.021*	−0.00011		−0.042

	p-value $\beta_{j,k} = 0, \forall j, k$	Estimate $\Sigma \Sigma \beta_{j,k}$	p-value $\Sigma \Sigma \beta_{j,k} = 0$
System	0.003*	−0.0005	0.036*

Notes: R is nearby return and X is change in aggregate CIT positions. The models are estimated across the K markets as a SUR system. The intercepts are estimated as a single-pooled parameter across all markets. The number of observations per commodity is 1,447.
*Statistically significant at the 5 percent level.

= 1 the cumulative test is redundant; this is the case for all commodities in table 6.2 except for live cattle. In order to assess the economic magnitude of estimated impacts, column six displays the one standard deviation cumulative impact of aggregate CIT positions on returns. In all cases, point estimates of the cumulative impact of a one standard deviation change in CIT positions on daily returns is very small, ranging from only −0.127 percent to 0.034 percent and averaging −0.022 percent.[20] In other words, a one-standard deviation increase in the aggregate net long position of CITs leads to a subsequent decline in daily futures prices averaging only about two basis points.

The system-wide tests at the bottom of table 6.2 show that the null of no CIT impact across all twelve markets is rejected despite the fact that significant impacts are found in three of the twelve individual market tests. The estimated cumulative system impact is negative, which again indicates

20. The average one standard deviation daily change in aggregate net-long CIT positions for the twelve markets is about 1,000 contracts, with corn (2,760) the largest and feeder cattle (109) the smallest.

that when CITs increase their aggregate position level agricultural futures prices subsequently decline. One interpretation of this result is that the large order flow of CITs temporarily pushes price above fundamental value, and since the impact is temporary, current CIT position changes and subsequent returns are negatively correlated. This is the classic problem of illiquidity arising from the asynchronous arrival of traders to the marketplace (Grossman and Miller 1988). This interpretation is also consistent with the results of a recent study by Henderson, Pearson, and Wang (2012), who find significant order flow impacts associated with the futures hedging trades of commodity-linked note issuers.

An alternative interpretation of the negative system impact is that CIT trading results in a repricing of risk in commodity futures markets. For example, Hamilton and Wu (2012) develop a theoretical model where the long "investment hedging" demand of index investors is met by short "arbitrageurs" in the futures market. The risk-averse arbitrageurs are compensated for taking on this risk by an embedded upward bias in futures prices before expiration. In this framework, the initiation of long positions by CITs drives the current futures price above the expected price at expiration. Futures prices then subsequently decline as expiration approaches to reward short arbitrageurs for providing risk transfer services to CITs—exactly the opposite direction of the bias predicted by the traditional Keynesian theory of risk premiums in commodity futures markets (e.g., Irwin and Sanders 2012b).[21] In the context of agricultural futures markets, this implies that physical market participants, such as farmers and grain merchants, are paid a positive risk premium for taking what have traditionally been regarded as short hedging positions.

Regardless of which one of the previous interpretations is ultimately correct, it is important to emphasize that the size of the estimated system impact, only about two basis points, is too small to be consistent with the Masters Hypothesis. Overall, the aggregate return test results are inconsistent with the claim that buying pressure from financial index investment in recent years caused a massive bubble in agricultural futures prices. In this sense the results are similar to the bulk of previous research on the issue.

Tests of the null hypothesis that CITs do not impact implied volatility are reported in table 6.3. The lag structure is (5,1) or (4,1) for all markets. The single lag of CIT positions is restricted to be equal across equations, and therefore, all p-values are equivalent. The null hypothesis is not rejected in any of the twelve markets and the estimated size of the cumulative impact is very small; on average, the estimated cumulative impact of a one standard

21. Hamilton and Wu (2012) do not find any significant evidence of a CIT-risk premium impact in the same twelve agricultural futures markets studied here. However, their empirical tests are based on the weekly data available publically from the CFTC. The small impact detected in our study may be due to the use of higher frequency daily data.

Table 6.3   **Granger causality test results for the null hypothesis that the change in aggregate commodity index trader (CIT) net position does not cause implied volatility, January 2004 through September 2009**

$$V_{t,k} = \alpha_{t,k} + \sum_{i=1}^{m} \gamma_{i,k} V_{t-i,k} + \sum_{j=1}^{n} \beta_{j,k} X_{t-j,k} + Dum + \varepsilon_{t,k} \text{ for each market } k \text{ and time } t$$

Market, k	m, n	p-value $\beta_j = 0, \forall j$	Estimate $\Sigma \beta_j$	p-value $\Sigma \beta_j = 0$	One std. dev. impact
Cocoa	5, 1	0.750	−0.000003		−0.001
Coffee	2, 1	0.750	−0.000003		−0.001
Cotton	5, 1	0.750	−0.000003		−0.002
Sugar	4, 1	0.750	−0.000003		−0.008
Feeder cattle	5, 1	0.750	−0.000003		−0.0004
Lean hogs	2, 1	0.750	−0.000003		−0.003
Live cattle	4, 1	0.750	−0.000003		−0.002
Corn	1, 1	0.750	−0.000003		−0.009
Soybeans	1, 1	0.750	−0.000003		−0.004
Soybean oil	3, 1	0.750	−0.000003		−0.002
Wheat CBOT	3, 1	0.750	−0.000003		−0.005
Wheat KCBOT	4, 1	0.750	−0.000003		−0.001

	p-value $\beta_{j,k} = 0, \forall j, k$	Estimate $\Sigma\Sigma \beta_{j,k}$	p-value $\Sigma\Sigma \beta_{j,k} = 0$
System	0.750	−0.000003	0.750

Notes: V is nearby implied volatility and X is change in aggregate CIT positions. The models are estimated across the K markets as a SUR system. Dummy variables for months are used. Coefficients for the first lag of CIT positions and May through October dummy variables are estimated as a single-pooled parameter across all markets. The number of observations per commodity is 1,447.

deviation change in CIT positions on implied volatility is a miniscule −0.003 percent, less than one basis point. Not surprisingly, the system-wide test is also insignificant. While the direction of the volatility impact estimated here is consistent with the evidence in previous studies (Brunetti, Buyuksahin, and Harris 2011; Sanders and Irwin 2011a; Irwin and Sanders 2012c), the magnitude is much smaller. It is not clear whether this is due to differences in sample periods, data sources for CIT positions, or frequency of observations (e.g., daily vs. weekly).

We conducted two robustness checks for the tests reported in this section. First, we conducted a parallel set of Granger causality tests using the percentage change in aggregate net long CIT positions. Results are qualitatively similar to those reported in the text using changes in the number of contracts. We also tested an alternative measure of volatility—Parkinson's (1980) high-low estimator. Again, similar results were found to those based on implied volatility. These additional results are available from the authors on request.

6.4.3   Returns or Volatility Do Not Cause Aggregate CIT Positions

The previous section examined the influence of aggregate index positions on prices and volatility; this section investigates the reverse relationship—the influence of returns or volatility on aggregate index positions. The same SUR framework is used to estimate the reverse-causality regressions, except now the dependent variable in equations (1) and (2) is the change in CIT positions. Table 6.4 presents the reverse-causality regression results for returns and CIT positions. The minimum Bayesian information criterion (BIC) lag structure (m, n) ranges from one to five for m and from one to four for n. The null hypothesis that returns do not lead positions is rejected at the 5 percent level for eight of the twelve markets. All cumulative impacts are positive. For example, a one standard deviation increase in returns of 1.5 percent in lean hogs increases CIT positions by approximately thirty-six contracts, a relatively small increase in positions. The system-wide tests at the bottom of the table indicate a highly significant impact of returns across all twelve markets, but the magnitude is still relatively small.

Table 6.4   **Granger causality test results for the null hypothesis that the change in returns does not cause the change in aggregate commodity index trader (CIT) net position, January 2004 through September 2009**

$$X_{t,k} = \alpha_{t,k} + \sum_{i=1}^{m} \gamma_{i,k} R_{t-i,k} + \sum_{j=1}^{n} \beta_{j,k} X_{t-j,k} + \varepsilon_{t,k} \text{ for each market } k \text{ and time } t$$

Market, k	m, n	p-value $\gamma_i = 0, \forall i$	Estimate $\sum \gamma_i$	p-value $\sum \gamma_j = 0$	One std. dev. impact
Cocoa	5, 2	0.053	18.14	0.080	37
Coffee	1, 2	0.053	9.84		20
Cotton	1, 4	0.028*	16.51		31
Sugar	1, 2	0.219	33.34		68
Feeder cattle	1, 2	0.425	2.32		2
Lean hogs	1, 3	0.016*	24.27		36
Live cattle	1, 3	0.024*	30.94		31
Corn	1, 3	0.000*	132.13		266
Soybeans	2, 2	0.000*	117.69	0.000*	220
Soybean oil	1, 3	0.023*	21.43		40
Wheat CBOT	1, 3	0.000*	62.66		138
Wheat KCBOT	1, 1	0.004*	14.34		29

		p-value $\gamma_{i,k} = 0, \forall i, k$	Estimate $\sum\sum \gamma_{i,k}$	p-value $\sum\sum \gamma_{i,k} = 0$	
System		0.000*	483.61	0.000*	

Notes: R is nearby return and X is change in aggregate CIT positions. The models are estimated across the K markets as a SUR system. Intercepts and coefficients for the third lag of CIT positions are estimated as a single-pooled parameter across all markets. The number of observations per commodity is 1,447.

*Statistically significant at the 5 percent level.

Table 6.5   Granger causality test results for the null hypothesis that implied volatility does not cause the change in aggregate commodity index trader (CIT) net position, January 2004 through September 2009

$$X_{t,k} = \alpha_{t,k} + \sum_{i=1}^{m} \gamma_{i,k} V_{t-i,k} + \sum_{j=1}^{n} \beta_{j,k} X_{t-j,k} + Dum + \varepsilon_{t,k} \text{ for each market } k \text{ and time } t$$

Market, k	m, n	p-value $\gamma_i = 0, \forall i$	Estimate $\Sigma \gamma_i$	p-value $\Sigma \gamma_j = 0$	One std. dev. impact
Cocoa	5, 2	0.000*	−2.28	0.054	−19
Coffee	3, 3	0.313	−1.87	0.249	−12
Cotton	1, 4	0.040*	−3.79		−30
Sugar	1, 2	0.004*	−21.08		−161
Feeder cattle	1, 2	0.131	1.19		6
Lean hogs	1, 2	0.817	0.20		3
Live cattle	1, 3	0.134	−4.71		−21
Corn	5, 3	0.000*	−4.86	0.480	−42
Soybeans	1, 1	0.145	−4.46		−36
Soybean oil	1, 3	0.181	−4.03		−24
Wheat CBOT	2, 1	0.000*	−9.52	0.009*	−86
Wheat KCBOT	1, 1	0.683	0.50		4

	p-value $\gamma_{i,k} = 0, \forall i, k$	Estimate $\Sigma\Sigma \gamma_{i,k}$	p-value $\Sigma\Sigma \gamma_{i,k} = 0$
System	0.000*	−48.94	0.000*

Notes: V is nearby implied volatility and X is change in aggregate CIT positions. The models are estimated across the K markets as a SUR system. Dummy variables for months are used. Coefficients for the third lag of CIT positions and the fifth lag of implied volatility are estimated as a single-pooled parameter across all markets. The number of observations per commodity is 1,447.
*Statistically significant at the 5 percent level.

Table 6.5 presents the reverse-causality regression results for implied volatility and CIT positions. The null hypothesis that implied volatility does not impact changes in CIT net positions is rejected in five of the twelve markets at the 5 percent level and the cumulative impact in each of these five markets is negative. For example in cocoa, a one standard deviation increase in implied volatility of 8.2 percent leads to a nineteen-contract decrease in CIT positions. The overall system coefficient is also negative and significant, but again the magnitude of the impact is very small.

In sum, index positions have a small but positive relationship to past price movements indicating a trend-following component to net financial index investment flows into agricultural futures markets. Furthermore, index positions have a weak but inverse relationship to price volatility. The combined findings on returns and volatility show that CITs have a tendency to increase aggregate positions when they perceive a clear upward trend in prices as compared to choppy market conditions. This provides the first evidence that index investors are not solely passive buy-and-hold investors, but are to some degree price-sensitive trend followers, similar to more traditional speculators in agricultural futures markets (Bryant, Bessler, and Haigh 2006; Sanders, Irwin, and Merrin 2009).[22] The results challenge the view that index investors should not be classified as speculators due to the "pure" diversification motive underlying their trading (Stoll and Whaley 2010).

6.5   Granger Causality Tests of Roll Period CIT Positions and Returns or Volatility

In the previous section, aggregate *new net flows* of index investment into agricultural futures markets were not found to impact subsequent daily returns or volatility in agricultural futures markets. This is not entirely surprising since the average standard deviation of daily changes in aggregate CIT positions across the twelve markets is only approximately 1,000 contracts. In contrast, the vast majority of *existing* index positions must be rolled from one futures contract maturity to another before expiration. This is clearly illustrated in figure 6.2 for the corn market. Recall for 2007, the aggregate position is quite stable around 350,000 contracts for most of the year (top black line), but this entire position must be rolled every few months from one contract to another (lower lines). As Stoll and Whaley (2010) point out, if index investment does impact market prices it may be more likely to do so in the roll period because the size of index position changes during the roll period dwarfs the size of changes in nonroll periods.

6.5.1   Econometric Models

Similar to the analysis of aggregate index investment impacts, bivariate Granger causality regression is used to analyze lead/lag dynamics between CIT positions and returns during roll periods. Because the rolling of positions is essentially the simultaneous selling of positions in the nearby contract and buying of positions in the first deferred contract (see the bottom panel in figure 6.2), regressions are specified separately for each contract series in a given market as follows:

$$(3) \qquad NR_t = \alpha + \sum_{i=1}^{m} \gamma_i NR_{t-i} + \sum_{j=1}^{n} \beta_j NX_{t-j} + \varepsilon_t$$

$$(4) \qquad DR_t = \alpha + \sum_{i=1}^{m} \gamma_i DR_{t-i} + \sum_{j=1}^{n} \beta_j DX_{t-j} + \varepsilon_t,$$

22. A possible confounding factor is the behavior of swap dealers who manage the bulk of CIT positions in agricultural futures markets. It is possible that index investors have "pure" diversification motives but swap dealers manage the hedging positions in futures markets in an active manner. In other words, swap dealers may not mechanically hedge swap positions in futures but instead engage in a "selective hedging" strategy in an effort to enhance the total profits of their book of swap business. If this is the case, then the trend-following component detected in CIT positions should be attributed to swap dealer behavior, not the underlying index investors.

where NR_t is the return for day t in the nearby contract during the roll period, NX_{t-j} is the change in CIT positions for day $t-j$ in the nearby contract during the roll period, DR_t is the return for day t in the first deferred contract during the roll period, and DX_{t-j} is the change in CIT positions for day $t-j$ in the first deferred contract during the roll period. This specification allows estimation of separate price pressure effects as index investors simultaneously roll positions out of the nearby contract and into the first deferred contract. Most previous studies have restricted the estimates of price pressure effects to be the same for the two contract series (Mou 2010; Stoll and Whaley 2010; Brunetti and Reiffen 2011; Garcia, Irwin, and Smith 2011; Irwin et al. 2011). In contrast, we test whether this restriction is consistent with the data before imposing it in the estimation. Equations (3) and (4) are estimated as a SUR system using the same procedure described earlier except that instead of a system across markets, the system is estimated for the two regressions for each individual market. The large variation in CIT positions during the roll window should make these statistical tests among the most powerful considered in this study.

Our prior analysis shows that a substantial part of CIT rolling activity may be omitted if attention is restricted to the conventional Goldman roll window. Instead, we define the roll window to begin on the tenth business day of the calendar month that falls two months before the contract expiration month and ends on the tenth business day of the month before expiration (figure 6.4, roll period number two). For example, the March 2008 contract maturity roll period spans mid-January 2008 to mid-February 2008. This window consistently includes approximately 90 percent of CIT rolling activity in agricultural futures markets. Note that nonroll days are not included in the analysis; although, lags that occur prior to the defined roll period may be included as explanatory variables. However, no observations are lagged across roll period windows.[23]

Interpretation of the β coefficients in equations (3) and (4) must be done with care. Specifically, if CIT rolling activity impacts returns in the nearby contract as CITs roll out this would be in the form of decreasing returns due to selling pressure (negative position changes). Conversely, the impact in the first deferred contract would be in the form of increasing returns due to buying pressure (positive position changes). In both situations the relationship between CIT position changes and returns is positive, and therefore, implies positive β coefficients. Note that the β coefficients can also be used to infer index investment impact on the spread between the nearby and first deferred contract. Assuming the nearby price is lower than the deferred price

---

23. To clarify, the variables are lagged prior to removing the days outside the roll window. For example, returns on day t may be the independent variable and lag of positions on day $t-1$ may be the explanatory variable. If t is the first day of the roll period, then $t-1$ positions would not be in the roll period. In this estimation $t-1$ positions are still used in the estimation as the roll period definition is only applied to the independent variable t.

(i.e., the market is normally in a state of contango), then the spread between the two contracts increases if nearby prices decrease and/or first deferred prices increase during the roll window.

In addition to testing returns, SUR systems are also specified to estimate lead/lag dynamics between CIT positions and implied volatility in a given market,

$$(5) \qquad NV_t = \alpha + \sum_{i=1}^{m} \gamma_i NV_{t-i} + \sum_{j=1}^{n} \beta_j NX_{t-j} + \varepsilon_t$$

$$(6) \qquad DV_t = \alpha + \sum_{i=1}^{m} \gamma_i DV_{t-i} + \sum_{j=1}^{n} \beta_j DX_{t-j} + \varepsilon_t.$$

where NV_t is implied volatility on day t for the nearby contract, DV_t is implied volatility on day t for the first deferred futures contract, and other variables are as defined above.

Roll Period CIT Positions Do Not Cause Returns or Volatility

Tests of the null hypothesis that CIT position changes do not impact returns during roll windows are reported in table 6.6. The minimum BIC

Table 6.6   Granger causality test results for the null hypothesis that the change in aggregate commodity index trader (CIT) net position does not cause returns during roll windows, January 2004 through September 2009

$$NR_t = \alpha_t + \sum_{i=1}^{m} \gamma_i NR_{t-i} + \sum_{j=1}^{n} \beta_j NX_{t-j} + \varepsilon_t \qquad\qquad DR_t = \alpha_t + \sum_{i=1}^{m} \gamma_i DR_{t-i} + \sum_{j=1}^{n} \beta_j DX_{t-j} + \varepsilon_t$$

Market, k	m, n	p-value $\beta_j = 0, \forall j$	Estimate $\Sigma \beta_j$	p-value $\Sigma \beta_j = 0$	One std. dev. nearby impact	One std. dev. deferred impact
Cocoa	1, 5	0.000*	−0.000026	0.143	−0.02	−0.02
Coffee	1, 5	0.857	−0.000005	0.196	−0.01	−0.01
Cotton	1, 1	0.000*	−0.000044	0.000*	−0.10	−0.10
Sugar	1, 4	0.490	−0.000003	0.157	−0.02	−0.02
Feeder cattle	1, 1	0.069	−0.000022	0.069	−0.01	−0.01
Lean hogs	1, 1	0.002*	−0.000013	0.002*	−0.04	−0.04
Live cattle	1, 1	0.001*	−0.000007	0.001*	−0.02	−0.02
Corn	1, 5	0.633	−0.000002	0.089	−0.02	−0.02
Soybeans	2, 1	0.704	−0.000001	0.704	0.00	0.00
Soybean oil	1, 1	0.560	−0.000001	0.560	0.00	0.00
Wheat CBOT	1, 5	0.088	−0.000004	0.037*	−0.02	−0.02
Wheat KCBOT	1, 4	0.001*	−0.000035	0.017*	−0.03	−0.03

Notes: NR is nearby return, DR is first deferred return, NX is nearby change in CIT positions, DX is first deferred change in CIT positions, NX is the change in nearby CIT positions, and DX is the first deferred change in CIT positions. The models are estimated across the two contract maturities for each market as a SUR system. Observations vary by commodity due to differences in the number of maturing contracts, but each commodity has approximately 630 observations.
*Statistically significant at the 5 percent level.

lag structure (m, n) ranges from one to two for m and one to five for n. The hypothesis that coefficients on lagged CIT position changes are the same for the nearby and first deferred contract regressions was rejected only for the cotton market. Therefore, the restriction that the coefficients are the same was imposed in the estimation for the other eleven markets. Note that p-values and cumulative coefficient estimates are based on system tests for the two regression equations for each market. Specifically, the p-values reported in the third column apply to the null hypothesis that CIT position changes during the roll window do not impact returns in both the nearby and first deferred regressions. This joint null hypothesis is rejected at the 5 percent level in five of the twelve markets. Estimated cumulative impacts are negative in all twelve markets, the opposite of the expected outcome if CIT rolling activity pressures nearby prices downward and first deferred prices upward. For example, a one standard deviation decrease in nearby CIT positions in cotton increases nearby returns by 0.10 percent; likewise, a simultaneous one standard deviation increase in deferred CIT positions in cotton decreases deferred returns by –0.10 percent. This in effect narrows the spread between the nearby and first deferred contract by 0.20 percent, or almost twenty basis points, assuming the nearby price is lower than the deferred price (i.e., the market is normally in a state of contango). Significant cumulative impacts are found in five markets: cocoa, cotton, lean hogs, live cattle, and KCBOT wheat. It is interesting to note that these five markets represent either nonstorable commodities (lean hogs, live cattle) or relatively low volume agricultural futures markets (cocoa, cotton, KCBOT wheat). These markets historically have had limited participation by commercial hedgers and/or poor liquidity, and therefore, would be most likely to benefit by the additional trading activity and liquidity associated with index investors.

The results reported in table 6.6 imply that CIT positions contribute, on average, to narrowing spreads between agricultural futures contracts and contrast with the findings in previous studies that CIT positions either have no impact on spreads (Stoll and Whaley 2010; Garcia, Irwin, and Smith 2011; Irwin et al. 2011; Hamilton and Wu 2012), or increase spreads (Mou 2011). The one other study that reports a negative relationship is Brunetti and Reiffen (2011), which is, interestingly, the only other study of spreads that used LTRS data on CIT positions. Since the LTRS data contains daily CIT positions by maturity month, this should presumably allow more accurate estimation of spread impacts than weekly tests based on aggregate CIT positions or tests based on alternative position estimation approaches.[24]

Brunetti and Reiffen (2011) argue that the narrowing of spreads associated with increasing CIT positions can be explained by the impact index investment has on risk premiums. Specifically, index investment increases the

---

24. Mou (2010) uses a yearly estimate of CIT investment divided by average market value.

supply of market risk-bearing capacity and lowers the overall cost of hedging. Since CIT positions are concentrated in near maturity contracts, spreads narrow due to the larger impact on the risk premium for near contracts relative to deferred contracts. Another possibility is a "sunshine trading effect" (Admati and Pfleiderer 1991), where the credible preannouncement that a trade is not based on private information changes the nature of informational asymmetries in the market. This preannouncement can have the effect of coordinating the supply and demand of liquidity in the market and reducing the trading costs of those who preannounce such trades. While our work shows that the rolling activity of CITs occurs over a wider window than the narrow five-day Goldman roll, it is nonetheless true that the majority of CIT rolling occurs in this narrow window using preannounced and mechanical rules for rolling positions. Hence, it is plausible that the net effect of the rolling of CIT positions is to narrow spreads. This is also consistent with the findings of a recent study by Bessembinder et al. (2012), who report that roll trades by exchange-traded funds (ETFs) in the crude oil futures market are associated with narrower bid-ask spreads, greater market depth, and a larger number of traders providing liquidity services on roll versus nonroll dates.

Tests of the null hypothesis that CIT position changes do not impact implied volatility during roll windows are reported in table 6.7. If CITs impact realized volatility during the roll period, then both the nearby and deferred contracts are expected to exhibit increases in volatility as index traders rolling causes rapid fluctuations in prices due to their trading activity.[25] Note that under this scenario β coefficients in equation (5) for the nearby contract would be negative and β coefficients in equation (6) for the deferred contract would be positive. The hypothesis that coefficients on lagged CIT position changes are the same for the nearby and first deferred contract regressions was rejected only for the cocoa market. Therefore, the restriction that the coefficients are the same was imposed in the estimation for the other eleven markets.

The results in table 6.7 indicate the null hypothesis of no impact on implied volatility is rejected for only two of the twelve markets (cocoa and feeder cattle). Cumulative impacts are positive for nine of the twelve markets. However, one must examine the one standard deviation impact to disentangle the signs for the nearby and deferred contracts. Here we see that nearby coefficients generally are all positive, implying that CITs exiting the nearby contract tend to reduce implied volatility; whereas, just the opposite result is found for the first deferred contract. For both the nearby and first deferred contracts the magnitude of the impact on implied volatility is very small. As an example, a one standard deviation decrease in nearby CIT positions

---

25. This is slightly different than examining volatility when aggregate CIT positions are the explanatory variable. In this short roll period, the transfer of open interest from the nearby to first deferred would be expected to increase volatility in both contracts.

Table 6.7   **Granger causality test results for the null hypothesis that the change in aggregate commodity index trader (CIT) net position does not cause implied volatility during roll windows, January 2004 through September 2009**

$$NV_t = \alpha_t + \sum_{i=1}^{m} \gamma_i NV_{t-i} + \sum_{j=1}^{n} \beta_j NX_{t-j} + \varepsilon_t \qquad DV_t = \alpha_t + \sum_{i=1}^{m} \gamma_i DV_{t-i} + \sum_{j=1}^{n} \beta_j DX_{t-j} + \varepsilon_t$$

Market, k	m, n	p-value $\beta_j = 0, \forall j$	Estimate $\Sigma \beta_j$	p-value $\Sigma \beta_j = 0$	One std. dev. nearby impact	One std. dev. deferred impact
Cocoa	1, 1	0.002*	0.000393	0.000*	0.33	0.29
Coffee	1, 1	0.749	−0.000008	0.749	−0.01	−0.01
Cotton	1, 1	0.789	−0.000003	0.789	−0.01	−0.01
Sugar	1, 1	0.423	0.000004	0.423	0.03	0.03
Feeder cattle	1, 1	0.014*	0.000093	0.014*	0.03	0.03
Lean hogs	1, 1	0.393	0.000014	0.393	0.04	0.04
Live cattle	1, 1	0.224	0.000006	0.224	0.02	0.02
Corn	1, 1	0.959	0.000000	0.959	0.00	0.00
Soybeans	2, 1	0.717	0.000002	0.717	0.01	0.01
Soybean oil	1, 1	0.759	−0.000005	0.759	−0.01	−0.01
Wheat CBOT	2, 1	0.927	0.000000	0.927	0.00	0.00
Wheat KCBOT	1, 1	0.076	0.000048	0.076	0.05	0.04

Notes: NV is nearby implied volatility, DV is first deferred implied volatility, NX is nearby change in CIT positions, DX is first deferred change in CIT positions, NX is the change in nearby CIT positions, and DX is the first deferred change in CIT positions. The models are estimated across the two contract maturities for each market as a SUR system. Observations vary by commodity due to differences in the number of maturing contracts, but each commodity has approximately 630 observations.
*Statistically significant at the 5 percent level.

in soybeans increases nearby and first deferred implied volatility just 0.01 percent, or one basis point. The only market with a notable impact is cocoa, where the one standard deviation impact in both series is about 0.30 percent. Overall, the evidence suggests that the impact of CIT position changes on implied volatility during roll periods is negligible.

We conducted several robustness checks for the roll period tests reported in this section. The first is motivated by the argument that CITs do not make decisions during the roll period based on expectations of future returns, which would make positions and prices exogenous. For this reason, equations (3) and (4) were also estimated without lagging CIT positions, that is, $j = 0$ instead of $j = 1$. The results were qualitatively similar to the results using lagged CIT positions. As before, the second check uses the percentage change in aggregate net long CIT positions. Results are qualitatively similar to those reported in the text using changes in the number of contracts. The third check is to use Parkinson's (1980) high-low estimator in volatility tests. We again found similar results to those based on implied volatility. All of these additional results are available from the authors on request.

As a final robustness check we computed the simple contemporaneous correlation between CIT position changes, returns, and implied volatility.

Table 6.8   Contemporaneous correlation between change in commodity index trader (CIT) position and return or implied volatility during alternative roll windows, January 2004 through September 2009

	Extended Goldman roll		Goldman roll	
Market	Nearby	Deferred	Nearby	Deferred
	A. Returns			
Cocoa	−0.01	0.04	−0.05	−0.02
Coffee	−0.01	0.02	−0.11	0.08
Cotton	0.01	0.01	0.01	0.00
Sugar	−0.04	0.05	−0.16	0.10
Feeder cattle	0.08*	−0.07	0.11	−0.07
Lean hogs	0.02	0.05	0.12	0.04
Live cattle	0.06	−0.04	0.19*	−0.16*
Corn	0.00	0.01	0.02	−0.04
Soybeans	−0.04	0.05	−0.16	0.10
Soybean oil	−0.03	0.05	−0.02	−0.03
Wheat	0.04	0.00	0.09	−0.04
Wheat KS	0.02	0.01	0.16	−0.05
Average	0.01	0.01	0.02	−0.01
	B. Implied volatility			
Cocoa	−0.01	−0.13*	−0.16*	−0.03
Coffee	0.14*	−0.20*	0.53*	−0.56*
Cotton	0.13*	−0.19*	0.53*	−0.54*
Sugar	0.09*	−0.15*	0.10	−0.28*
Feeder cattle	0.14*	−0.14*	0.01	−0.04
Lean hogs	0.00	−0.08*	0.09	−0.33*
Live cattle	0.14*	−0.16*	0.55*	−0.52*
Corn	0.00	−0.05	0.08	−0.19*
Soybeans	0.09*	−0.15*	0.10	−0.28*
Soybean oil	0.12*	−0.18*	0.35*	−0.41*
Wheat	0.06	−0.16*	0.21*	−0.38*
Wheat KS	0.00	−0.06	0.07	−0.12
Average	0.07	−0.14	0.20	−0.31

*Statistically significant at the 5 percent level.

We computed these correlations for both the data-defined roll period (number two) and the conventional Goldman roll (number four) in order to check the sensitivity of the findings to alternative definitions of the roll period. One can view this test as the most favorable with regard to detecting market impact of CITs because it is based solely on contemporaneous observations and it is the period of largest changes in CIT positions. Table 6.8 presents the estimated contemporaneous correlations between changes in CIT positions and returns or volatility. Panel A shows that, with just a few exceptions, the correlations are very small; only nine out of the forty-eight are larger than 0.10 in absolute value. Just three of the forty-eight correlations are statistically significant. The average correlation is only −0.01 and 0.02. This provides even less evidence of CIT impact on returns during roll periods than the Granger causality tests. In contrast, panel B shows widespread evidence of contemporaneous correlation between CIT position changes and implied volatility—thirty-two of the forty-eight correlations are statistically significant. A clear tendency emerges of a positive correlation for nearby implied volatility and negative for first deferred implied volatility. Interestingly, this pattern indicates volatility for both the nearby and deferred futures contracts declines during roll periods, that is, volatility declines as CITs exit the nearby contract and enter the first deferred contract. The size of the correlations is also striking, with an average of 0.20 for nearby and –0.31 first deferred across all twelve markets during the Goldman roll window.

6.6   Summary and Conclusions

The nature and cause of recent spikes in commodity prices is the subject of an acrimonious and worldwide debate. Hedge fund manager Michael W. Masters has led the charge that unprecedented buying pressure from new financial index investors created a massive bubble in commodity futures prices at various times in recent years. Irwin and Sanders (2012c) use the term Masters Hypothesis as a shorthand label for this argument. Several well-known international organizations have been among the most ardent supporters of the Masters Hypothesis (see Robles, Torero, and von Braun 2009; De Schutter 2010; Herman, Kelly, and Nash 2011; UNCTAD 2011), arguing that financial index investors were one of the main drivers of spikes in food commodity prices that have occurred since 2007. Because consumers in less-developed countries devote a relatively high proportion of disposable income to food purchases, sharp increases in the price of food can be quite harmful to the health and well-being of large numbers of people.

A number of recent studies investigate whether an empirical relationship can be detected between financial index positions and subsequent price movements in agricultural futures markets (e.g., Gilbert 2009, 2010; Stoll and Whaley 2010; Capelle-Blancard and Coulibaly 2011; Sanders and Irwin 2011a, b; Hamilton and Wu 2012; Gilbert and Pfuderer 2012). While most of these studies do not support the Masters Hypothesis, the data used in nearly all of these studies are subject to important limitations. Specifically, public data on financial index positions in agricultural futures markets are only available on a weekly basis, in aggregate form, and not before 2006 when growth in index positions was most rapid.

The purpose of this chapter is to analyze the market impact of financial index investment in agricultural futures markets using nonpublic data from the Large Trader Reporting System (LTRS) maintained by the US Commodity Futures Trading Commission (CFTC). The LTRS data are superior to publicly available data because commodity index trader (CIT) positions are available on a daily basis, positions are disaggregated by contract maturity, and positions before 2006 can be reliably estimated. The twelve agricultural futures markets included in the study are: corn, soybeans, soybean oil, and wheat traded at the Chicago Board of Trade (CBOT); wheat traded at the Kansas City Board of Trade (KCBOT); feeder cattle, lean hogs, and live cattle traded at the Chicago Mercantile Exchange (CME); and cocoa, cotton, coffee, and sugar traded at the Intercontinental Exchange (ICE). This is the first study to use the daily LTRS data files for all twelve agricultural futures markets included in the CFTC's Supplemental Commitments of Traders report.

Bivariate Granger causality tests use CIT positions in terms of both the change in *aggregate new net flows* into index investment and the *rolling of existing* index positions from one contract to another. Analysis based on the aggregate new net flows of index investor positions affords the most direct test of the Masters Hypothesis because aggregate positions represent the new investment decisions of financial index investors. Analysis based on the rolling of existing financial index positions is also important to consider because the size of index position changes in roll periods is substantially larger than the size of position changes in nonroll periods. Stoll and Whaley (2010) argue that roll period tests are most likely to exhibit a price pressure effect due to the size of index position changes during these periods. Previous studies typically assume that the roll window is the conventional five-day Goldman roll. The disaggregated LTRS data allows us to define a more accurate data-dependent roll period.

A seemingly unrelated regression (SUR) system framework is used to estimate lead-lag dynamics in order to increase the power of causality tests. A total of 1,147 daily observations over January 2004 to September 2009 are available from the LTRS for each of the twelve agricultural futures markets. The null hypothesis of no impact of aggregate CIT positions on daily returns is rejected in only three of the twelve markets. Point estimates of the cumulative impact of a one standard deviation increase in CIT positions on daily returns are negative and very small, with the negative impact averaging only about two basis points. Parallel tests generally fail to reject the null hypothesis that aggregate CIT positions impact implied volatility. Reverse-causality tests show that aggregate CIT positions have a small positive relationship to past daily returns and a weak negative relationship to implied volatility. The combined findings on returns and volatility show that CITs have a tendency to increase aggregate positions when they perceive a clear upward trend in prices as compared to choppy market conditions. This provides the first evidence that index investors are not solely passive buy-and-hold investors, but are to some degree price-sensitive trend followers, similar to more traditional speculators in agricultural futures markets (Bryant, Bessler, and Haigh 2006; Sanders, Irwin, and Merrin 2009).

The null hypothesis that CIT positions do not impact daily returns in the data-defined roll period for CITs is rejected at the 5 percent level in five of the twelve markets and estimated cumulative impacts are negative in all twelve markets; the opposite of the expected outcome if CIT rolling activity simultaneously pressures nearby prices downward and first deferred prices upward. These results imply that CIT positions contribute to narrowing spreads between agricultural futures contracts. Additional tests indicate that the impact of CIT position changes on implied volatility during roll periods is negligible.

In sum, the results of this study add to the growing body of literature indicating that buying pressure from financial index investment in recent years did not cause massive bubbles in agricultural futures prices. The Masters Hypothesis is simply not a valid characterization of reality. This is not to say that the large influx of index investment did not have any impact in agricultural futures markets. We find some evidence that index investment may have resulted in a very slight upward pressure on futures prices before expiration and contributed to a small narrowing of price spreads during the period when index investors roll trades across futures contracts. The upward pressure on agricultural futures prices before expiration can be explained as either a temporary order flow impact (Henderson, Pearson, and Wang 2012) or a repricing of risk (Hamilton and Wu 2012). The narrowing of spreads is likely due to a sunshine trading effect (Admati and Pfleiderer 1991) where the preannouncement of CIT rolling activities coordinates the supply and demand of liquidity and reduces trading costs. These conclusions are consistent with the argument of Irwin and Sanders (2012a) that index investment may have several long-lasting and beneficial economic impacts, including a decrease in the cost of hedging for traditional physical market participants, a dampening of price volatility, and better integration of agricultural futures markets with financial markets. Finally, it should be noted that the results of this study do not rule out the possibility of small and short-lived bubble components in agricultural futures prices that are not associated with commodity index investment.

Important implications for public policy follow from the conclusion that the Masters Hypothesis is not valid. First, new limits on speculation in agricultural futures markets are not grounded in well-established empirical findings and could impede the price discovery and risk-shifting functions of these markets. Second, the focus on speculation has wasted precious time, attention, and effort that could be more productively directed toward the multiple challenges that global agriculture will face in the coming decades. The recent effort to put these challenges on the political agenda of international organizations such as the G20 is an encouraging start (Blas 2012).

Appendix

Table 6A.1   **OLS Granger causality test results for the null hypothesis that the change in aggregate commodity index trader (CIT) net position does not cause returns, January 2004 through September 2009**

$$R_{t,k} = \alpha_t + \sum_{i=1}^{m} \gamma_{i,k} R_{t-i,k} + \sum_{j=0}^{n} \beta_{j,k} X_{t-j,k} + \varepsilon_{t,k} \text{ for each market } k \text{ and time } t$$

Market, k	m, n	p-value $\beta_j = 0, \forall j$	Estimate $\sum \beta_j$	p-value $\sum \beta_j = 0$	One std. dev. impact
Cocoa	1, 1	0.841	0.00003		0.011
Coffee	1, 1	0.290	0.00013		0.055
Cotton	1, 1	0.766	0.00002		0.015
Sugar	1, 1	0.685	0.00001		0.022
Feeder cattle	1, 1	0.816	−0.00005		−0.006
Lean hogs	2, 1	0.001*	−0.00017		−0.130
Live cattle	1, 2	0.037*	−0.00004	0.479	−0.027
Corn	1, 1	0.127	−0.00003		−0.080
Soybeans	1, 1	0.154	0.00007		0.070
Soybean oil	1, 1	0.053	−0.00013		−0.095
Wheat CBOT	1, 1	0.029*	−0.00009		−0.126
Wheat KCBOT	1, 1	0.429	−0.00011		−0.042

Notes: R is nearby return and X is change in aggregate CIT positions. The models for each individual market are estimated using OLS. The number of observations per commodity is 1,447.
*Statistically significant at the 5 percent level.

Table 6A.2   **OLS Granger causality test results for the null hypothesis that the change in aggregate commodity index trader (CIT) net position does not cause implied volatility, January 2004 through September 2009**

$$V_{t,k} = \alpha_t + \sum_{i=1}^{m} \gamma_{i,k} V_{t-i,k} + \sum_{j=0}^{n} \beta_{j,k} X_{t-j,k} + Dum + \varepsilon_{t,k} \text{ for each market } k \text{ and time } t$$

Market, k	m, n	p-value $\beta_j = 0, \forall j$	Estimate $\sum \beta_j$	p-value $\sum \beta_j = 0$	One std. dev. impact
Cocoa	5, 1	0.681	0.00005		0.020
Coffee	2, 1	0.805	−0.00003		−0.012
Cotton	5, 1	0.148	0.00018		0.108
Sugar	4, 1	0.954	0.00000		0.003
Feeder cattle	5, 1	0.154	0.00141		0.154
Lean hogs	2, 1	0.493	−0.00017		−0.126
Live cattle	4, 1	0.080	−0.00010		−0.068
Corn	1, 1	0.029*	−0.00004		−0.096
Soybeans	1, 1	0.443	0.00003		0.028
Soybean oil	3, 1	0.655	−0.00003		−0.020
Wheat CBOT	3, 1	0.977	0.00000		−0.001
Wheat KCBOT	4, 1	0.918	0.00001		0.005

Notes: V is nearby implied volatility and X is change in aggregate CIT positions. The models for each individual market are estimated using OLS. Dummy variables for months are used. The number of observations per commodity is 1,447.
*Statistically significant at the 5 percent level.

Table 6.A.3 **OLS Granger causality test results for the null hypothesis that the change in returns does not cause the change in aggregate commodity index trader (CIT) net position, January 2004 through September 2009**

$$X_{t,k} = \alpha_t + \sum_{i=1}^{m} \gamma_{i,k} R_{t-i,k} + \sum_{j=0}^{n} \beta_{j,k} X_{t-j,k} + \varepsilon_{t,k} \text{ for each market } k \text{ and time } t$$

Market, k	m, n	p-value $\gamma_i = 0, \forall i$	Estimate $\Sigma \gamma_i$	p-value $\Sigma \gamma_j = 0$	One std. dev. impact
Cocoa	5, 2	0.045*	21.97	0.036*	45
Coffee	1, 2	0.026*	12.49		25
Cotton	1, 4	0.018*	19.59		37
Sugar	1, 2	0.110	46.08		94
Feeder cattle	1, 2	0.242	3.49		3
Lean hogs	1, 3	0.189	17.24		25
Live cattle	1, 3	0.007*	49.79		50
Corn	1, 3	0.000*	160.00		322
Soybeans	2, 2	0.000*	154.02		288
Soybean oil	1, 3	0.019*	24.09		45
Wheat CBOT	1, 3	0.000*	68.84		152
Wheat KCBOT	1, 1	0.003*	14.79		29

Notes: R is nearby return and X is change in aggregate CIT positions. The models for each individual market are estimated using OLS. The number of observations per commodity is 1,447.

*Statistically significant at the 5 percent level.

Table 6A.4 **OLS Granger causality test results for the null hypothesis that implied volatility does not cause the change in aggregate commodity index trader (CIT) net position, January 2004 through September 2009**

$$X_{t,k} = \alpha_t + \sum_{i=1}^{m} \gamma_{i,k} V_{t-i,k} + \sum_{j=0}^{n} \beta_{j,k} X_{t-j,k} + Dum + \varepsilon_{t,k} \text{ for each market } k \text{ and time } t$$

Market, k	m, n	p-value $\gamma_i = 0, \forall i$	Estimate $\Sigma \gamma_i$	p-value $\Sigma \gamma_j = 0$	One std. dev impact
Cocoa	5, 2	0.000*	-2.57	0.035*	-21
Coffee	3, 3	0.539	-1.68	0.346	-11
Cotton	1, 4	0.000*	-7.55		-60
Sugar	1, 2	0.001*	-26.55		-202
Feeder cattle	1, 2	0.530	-0.36		-2
Lean hogs	1, 2	0.462	-1.09		-18
Live cattle	1, 3	0.003*	-12.84		-57
Corn	5, 3	0.021*	-20.55	0.009*	-178
Soybeans	1, 1	0.006*	-9.82		-79
Soybean oil	1, 3	0.030*	-7.26		-43
Wheat CBOT	2, 1	0.000*	-14.32	0.001*	-129
Wheat KCBOT	1, 1	0.758	-0.39		-3

Notes: V is nearby implied volatility and X is change in aggregate CIT positions. The models for each individual market are estimated using OLS. Dummy variables for months are used. The number of observations per commodity is 1,447.

*Statistically significant at the 5 percent level.

References

Acharya, V. V., L. A. Lochstoer, and T. Ramadorai. 2010. "Limits to Arbitrage and Hedging: Evidence from Commodity Markets." Working Paper, London Business School.

Adammer, P., M. T. Bohl, and P. M. Stephan. 2011. "Speculative Bubbles in Agricultural Prices." Working Paper, Department of Economics, Westphalian Wilhelminian University of Munster.

Admati, A. R., and P. Pfleiderer. 1991. "Sunshine Trading and Financial Market Equilibrium." *Review of Financial Studies* 4:443–81.

Bellemare, M. F. 2012. "Rising Food Prices, Food Price Volatility, and Political Unrest." Working Paper, Sanford School of Public Policy, Duke University.

Bessembinder, H., A. Carrion, L. Tuttle, and K. Venkataraman. 2012. "Predatory or Sunshine Trading? Evidence from Crude Oil ETF Rolls." Working Paper, Department of Finance, University of Utah.

Blas, J. 2012. "Food Prices: Leaders Seek a Long-Term Solution to Hunger Pains." *Financial Times*, June 18. http://www.ft.com/intl/cms/s/0/a6137e70-b15e-11e1-9800-00144feabdc0.html#axzz1yBlAAZ4Z.

Brunetti, C., B. Buyuksahin, and J. H. Harris. 2011. "Speculators, Prices, and Market Volatility." Working Paper, Carey Business School, Johns Hopkins University.

Brunetti, C., and D. Reiffen. 2011. "Commodity Index Trading and Hedging Costs." Finance and Economics Discussion Series 2011-57. Washington, DC: Divisions of Research and Statistics and Monetary Affairs, Federal Reserve Board.

Bryant, H., D. A. Bessler, and M. S. Haigh. 2006. "Causality in Futures Markets." *Journal of Futures Markets* 26:1039–57.

Buyuksahin, B., and M. A. Robe. 2011. "Speculators, Commodities, and Cross-Market Linkages." Working Paper, Kogod School of Business, American University.

Capelle-Blancard, G., and D. Coulibaly. 2011. "Index Trading and Agricultural Commodity Prices: A Panel Granger Causality Analysis." *Economie Internationale* 126:51–72.

Cheng, I. H., A. Kirilenko, and W. Xiong. 2012. "Convective Risk Flows in Commodity Futures Markets." Working Paper, Department of Economics, Princeton University.

Commodity Futures Trading Commission (CFTC). 2006. "Commodity Futures Trading Commission Actions in Response to the Comprehensive Review of the Commitments of Traders Reporting Program." June 21. http://www.cftc.gov/ucm/groups/public/@commitmentsoftraders/documents/file/noticeonsupplemental cotrept.pdf.

———. 2012a. "About the Commitments of Traders." http://www.cftc.gov/market reports/commitmentsoftraders/cot_about.html.

———. 2012b. "Large Trader Reporting Program." http://www.cftc.gov/Industry Oversight/MarketSurveillance/LargeTraderReportingProgram/index.htm.

De Long, J. B., A. Shleifer, L. H. Summers, and R. J. Waldmann. 1990. "Noise Trader Risk in Financial Markets." *Journal of Political Economy* 98:703–38.

De Schutter, O. 2010. "Food Commodities Speculation and Food Price Crises: Regulation to Reduce the Risks of Price Volatility." Briefing Note 02. United Nations Special Rapporteur on the Right to Food. http://www.srfood.org/images/stories/pdf/otherdocuments/20102309_briefing_note_02_en_ok.pdf.

Dwyer, A., J. Holloway, and M. Wright. 2012. "Commodity Market Financialisation: A Closer Look at the Evidence." *Reserve Bank of Australia Bulletin*, March Quarter. http://www.rba.gov.au/publications/bulletin/2012/mar/8.html.

Enders, W. 1995. *Applied Econometric Time Series*. New York: John Wiley and Sons.

Engelke, L., and J. C. Yuen. 2008. "Types of Commodity Investments." In *The Handbook of Commodity Investing*, edited by F. J. Fabozzi, F. Roland, and D. G. Kaiser. New York: John Wiley and Sons.

Etula, E. 2010. "Broker-Dealer Risk Appetite and Commodity Returns." Staff Report no. 406. New York: Federal Reserve Bank of New York.

Fama, E. F. 1970. "Efficient Capital Markets: A Review of Theory and Empirical Work." *Journal of Finance* 25:383–417.

Fattouh, B., L. Kilian, and L. Mahadeva. 2012. "The Role of Speculation in Oil Markets: What Have We Learned So Far?" Working Paper, Oxford Institute for Energy Studies.

Fenton, J., and G. Martinaitas. 2005. "Large Trader Reporting: The Great Equalizer." *Futures Industry* July/August:34–9.

G20. 2011. "Report of the G20 Study Group on Commodities." http://www.g20.org/images/stories/canalfinan/gexpert/01reportG20.pdf.

Garcia, P., S. H. Irwin, and A. Smith. 2011. "Futures Market Failure?" Working Paper, Department of Agricultural and Consumer Economics, University of Illinois at Urbana-Champaign.

Gilbert, C. L. 2009. "Speculative Influences on Commodity Futures Prices, 2006–2008." Working Paper, Department of Economics, University of Trento.

Gilbert, C. L. 2010. "How to Understand High Food Prices. *Journal of Agricultural Economics* 61:398–425.

Gilbert, C. L., and S. Pfuderer. 2012. "Index Funds Do Impact Agricultural Prices." Working Paper, Department of Economics, University of Trento.

Grosche, S. 2012. "Limitations of Granger Causality Analysis to Assess the Price Effects from the Financialization of Agricultural Commodity Markets under Bounded Rationality." Discussion Paper 2012:1. Bonn: Institute for Food and Resource Economics, University of Bonn.

Grossman, S. J. 1986. "An Analysis of 'Insider Trading' on Futures Markets." *Journal of Business* 59 (part 2): S129–46.

Grossman, S. J., and M. H. Miller. 1988. "Liquidity and Market Structure." *Journal of Finance* 43:617–33.

Gutierrez, L. 2011. "Looking for Rational Bubbles in Agricultural Commodity Markets." Paper presented at the European Agricultural Economics Congress, Zurich, Switzerland, August 30–September 2.

Hamilton, J. D. 1994. *Time Series Analysis*. Princeton, NJ: Princeton University Press.

Hamilton, J. D., and J. C. Wu. 2011. "Risk Premia in Crude Oil Futures Prices." Working Paper, Department of Economics, University of California, San Diego.

———. 2012. "Effects of Index-Fund Investing on Commodity Futures Prices." Working Paper, Department of Economics, University of California, San Diego.

Harvey, A. C. 1991. *The Econometric Analysis of Time Series*, 2nd ed.. Cambridge, MA: MIT Press.

Henderson, B. J., N. D. Pearson, and L. Wang. 2012. "New Evidence on the Financialization of Commodity Markets." Working Paper, Department of Finance, George Washington University.

Herman, M. O., R. Kelly, and R. Nash. 2011. "Not a Game: Speculation vs. Food Security." Oxfam Issues Briefing, October 3. http://www.oxfam.org/sites/www.oxfam.org/files/ib-speculation-vs-food-security-031011-en.pdf.

Hoover, K. D. 2001. *Causality in Macroeconomics*. Cambridge: Cambridge University Press.

Hull, J. C. 2000. *Options, Futures, and Other Derivatives*, 4th ed. Upper Saddle River, NJ: Prentice Hall.

Irwin, S. H., P. Garcia, D. L. Good, and E. L. Kunda. 2011. "Spreads and Non-Convergence in CBOT Corn, Soybean, and Wheat Futures: Are Index Funds to Blame?" *Applied Economic Perspectives and Policy* 33:116–42.

Irwin, S. H., and D. R. Sanders. 2011. "Index Funds, Financialization, and Commodity Futures Markets." *Applied Economic Perspectives and Policy* 33:1–31.

Irwin, S. H., and D. R. Sanders. 2012a. "Financialization and Structural Change in Commodity Futures Markets." *Journal of Agricultural and Applied Economics* 44:371–96.

———. 2012b. "A Reappraisal of Investing in Commodity Futures Markets." *Applied Economic Perspectives and Policy* 34:515–30.

———. 2012c. "Testing the Masters Hypothesis in Commodity Futures Markets." *Energy Economics* 34:256–69.

Irwin, S. H., D. R. Sanders, and R. P. Merrin. 2009. "Devil or Angel? The Role of Speculation in the Recent Commodity Price Boom (and Bust)." *Journal of Agricultural and Applied Economics* 41:393–402.

Janzen, J. P., A. Smith, and C. A. Carter. 2012. "Commodity Price Comovement: The Case of Cotton." Proceedings of the 2012 NCCC-134 Conference on Applied Commodity Price Analysis, Forecasting, and Market Risk Management. http://www.farmdoc.illinois.edu/nccc134/conf_2012/pdf/confp02-12.pdf.

Kemp, J. 2010. "Volatility Indices Round out Markets." *Commodities Now*, March 9. http://www.commodities-now.com/news/portfolio-management/1978-volatility-indices-round-out-commodity-markets.html.

Masters, M. W. 2008. "Testimony before the Committee on Homeland Security and Governmental Affairs, United States Senate." May 20. http://hsgac.senate.gov/public/_files/052008Masters.pdf.

———. 2009. "Testimony before the Commodity Futures Trading Commission." August 5. http://www.cftc.gov/ucm/groups/public/@newsroom/documents/file/hearing080509_masters.pdf.

Masters, M. W., and A. K. White. 2008. "The Accidental Hunt Brothers: How Institutional Investors are Driving up Food and Energy Prices." http://www.loe.org/images/content/080919/Act1.pdf.

Meyer, G., and C. Cui. 2009. "US Oil Fund Finds Itself at the Mercy of Traders." *The Wall Street Journal*, March 6. http://online.wsj.com/article/SB12362987470 1846317.html.

Mou, Y. 2010. "Limits to Arbitrage and Commodity Index Investment: Front-Running the Goldman Roll." Working Paper, Columbia School of Business, Columbia University.

Newbold, P. 1982. "Causality Testing in Economics." In *Time Series Analysis: Theory and Practice I*, edited by O. D. Anderson, 701–16. Amsterdam: North Holland Publishing Company.

Parkinson, M. 1980. "The Extreme Value Method for Estimating the Variance of the Rate of Return." *Journal of Business* 53:61–5.

Phillips, P. C. B., and J. Yu. 2010. "Dating the Timeline of Financial Bubbles during the Subprime Crisis." Cowles Foundation Discussion Paper no. 1770. New Haven, CT: Yale University.

Pirrong, C. 2010. "No Theory? No Evidence? No Problem!" *Regulation* 33:38–44.

Robles, M., M. Torero, and J. von Braun. 2009. "When Speculation Matters." IFPRI Issue Brief 57. Washington, DC: International Food Policy Research Institute. http://www.ifpri.org/publication/when-speculation-matters.

Sanders, D. R., and S. H. Irwin. 2010. "A Speculative Bubble in Commodity Futures Prices? Cross-Sectional Evidence." *Agricultural Economics* 41:25–32.

———. 2011a. "The Impact of Index Funds in Commodity Futures Markets: A Systems Approach." *Journal of Alternative Investments* 14:40–9.

———. 2011b. "New Evidence on the Impact of Index Funds in US Grain Futures Markets." *Canadian Journal of Agricultural Economics* 59:519–32.

Sanders, D. R., S. H. Irwin, and R. P. Merrin. 2009. "Smart Money? The Forecasting Ability of CFTC Large Traders." *Journal of Agricultural and Resource Economics* 34:276–96.

———. 2010. "The Adequacy of Speculation in Agricultural Futures Markets: Too Much of a Good Thing?" *Applied Economics Perspectives and Policy* 32:77–94.

Singleton, K. J. 2011. "Investor Flows and the 2008 Boom/Bust in Oil Prices." Working Paper, Graduate School of Business, Stanford University.

Stoll, H. R., and R. E. Whaley. 2010. "Commodity Index Investing and Commodity Futures Prices." *Journal of Applied Finance* 20:7–46.

Summers, L. H. 1986. "Does the Stock Market Rationally Reflect Fundamental Values?" *Journal of Finance* 41:591–601.

Tang, K., and W. Xiong. 2010. "Index Investing and the Financialization of Commodities." NBER Working Paper no. 16385, Cambridge, MA.

United Nations Conference on Trade and Development (UNCTAD). 2011. "Price Formation in Financialized Commodity Markets: The Role of Information." http://unctad.org/en/docs/gds20111_en.pdf.

United States Senate, Permanent Subcommittee on Investigations (USS/PSI). 2009. *Excessive Speculation in the Wheat Market.* Washington, DC: US Government Printing Office.

World Bank (WB). 2011. "Food Price Hike Drives 44 Million People into Poverty." Press Release no. 2011/333/PREM, February 15. http://web.worldbank.org /WBSITE/EXTERNAL/NEWS/0,,contentMDK:22833439~pagePK:64257043 ~piPK:437376~theSitePK:4607,00.html.

Wright, B. 2011. "The Economics of Grain Price Volatility." *Applied Economic Perspectives and Policy* 33:32–58.

Comment   Aaron Smith

Speculation

Does speculation cause high food prices? When phrased this way, as it often is in the public discourse, the answer to the question is obviously "yes." Every decision made by producers, consumers, merchants, processors, and arbitrageurs requires some degree of speculation. For example, merchants and processors speculate about how much the commodity will be worth in the future when deciding how much they are willing to pay for it now. If the collective expectation of these economic agents is that the commodity is likely to be relatively scarce next year, then they act to place more inventories in storage, thereby bidding up the current price. We observed this phenomenon in action in July and August of 2012. Corn and soybean prices jumped

Aaron Smith is associate professor of agricultural and resource economics at the University of California, Davis.

For acknowledgments, sources of research support, and disclosure of the author's material financial relationships, if any, please see http://www.nber.org/chapters/c12815.ack.

as a severe drought reduced the expected size, not of available supply, but of the upcoming crop.

When presented with these market features, critics of commodity speculation qualify their critique. The issue, they say, is whether excessive speculation drives prices, to which the natural response is "what is excessive speculation?"

The phrase "excessive speculation" has been used in connection with regulating commodity trading since at least the Grain Futures Act of 1922. Peck (1980) reports that the phrase appeared repeatedly in the hearings leading to the passing of that legislation as well as in the act itself. It also appears in the Commodity Exchange Act of 1936, the Commodity Futures Trading Act of 1974, and the Dodd-Frank Wall Street Reform and Consumer Protection Act of 2010, which constitute the three major revisions to commodity trading legislation in the United States since 1922. In each case, the legislation states that excessive speculation causes "an undue and unnecessary burden on interstate commerce" and that it can be rectified by imposing "limits on the amounts of trading which may be done or positions which may be held by any person" in commodity futures markets. Thus, excessive speculation is defined by a remedy rather than a disease; it is a solution in search of a problem.[1]

Most economists, if asked to define excessive speculation, would define it as trading that causes prices to differ from "fundamentals." To be operational, this definition requires that the fundamental be defined. Here, I define as fundamental the price sequence that would result from competitive markets populated by equally informed traders with rational expectations. Gustafson (1958) first formalized this concept, which we now know as the competitive rational storage model. Wright (2011) provides an accessible summary of the model and its application to food price volatility. Estimating the path of prices implied by the competitive rational expectations model is notoriously difficult, which means that quantifying excessive speculation by this metric is similarly difficult.

The "Masters Hypothesis," which Aulerich, Irwin, and Garcia (AIG)[2] address in this chapter, takes a simpler approach and defines excessive speculation by the actions of a particular type of trader, namely index funds that take long (i.e., buy) positions in commodity futures markets. Proponents of the Masters Hypothesis allege that this trading behavior is not based on current or future expected supply and demand for the commodity and causes prices to increase dramatically. Aulerich, Irwin, and Garcia reject this hypothesis emphatically, showing that there is little relationship between futures positions held by index traders and prices. They test the hypothesis

---

1. I credit Craig Pirrong for this last phrase. On his blog, he used the phrase "a solution in search of a problem" to describe position limits. See http://streetwiseprofessor.com/?p=4627.

2. I considered not using this acronym because of its association with excessive speculation but irony demanded that I keep it.

for twelve agricultural commodities over several trading periods (e.g., roll and nonroll periods). In the few cases with a statistically significant relationship, it is small and often of the opposite sign to that predicted by the Masters Hypothesis. When combined with other papers by Scott Irwin and his coauthors (e.g., Irwin and Sanders 2011, 2012; Sanders and Irwin 2011; and Irwin, Sanders, and Merrin 2009), these results refute the simplistic yet popular notion that index funds cause high commodity prices.

In this chapter, AIG use even better data than in prior studies to measure index fund positions. Their empirical work is thorough and convincing, so I see little value in asking them to run more regressions or make any other changes. Rather, in this comment I step back and comment more generally on excessive speculation and its effect on commodity markets.

Potential Effects of Excessive Speculation on Food Commodity Markets

Tales of speculative excess are typically associated with assets such as equities or houses. Commodities differ from these assets because they are produced and consumed. This means that the price of a commodity always equals its marginal consumption value. This feature adds an anchor to prices; if the price gets too high then consumers will stop buying the commodity and producers will expand production, thereby increasing inventory.

The competitive rational storage model provides a way to formalize the connection between the consumption value of a commodity and the speculative effects on prices. Equilibrium in this model implies a kinked total-demand curve, as shown in figure 6C.1 (Wright 2011). When prices are low,

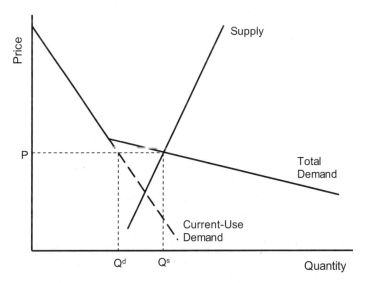

Fig. 6C.1   Equilibrium in rational storage model

rational firms choose to place some units of the commodity in storage, and total demand equals demand for current use plus demand from inventory holders. Thus positive inventory implies that total demand is more elastic than demand for current use. When prices are high, storage is unprofitable, inventory goes to zero, and total demand equals current-use demand.

Figure 6C.1 depicts an equilibrium in which inventory is positive. If excessive speculation were to push prices above this equilibrium, then the quantity in storage would increase. The magnitude of the inventory increase depends on the elasticities of demand and supply; the smaller are these elasticities, the smaller would be the inventory increase.

Are the relevant elasticities large enough that we would see the traces of a speculative food price increase in accumulated inventory? To answer this question, I use estimates of the supply and demand elasticities for US corn. Given that inventory equals quantity supplied minus quantity demanded ($I = Q^s - Q^d$), the elasticity of inventory supplied to the market is

$$\frac{P}{I}\frac{\partial I}{\partial P} = \frac{Q}{I}\left(\frac{P}{Q}\frac{\partial Q^s}{\partial P} - \frac{P}{Q}\frac{\partial Q^d}{\partial P}\right).$$

Between 1990 and 2010, the average ending stocks to use (I/Q) was 0.15. Hendricks, Sumner, and Smith (forthcoming) estimate that the annual elasticity of supply of US corn equals about 0.3, and Berry, Roberts, and Schlenker (2012) report a similar estimate (chapter 2, this volume). On the demand side, Adjemian and Smith (2012) estimate that the annual flexibility (inverse elasticity) of total demand equals −1.35 on average between 1980 and 2010, but had increased steadily in the past few years as corn-ethanol production increased. Based on a conservative interpretation of their estimates for recent years, I choose a demand flexibility of −3.3, that is, an elasticity of −0.3.

Plugging in these numbers yields an elasticity of inventory supply of

$$\frac{P}{I}\frac{\partial I}{\partial P} = \frac{1}{0.15}(0.3 - (-0.3)) = 4.$$

Consider a 30 percent speculative price spike. The standard deviation of annual price changes since 1980 is about 30 percent, so such a shock is not extreme. With an inventory supply elasticity of four, crop-year-ending inventory would increase by 120 percent in response to such a speculative shock. At lower inventory levels, such as those seen in the past two years, we would expect the percent inventory response to be even greater. Since 1980, corn inventory has increased by more than 100 percent in only three years: 1985, 1996, and 2004. In each of those years price declined; that is, inventory accumulated because of high production. Thus, a 120 percent inventory increase coinciding with a 30 percent price increase would be very obvious in the data if it had occurred.

This analysis would overstate the observed change in inventory if speculative shocks are correlated with prices. For example, suppose speculators follow momentum strategies; they observe prices rising in response to poor weather and move into the market on the long side exacerbating the price rise. Under rational expectations the poor weather would cause a reduction in inventory, but the excessive speculative offsets that decline. The effect of excessive speculation is therefore that inventory declines by less than it otherwise would have. However, the lack of inventory depletion in the face of a temporary weather shock would be just as large an error as the 120 percent inventory accumulation in the previous paragraph and appears inconsistent with the path of annual corn prices in the United States.

This analysis applies to the annual horizon. At shorter horizons, such as weeks or days, supply and demand respond much less to a price shock and the corresponding inventory buildup would be smaller. Put another way, the physical forces that would act to correct speculative excess over a year are less powerful at short horizons. Conceivably, speculative trading could cause prices to be more volatile than those implied by competitive rational expectations equilibrium and this excess volatility could come without large quantity effects.

Price Discovery

The discussion above suggests that any effects of excessive speculation on food prices likely occur at high frequencies. Such effects would imply that futures markets do not function efficiently as venues of price discovery. For this reason, studying price discovery provides a promising path for future research on the connection between futures market trading and prices. In other words, how do markets aggregate information and opinions?

In contrast, much of the previous literature on futures market speculation focuses on risk premia. It asks how speculation affects the price hedgers must pay to reduce risk. In the past thirty years, average payoffs on agricultural futures have been close to zero, which suggests that average risk premia are very small. Thus, for risk premia to be important in price determination, they must sometimes be negative and at other times be positive. Moreover, to have significant effects on spot prices, risk premia must have significant effects on quantities consumed, produced, and stored. There is little evidence in the agricultural risk literature that risk premia are volatile enough to have large enough quantity effects to noticeably affect prices. For example, Acharya, Lochstoer, and Ramadorai (2012) show that hedging demand (driven by default risk) and speculator supply (driven by broker-dealer balance sheets) have statistically significant but small effects on risk premia in energy markets. But would anyone attribute a 30 percent price spike to a change in risk premia?

If prices were to differ significantly from the fundamental over a period of days or weeks, it seems that a more likely source than risk premia is a failure of efficient price discovery. Promising veins of price-discovery research focus on differences of opinion among traders and limits to arbitrage. In difference-of-opinion models, traders do not believe that prices fully incorporate the available information about fundamentals. Rather, they trust their own information. Banerjee (2011) shows that prices tend to underreact to fundamental shocks in this setting, which generates price drift toward the new fundamental. This kind of model appears consistent with the results of Hong and Yogo (2012), who find that futures market open interest (total number of positions held) predicts future prices better than do current prices. They infer that traders act on fundamental shocks, thereby increasing open interest, but that prices underreact to these shocks. Thus, open interest provides a better signal of future demand than does price.

Interestingly, this difference-of-opinion equilibrium implies that trading reduces rather than amplifies volatility. Most of the discussion about excessive speculation assumes the opposite. Limits-to-arbitrage models tend to imply increased volatility relative to the unlimited arbitrage case. In such models, fully informed rational traders exist but are unable to correct pricing errors because of the risk that in future periods irrational traders may drive the price further from its fundamental. Some sources of limits to arbitrage in financial markets do not apply to commodity futures markets (notably short sales constraints), but others such as noise trader risk (De Long et al. 1990) may be quite relevant. There is scope to explore the potential for differences of opinion and limits to arbitrage to hamper price discovery in commodity markets.

In conclusion, I commend AIG for emphatically refuting the Masters Hypothesis. It is important for economists to bring facts and rigorous data analysis to bear on issues that have received such publicity, especially if they appear to be influencing policy. I hope that their work allows us to move the discussion toward the efficiency of the price discovery process in the short run.

References

Acharya, V., L. Lochstoer, T. Ramadorai. 2012. "Limits to Arbitrage and Hedging: Evidence from Commodity Markets." Working Paper, New York University.

Adjemian, M. K., and A. Smith. 2012. "Using USDA Forecasts to Estimate the Price Flexibility of Demand for Agricultural Commodities." *American Journal of Agricultural Economics* 94 (4): 978–95.

Banerjee, S. 2011. "Learning from Prices and the Dispersion in Beliefs." *Review of Financial Studies* 24 (9): 3025–68.

Berry, S. T., M. J. Roberts, and W. Schlenker. 2012. "Identifying Agricultural Demand and Supply Elasticities: Implications for Food Price Volatility." NBER Food Price Volatility Conference, National Taiwan University, June 15–16.

De Long, J. B., A. Shleifer, L. H. Summers, and R. J. Waldmann. 1990. "Noise Trader Risk in Financial Markets." *Journal of Political Economy* 98 (4): 703–38.

Gustafson, R. L. 1958. "Carryover Levels for Grains: A Method for Determining

Amounts that are Optimal under Specified Conditions." USDA Technical Bulletin 1178. Washington, DC: United States Department of Agriculture.

Hendricks, N. P., D. A. Sumner, and A. Smith. Forthcoming. "Agricultural Supply Dynamics: The Illusion of Partial Adjustment." *American Journal of Agricultural Economics.*

Hong, H. and M. Yogo. 2012. "What Does Futures Market Interest Tell Us about the Macroeconomy and Asset Prices?" *Journal of Financial Economics* 105 (3): 473–90.

Irwin, S. H., and D. R. Sanders. 2011. "Index Funds, Financialization, and Commodity Futures Markets." *Applied Economic Perspectives and Policy* 33:1–31.

———. 2012. "Testing the Masters Hypothesis in Commodity Futures Markets." *Energy Economics* 34:256–69.

Irwin, S. H., D. R. Sanders, and R. P. Merrin. 2009. "Devil or Angel? The Role of Speculation in the Recent Commodity Price Boom (and Bust)." *Journal of Agricultural and Applied Economics* 41:377–91.

Peck, A. E. 1980. "The Role of Economic Analysis in Futures Market Regulation." *American Journal of Agricultural Economics* 62 (5): 1037–43.

Sanders, D. R., and S. H. Irwin. 2011. "The Impact of Index Funds in Commodity Futures Markets: A Systems Approach." *Journal of Alternative Investments* 14:40–9.

Wright B. D. 2011. "The Economics of Grain Price Volatility." *Applied Economic Perspectives and Policy* 33:32–58.

7
Food Price Volatility and Domestic Stabilization Policies in Developing Countries

Christophe Gouel

7.1 Introduction

In early 2009, Manmohan Singh was reelected as prime minister of India following a successful election campaign in which he emphasized his success in protecting his country from the outcomes of the 2007 to 2008 world food crisis. While world rice prices increased by 160 percent between June 2007 and June 2008, in India this increase was only 7.9 percent (World Bank 2010). In 2007, when the world rice price increase was accelerating, the Indian government was already aware of and concerned about the high world price of wheat, which would have made large wheat imports very costly. To secure domestic grain availability, in October 2007, India banned non-Basmati rice exports. The ban was soon relaxed and a minimum export price above the Indian export parity price was imposed, which had to be increased regularly as world prices were rising.[1]

The Haitian government was less successful in its attempts to weather the crisis. Haiti imports 82 percent of its rice consumption, and in April

Christophe Gouel is an economist at the French National Institute for Agricultural Research (Institut National de la Recherche Agronomique [INRA]) and a research associate at the French Research Center in International Economics (Centre d'Études Prospectives et d'Informations Internationales [CEPII]).

This research was generously supported by the Knowledge for Change Program (KCP), and by the FOODSECURE project funded under the 7th Framework Programme for Research and Development, DG-Research, European Commission. Much of this work was done while I was working as a consultant for the World Bank. I would like to thank Mathilde Douillet, Franck Galtier, Will Martin, and participants at the NBER "Economics of Food Price Volatility" conference for helpful comments. For acknowledgments, sources of research support, and disclosure of the author's material financial relationships, if any, please see http://www.nber.org/chapters/c12816.ack.

1. For more on Indian rice policies see Slayton (2009), World Bank (2010), and Timmer (2010).

2008, after an annual increase of 81 percent in the price for imported rice, the Haitian president, acknowledging his helplessness, was reported to have said to protesters: "come get me at the palace and I will demonstrate with you."[2] The Haitian prime minister was soon voted out and decisions were taken to subsidize the price of rice. Many countries experienced food riots that threatened the stability of their governments but the situations in Haiti and India illustrate that public intervention in a period of high food prices is a matter of political survival in countries with large poor populations. Governments have to be "seen to be doing something" (Poulton et al. 2006). Inaction is not an option. But without appropriate preparation for such situations and pressed by emergencies, many countries rely on costly policies, such as universal food subsidies, or beggar-thy-neighbor policies, such as trade policy adjustments. The food crisis has increased the consciousness of many governments of the unreliability of world markets,[3] and that the stable food prices experienced in the previous decades must not be taken for granted. Anecdotal evidence and experience of what happened following the 1973 to 1974 crisis would suggest that the recent crisis could trigger a wave of new stabilization policies relying on storage and self-sufficiency.

However, these developments would go against the recommendations made since the 1980s by academics and policy analysts that direct market intervention should be avoided, people should be assisted to cope with risks by their governments through the use of safety nets or the development of market-based risk management instruments, agriculture should be supported through investment in long-run productivity growth, and trade and private storage should be relied on to compensate for supply shortfalls (World Bank 2006).[4] The food crisis has led many researchers and experts to question the dominant approach (Timmer 2012, Galtier 2009, Abbott 2012b, HLPE 2011, Oxfam 2011). The dominant approach has attracted criticism because safety nets have proved complex to use in times of crisis, market-based risk management instruments have not yet been successfully developed, and the countries that were relying on the world market for their imports were the ones that suffered the most during the crisis. Indeed, the countries that weathered the food crisis best were those countries with very interventionist policies related to both trade and storage, such as China and India. Despite international recommendations, stabilization policies are widespread in most developing and emerging countries. For example, Demeke, Pangrazio, and Maetz (2009), based on information obtained from eighty-one countries, show that sixty-eight of them used trade policy mea-

---

2. *New York Times*, April 18, 2008, "Across Globe, Empty Bellies Bring Rising Anger."
3. The recent global "land rush," which is strongly driven by net food importing countries (Arezki, Deininger, and Selod 2011), is a good illustration of this new distrust in world markets.
4. A framework labeled "best practice" by Timmer (2010) and Abbott (2012b), and "optimum strategy" by Galtier (2009).

sures during the 2007 to 2008 food crisis, and thirty-five released public stocks at subsidized prices.

The present chapter attempts to make sense of this divide between policy advice and practice. Drawing on the theoretical literature and on accounts of policy responses to price volatility, this chapter tries to answer the following questions: What are the justifications for domestic stabilization policies? Following the food crisis, is the policy framework put forward by international organizations still relevant, or should countries rely more on price-stabilization policies? And if so, what type of price stabilization?

The liberal paradigm is facing reasonable criticism. Why should food importing countries trust a world market that is susceptible to sudden spikes and can even disappear if major exporters close their borders? In our view, the weakness of the dominant approach to a large extent is related to the fact that it requires countries to trust each other and to adopt the same cooperative policies. Indeed, the impact of domestic policies on stability of world prices is negative in the case of countercyclical trade measures and potentially positive in the case of storage policies. Those policies also are interdependent in the sense that each country's domestic policy choices might affect the policy choices of its trade partners. Because domestic stabilization policies can be rationalized as the outcome of a noncooperative equilibrium in which countries coordinate through a vicious circle of negative feedbacks, their reform faces considerable challenges.

Coordination on a noncooperative equilibrium and distrust among agents are not just international problems; they apply also to the domestic sphere, where in many countries public intervention crowds out private agents because of political uncertainty, and regulations limiting profit from arbitrage (Wright and Williams 1982b; Tschirley and Jayne 2010). The caution of private agents confirms government's belief that it must step in to ensure basic storage and trade, deterring even more a normal market behavior. This mechanism implies that any reform of domestic policies toward fewer market interventions must also deal with the issue of building domestic trust.

This chapter explains the various aspects of this policy conundrum. Section 7.2 provides a summary of the motivations for stabilizing food prices. It focuses on the potential efficiency costs of price instability and shows that there are still significant uncertainties regarding these costs. The standard assessments that rely on assumption of market incompleteness and the expected utility framework lead to small welfare costs and hence challenge the usefulness of public intervention. In contrast, recent research highlights the potential costs of food price spikes to poor households. Section 7.3 draws on the theoretical and applied literature on price stabilization policies to discuss the design and the effects of stabilization policies concentrating on storage and trade policies, and the alternative of safety nets. In section 7.4, we explore what can be learned from historical stabilization policies and their effects. Section 7.5 presents some policy implications of this discussion and concludes the paper.

7.2   Motivations for Stabilizing Food Prices

This section analyzes the cost of food price instability, the reasons why public intervention might be defensible, and the reasons why it is justifiable in practice. It focuses mostly on justifications for intervention that are independent of the underlying causes of price volatility. Sections 7.3 and 7.4 discuss justifications for intervention that arise endogenously from the existence of other interventions and that have a feedback effect on price volatility. This applies, for example, to the cases of trade policies abroad and lack of commitment not to intervene, but in these two cases the reasons to intervene in the first place are those discussed in the present section. There is a third category of justifications: situations where the market failure justifying intervention is also one of the causes of food price volatility. This can occur if price volatility is the result of expectations errors (see section 7.2.4) or if private storage is different from its competitive level. Those last causes have attracted limited attention in the literature and thus are not reviewed in this chapter.

7.2.1   Incomplete Markets and Standard Assessments of the Costs of Price Instability

The assumption that risk markets are incomplete is used frequently to justify public intervention in volatile commodity markets (Newbery and Stiglitz 1981; Innes 1990). Although this assumption may be reasonable, the extent of markets' incompleteness is a difficult empirical issue; therefore, for convenience, assessments of the welfare cost of price instability generally assume that the markets for risk management are missing.

In this chapter, the standard assessment of the welfare effect of price instability is considered to be the method that emerged in the 1980s to measure the cost of instability using the expected utility framework. This approach superseded the earlier Marshallian surplus analysis, which is described in Wright (2001).

Consumers

Under the expected utility hypothesis, Turnovsky, Shalit, and Schmitz (1980) analyze the welfare change for consumers from price stabilization at its arithmetic mean, and represent it by an equivalent variation measure approximated to the second order by:

(1) $$[\gamma(\eta - \rho) - \alpha]\gamma \frac{\Delta\sigma_P^2}{2},$$

where α and η are the price and the income elasticities of demand, $\Delta\sigma_P^2$ is the reduction in the square of the coefficient of variation of price, and γ and ρ are the commodity budget share and the relative risk aversion parameters at mean price. This measure implicitly assumes that consumers are unable to insure against price volatility, to store grain, or to save.

If we ignore variations in the marginal utility of income (the term $\gamma(\eta - \rho)$), this welfare measure is necessarily negative with a downward sloping demand curve. In this case, it reduces to a surplus measure, and with a downward-sloping demand curve, surplus gains from low prices more than compensate for losses at high prices (Waugh 1944). Table 7.1 presents the welfare measure in equation (1) for various parameter values. For low budget shares, $\gamma = 0.01$, or in the absence of income effects, $\eta = \rho = 0$, the welfare change is close to a surplus measure, and the consumer suffers from stabilization. This implies that stabilization at the mean price is detrimental to consumers from developed countries, since a low share of their budget goes on food staples. However, because of this low budget share, the welfare losses would be relatively innocuous since they do not exceed -0.032 percent of income when 1 percent of income is devoted to a staple.

Risk aversion can compensate for the risk-loving component associated with a downward-sloping demand curve, and make stabilization beneficial only if budget share and risk aversion are sufficiently high. With high risk aversion ($\rho = 4$) and high budget share ($\gamma = 30\%$), gains do not exceed 0.7 percent and 1.5 percent of income for coefficients of variation of price of 20 percent and 30 percent (a range of volatility typical of the real prices on world food markets; Gilbert and Morgan [2010]). While a food budget share of 50 percent to 60 percent is common in low-income countries (Seale, Regmi, and Bernstein 2003), expenditure on one staple reaches 30 percent only for the poor population subgroups, and this level is less likely in countries where consumption of stables is diversified, such as in eastern Africa where staples consumption is divided among maize, wheat, rice, and cassava (Tschirley and Jayne 2010).

There are many variants of the welfare measure represented by equation (1). Newbery and Stiglitz (1981, 123) propose a measure that accounts for price and income risk and their correlation. Wright and Williams (1988b) note that in reality commodity policies achieve price stabilization by stabilizing quantities not prices; hence, welfare change should be assessed with respect to stabilization at the mean quantity. This measure demonstrates the importance of demand curvatures in welfare gains. If the demand function is nonlinear, stabilizing quantities consumed at their mean affects the mean price, which in turns affects welfare change. Although this may lead to welfare changes very different from equation (1), the difference concerns the incidence of the policy; that is, the repartition of gains between consumers and producers rather than efficiency (we return to this issue in section 7.3.4).

Table 7.1   Ex-ante equivalent variation for a consumer from perfect price stabilization at mean price for various parameters

η	α	ρ:	0			2			4		
		γ:	0.01	0.15	0.3	0.01	0.15	0.3	0.01	0.15	0.3
Medium fluctuations (σ$_P$ = 20%)											
0	-0.1		-0.002	-0.030	-0.060	-0.002	0.060	0.300	-0.001	0.150	0.660
0.25	-0.1		-0.002	-0.041	-0.105	-0.002	0.049	0.255	-0.001	0.139	0.615
0.25	-0.4		-0.008	-0.131	-0.285	-0.008	-0.041	0.075	-0.007	0.049	0.435
0.5	-0.4		-0.008	-0.143	-0.330	-0.008	-0.053	0.030	-0.007	0.038	0.390
0.5	-0.7		-0.014	-0.233	-0.510	-0.014	-0.143	-0.150	-0.013	-0.053	0.210
Large fluctuations (σ$_P$ = 30%)											
0	-0.1		-0.005	-0.068	-0.135	-0.004	0.135	0.675	-0.003	0.338	1.485
0.25	-0.1		-0.005	-0.093	-0.236	-0.004	0.110	0.574	-0.003	0.312	1.384
0.25	-0.4		-0.018	-0.295	-0.641	-0.017	-0.093	0.169	-0.016	0.110	0.979
0.5	-0.4		-0.018	-0.321	-0.743	-0.017	-0.118	0.067	-0.016	0.084	0.878
0.5	-0.7		-0.032	-0.523	-1.148	-0.031	-0.321	-0.338	-0.030	-0.118	0.473

Notes: Relative risk aversion, ρ; commodity budget share, γ; income elasticity, η; price elasticity, η′; price elasticity, α; coefficient of variation of price, σ$_P$; welfare changes are calculated using equation (1) and expressed as percentage of income.

Nocetti and Smith (2011) extend the analysis to a situation where consumers can save. None of these works is able to challenge the initial finding of only small welfare changes from price stabilization.

In addition, in this framework, the welfare costs presented above should be considered upper bounds. All possibilities of risk-coping strategies have been assumed away. For example, consumers cannot save. And the welfare changes are calculated by comparing welfare under price instability with welfare when prices are stabilized at their means. This ideal stabilization is not feasible (Townsend 1977), and feasible stabilization policies are costly.

Peasants and Rural Households

In poor countries, it is common for rural households to engage in agricultural production for their own consumption. And in the context of rural poor markets where market failures prevail, these production and consumption decisions tend to be nonseparable (de Janvry and Sadoulet 2006). This has decisive implications for the effect of price uncertainty on welfare. Barrett (1996) and Myers (2006) propose expressions similar to equation (1) to assess the welfare cost of food price volatility in this case. For peasant households, what is crucial to determine the effect of price fluctuations is the size and the sign of their marketed surplus. For households that are net food buyers, it does not change much from the effects described above for consumers. Affluent consumers are unlikely to suffer from price fluctuations, and may even prefer them. Poor consumers, who spend a large share of their budget on a commodity and are quite risk averse, are more likely to suffer from price fluctuations, but not overly so. However, net sellers are likely to prefer price stability since it helps to stabilize a large share of their income because they have to make their productive decisions before uncertainty is resolved. Poor producers with a limited marketed surplus are unlikely to experience large welfare gains, contrary to affluent producers. The larger the producer and the marketed surplus, the greater the preference for stability. So stabilization gains will accrue mostly to affluent producers, and potentially will be regressive.

For producers, the consequences of price instability most often discussed are the behavioral not the welfare consequences; the argument being that instability leads to production levels lower than if prices were stabilized at their expected values (Sandmo 1971). Because producers have to commit resources before uncertainty is resolved, they decrease their production levels to decrease their risk exposure. In poor countries, however, there are arguments and evidence against this behavior (Fafchamps 2003, chap. 6). If we account for the lack of formal markets for some inputs, such as labor and land, and if we account also for the survival risk created by underproduction under price risk, households may not systematically under produce. For example, households that are food insecure and risk averse are likely to overproduce to ensure their food intake, and the inverse farm size-productivity relationship could be seen as illustrative of this behavior (Barrett 1996).

Among the many strategies used by the poor to cope with risk, the choice between commercial and subsistence farming is noteworthy. Due to limited market integration, food prices in rural regions can be very volatile. When faced with the choice of allocating land and labor between a food crop and a nonconsumed cash crop, in a context of price instability poor farmers may allocate a larger share of resources to the food crop than if food prices were stable, as insurance against consumption price uncertainty (Fafchamps 1992). Consequently, food price instability may hinder the transition toward more market-oriented specialization, and some risk-coping strategies could actually hinder development.

7.2.2   Price Volatility or Downward and Upward Price Risks?

The standard assessment of the welfare cost of food price volatility, which relies on the expected utility framework and the assumption of incomplete markets, leads to provocative results. It suggests that, in most cases, the cost to consumers is small if not negative. The only people who can expect significant gains from price stabilization are the producers—and especially affluent producers, which would make price stabilization where most benefits accrue to the most well off, highly regressive. This welfare assessment implies that governments should avoid price stabilization policies and focus resources on policies that promote increased food productivity (a conclusion similar to Lucas [2003], in macroeconomics, for whom the small cost of business-cycle fluctuations seems to go against active stabilization policies). This conclusion conflicts with the attention paid to food price volatility since 2007, and the decades of major public interventions it has prompted. On this, Barrett and Bellemare (2011) propose a provocative argument: food price volatility does not matter, high food prices do matter. They show that civil unrest is correlated not to food price volatility but to food price spikes. Bellemare (2011) builds on this idea and instruments the food price index with natural disasters to demonstrate that high food prices are the cause of political unrest (see also Arezki and Brückner 2011).

Food riots are an indication that high food prices create severe hardship for people and it is unlikely that periods of low food prices will compensate for these events as postulated by the standard framework in which there is symmetry between high and low food prices. A symmetric welfare effect of high and low prices is understandable for affluent consumers or for nonessential consumption goods, but the situation is different for food and poor households. When the price of a staple food increases, poor households search to protect their caloric intake. They reduce their dietary diversity, even to the extent of consuming more of a more expensive staple (Giffen good behavior), because it is still the cheapest way to obtain calories (D'Souza and Jolliffe 2012). This reduction in food diversity implies a shift from nutrient-rich food to cheaper and more caloric food, which can have lasting consequences for vulnerable populations with high nutrient requirements, such as young children or pregnant mothers (Brinkman et al. 2010).

These costs are clearly asymmetric, they cannot be compensated for by periods of low prices but they are also dynamic. Nutrition in childhood affects education outcomes, cognitive skills, and adult economic achievement (Glewwe, Jacoby, and King 2001; Hoddinott et al. 2008). In addition, as households struggle to protect their food intake, they are forced to reduce other expenses such as child schooling and health-related expenditures (Jacoby and Skoufias 1997). If periods of high prices prevent human capital accumulation it means that, in addition to static welfare losses, they generate dynamic welfare losses that compound over time and may matter much more in the assessment of welfare cost than static losses (Myers 2006).

This is not to imply that we should worry only about upward price spikes—and policymakers do not do so. Anderson and Nelgen (2012b, table 6) show that policymakers adjust trade policies in response to upward or downward price spikes by the same magnitude. The prevention of downward price spikes is likely to arise from a concern for producer welfare. In the case of the cost of price volatility for producers, is the concern more about price volatility or about downward price spikes? Volatility is definitely a concern for producers. Price volatility can induce large swings in realized profit, and therefore in the marginal utility of income. It can also affect production decisions, since resources have to be committed before prices and yields are known. However, it is true that within the standard framework there is symmetry between low and high prices, whereas low price periods are clearly different for producers because they increase the threat of default (Leathers and Chavas 1986). In a creative destruction approach the default of some firms allows the elimination of the least productive firms, but in a context of price volatility it may just be that firms default due to the absence of a perfectly contingent market. Although price volatility is a concern for producers, it could be argued that for them downward price spikes are at least an equivalent concern.

This distinction between price volatility and downward and upward price spikes could be considered merely rhetorical, because these spikes are the two components of volatility—you cannot have one without the other. But this discussion raises the point that standard welfare measures may not be able to capture the real cost of volatility. This discussion is also informative for policy design by focusing on the most important justifications for public intervention.[5] Although development economics research demon-

---

5. One example of this framework applied to policy design is Giordani, Rocha, and Ruta (2012). They assume agents are loss averse: they value losses more than gains. Consumers experience losses when prices exceed some reference price, and vice versa for producers. It is consistent also with the contradictory injunctions from nongovernmental and international organizations, for which food prices are always either too low or too high (Swinnen and Squicciarini 2012).

strates that food security and related coping strategies to preserve it are likely to be more important for welfare assessments than standard measures of welfare change under expected utility, they do not provide any monetary assessments. To allocate resources to their most profitable use, we would like to deal with the marginal cost of stabilization policies and their marginal benefits. At the present time this is not possible, and even in the future is likely to be difficult. Contrary to infrastructure spending that has tangible outcomes, the benefits from price stabilization are intangible and depend heavily on households' coping strategies. They depend on improvements in health, nutrition, schooling, child labor, and savings. As Grosh et al. (2008, chap. 3) note in relation to measuring the benefits of spending on safety nets, many economists believe that such a measure is not feasible. And even if it were, it would remain an academic exercise and a function of many behavioral assumptions and hypotheses about the future state of the economy.

In the absence of more precise conclusions about the welfare cost of price instability, in what follows we assume that, at least in poor countries, the difficulty of coping with high food prices creates large and potentially irreversible welfare losses.

7.2.3   Political Economy and Redistribution

Previous discussions have focused on market failures as justification for food price stabilization policies, but market failures are not necessary for socially unacceptable outcomes to emerge. Even with complete and well-functioning markets, price booms can result in dire poverty and starvation for the poorest. These are not socially desirable outcomes, and a free market will not prevent them. So given the large distributive effects at stake, public intervention would be likely to emerge even without the market failures mentioned above.

Anderson et al. (2010) remind us that public support for agriculture increases with national per capita income and its importance is greater when a country's agricultural comparative advantage is weaker. It is unlikely to emerge from any market failure, but it represents the increasing role of farm lobbies as countries develop. This political economy motivation for stabilization policies is especially strong in developed countries where it is difficult to find compelling market failures to justify this scale of intervention. It is probably also present in some developing countries—and increasing with economic growth. For example, the way the minimum support price can be increased in India without any consideration for plentiful public stocks and further utilization of these stocks is a good indication of the influence of farmers in the policy process.

Other justifications for such public interventions have been discussed (see, e.g., Rashid, Cummings, and Gulati [2007] for the Asian case), such as lack of transport and communication infrastructures, and limited foreign currency reserves, which reduce the ability of a country to import food.

Although valid forty years ago, these justifications have lost some traction. In section 7.4 we discuss two common and still relevant justifications for stabilization: lack of private storage, and limited reliability of world markets. The problem is that these justifications are self-fulfilling. They arise from a vicious circle around public intervention and agents' behavior.

7.2.4   Stabilization Policies as Second-Best Interventions

The reasons for intervention outlined above do not imply that the price distribution is suboptimal. They state that agents have difficulties to cope with price shocks but not that price shocks are evidence of market failure. In this framework, price stabilization policies are, at best, second-best policies. The first-best policy would be to provide insurance/futures markets but their behavior could be mimicked through safety nets that would provide countercyclical transfers.

This is true if we believe that price instability is driven by supply and demand shocks, and mediated by the optimal reactions of rational agents. There is an alternative vision: price dynamics is not optimal because it is driven by expectations errors as in a cobweb. This is not a new idea, and has not gained ground in discussions of stabilization policies (see Gouel [2012] for a survey of the debate). This approach assumes that agents—or at least some agents in a model with heterogeneous expectations (Brock and Hommes 1997)—will base their decisions on rule-of-thumb expectations, implying that they will make systematic forecasting errors and not allocate resources according to their expected scarcity. In this case, price volatility arises endogenously from market behavior. It implies potentially large welfare costs of instability and this argument has been used to support price stabilization policies (Boussard et al. 2006). However, this approach involves many theoretical inconsistencies and is not supported by the empirical evidence (Gouel 2012).

A related issue is the ongoing debate on the role of the recent financialization of commodity markets in the food crisis. This debate is more empirical than theoretical, but proof of a positive link between increased speculation and commodity price volatility could be interpreted as evidence that the introduction of new agents may have influenced prices so that they inadequately represent the supply and demand equilibrium. Currently there is no clear theoretical justification behind the potential impact of financialization. Irwin and Sanders (2012) propose three plausible justifications: (a) lack of liquidity, which would have prevented the absorption of the large order flow of index funds; (b) index investors being noise traders; and (c) the development of index investors makes it more difficult for other traders to distinguish signals from noise. In any case, it could be seen as supporting a cobweb-like conclusion that prices do not reflect the equilibrium in which all agents take informed decisions. However, with a few exceptions (e.g., von Braun and Torero 2009), the belief that speculation played an important role in the price spike has not led people to conclude that governments should intervene to stabilize markets but rather that they should introduce rules that would make speculation less destabilizing.

7.3   Lessons from the Theory of Price Stabilization Policies

We need to make an artificial distinction between the theoretical literature and the lessons drawn from experience because empirical analysis of commodity markets is at an early stage—at least in terms of its ability to match structural models with the data.[6] This section presents theoretical and applied results for price stabilization policies. They are drawn from models that represent commodity markets in which policies are introduced. For applied models, they are calibrated to represent the economies of interest and to simulate price dynamics similar to those observed.

7.3.1   Theory of Buffer-Stock Policy

In this section, we focus on broad issues related to the design of storage policy for price stabilization. We do not consider, for example, issues such as how to account for price trends, or how storage for interannual stabilization interacts with intraannual storage. These are not simple issues, but as we show in section 7.4, the practical difficulties related to storage policies come more from their political economy than from any lack of theoretical understanding, even though a theoretical design of second-best storage policies presents significant unresolved challenges.

The importance of interannual storage in policy debate and in applied policies stems from its perceived ability to smooth quantitative shocks and from observation that a low-stock situation has been a necessary condition for price spikes since the 1960s (Gilbert 2011). Stocks accumulate when supply is larger than need, and are released in times of scarcity. This provides some price stabilization but only to the extent that stocks are available when prices rise. In competitive markets, storage can be profitable since it exploits the difference between low and high prices. Recognizing the existence of profit-oriented storers is crucial, because any food price policy will affect their incentives. A first consequence of their existence is that they provide some stability in the market even without public intervention (Wright and Williams 1982a). However, based on the discussion in section 7.2, it is likely that private storers do not take account of some of the costs accruing to the population in times of very high or very low food prices. So, higher price stability, provided by more storage, could improve welfare.

Increasing stock levels beyond competitive levels is the basis of any storage policy aimed at achieving higher price stability. There are many ways to

---

6. This is changing, though, and some studies present encouraging estimates of storage models (see, e.g., Cafiero et al. 2011).

achieve it but it should be noted first that increasing stock levels is costly. If private storers are already arbitraging the difference between current and expected prices, any policy that increases storage beyond competitive levels will not cover its costs through market operations, and may even reduce profitability and thus amounts of private storage. As long as private markets are functioning properly—which may be assuming a lot in poor countries—any public policy aimed at increasing storage beyond competitive levels will be fiscally costly. This does not reduce the potential for storage policy to increase welfare but it should not be assumed from the start that a public storage policy will result in breakeven because storers buy low and sell high. This may occur —and over several years—but by design public storage policy must be costly in order to exceed what is being done by private arbitrageurs.

An important question, linked to the discussion in the previous section, is how policymakers want to alter price distribution. As already emphasized, the literature generally retains that price stabilization policies are second-best policies, so it is likely that there is nothing wrong initially with the price distribution except that agents may find it difficult to cope with. If the problem is mostly one of risk aversion, equation (1) tells us that the cost of price volatility for consumers will decrease with a decrease in price variance. In this case, Gouel (2013) shows that the optimal storage rule is very similar to the competitive storage rule (on second-best storage policies, see also Gardner [1979] and Newbery [1989]). For low food availability, no stock is accumulated and all stocks are sold. When availability is superior to normal consumption, part of the excess is accumulated. The difference between the competitive and optimal storage rule is that under the optimal rule stock accumulation starts at lower food availability and the marginal propensity to store is always higher. The occurrence of low prices decreases because of the increased stock accumulation, and the higher mean stock level allows avoidance of more price spikes than under the competitive level. As a consequence, any public agency implementing such a rule would completely crowd out private storage since the reduced instability would not be enough to sustain the profitability of arbitrageurs. If public storage is less efficient than private storage, this crowding out will increase the costs of the policy well beyond the additional storage that it requires. Another issue arises because crowding out means that such a policy may inhibit the development of a private marketing system, making future transition to a freer trade regime more difficult.

There are reasons to expect incomplete crowding out. This will be the case if private storage is motivated not just by speculation or if it has some structural differences from public storage. Wright and Williams (1982a), and Williams and Wright (1991, chap. 15) touch on this by analyzing the management of strategic petroleum reserves. Two features explain the coexistence of both public and private stocks: in the first study, private storers are assumed to receive a convenience yield from the holding of stocks, implying that they hold stock even if the apparent return is negative; in the second study, they suppose that public stock is not held at the same location as private stock—for example, private stocks may be located closer to the market—so that private storers face a different price instability, which may sustain their activity. For these reasons, and because private storers hold stocks to smooth the natural seasonality of agriculture production, it is reasonable to think that, in practice, an optimal public storage policy would not completely crowd out private storage. But there will be very little scope for private storage to obey a speculative motive in the presence of welfare-maximizing public storage.

Since an optimal storage rule designed to address issues of risk aversion is similar to a competitive storage rule, optimal storage could also be achieved by giving appropriate incentives to private storers. Gouel (2013) shows that the gains from a public storage rule can be reached simply by giving storers a subsidy proportional to the stored quantities. This policy has the advantage of avoiding the involvement of government in grain marketing and decentralizing the policy to private agents. Subsidies have been used to stimulate private storage in Latin American countries and in the United States, but often in the less efficient form of interest-rate subsidies (Gardner and López 1996).

In policy discussions, a more frequent option than a storage rule that would be close to a competitive rule is a price band. Price bands can be justified on two grounds. One is that an optimal storage policy can be complex to design and to explain to private agents and may not be robust to uncertainties, so relying on a simple storage rule may be a good way to reap some of the benefits from stability without too many complications (Gardner 1979; Gouel 2013). The other is the idea that price instability is not the most important problem. What concerns agents are very high or very low prices, and while normal price instability can be smoothed by private storers, government should intervene to prevent extreme prices. These justifications can lead to opposite recommendations with respect to lower and upper bounds. In the former case, the optimal price band is a price peg, a policy where the lower and upper bounds are identical, with an intervention price close to the steady state (Gouel 2013). Although there is no formal analysis of a price band designed to prevent extremes, the intuition is that this case would call for a wide price band, which would limit interventions to serious shortages or surpluses and permit private sector intervention between bounds (World Bank 2012). However, simulation studies so far find that the wider the band, the costlier is the policy (Miranda and Helmberger 1988; Williams and Wright 1991; Gouel 2013).

Whatever the bounds, price-band policies have some common features. Contrary to common expectations that prices will fluctuate between bounds, they spend a lot of time at the bounds, challenging them (Williams and Wright 1991, chap. 14). A price band is also very different from a competitive storage rule. Because of the commitment to defend a lower bound, the marginal propensity to store at high food availability is equal to one, while competitive storers have a marginal propensity to store that increases with availability but stays below unity. So when the floor price is reached, stock accumulation is much higher under a price band than what would be achieved by competitive storers. Because of this high marginal propensity to store, price bands can easily lead to overaccumulation and even explosive behavior when the bounds are inappropriate (Miranda and Helmberger 1988; Williams and Wright 1991, chap. 14). This can be prevented by fixing a limit on the stock level, which greatly improves the behavior of a price band (Gouel 2013). With such a policy, nothing is accumulated until the lower bound is reached, and since there is no intervention between the bounds, there may continue to be sufficient volatility to sustain private activity. With respect to private storage, a price band has ambiguous effects. Since it trims from the distribution prices above and below the bounds, it removes some of the incentives to store. On the other hand, public storage under a price band presents predictable public interventions that can be exploited strategically by private storers to make profit, and even subject it to speculative attacks (Salant 1983). This private speculative activity taking place along a price-band policy might be perceived negatively since it interacts strategically with the government program. Theoretically, this intuition would be wrong. A price-band policy without private activity is more likely to generate welfare losses compared to a laissez-faire situation (Gouel 2013) since arbitrage possibilities continue to be available. A price-band policy can increase storage beyond competitive levels only with the help of speculators.

The need of private storers to make a price band welfare improving contrasts with the observation that countries implement buffer-stock policies partly because of their distrust of private markets. It contrasts also with the regulations on private activity that often accompany these policies, such as panterritorial pricing, and restrictions on intranational or international trade.

That a price band means buying low and selling high does not imply that this policy is fiscally profitable. It might be without the intervention of private storers, but as long as speculators are not prevented from seizing the profit opportunities—and they should not be since they provide valuable stabilization—public storage under a price band results in a loss. In particular, contrary to expectations and many policy recommendations, wide bands are very costly to defend. Common expectations are that wide bands ensure rare interventions and allow private storers to do their work, and that the large spread between buying and selling prices reduces the cost of the policy. This latter expectation does not hold: the high selling price will cover the purchasing costs but the large spread implies that the time between accumulation and release of grain may be long, creating large opportunity and storage costs.

7.3.2   Countercyclical Trade Policies

Second-best trade policies have received comparatively much more attention than second-best storage policies, particularly in relation to the issue
of the nonoptimality of free trade under uncertainty, which inspired a large
literature in the 1970s and 1980s. The first formalization of this issue was
achieved by Brainard and Cooper (1968). Based on a portfolio approach,
they showed that diversification in a primary-producing country decreases
fluctuations in national income, which increases national welfare if the
country is risk averse. Based on a comparable framework, including risk
aversion in a context where productive choices are made before uncertainty
is resolved, several papers challenge the idea of the optimality of free trade
under uncertainty (Batra and Russell 1974; Turnovsky 1974; Anderson and
Riley 1976).

Helpman and Razin (1978) point out that this result hinges crucially on
the assumption of incomplete risk-sharing markets. They show that the
main results of Ricardian and Heckscher-Ohlin theories of international
trade, including the optimality of free trade, carry over to uncertain environments if risk can be shared appropriately. In their model, this is the case
because the stock market allows households to diversify their capital, and
cross-border trade in financial assets opens the possibility for international
risk-sharing arrangements.

Helpman and Razin's seminal contributions clarify decisively the conditions underlying potential deviations from standard results and pave the way
to numerous insightful elaborations. Yet, as argued in section 7.2, there is
a variety of reasons why the conditions required for their results might not
hold. For instance, in the case that households need to invest their capital
in a particular activity without any possibility to diversify, to insure, or to
trade the corresponding risk. In this context, which is plausible especially
for rural households in developing countries, Eaton and Grossman (1985)
show that the optimal trade policy for a small open economy is not free trade.
The optimal policy is countercyclical and helps to redistribute resources
between groups depending on the terms-of-trade shocks. In addition, this
optimal policy entails, on average, an antitrade bias. Similar conclusions
emerge if market incompleteness is the result of lack of international trade
in financial assets (Feenstra 1987). In a specific-factor model with risk-averse
factor owners, Cassing, Hillman, and Long (1986) also show that a state-
contingent tariff policy can increase the expected utility of all agents.

These works are not concerned primarily with food products and food
security but they make the point that when other arrangements are not
available, a departure from free trade may be motivated by domestic risk
sharing. Food security concerns would probably even further reinforce the
rationales to redistribute resources from producers to consumers in times
of food price spikes. With the exception of Newbery and Stiglitz (1984), a

notable feature of work that supports interventionist trade policies is that it considers small-open countries. Although these kinds of policies may make perfect sense for a single country, extending this conclusion to the whole world would lead to a fallacy of composition. When applied globally and to the extent that countries have similar risk preferences, trade policies may not allow any risk sharing and may even be procyclical. Martin and Anderson (2012) study the collective action problem that arises if countercyclical trade policies are generalized. Their generalization, first, results in their being ineffective. Importers tax imports when the world price is low, and decrease tariffs or use import subsidies when the world price is high. Exporters do the opposite. They subsidize exports when world prices are low and restrict them in times of high world prices. These trade policies offset each other, which can leave domestic prices unchanged with respect to free trade and make the world price more volatile, giving the illusion of a successful policy when the domestic price is compared to the world price. Second, not all countries apply such policies, or if they do they may face budgetary constraints limiting their adjustment. Those countries that refrain from using trade policies or that are constrained about adjustment to their interventions may suffer from the worldwide use of trade policies. The use of countercyclical trade policies, thus, results in a typical prisoner's dilemma.

In reality, adjustments to trade policies are constrained by bilateral and multilateral trade agreements, but the scope for adjustment is nevertheless quite large. When instituting export restrictions on foodstuffs World Trade Organization (WTO) members only have to give consideration to the effects on importing members, and provide notification. Import tariffs are constrained by their bound levels, but bound levels for agricultural products are high and allow large tariff adjustments (Bouët and Laborde 2010). Export subsidies are allowed for twenty-five WTO members and are subject to commitments but all developing countries can use them to cover marketing and transport costs. Variable levies that adjust the levy on imports to defend domestic price targets were banned by the Uruguay Round Agreement on Agriculture. However, discretionary tariff adjustments are allowed as long as tariff rates stay below their bound levels, and have been used often over the last forty years (Anderson and Nelgen 2012b).

7.3.3   Combining Trade and Storage Policies

Most results for storage policies are derived in closed economy settings or under the implicit assumption that the model represents the whole world. We know much less about how to implement storage policies in an open economy. For example, we know very little about the interactions between price-band policies and trade. This is a very important issue because, despite the widespread pursuit of self-sufficiency, most countries engage in cereal trade and trade strongly affects storage decisions.

There are a few theoretical relations between trade and storage under free trade that are important to understand in order to consider the effect of combined storage and trade policies. For each country, shocks to yields can be decomposed into an aggregate component, deviation of world yield from its mean allocated to each country according to its land share, and an idiosyncratic component, which is the difference between realized domestic yields and their aggregate components. In a world without trade costs and trade policies, trade would perfectly alleviate the idiosyncratic components since by construction they sum to zero. All countries would share the same price, determined by the aggregate shock to world yield and existing stocks, and stocks would help to reduce the volatility caused by the aggregate shocks. With trade costs, as long as countries are not trading continuously, trade cannot completely smooth away idiosyncratic shocks since spatial arbitrage is costly. Hence storage with trade costs plays a different role. It contributes to smoothing both the aggregate shocks and the part of idiosyncratic shocks that cannot be smoothed by trade. But except when trade costs are so large that they prevent trade, the respective ideal contributions of trade and storage in smoothing shocks in a laissez-faire world are for trade to smooth idiosyncratic shocks and for stocks to smooth aggregate shocks. Because of these respective functions, the use of trade and storage policies as national policies to smooth domestic prices appears problematic. Trade policies will reduce the global smoothing of idiosyncratic shocks, which free trade allows, and efficient storage is more about world risk than national risk.

That the main contribution of stocks is to smooth aggregate world shocks does not imply that the location of the stocks is indifferent. Because of trade costs, it is not. Storing grains entails many costs, including the opportunity cost of the money that has to be spent immediately to reap future benefits. Importing grains with the objective of speculating implies paying opportunity costs over trade costs, since trade costs have to be paid immediately. The consequence is that in an importing country, storers should not import based on a speculative motive but only for proximate consumption. Speculative storage should be confined to exporting countries (Williams and Wright 1991). This does not mean that there are no reasons to store in importing countries. Shipping takes time, which justifies some stockholding by an importing country (Coleman 2009), however this does not modify the previous argument that, in general, arbitrageurs should prefer storing the commodity closer to its production to reduce interest costs.

However, this is a worldwide perspective. With respect to a single country, trade is not always a blessing. It can help reduce volatility, because world price volatility can be expected to be lower than domestic price volatility in an autarkic country thanks to the smoothing of idiosyncratic shocks. Trade also helps to alleviate a limit of storage, its nonnegativity. Storage, whether public or private, cannot prevent all price spikes because stocks occasionally are exhausted, but trade gives access to a supply source that is less likely to be exhausted. On the other hand, because of bad weather events or strong demand abroad, the world price can spike despite adequate domestic supply, and a country will face high prices that are unrelated to its domestic conditions. This opens the way to the numerous trade interventions we observe. It may be tempting to exploit the world market when it serves the interests of a country, and to withdraw from it when scarcity prevails abroad.

To analyze the interaction between trade and storage policy, we consider first the situation of a country close to self-sufficiency, which is the best suited to having a storage policy with some independence from the world market. Gouel and Jean (forthcoming) analyze this situation by considering the optimal design of a food price stabilization policy in a small open economy that is normally self-sufficient. Based on this assumption, the domestic price evolves between export- and import-parity prices, and when it is not connected to the world market, any changes in stock levels affect the domestic price. The implications of increasing domestic price stability through storage or through trade policy are different. Storage policy on its own is not effective at preventing high prices because periods of price spikes occur when a country is very likely to be connected to the world market, through exports or imports. Storage could prevent spikes from domestic scarcity but stock release would need to be sufficiently high to completely crowd out imports. However, storage policy alleviates low prices by increasing stock accumulation and so leads to asymmetric price stabilization by reducing the occurrence more of low than high prices, which increases the mean price. This has consequences for trade. The increased stock levels reduce imports and increase exports.

In this setting, a countercyclical trade policy is much more efficient than a storage policy to stabilize prices. In particular, it reduces the occurrence of high prices by using export restrictions and import subsidies. Because trade policy reduces price volatility and the occurrence of price spikes, it reduces the incentives of private storers, and storage decreases by 20 percent in the simulations. Stabilization is more efficiently achieved by combining trade and storage policies since trade policy limits the "leakage" of storage policy to the world market and is efficient in preventing high prices, while storage is better at preventing low prices. Export restrictions are an essential component of this policy: not using them hugely reduces the potential gains and allows more of the effect of world price spikes to be transmitted to the market.

A country need not be self-sufficient to have an active and effective storage policy. For example, Larson et al. (2014) analyze the possibility of defending a price ceiling on wheat with public storage to alleviate very high prices (i.e., the last decile of the distribution), for Middle East and North African (MENA) countries. The MENA countries are very dependent on wheat imports (for 40 percent of their consumption), and wheat represents a very high share of national caloric intake. A storage policy is shown to be effective for reducing the frequency of price spikes for MENA, but also for the rest of the world, since MENA countries are always connected to the world market because of their large import needs. It leads also to some international crowding out. Without public policy, speculative storage should be absent in MENA countries because they are consistently importing. A public storage policy in MENA reduces private storage in the rest of the world since it decreases price volatility by preventing high prices and by decreasing episodes of low prices through stock accumulation. This crowding out tends to be costly, because as noted above it means that storage is undertaken in a less efficient location, so interest costs have to be paid on top of transport costs.

Although many of the results for storage policies in closed economies hold for open economies, in the latter case there is a fundamental difference, which is the possibility of leakage of the policy to the world market. As long as a country is not well insulated by trade policies from world price variations, it has to displace trade volumes to be able to stabilize domestic prices through storage. This can be costly. If trade is not crowded out, the additional storage mostly helps to stabilize the world market. Price stabilization policies, even if individually rational for each country, create serious collective action problems. Public storage policies that could have positive international spillovers are of limited interest domestically if not flanked by trade policies to countries that are not isolated from the world market. On the other hand, trade policies have negative spillovers because they provide stabilization for a country at the expense of its trade partners. This can be linked to a previous point that in an open economy storage should be more about dealing with aggregate world shocks and trade should be more concerned with idiosyncratic shocks. A storage policy without an accompanying trade policy increases world stability by providing more smoothing of aggregate shocks. However, a trade policy will prevent the smoothing of idiosyncratic shocks. It should be apparent from this that it is not possible for an open economy to stabilize its domestic food prices without affecting its partners. Whether they are affected negatively or positively depends on the mix of trade and storage policies applied.

7.3.4   Large Redistributive Effects

Since the work of Newbery and Stiglitz (1981), a recurrent criticism of stabilization policies is that they generate redistribution between consumers and producers more than efficiency gains. Indeed, stabilizing prices through storage or trade policies can affect agents' welfare in convoluted and counterintuitive ways. This is because it is difficult if not impossible to reduce price variance without changing the mean as well as other moments. If we assume that agents are sufficiently risk averse, they may enjoy welfare gains from a reduced variance in prices, and we can expect aggregate efficiency gains for the economy. However, changes in the mean price will lead to transfers between consumers and producers that for some groups will potentially exceed the efficiency gains obtained from a reduced risk. The direction of the transfers between agents will be determined mainly by changes in the mean price and there are good reasons to expect stabilization policies to affect the mean price.

Stabilization may affect the mean price in both directions, and it is difficult to propose general results for the incidence of stabilization policies because it is influenced by several parameters. For example, the incidence identified for long-run results can be reversed when dynamics is accounted for and long-run welfare changes are discounted. Welfare gains can be reversed depending on the hypotheses made about the nature of the shocks: multiplicative or additive, related to the demand curvature or the values of the elasticities. Since incidence is so dependent on setting, we describe some general mechanisms that affect the distribution of gains among agents (for more details on the incidence of price stabilization policies, see Wright [1979]; Wright and Williams [1988a]).

Static Incidence

Here we focus on static transfers, those that arise from a static model or from the stationary regime of a dynamic model. The mean price around which a policy stabilizes domestic prices depends on the details of the policy, but some general conclusions about this mean price can be drawn by considering how price instability affects demand and supply behavior.

The curvature of the demand function is a crucial element driving how stabilization policies affect the mean price. In many policies, the real objective is to stabilize food consumption not prices, and even if this is not the objective, stabilizing quantities is more convenient in practice since prices are the endogenous result of market equilibrium whereas it is possible to affect quantities through storage. If we focus on demand and neglect the supply reaction, a mean-quantity-preserving contraction will maintain the mean price constant if the demand function is linear. If demand is convex, a mean-quantity-preserving contraction (spread) leads to a lower (higher) mean price because the convexity implies that prices react more to changes in high consumption levels than to changes in low consumption levels.

Supply reaction also matters for assessing incidence. The welfare of producers changes because of the new price distribution, but they also react to this distribution by changing their supply. Let us consider a situation à la Sandmo (1971) in which producers are risk averse and produce less when faced with stochastic prices than in a certain environment, and complete the market by introducing futures that allow producers to hedge their price risk with the result that they will produce more. This is individually profitable. Each producer, by securing the selling price on the futures market, is able to commit more resources and enjoy more benefits. However, this can be collectively self-defeating. Increased production by all farmers results in a price distribution with a lower mean, which may decrease producers' welfare for inelastic demand and elastic supply (Myers 1988; Lence 2009). In the absence of other market failures, completing the market increases economic efficiency and generates aggregate welfare gains but with no guarantee that risk-averse agents will benefit.

That incidence results might be dominated by mean price changes is a consequence of the low valuation of risk in expected utility models. Surplus measures dominate welfare assessments and efficiency gains are dwarfed by transfers. However, we have argued that price instability creates costs that are not well accounted for, and the low values obtained from the expected utility framework are difficult to reconcile with the social unrest and endless public intervention in these markets. We cannot ignore the possibility that these potentially larger efficiency costs mean that incidence results could be dominated less by mean price changes and more by a decrease in extreme events. The dominance of transfers over efficiency gains is a reason for Newbery and Stiglitz's (1981) skepticism about stabilization policies. This reasoning, which has become very influential and is the basis of many subsequent works, depends crucially on the way welfare gains are assessed. But even if there are good reasons to expect higher efficiency gains than previously assumed, these gains will not be evenly spread in society and these policies will probably have large redistributive effects. In a world where agents are heterogeneous, some will gain a little from price stabilization or from reductions in extreme price events; some, because they are poorer or because they are highly specialized producers, will benefit a lot; and some may be indifferent to instability but will be affected by any mean price change. Since stabilization policies are untargeted policies, they affect all agents indifferently and it is very likely that to achieve the underlying efficiency gains, they will generate transfers. The literature on incidence, however, may be an incomplete guide to this issue since it assumes extremely low efficiency gains.

Dynamic Incidence

Stabilization policies are inherently dynamic, which means that their incidence should not be assessed only on the long-run equilibrium. It is also important to account for the way welfare gains are affected in the transition to this equilibrium. A public storage policy usually aims at stabilizing prices by accumulating stocks beyond competitive levels. So a storage policy begins with a transitory phase of stock accumulation before reaching its long-run behavior. Since stock purchases are higher than they would be without intervention, prices will be temporarily higher. We explained above that a stabilization policy in the long run may lead to a price distribution with a lower mean, either because of supply reaction or of demand convexity, thus potentially hurting producers' welfare. Because these long-run lower prices are discounted with respect to short-run high prices caused by stock accumulation, producers may actually enjoy a storage policy. This is the important conclusion in Miranda and Helmberger (1988) and Wright and

Williams (1988a), that the actual incidence of market-stabilizing policies is often dominated by what occurs in the transitory phase. The importance of transitional dynamics also implies that initial conditions matter a lot: it is not the same to start a policy when availability is high or low.

The other crucial point that affects the dynamic incidence of policies is capitalization. Agricultural production requires the use of a fixed factor, land. To the extent that other inputs are supplied elastically, the value of land is likely to include the effect of agricultural policies, potentially depriving farmers of welfare gains. Since the market value of farmland reflects the expected benefits tied to its operation and how much people are willing to pay to benefit from the insurance provided by farm programs, this value will increase with the introduction of policies that increase revenue or decrease revenue risk. Thus, the main beneficiaries of such a policy will be the owners of the farmland at the time the policy is implemented. In reality, the pass-through from policy benefits to land market values is not complete, but capitalization still allocates much of the gain to the current land owner (Kirwan 2009; Goodwin, Mishra, and Ortalo-Magné 2012).

7.3.5   The Alternative of Safety Nets

This chapter is not concerned directly with safety nets, but a presentation of stabilization policies would not be complete without some discussion of what often is considered to be their alternative. In the context of the failure of the international commodity agreements (Gilbert 1996) and the high cost and mixed record of domestic stabilization policies, the main policy recommendation in the 1980s and 1990s was that countries should rely more on market-based risk management instruments and safety nets (Varangis, Larson, and Anderson 2002; World Bank 2006; or Timmer 1989 for a critique).

Market-based risk management instruments are supposed to provide farmers, traders, food agencies, and even individuals with access to instruments that allow the sharing of price and weather risks and the smoothing of income fluctuations. Put simply, these instruments should help to complete markets. On the other hand, safety nets are supposed to help the poor and vulnerable cope with shocks. Safety nets are noncontributory targeted transfers, whose function is to provide assistance to the poor and to prevent destitution following shocks (Grosh et al. 2008). They exist in various forms such as cash transfers, food stamps, in-kind transfers, and food-for-work and cash-for-work programs. With respect to food price risk, they complement market-based risk management instruments by providing some insurance to the poor who have a limited access to formal coping mechanisms.

This is theoretically appealing since the case for public intervention is based not on excessive volatility, but on people's lack of capacity to deal with this risk. So countercyclical safety nets should bring us closer to the first-best than could price-stabilization policies. And even should this not be the case, as long as safety nets provide cash or inframarginal in-kind transfers, they are unlikely to generate large efficiency losses. Also safety nets can be complementary even to stabilization policies. The source of food price fluctuations, weather events, or demand shocks can destabilize incomes. Hence the release of food from public stocks may not be enough to protect the purchasing power of the poor (Sen 1981; Alderman and Haque 2006) and safety nets would be a necessary complement to stabilization policies. In-kind safety nets can also be considered complements to storage policies because they provide a natural way to dispose of grains when stocks need to be rotated, although open-market sales would permit stock rotation without the logistical hurdle of a system of ration shops.

The use of countercyclical safety nets is not straightforward. Most of the time, safety nets are not designed to fulfill an insurance function, but rather to reduce poverty and help raise people above the poverty level. This income-transfer function is easier and better known than the insurance function. For example, the administration of countercyclical safety nets is challenging, because resources tend to be procyclical; they are more available in good than in bad times. This is especially true for safety nets providing in-kind transfers since grain procurement is cheaper when harvests are good and prices are low. So using safety nets as insurance presents some hurdles (Alderman and Haque 2006). One of these is the ability to scale safety nets up or down, depending on needs. In addition to administrative capabilities, this requires flexible financing. Targeting should also be dynamic. Food price shocks deteriorate the situation of the already-poor net food buyers and also may push into poverty people who initially were not poor enough to be covered by the safety net.

Safety nets are often presented as a good policy alternative to price stabilization policies, because they are targeted, they do not attempt to manipulate food prices, and they do not destabilize world markets. However, these transfers could create pecuniary externalities at the world level. Through cash or through in-kind transfers, safety nets protect the purchasing power of the poor from increased food prices and help them maintain their food consumption. If applied, they will reduce the exportable surplus of an exporting country and increase the excess demand of an importing country. So safety nets create pecuniary externalities for other countries by increasing domestic demand for food, and in this respect do not differ much from countercyclical trade policies (Do, Levchenko, and Ravallion, chap. 9, this volume), which try to secure local food supply and have been heavily criticized for fueling food crises. Safety nets, however, are advocated as good policy practice. In section 7.4, we show that the practical use of these policies creates crucial differences: trade policies tend to overreact to upward price shocks, for example, with countries banning exports and accumulating stocks in the midst of the food crisis, while safety nets underreact (Grosh et al. 2011)—probably because of the aforementioned difficulties to adjust them in times of crisis.

7.4   Lessons from Historical Experience

This section looks at the effectiveness and limitations of some examples of past food policies. Unfortunately, since statistical evidence on their effects is still limited, it focuses on narratives of stabilization policy successes and failures. As a consequence, even though we can highlight cases where trade and storage policies have been extremely costly or cases where interventions have not led to poverty reduction, or reduced hunger and malnutrition, these interventions cannot be compared to a benchmark situation; there is no counterfactual.

7.4.1   Safety Nets during the Recent Food Crisis

Have safety nets protected the poor during the recent food crisis? Although most countries already had some kind of safety net in place, these measures were not always appropriate to protect against rising food prices. And since safety nets are difficult to develop in the timeframe of a food crisis, countries without preexisting and adequate programs have tended to rely on untargeted and distortive policies, such as universal food subsidies or trade policies, import tariff decreases, import subsidies, and export restrictions. The situation is by nature highly heterogeneous among countries. For example, in North African countries, the coverage provided by targeted safety nets is very limited and targeting often inadequate (World Bank 2009). These countries rely much more on general subsidies on flour, sugar, and cooking oil. As a result, in 2007 to 2008, the overall policy response was to increase subsidies and reduce tariffs. Existing staple food subsidies proved difficult to reform because they are an essential part of the social order.

Grosh et al. (2011) provide a picture of safety-net readiness for food price volatility and its recent evolution. They provide detailed analysis of thirteen low-income countries that faced high food price increases. They show that even in countries relatively well prepared coverage was only partially adequate. To be able to react in time countries relied on existing safety nets, most of which were based on static targeting because their original purpose was income transfer. However, the crisis increased interest in safety nets, and Grosh et al. (2011) found that the countries they studied were better prepared in 2011 than in 2008, with many projects launched and extended since that time.

Despite these difficulties, where safety nets were in place they played a crucial role in protecting the poor from food price increases (Demeke, Pangrazio, and Maetz 2009; Grosh et al. 2011). In the Latin American countries, the benefits of conditional cash transfer (CCT) programs were increased (Brazil, Mexico). Many countries scaled up school feeding programs to deter parents from removing their children from school (e.g., Haiti, Madagascar, Philippines). Other interventions included increasing subsidies in public distribution systems (e.g., Bangladesh and India), and raising wage rates in public work programs (Ethiopia).

An important lesson from the use of safety nets in the food crisis is that even countries with large safety net systems used complementary price stabilization policies. In Jamaica and Mexico, despite existing and well-considered CCT programs, the first reaction was not to scale up these programs but to rely on untargeted price subsidies. Their CCT programs were used as a second step (Grosh et al. 2011). Price stabilization in India, pursued through an export ban on non-Basmati rice and wheat, was so effective (real price of food grains increased by 4.7 percent in 2007 to 2008 compared to 2006 to 2007) that it caused partial redundancy of adjustments to existing safety nets, although food subsidies increased by 32 percent in the period (World Bank 2010).

This use of price stabilization policies in a context of existing safety nets may be related to the difficulties involved in scaling up and targeting this protection (Alderman and Haque 2006; Grosh et al. 2011) but may also be due to two other considerations. For countries close to self-sufficiency, such as India, it might be fiscally less costly to ban exports than to increase transfers. In addition, well-targeted safety nets leave a large share of the middle class unprotected. Since international trade agreements do not seriously constrain the use of export restrictions on food, the political cost of their use is low compared to the political gains obtained from protecting the middle class not covered by social protection policies. Governments are rewarded for such actions. As noted by Timmer (2010), the Indian prime minister and the Indonesian president were reelected in 2009 after campaigns that emphasized their ability to limit the impact of the food crisis on their countries.

In sum, in countries with already well-established safety nets, they have proved useful for protecting the poor from high food prices. Following the 2007 to 2008 crisis many new projects are in development and are benefiting from technological improvements. For example, the United Nations World Food Programme is moving to a logic of food assistance agencies and is helping countries develop safety nets using cash and voucher transfers, relying on smart cards and cell phones (Omamo, Gentilini, and Sandström 2010). But there are some real difficulties: a dynamic targeting is proving difficult, good administrative capacities are important to achieve policy adjustments at short notice, and the political economy is not always favorable to such reforms (e.g., in the Middle East and North Africa where reform of universal food subsidies has proved difficult). Nevertheless, these problems are no greater than those faced by governments when they try to stabilize prices— as we see below.

7.4.2   The Problems Faced by Buffer-Stock Policies

Weak Selling Provisions of National Storage Policies

As explained above, the incidence of storage policies is inherently dynamic. Producers may enjoy a market-stabilizing policy not because of its long-run properties—potentially detrimental to them when demand function is convex—but because of the initial accumulation phase that pushes prices to high levels. It also means that, once the first accumulation is achieved, farmers may lobby to delay stock selling, push for further stock accumulation, or for disposal through export subsidies. This occurred in many situations where the rule governing public stock accumulation was defined much more precisely than the rule governing stock release.

India offers a snapshot of this behavior. In the introduction we described how well India weathered the 2007 to 2008 food crisis. This was due to its countercyclical trade policies, and particularly, its export ban. However, Indian storage policy has probably little to do with this success. Since the end of the 1960s Indian food policy has achieved some of its objectives: no famine, domestic price stability, and self-sufficiency in major cereals. Public intervention dominates Indian food grain markets. Farmers benefit from a minimum support price through which 58 percent of the rice and wheat marketed surplus is channeled to public stocks. Public stocks are used to supply in-kind safety nets and to stabilize markets. Finally, various laws restrict private involvement in grain markets, such as limitations to interstate and international trade, and antihoarding laws.

The recent management of Indian public stocks would suggest that these interventions are very costly and that better outcomes could be expected with the same public funding. Because of political pressures and to maintain the farmers' incentives to supply public stocks in periods of rising world prices, government rapidly raised minimum support prices in the 1990s and in the second half of the first decade of the twenty-first century, which led to increased procurement. Although stock accumulation increased, stock releases did not keep up (see figure 7.1). An important share of stocks is used to supply ration shops and other in-kind safety nets. But to limit fiscal costs, the public distribution of subsidized food was not adjusted to accord with stock levels. There is no rule to dispose of remaining stocks, which are supposed to help stabilize the market through discretionary releases. The large stocks accumulated were reduced in the early twenty-first century through subsidized exports; a policy difficult to rationalize in a country with more than 200 million undernourished people. It is also difficult to rationalize the stock accumulation during the 2007 to 2008 crisis. While cereal prices were reaching very high levels on the world market, Indian rice stocks were increasing (as Dorosh [2009] notes, this had a large opportunity cost: two to three million tons of rice exported at $300 per ton—a conservative estimate—would have represented $600 to $900 million in export revenues). Similarly, in 2009 to 2010 India suffered from a severe dry monsoon season, and rice production decreased from 99 million tons from 2008 to 2009 to 89 million tons. This was accompanied by a reduction in consumption of 5.6 million tons but a stock increase of 1.5 million tons (USDA 2012). From these anecdotes, it is unclear how much Indian storage policy is counter-

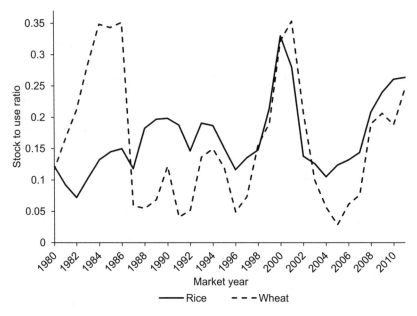

Fig. 7.1   Wheat and rice stocks in India
Source: USDA (2012).

cyclical and is helping market stabilization, given that stock release does not seem to follow high prices and stock accumulation persists during high price episodes.

The story of the Australian Wool Corporation is also exemplary of this mechanism because its failure was the result of its direct management by wool producers (see Bardsley [1994] for the whole story). Australia stabilized the price of wool successfully through the 1970s and 1980s. The Wool Reserve Price Scheme, funded by a tax on production, defended a floor price set annually by the government after consultation with the industry. However, there was no selling provision. Beyond stock purchase, stock management was discretionary. In 1987 management was handed over to the wool industry, which immediately increased the floor price by 70 percent. Supply increased accordingly, but the high prices deterred demand, which turned to cotton and synthetic fibers. At the end of the 1980s, the Wool Corporation bought for storage half of all the wool offered for sale. The high stock accumulation soon exhausted the funding coming from the tax on production and further accumulations were financed by borrowing against the wool stockpile. However, this did not lead the industry to decrease the floor price. The industry was facing skewed incentives: large gains from selling high current production versus limited future losses from the corporation because the industry was liable for the equity but not for the outstanding debts. In 1991 the Australian government suspended the scheme. The remaining stockpile was close to one year's production and the debt represented between 60 percent and 90 percent of one year's sales.

Storage in International Commodity Agreements (ICAs)

We can get more insight into the practice of storage policies by considering the history of ICAs. Because these agreements involve many consuming and producing countries, interventions were required to allow more transparency and less discretion than is possible for a sovereign country. In addition, another interest of these global policies is that, beyond anecdote, it is difficult to assess the effectiveness of a storage policy for stabilizing prices in a single country since storage policies are often associated with trade policies, whose effects are likely to be very important.

The ICAs with provisions for market control emerged in the postwar period under the auspices of the United Nations and concerned cocoa, coffee, rubber, sugar, and tin. They were treaties between producing and consuming countries. They defined regulation on international trade and storage to achieve remunerative and stable prices. Although some ICAs are still active, they no longer include "economic clauses" and their role is to facilitate intergovernmental consultations and market transparency (for a detailed description of market interventions under ICAs, see Gilbert [1996, 2011]). The primary objective of some ICAs was to prevent very low prices rather than to stabilize prices. In this respect, the international coffee and sugar agreements relied on export controls, not buffer stock. Nonetheless, storage played a crucial role; when supply is very inelastic in the short run, control of exports is easier through domestic storage than through supply restriction. The agreements on cocoa, rubber, and tin relied explicitly on buffer stocks. All were based on bandwidth rules. The buffer-stock managers had to defend ceiling and floor prices by stock sales and purchases.

The history of ICAs with stockholding provisions provides the following lessons. Intervention was possible over a long time (twenty-eight years for the tin agreements) because the price targets were regularly adjusted. Storage policies based on a bandwidth rule require regular adjustments to account for structural changes (e.g., production costs and consumer tastes). This raises several issues. First, it can be conceptually complex. The existence of the intervention can mean that a representative free-trade price on which to base adjustment is lacking. Second, these successive adjustments inflame each time the inherent conflict between producing and consuming countries about the right price level. For example, the cocoa agreements were unsuccessful in the 1970s because the ceiling price was always below the market price. In the early 1980s, the third cocoa agreement fared no better. Its financial resources were exhausted in the first three months by attempts to defend an unrealistically high floor price, which remained above the market price for most of the life of the agreement. Third, when price targets are set in line with economic fundamentals, the policy may have limited effects if it accommodates the price changes too well. This was the situation for the international natural rubber agreements. These agreements allowed large bands, with a ceiling price 28.6 percent above the reference price and a floor price 25.2 percent below it. The large bands meant that interventions were limited. The agreements were successful in preventing the price from falling below the floor, but not in preventing prices above the ceiling. Gilbert (1996) argues that natural rubber agreements lasted two decades precisely because they were relatively innocuous.

Some of the commodities covered by ICAs were traded on organized futures markets, as is the case for most grains. This raises issues about interaction with speculators; Salant (1983) argues theoretically that the coexistence of public stock and private arbitrageurs create the possibility for speculative attacks on the stabilization scheme. In practice, this was scarcely a concern except at the end of the international tin agreements (ITA) in 1985 (Anderson and Gilbert 1988). Speculators' activities did not lead directly to the collapse of the ITA, however. During more than twenty years, the ITAs managed successfully to defend the floor price using both buffer stock and export control. Following the important price increase in the late 1970s, the bands were adjusted to represent the prevailing prices but in the early 1980s the market was turning to a situation of excess supply resulting in the International Tin Council (ITC) accumulating large stocks to defend the floor. When it faced its legal storage constraint, the ITC engaged in futures trades to support prices. But then faced with the threat of short sales that would have led to huge losses, the buffer-stock manager engaged in a massive market corner that ended with a market collapse when the ITC ran out of liquidity.

Lessons from Public Storage Experiences

Before drawing lessons from these experiences of public storage, we again emphasize the need for caution. The absence of adequate counterfactuals prevents derivation of definitive conclusions from these experiences and opens the way to personal interpretations. This applies less to conclusions about safety nets, which can be evaluated through random assignments. For trade policies, there are a lot of available data, and counterfactual models, although imperfect, can be built to simulate the counterfactual. For storage, however, data on stock levels are poor quality and the models not sufficiently rich to represent the complexity of actual food markets. For example, we described above several issues related to public storage management in India. Despite its many flaws, Indian food policy has managed to prevent a major food crisis over the last forty years and has weathered large production shocks that significantly reduced domestic supply (with five supply shortfalls exceeding 10 percent). But even senior Indian government officials (Basu 2010) recognize that welfare could be improved by a better food grain policy. The previous description shows that Indian storage policy could be improved by clearer release rules and a less procyclical behavior. However, making a judgment about the alternative to laissez-faire is more difficult. Would private storers have done the job? Would they have been willing to undertake sufficient interannual storage for India to deal with a 10 percent production decrease? Would India have been able to procure cereals on the world market in the case of supply shortfall?

The histories of storage in Australia and India summarized above show that storage policies, because of their ability to temporarily raise prices, are highly susceptible to being captured by farm lobbies. But other experiences of storage policies such as the European ones that resulted in butter mountains and a wine lake could tell the same story. This political economy issue was illustrated by the fact that these domestic storage policies lacked clear rules and may even have pursued multiple and contradictory objectives. The confusion was between preventing low prices and reducing price volatility. The former objective was always seriously defended but the lack of precise selling prices made the latter less achievable. The failures of the wool and tin stabilization programs demonstrate also that, when these programs are poorly designed, one of their most important market effects may be their collapse, since the stocks accumulated under explosive intervention rules can depress the market for a long time. These limitations might suggest that better outcomes would be achieved through more rules-based storage policies, delegated perhaps to independent organizations.

The story of ICAs, which relied on clear rules and were delegated, proves this intuition wrong. From his study of ICAs, Gilbert (1996, 2011) does not conclude that price stabilization policies are infeasible and bound to break down, but that they involve problems likely to threaten their long-run stability. These problems revolve around the issue of reference price and bandwidth updating, which is both conceptually complex and politically challenging since it reveals the inherent conflict between producing and consuming countries over schemes that have obvious large costs but unclear benefits. In addition, where such schemes proved effective, this was more in relation to preventing low prices than stabilizing prices.

7.4.3   The Apparent Effectiveness of Trade Policies

In the past, buffer-stock policies were quite widespread. The end of ICAs, successive reductions in Europe of direct market support, and structural adjustments in many developing countries have resulted in these policies being used much less since the early 1990s. Many countries continue to maintain stocks for emergencies or food-based safety nets but less so to achieve stabilization. This does not apply to countercyclical trade policies that are widespread. In the countries surveyed by Demeke, Pangrazio, and Maetz (2009), trade policy adjustments, whether tariff reductions or export restrictions, were the most commonly adopted policy measures during the 2007 to 2008 food crisis (in sixty-eight out of eighty-one countries). Their use is not

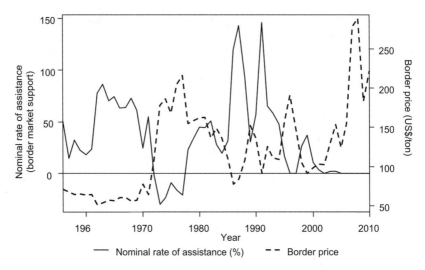

Fig. 7.2   Nominal rate of assistance and border price on French wheat market
Source: Anderson and Nelgen (2012c).

restricted to crisis situations. Anderson and Nelgen (2012b) analyze a panel of seventy-five countries that account for 90 percent of global agriculture and show that these adjustements occur equally at low and high prices, in importing and exporting countries, and in developing and high-income countries.

Unlike storage policies, which occasionally have been procyclical, trade policies are fairly consistently countercyclical. Tariffs increase when the world price is low and decrease when it is high. Exporting countries tend to restrict exports during price spikes and to promote them during price downturns. The data show that trade policy measures are negatively correlated with deviations in the international price from its trend (Anderson and Nelgen 2012b, table 1). Among the developed countries, an archetypical example of such an adjustment is the European Common Agricultural Policy (CAP). To promote domestic agricultural production, the CAP stabilized the prices of several commodities and guaranteed a minimum price to farmers enabled by public storage with the help of trade policies. In the case of wheat, trade policies were crucial since Europe was a net importer of wheat until the end of the 1970s and an exporter thereafter. Figure 7.2 illustrates the protection granted to French wheat producers based on border adjustments and the countercyclical nature of these adjustments with respect to border price. As an importer, France's domestic prices were prevented from going below the intervention price through the use of variable levies or duties that adjusted automatically to the world market price in order to protect the intervention price. When world prices spiked in 1973 to 1974, Europe used export taxes to limit domestic price increases (negative rate of assistance).

When Europe became a net wheat exporter, variable levies were no longer sufficient to prevent low prices and Europe had to rely on export subsidies. Recent CAP reforms, by decreasing wheat intervention prices, have reduced the need for border protection. Price stability in the European market has never been complete because the policy was mostly aimed at protecting producers from downward price spikes, but only a limited share of the world price movements was transmitted.

By using similar trade policies to those applied in Europe, many countries achieved some isolation from the global market. On average, in their sample Anderson and Nelgen (2012b) find short-run price transmission elasticity from world to domestic price close to 0.5. This imperfect transmission likely comes from trade policies. The elasticity is 0.72 for soybean, which is known to be heavily traded (more than 30 percent of production is traded according to the USDA [2012], against less than 8 percent and 20 percent for rice and wheat) and for which the rate of protection is not significantly correlated to the world price, unlike other commodities (Anderson and Nelgen 2012b, table 1). As a comparison, the short-run elasticities for rice and wheat are 0.52 and 0.47.

These trade policy adjustments did not always translate into a more stable domestic market. For example, Anderson and Nelgen (2012b, table 9) find that in African countries domestic agricultural prices on average are more unstable than border prices. They suggest that this may be caused by poor policy timing. It could also be that export restrictions are difficult to enforce in countries with porous borders, which applies to many African countries. In this situation, export restrictions raise transaction costs and informal trade flows but do not always decrease trade (Staatz et al. 2008). Another reason could be that discretionary interventions create uncertainty, which hinders private traders' activities. This effect is confirmed by Chapoto and Jayne (2009), who show that in eastern and southern Africa the most inter-ventionist countries tend to end up with more volatile and uncertain prices than the other countries (see also Porteous [2012], on the destabilizing effect of trade policies in Africa).

In developing Asian countries, trade policies have been more effective. Their domestic agricultural prices have been 30 percent more stable than border prices. For some (Dawe 2001; Timmer 2010), this Asian success at price stabilization is used frequently to illustrate what can be achieved by stabilization policies: securing good incentives for farmers' long-run invest-ment and providing stable and affordable supply for poor consumers. How-ever, the Asian success in stabilizing prices is apparent only. Although Asian policymakers may have congratulated themselves on achieving domestic stability in an unstable world market, the world rice price does not represent global scarcity, but only the extent to which these countries are willing to trade. It is widely acknowledged that the major cause of the 2007 to 2008 rice price spike was the generalized use of restrictive trade policies by exporting countries (Timmer 2010). For each country taken individually, a counter-cyclical trade policy appears to work because its domestic price is less than the world price. However, for the countries collectively, this policy is self-defeating as the world market becomes thinner and more unstable (Martin and Anderson 2012). In addition, these policies cannot be effective for all countries. Anderson, Ivanic, and Martin (chap. 8, this volume), analyzing the combined effect of all policies, show that India and the Philippines tried to insulate their domestic rice markets from the increase in world prices but their policy adjustments were not enough to offset the price-increasing implications of all other countries' collective adjustments. Their rice price did not increase as much as the world price, but increased more than it would have done in the absence of worldwide insulation. Martin and Anderson (2012) compare this to the collective-action problem arising when a crowd stands up in a stadium to get a better view. Remaining seated is not an option because the view is obliterated, and standing up collectively is ineffective.

The extent to which these trade-policy adjustments contribute to world price volatility through their terms-of-trade effects can be assessed by building models to represent the world food market and analyzing the counterfactual situation of a world without trade-policy adjustments. This is obviously subject to many criticisms given the difficulties in estimating models that explain commodity price volatility (Cafiero et al. 2011). Anderson and Nelgen (2012a) provide such a back-of-the-envelope assessment using observed policy changes. For rice, the contribution is significant; they estimate that trade policy changes explain 40 percent of the 2006 to 2008 rice price spike compared to 27 percent in 1972 to 1974. It mattered also for wheat and maize, where changes to trade barriers contributed respectively to 19 percent and 10 percent of the spike.

Beyond terms-of-trade effects, trade policies affect volatility by hindering risk sharing of yield shocks. There are a few statistical illustrations of the consequences of a smaller market on instability. Jacks, O'Rourke, and Williamson (2011) use years of war as a natural experiment to show that since 1700 commodity prices were more volatile when the world market was smaller. Persson (1999) reaches a similar conclusion for the case of early modern Europe. He shows that price volatility declined with falling trade costs and the reduced administrative barriers to trade. These results make sense given the limited volatility of world yield compared to domestic yield. Table 7.2 presents the coefficients of variation of yield of the three main cereals for ten large producing countries and for the world. There is no country where yield volatility is less than at world level. It is not uncommon for yield volatility in major producers to be twice as high as at world level. Given the smoothness of cereal yields at world level, it is hardly surprising that any measure that disturbs this smoothing of shocks will increase the volatility of global prices since the residual market will have to bear much larger shocks.

Table 7.2   Coefficient of variation of yield in the ten largest cereal producers and in the world, 1960–2012

	Maize (%)	Rice (%)	Wheat (%)
Argentina	6.02	5.52	7.81
Bangladesh	—	2.32	8.56
Brazil	3.63	2.32	10.89
Canada	5.40	—	8.41
China	3.70	2.62	3.14
European Union (27)	7.35	5.74	4.27
Indonesia	3.97	2.93	—
India	4.95	3.64	2.97
Russia	21.04	6.31	12.33
United States	5.84	3.43	4.97
World	2.82	1.29	2.32

Source: Obtained after HP-filtering (smoothing parameter of 400) of original yield data from USDA (2012).

7.4.4   Mixed Outcomes from Experiences of Liberalization

From the foregoing, it might seem that the cost of stabilization or the difficulty involved in managing storage policies would make greater liberalization profitable. However, the issue is less straightforward. It is true that real policies crowd out private activity because stabilization policies reduce the benefits from private arbitrage, but potential interventions can have the same effect since the expectations of public involvement in the market in times of crisis reduce the benefits from arbitrage as well as creating a lot of uncertainty. This situation is analyzed theoretically in Wright and Williams (1982a). They show that if government is unable to commit to not intervening in times of shortage—in their case by imposing a price ceiling—private storers stock much less than under this commitment. The insufficiency of private stock levels implies that welfare can be improved through public stockpiling. This is not just a theoretical consideration; the configuration has emerged in several countries as we show below.

The case of eastern and southern Africa are the most frequently analyzed for the challenges related to reforming food policies. The countries in this region inherited from the colonial period food policies that relied on state marketing aimed at promoting settlers' production through cross-subsidies using taxes on African farmers' production (Jayne and Jones 1997). They involved many regulations including panseasonal and panterritorial pricing, and restrictions on private grain movements. The new policies that were introduced at independence promoted smallholder agriculture but did not reduce state involvement. In the mid-1980s, the combination of mounting fiscal costs and structural adjustment programs in Africa pushed these countries toward liberalization of their food policies.

However, in most cases, liberalization has not been complete and several countries have maintained some state-owned grain trading enterprises, which, although coexisting alongside private traders, still play an important role in food policies. This is the case in Zambia where the Food Reserve Agency manages food security stocks and purchases substantial quantities, mostly maize (Tschirley and Jayne 2010). In addition, government maintains comprehensive regulation of trade through the issuing of export and import licenses. Since 2000, Zambia has experienced three periods of prices exceeding import parity prices, which at first sight might seem to be severe market failure, but is not. These situations arose as a result of distrust between government and traders. In 2001 to 2002, in the expectation of a supply shortfall, government announced large public, subsidized imports. Following this announcement, private traders abstained from importing. However, the public imports were delayed and prices soared. In 2002 to 2003, faced with another potential crisis, government tried to involve the private sector in the import decision but limited the discussion to large commercial millers who produce expensive maize meals, excluding from discussion small-scale millers. Price again rose above the import parity price because of insufficient imports. In 2005 to 2006, following forecasts of a poor maize harvest, government announced that the 15 percent tariff on maize would be waived. Private traders delayed their imports until the decision was implemented. The delay pushed prices above the import parity price. There are similar stories that could be told about the case of Malawi (Tschirley and Jayne 2010).

This lack of trust between private agents and government is problematic in some eastern and southern African countries because their food policy reforms are in midstream: they do not have real public stabilization policies but they do not trust private traders, which are reluctant to step in fearing erratic government intervention. This distrust is not reserved to Africa; it is observed in India where public regulation prevents hoarding, and regional and international trade. This makes reform of food policies in India and many other interventionist countries extremely challenging.

Bangladesh, like India and Pakistan, inherited from its colonial era food policies based on food grain procurement at minimum support prices to support farmers, public management of international trade, and stock policies aimed at stabilizing domestic prices and providing supply for public distribution systems. Bangladesh reformed its food policies in the early 1990s. The reforms involved trade liberalization, limitation of the role of public stocks to emergencies and targeted safety nets, and elimination of ration shops. Notably, the reforms were accompanied by measures meant to build private sector confidence in future limited public interventions: the absence of antihoarding regulation, dialogue between traders and government, and low tariffs on grains (Dorosh 2009). This policy has succeeded in reducing food price volatility and food shortages. When rice production was reduced in 1998 by severe flooding, the domestic price increase was limited by the import parity price and traders compensated for the production shortfall by imports. During the 2007 to 2008 campaign, Bangladesh simultaneously suffered serious flooding, the effects of Cyclone Sidr, and the global food crisis. The same strategy was applied: private sector imports compensated for shortfalls despite reduced supply in a tightening world market; safety nets were scaled up (46 percent budget increase); and agricultural production was supported to ensure a good harvest from winter-season rice. These measures limited food price inflation and the threat of a large-scale food crisis. However, the severity of the shocks and the need to import from the world market during the crisis led to a doubling of the rice price (World Bank 2010) and a worsening of food insecurity for many poor people. Bangladesh's food policy reforms have been praised as an important step toward a modern food market (Ahmed, Haggblade, and Chowdhury 2000), but the recent crisis has highlighted the difficulty to weather a perfect storm affecting both domestic production and the world market, when the other countries are less committed to liberal policies.

7.5   Conclusion

From this literature review, we have identified the reasons for the negative conclusions drawn by economists in relation to price stabilization policies. For some time, one of these reasons was related to the limited welfare gains arising from the expected utility framework. Although economists may have found it tricky to assess the welfare cost of food price instability, there is a suspicion that more stability could deliver significant gains, not least from additional political stability. However, the literature seems doubtful about the possibility that price stabilization policies could deliver such gains without the country involved or its partners having to pay a cost that is disproportionately high compared to the gains. This is explained, first, by the difficulty to design a stabilization policy that would not adversely affect trade partners or hinder market development. A buffer-stock policy requires some isolation from the world market to stabilize the domestic price so it needs to be backed by adequate trade policy. Second, storage policies historically have been costly and have failed to deliver the expected stabilization, because they have been captured by farmers' lobbies resulting in weak selling provision and overaccumulation in order to maintain high prices artificially. Last, successful stabilization policies have relied heavily on trade policies exploiting the world market to achieve domestic objectives. Hence, trade policy more than buffer stocks is the instrument that effectively stabilized domestic prices in many countries, but also imposes the greatest cost on the focal country's partners. Thus, these policies lead to a typical prisoner's dilemma where the world market is trapped in a noncooperative equilibrium. As long as this equilibrium prevails, it makes sense for countries individually to pursue domestic price stability through trade policies even though collectively this is self-defeating.

The introduction to this chapter raised the question of whether the academically dominant approach of reliance on safety nets and world trade is still relevant or whether developing countries should rely on food-price stabilization policies. Based on the reviews of past experiences and the literature, we believe that the food crisis has not changed the general perspective. Indeed, for most economists, a world where all countries rely on direct transfers to assist consumers and producers, where government refrains from changing the price distribution, and where trade smoothes production shocks globally would be close to the first best. It is true that countercyclical safety nets have proved challenging, but experiences suggest that good management of price stabilization policies is no less difficult. What seems to be the most important problem in standard international advice is that it relies on the idea that all countries will adopt the same cooperative policies. As long as this is not the case, a country adopting a free-trade policy will act as a residual market that must absorb a disproportionate share of global volatility. In addition, reliance on a world market requires its existence at all times, which is not guaranteed if major exporters use export bans.

The apparent effectiveness of trade policies makes it difficult to break the vicious circle of noncooperative policies. This problem of multiple equilibria could explain the different stances of economists on the issue of food-price stabilization policies. On the one hand, international organizations should not be expected to advise countries about policies in which benefits will come at the expense of their partners. Their policy advice should be consistent— domestically and internationally. Their policy recommendations will focus naturally on the most cooperative outcome. On the other hand, some (e.g., Timmer, forthcoming; Abbott 2012a, 6), although acknowledging the benefits of a market with limited trade interventions, do not believe it is achievable in the present policy situation. Hence, in our judgment there are two crucial policy and research questions: (a) how do we pass from the current, noncooperative equilibria in which countries, distrustful of the world market and of a private marketing system, apply insulating and stabilizing policies to a cooperative equilibrium that would allow a better sharing of risk; and (b) taking account of the present situation, what policies that would not worsen the situation can economists recommend to countries wanting to protect their populations from food price instability? Related to both questions, we offer some perspectives on the respective issues of trade policies, safety nets, and storage policies.

The current difficulties related to the rice market are in part a legacy of the 1972 to 1973 crisis (Timmer 2010). Following the collapse of the rice market in 1972 to 1973 and the scramble for affordable rice imports, countries such as India and Indonesia focused on greater self-sufficiency and developed policies to achieve it. Following the 2007 to 2008 food crisis, were more countries to emulate these examples, this would reduce the rice market even further. Is it possible to curb the tendency to restrict trade further? The theoretical answer from the literature on self-enforcing trade agreements (e.g., Bagwell and Staiger [1990] for trade policies in a volatile environment) would be that as long as the discount rate is not too low a cooperative equilibrium can be sustained by threat of future punishment. However, even if the payoff from cooperation is collectively high, being sovereign, countries will accept to cooperate only if this is in their own self-interest. A consequence—and a standard feature of self-enforcing trade agreements—is that the first-best policy of free trade may not satisfy the interests of every country for all large shocks. Thus, the countries that are best positioned to extract gains from noncooperative policies may retain the right to some deviations from the first best in a cooperative equilibrium in order to satisfy their participation constraints. So even under cooperation, to satisfy each country's national interest, some deviations from free trade should be expected and countries relying on the world market for their food supply should account for these deviations.

In practice, this type of coordination, even if incomplete, occurs mostly with the help of trade agreements or within the World Trade Organization (WTO), and the outlook for such agreements is not good. Nevertheless, the Uruguay round negotiations brought discipline to a similar situation: the export subsidy escalation between the European Union (EU) and the United States Export restrictions could be subject to the same discipline as tariffs and export subsidies: taxes, which must be consolidated, are allowable, but not quantitative restrictions—recently acceded WTO members have accepted similar disciplines during accession negotiations (Crosby 2008). The bound levels can be decreased gradually at each round of negotiations. This allows importing countries to predict more accurately the extents of policy adjustments. These trade policies for food security are more difficult to regulate than export subsidies, however. Export restrictions usually have a short life, and dispute settlements in the WTO take a long time and are supposed to address existing policies. In addition, proposals to regulate export restrictions were rejected by many member countries at the beginning of the Doha Round negotiations (WTO 2004) and are unlikely to be accepted now. A positive point with respect to trade policies is that the policy changes in high-income countries contributed much less to the 2007 to 2008 price spike than in 1973 to 1974 (Anderson and Nelgen 2012a). They reduced some tariffs to limit domestic price increases but refrained from their previous action of using export taxes. Nevertheless, the role of developed countries' policies in the recent food crisis should be acknowledged. It is true that these countries rely less on storage policies and time-varying trade policies, but recently the agricultural policies with the largest terms-of-trade effects are probably the biofuels policies in the United States and in the EU. In 2009, maize used for ethanol production in the United States represented 12 percent of maize world production. Vegetable oil used for biodiesel in the EU represented 5 percent of world vegetable oil production. The ability of developing countries' trade policies to affect the quantities supplied to the world market is dwarfed by the effects of these biofuels policies. To ask developing countries to commit to liberal trade policies while calories are sucked toward developed countries' fuel tanks is asking a lot from them.

Safety nets are mushrooming and countries will be able to rely on them in the future in preference to stabilization policies. Adjusting them in times of food crises will continue to be a challenge, but lessons have been learned from the 2007 to 2008 experience. Safety nets are a necessary first step toward reforms; they are needed in order to build trust with private agents. As governments politically cannot afford to be perceived to be inactive during food crises, private storers should rightly be concerned by governments pretending to abandon all possibilities to address hunger in times of high prices. If appropriate and scalable safety nets have not been developed, governments will be forced to rely on costly policies such as universal subsidies, or self-defeating policies such as erratic trade policy adjustments, that disincentivize private traders. A government commitment not to intervene directly on food prices is credible so long as government retains some options to protect the poor and vulnerable. So safety nets are essential to break noncooperative interactions between private traders and governments. This will not ensure that countries with more safety nets will avoid price stabilization policies completely. As we observed in the 2007 to 2008 food crisis, even countries with large safety net systems (e.g., India) used stabilization policies and are planning to increase storage facilities. Hence, an important research question would be to better understand this trade-off between stabilization policies and safety nets.

As countercyclical trade policy interventions are unlikely to decrease soon and the reliability of the world market is equally unlikely to increase, it should not be excluded that storage policies may still play a part in the policy mix in the future. While buffer-stock policies have proved difficult to manage and rarely delivered any additional stabilization, emergency stocks may appear to be a valuable alternative. Emergency stocks are stocks allowing to meet situations when there are short-run physical constraints on production and import preventing supply of needs. Although the topic of buffer-stock policies has been well researched, this is not the case for emergency stocks. The World Food Programme's (2011) feasibility study for the G20 on regional food reserves and the assessment of the Ethiopian strategic grain reserve by Rashid and Lemma (2011) provide insights into the design of and the benefits that can be expected from emergency stocks. Research on emergency grain stocks could also be inspired by studies related to the management of strategic petroleum reserves and their disposal in the case of supply disruption or the embargo that emerged in the 1980s.

References

Abbott, Philip C. 2012a. "Export Restrictions as Stabilization Responses to Food Crisis." *American Journal of Agricultural Economics* 94 (2): 428–34.

———. 2012b. "Stabilisation Policies in Developing Countries after the 2007–08 Food Crisis." In *Agricultural Policies for Poverty Reduction*, edited by J. Brooks, 109–68. Paris: OECD Publishing.

Ahmed, Raisuddin, Steven Haggblade, and Tawfiq-e-Elahi Chowdhury, eds. 2000. *Out of the Shadow of Famine: Evolving Food Markets and Food Policy in Bangladesh*. Baltimore: Johns Hopkins University Press for IFPRI.

Alderman, Harold, and Trina Haque. 2006. "Countercyclical Safety Nets for the Poor and Vulnerable." *Food Policy* 31 (4): 372–83.

Anderson, James E., and John G. Riley. 1976. "International Trade with Fluctuating Prices." *International Economic Review* 17 (1): 76–97.

Anderson, Kym, Johanna Croser, Damiano Sandri, and Ernesto Valenzuela. 2010. "Agricultural Distortion Patterns Since the 1950s: What Needs Explaining?" In *The Political Economy of Agricultural Price Distortions*, edited by Kym Anderson, 25–80. New York: Cambridge University Press.

Anderson, Kym, and Signe Nelgen. 2012a. "Agricultural Trade Distortions During the Global Financial Crisis." *Oxford Review of Economic Policy* 28 (2): 235–60.

———. 2012b. "Trade Barrier Volatility and Agricultural Price Stabilization." *World Development* 40 (1): 36–48.

———. 2012c. "Updated National and Global Estimates of Distortions to Agricultural Incentives, 1955 to 2010." Washington, DC: World Bank. Available at www.worldbank.org/agdistortions.

Anderson, Ronald W., and Christopher L. Gilbert. 1988. "Commodity Agreements and Commodity Markets: Lessons from Tin." *Economic Journal* 98 (389): 1–15.

Arezki, Rabah, and Markus Brückner. 2011. "Food Prices and Political Instability." IMF Working Paper no. 11/62, Washington, DC, March.

Arezki, Rabah, Klaus Deininger, and Harris Selod. 2011. "What Drives the Global 'Land Rush'?" World Bank Policy Research Working Paper no. 5864, Washington, DC, October.

Bagwell, Kyle, and Robert W. Staiger. 1990. "A Theory of Managed Trade." *American Economic Review* 80 (4): 779–95.

Bardsley, Peter. 1994. "The Collapse of the Australian Wool Reserve Price Scheme." *Economic Journal* 104 (426): 1087–105.

Barrett, Christopher B. 1996. "On Price Risk and the Inverse Farm Size-Productivity Relationship." *Journal of Development Economics* 51 (2): 193–215.

Barrett, Christopher B., and Marc F. Bellemare. 2011. "Why Food Price Volatility Doesn't Matter: Policymakers Should Focus on Bringing Costs Down." *Foreign Affairs*, July 12. http://foreignaffairsmagazine.tumblr.com/post/7574827066/why-food-price-volatility-doesnt-matter.

Basu, Kaushik. 2010. "The Economics of Foodgrain Management in India." Working Paper no. 2/2010, Ministry of Finance, Government of India, September.

Batra, Raveendra N., and William R. Russell. 1974. "Gains from Trade Under Uncertainty." *American Economic Review* 64 (6): 1040–8.

Bellemare, Marc F. 2011. "Rising Food Prices, Food Price Volatility, and Political Unrest." MPRA Paper no. 31888, June. University Library of Munich, Germany.

Bouët, Antoine, and David Laborde. 2010. "Assessing the Potential Cost of a Failed Doha Round." *World Trade Review* 9 (02): 319–51.

Boussard, Jean-Marc, Francoise Gerard, Marie Gabrielle Piketty, Mourad Ayouz, and Tancrède Voituriez. 2006. "Endogenous Risk and Long Run Effects of

Liberalization in a Global Analysis Framework." *Economic Modelling* 23 (3): 457–75.

Brainard, William C., and Richard N. Cooper. 1968. "Uncertainty and Diversification in International Trade." *Food Research Institute Studies* 8:257–85.

Brinkman, Henk-Jan, Saskia de Pee, Issa Sanogo, Ludovic Subran, and Martin W. Bloem. 2010. "High Food Prices and the Global Financial Crisis Have Reduced Access to Nutritious Food and Worsened Nutritional Status and Health." *Journal of Nutrition* 140 (1): 153S–161S.

Brock, William A., and Cars H. Hommes. 1997. "A Rational Route to Randomness." *Econometrica* 65 (5): 1059–96.

Cafiero, Carlo, Eugenio S. A. Bobenrieth, Juan R. A. Bobenrieth, and Brian D. Wright. 2011. "The Empirical Relevance of the Competitive Storage Model." *Journal of Econometrics* 162 (1): 44–54.

Cassing, J. H., A. L. Hillman, and N. V. Long. 1986. "Risk Aversion, Terms of Trade Uncertainty and Social-Consensus Trade Policy." *Oxford Economic Papers* 38 (2): 234–42.

Chapoto, Antony, and Thomas S. Jayne. 2009. "The Impacts of Trade Barriers and Market Interventions on Maize Price Predictability: Evidence from Eastern and Southern Africa." Food Security International Development Working Paper no. 56798, Department of Agricultural, Food, and Resource Economics, Michigan State University, December.

Coleman, Andrew. 2009. "Storage, Slow Transport, and the Law of One Price: Theory with Evidence from Nineteenth-Century US Corn Markets." *Review of Economics and Statistics* 91 (2): 332–50.

Crosby, Daniel. 2008. "WTO Legal Status and Evolving Practice of Export Taxes." *Bridges* 12 (5): 3–4.

Dawe, David. 2001. "How Far down the Path to Free Trade? The Importance of Rice Price Stabilization in Developing Asia." *Food Policy* 26 (2): 163–75.

De Janvry, Alain, and Elisabeth Sadoulet. 2006. "Progress in the Modeling of Rural Households' Behavior Under Market Failures." In *Poverty, Inequality and Development: Essays in Honor of Erik Thorbecke*, edited by Alain de Janvry and Ravi Kanbur, 155–82. New York: Springer.

Demeke, Mulat, Guendalina Pangrazio, and Materne Maetz. 2009. "Country Responses to the Food Security Crisis: Nature and Preliminary Implications of the Policies Pursued." Initiative on Soaring Food Prices, Food and Agriculture Organization of the United Nations.

Dorosh, Paul A. 2009. "Price Stabilization, International Trade and National Cereal Stocks: World Price Shocks and Policy Response in South Asia." *Food Security* 1 (2): 137–49.

D'Souza, Anna, and Dean Jolliffe. 2012. "Rising Food Prices and Coping Strategies: Household-level Evidence from Afghanistan." *Journal of Development Studies* 48 (2): 282–99.

Eaton, Jonathan, and Gene M. Grossman. 1985. "Tariffs as Insurance: Optimal Commercial Policy When Domestic Markets Are Incomplete." *Canadian Journal of Economics* 18 (2): 258–72.

Fafchamps, Marcel. 1992. "Cash Crop Production, Food Price Volatility, and Rural Market Integration in the Third World." *American Journal of Agricultural Economics* 74 (1): 90–9.

———. 2003. *Rural Poverty, Risk and Development*. Northampton, MA: Edward Elgar .

Feenstra, Robert C. 1987. "Incentive Compatible Trade Policies." *Scandinavian Journal of Economics* 89 (3): 373–87.

Galtier, Franck. 2009. "How to Manage Food Price Instability in Developing Countries?" Working Paper no. 5, MOISA, INRA.

Gardner, Bruce L. 1979. *Optimal Stockpiling of Grain*. Lexington, MA: Lexington Books.

Gardner, Bruce L., and Ramón López. 1996. "The Inefficiency of Interest-Rate Subsidies in Commodity Price Stabilization." *American Journal of Agricultural Economics* 78 (3): 508–16.

Gilbert, Christopher L. 1996. "International Commodity Agreements: An Obituary Notice." *World Development* 24 (1): 1–19.

———. 2011. "International Commodity Agreements and Their Current Relevance for Grains Price Stabilization." In *Safeguarding Food Security in Volatile Global Markets*, edited by Adam Prakash, 202–30. Rome: Food and Agriculture Organization of the United Nations.

Gilbert, Christopher L., and Wyn Morgan. 2010. "Food Price Volatility." *Philosophical Transactions of the Royal Society of London. Series B, Biological Sciences* 365 (1554): 3023–34.

Giordani, Paolo E., Nadia Rocha, and Michele Ruta. 2012. "Food Prices and the Multiplier Effect of Export Policy." CESifo Group Munich Working Paper no. 3783, Center for Economic Studies and Ifo Institute for Economic Research, April.

Glewwe, Paul, Hanan G. Jacoby, and Elizabeth M. King. 2001. "Early Childhood Nutrition and Academic Achievement: A Longitudinal Analysis." *Journal of Public Economics* 81 (3): 345–68.

Goodwin, Barry K., Ashok K. Mishra, and François Ortalo-Magné. 2012. "The Buck Stops Where? The Distribution of Agricultural Subsidies." In *The Intended and Unintended Effects of US Agricultural and Biotechnology Policies*, edited by Joshua S. Graff Zivin and Jeffrey M. Perloff, 15–50. Chicago: University of Chicago Press.

Gouel, Christophe. 2013. "Rules Versus Discretion in Food Storage Policies." *American Journal of Agricultural Economics*. 95 (4): 1029–44.

———. 2012. "Agricultural Price Instability: A Survey of Competing Explanations and Remedies." *Journal of Economic Surveys* 26 (1): 129–56.

Gouel, Christophe, and Sébastien Jean. Forthcoming. "Optimal Food Price Stabilization in a Small Open Developing Country." *World Bank Economic Review*, doi:10.1093/wber/lht018.

Grosh, Margaret, Colin Andrews, Rodrigo Quintana, and Claudia Rodriguez-Alas. 2011. "Assessing Safety Net Readiness in Response to Food Price Volatility." Social Protection Discussion Paper no. 1118. Washington, DC: World Bank.

Grosh, Margaret, Carlo del Ninno, Emil Tesliuc, and Azedine Ouerghi. 2008. *For Protection and Promotion: The Design and Implementation of Effective Safety Nets*. Washington, DC: World Bank.

Helpman, Elhanan, and Assaf Razin. 1978. *A Theory of International Trade Under Uncertainty*. New York: Academic Press.

High Level Panel of Experts on Food Security and Nutrition (HLPE). 2011. "Price Volatility and Food Security." The High Level Panel of Experts on Food Security and Nutrition, Committee on World Food Security, Report 1. http://www.fao.org/cfs/cfs-hlpe/en/.

Hoddinott, John, John A. Maluccio, Jere R. Behrman, Rafael Flores, and Reynaldo Martorell. 2008. "Effect of a Nutrition Intervention During Early Childhood on Economic Productivity in Guatemalan Adults." *Lancet* 371 (9610): 411–6.

Innes, Robert. 1990. "Uncertainty, Incomplete Markets and Government Farm Programs." *Southern Economic Journal* 57 (1): 47–65.

Irwin, Scott H., and Dwight R. Sanders. 2012. "Testing the Masters Hypothesis in Commodity Futures Markets." *Energy Economics* 34 (1): 256–69.

Jacks, David S., Kevin H. O'Rourke, and Jeffrey G. Williamson. 2011. "Commodity Price Volatility and World Market Integration Since 1700." *Review of Economics and Statistics* 93 (3): 800–13.

Jacoby, Hanan G., and Emmanuel Skoufias. 1997. "Risk, Financial Markets, and Human Capital in a Developing Country." *Review of Economic Studies* 64 (3): 311–35.

Jayne, T. S., and Stephen Jones. 1997. "Food Marketing and Pricing Policy in Eastern and Southern Africa: A Survey." *World Development* 25 (9): 1505–27.

Kirwan, Barrett E. 2009. "The Incidence of US Agricultural Subsidies on Farmland Rental Rates." *Journal of Political Economy* 117 (1): 138–64.

Larson, Donald F., Julian Lampietti, Christophe Gouel, Carlo Cafiero, and John Roberts. 2014. "Food Security and Storage in the Middle East and North Africa." *World Bank Economic Review* 28 (1): 48–73.

Leathers, Howard D., and Jean-Paul Chavas. 1986. "Farm Debt, Default, and Foreclosure: An Economic Rationale for Policy Action." *American Journal of Agricultural Economics* 68 (4): 828–37.

Lence, Sergio H. 2009. "Do Futures Benefit Farmers?" *American Journal of Agricultural Economics* 91 (1): 154–67.

Lucas, Jr., Robert E. 2003. "Macroeconomic Priorities." *American Economic Review* 93 (1): 1–14.

Martin, Will, and Kym Anderson. 2012. "Export Restrictions and Price Insulation during Commodity Price Booms." *American Journal of Agricultural Economics* 94 (1): 422–7.

Miranda, Mario J., and Peter G. Helmberger. 1988. "The Effects of Commodity Price Stabilization Programs." *American Economic Review* 78 (1): 46–58.

Myers, Robert J. 1988. "The Value of Ideal Contingency Markets in Agriculture." *American Journal of Agricultural Economics* 70 (2): 255–67.

———. 2006. "On the Costs of Food Price Fluctuations in Low-Income Countries." *Food Policy* 31 (4): 288–301.

Newbery, David M. G. 1989. "The Theory of Food Price Stabilisation." *Economic Journal* 99 (398): 1065–82.

Newbery, David M. G., and Joseph E. Stiglitz. 1981. *The Theory of Commodity Price Stabilization: A Study in the Economics of Risk*. Oxford: Clarendon Press.

———. 1984. "Pareto Inferior Trade." *Review of Economic Studies* 51 (1): 1–12.

Nocetti, Diego, and William T. Smith. 2011. "Price Uncertainty, Saving, and Welfare." *Journal of Economic Dynamics and Control* 35 (7): 1139–49.

Omamo, Steven Were, Ugo Gentilini, and Susanna Sandström, eds. 2010. *Revolution: From Food Aid to Food Assistance. Innovations in Overcoming Hunger*. Rome: World Food Programme.

Oxfam International. 2011. "Preparing for Thin Cows: Why the G20 Should Keep Buffer Stocks on the Agenda." Briefing Note. http://www.oxfam.org/en/grow /policy/preparing-for-thin-cows.

Persson, Karl Gunnar. 1999. *Grain Markets in Europe, 1500–1900: Integration and Deregulation*. Cambridge: Cambridge University Press.

Porteous, Obie C. 2012. "Empirical Effects of Short-Term Export Bans: The Case of African Maize." Working Paper, Department of Agricultural and Resource Economics, University of California, Berkeley.

Poulton, Colin, Jonathan Kydd, Steve Wiggins, and Andrew Dorward. 2006. "State Intervention for Food Price Stabilisation in Africa: Can It Work?" *Food Policy* 31 (4): 342–56.

Rashid, Shahidur, Ralph Cummings Jr., and Ashok Gulati. 2007. "Grain Marketing Parastatals in Asia: Results from Six Case Studies." *World Development* 35 (11): 1872–88.

Rashid, Shahidur, and Solomon Lemma. 2011. "Strategic Grain Reserves in Ethiopia: Institutional Design and Operational Performance." IFPRI Discussion Paper no. 01054, International Food Policy Research Institute.

Salant, Stephen W. 1983. "The Vulnerability of Price Stabilization Schemes to Speculative Attack." *Journal of Political Economy* 91 (1): 1–38.

Sandmo, Agnar. 1971. "On the Theory of the Competitive Firm under Price Uncertainty." *American Economic Review* 61 (1): 65–73.

Seale Jr., James L., Anita Regmi, and Jason Bernstein. 2003. "International Evidence on Food Consumption Patterns." Technical Bulletin no. 1904, October. Washington, DC: United States Department of Agriculture.

Sen, Amartya Kumar. 1981. *Poverty and Famines: An Essay on Entitlement and Deprivation.* Oxford: Oxford University Press.

Slayton, Tom. 2009. "Rice Crisis Forensics: How Asian Governments Carelessly Set the World Rice Market on Fire." Working Paper no. 163, Center for Global Development, March.

Staatz, John M., Niama Nango Dembele, Valerie A. Kelly, and Ramziath Adjao. 2008. "Agricultural Globalization in Reverse: The Impact of the Food Crisis in West Africa." Food Security Collaborative Working Paper no. 55466, Department of Agricultural, Food, and Resource Economics, Michigan State University, September.

Swinnen, Johan, and Pasquamaria Squicciarini. 2012. "Mixed Messages on Prices and Food Security." *Science* 335 (6067): 405–6.

Timmer, C. Peter. 1989. "Food Price Policy: The Rationale for Government Intervention." *Food Policy* 14 (1): 17–27.

———. 2010. "Reflections on Food Crises Past." *Food Policy* 35 (1): 1–11.

———. 2012. "Behavioral Dimensions of Food Security." *Proceedings of the National Academy of Sciences* 109 (31): 12315–20.

———. Forthcoming. "Managing Price Volatility: Approaches at the Global, National, and Household Levels." In *Stanford Synthesis Volume on Global Food Policy and Food Security in the 21st Century*, edited by Walter P. Falcon and Rosamond L. Naylor. Available at http://foodsecurity.stanford.edu/events/series/global_food_policy_series.

Townsend, Robert M. 1977. "The Eventual Failure of Price Fixing Schemes." *Journal of Economic Theory* 14 (1): 190–9.

Tschirley, David L., and T. S. Jayne. 2010. "Exploring the Logic Behind Southern Africa's Food Crises." *World Development* 38 (1): 76–87

Turnovsky, Stephen J. 1974. "Technological and Price Uncertainty in a Ricardian Model of International Trade." *Review of Economic Studies* 41 (2): 201–17.

Turnovsky, Stephen J., Haim Shalit, and Andrew Schmitz. 1980. "Consumer's Surplus, Price Instability, and Consumer Welfare." *Econometrica* 48 (1): 135–52.

United States Department of Agriculture (USDA). 2012. "Production, Supply and Distribution Online." http://www.fas.usda.gov/psdonline/.

Varangis, Panos, Donald Larson, and Jack R. Anderson. 2002. "Agricultural Markets and Risks—Management of the Latter, Not the Former." World Bank Policy Research Working Paper no. 2793, Washington, DC, February.

Von Braun, Joachim, and Maximo Torero. 2009. "Implementing Physical and Virtual Food Reserves to Protect the Poor and Prevent Market Failure." IFPRI Policy Brief no. 10, February. International Food Policy Research Institute.

Waugh, Frederick V. 1944. "Does the Consumer Benefit from Price Instability?" *Quarterly Journal of Economics* 58 (4): 602–14.

Williams, Jeffrey C., and Brian D. Wright. 1991. *Storage and Commodity Markets.* New York: Cambridge University Press.

World Bank. 2006. *Managing Food Price Risks and Instability in an Environment of Market Liberalization.* Washington, DC: World Bank.

———. 2009. *Improving Food Security in Arab Countries.* Washington, DC: World Bank.

———. 2010. *Food Price Increases in South Asia: National Responses and Regional Dimensions.* Washington, DC: World Bank.

———. 2012. "Using Public Foodgrain Stocks to Enhance Food Security." Agricultural and Rural Development, Economic and Sector Work 71280-GLB, July. Washington, DC: World Bank.

World Food Programme, International Center for Trade and Sustainable Development. 2011. "Emergency Humanitarian Food Reserves: Feasibility Study, Cost-Benefit Analysis and Proposal for Pilot Programme." http://ictsd.org/i/agriculture/114530/?view=details.

Wright, Brian D. 1979. "The Effects of Ideal Production Stabilization: A Welfare Analysis Under Rational Behavior." *Journal of Political Economy* 87 (5): 1011–33.

———. 2001. "Storage and Price Stabilization." In *Marketing, Distribution and Consumers*, edited by Bruce L. Gardner and Gordon C. Rausser, 1B, part 2, 817–61. Amsterdam: Elsevier.

Wright, Brian D., and Jeffrey C. Williams. 1982a. "The Economic Role of Commodity Storage." *Economic Journal* 92 (367): 596–614.

———. 1982b. "The Roles of Public and Private Storage in Managing Oil Import Disruptions." *Bell Journal of Economics* 13 (2): 341–53.

———. 1988a. "The Incidence of Market-Stabilising Price Support Schemes." *Economic Journal* 98 (393): 1183–98.

———. 1988b. "Measurement of Consumer Gains from Market Stabilization." *American Journal of Agricultural Economics* 70 (3): 616–27.

World Trade Organization (WTO). 2004. "WTO Agriculture Negotiations: The Issues, and Where We Are Now." http://www.wto.org/english/tratop_e/agric_e/negs_bkgrnd00_contents_e.htm.

Comment   Shenggen Fan

When countries experience food price spikes, their governments often feel compelled to implement price stabilization measures, which can follow a plan or be ad hoc, depending on the severity of the shock and the level of prior preparation of the countries. Planned actions may include countercyclical management of public food reserves, targeted safety nets, market-based risk management instruments, and investing in agricultural research and development. Governments may also take recourse to unplanned stabilization policies, such as universal food subsidies or trade policy adjustments. During

Shenggen Fan is director general of the International Food Policy Research Institute.

This discussion draws from Fan, Torero, and Headey (2011). For acknowledgments, sources of research support, and disclosure of the author's material financial relationships, if any, please see http://www.nber.org/chapters/c12817.ack.

the 2007 to 2008 food crisis, for example, India weathered the shock through its countercyclical trade policies, particularly by banning exports.

This chapter by Christophe Gouel provides a well-organized review and analysis of the different elements of food price stabilization policies that are especially relevant for developing countries. Coordination problems between governments in their food trade policies present some of the biggest challenges toward effectively responding to food price spikes. The lack of trust between public and private agents in the absence of effective safety nets to protect the poor is also an important challenge in the domestic food market. The chapter discusses these important challenges with great breadth and depth. In the next section, I present some ideas to further enrich the discussion of food price stabilization policies and link the International Food Policy Research Institutes (IFPRI)'s own work to overcome these policy challenges.

Summary of Discussion

The chapter discusses how countries' domestic food policies (mainly through trade and storage policies) can impact the stability of world prices. However, there is the need to recognize country heterogeneity in its discussion, such as whether countries are large or small (as measured by the size of their economy and population), and whether these countries are major exporters or importers of important tradable agricultural commodities. In particular, the chapter should pay more attention to countries such as Brazil, China, India, Russia, and the United States for their importance in affecting the global food trade system. The policies that these countries choose can easily affect global food prices and food security in low-income countries that depend on food imports to feed their population. Furthermore, the chapter should also differentiate between agricultural commodities that are being traded at world markets. Rice, wheat, and maize, for example, make up 90 percent of all cereal crops traded in the world and are interlinked, but also driven by different factors such as the trade and storage policies of major exporting and importing countries for the respective commodities.

As a response to food price shocks, the chapter discusses the significance of social safety nets serving to mimic the first best policy of providing insurance or futures markets by providing countercyclical transfers. IFPRI has also in the past been supporting efforts to either establish or expand social safety net programs to protect the most vulnerable groups, particularly women and young children, in developing countries from shocks. IFPRI, for example, has been engaged in evaluating the impact of Ethiopia's Productive Safety Net Program (PSNP), which is one of the largest social safety net programs in Africa, covering some 7.5 million primary beneficiaries in 2009. According to the World Bank, nearly 80 percent of the population in the poorest countries currently lacks effective safety net coverage, underscoring the importance of its expansion (World Bank 2012).

In the long term, there would be high returns to combining these safety nets with other interventions that increase productive capacity and improve the nutrition and health of the poor. Food price volatility risk can be substantially reduced by policies and investments that promote agricultural growth, in particular smallholder productivity, especially in the face of climate change. Extreme weather situations are major contributors to price volatility by affecting agricultural production as evidenced by the 2012 drought in the United States and other major producing countries. Policies that ensure that small farmers have opportunities to increase their productivity and income are likely to have high returns. There are also a number of potentially promising steps for national governments, as well as global and regional institutions, such as improved smallholder access to inputs such as seeds and fertilizer—through lower transport and marketing costs, improved market infrastructure, and greater competition, as well as financial and extension services and weather-based crop insurance.

An international working group should also regularly monitor the world food situation. Key institutions, including the Food and Agriculture Organization of the United Nations (FAO), the United Nations Conference on Trade Development (UNCTAD), the World Bank, the World Food Programme (WFP), and the United States Department of Agriculture (USDA), in collaboration with local partners, should pay close attention to developments in food supply, consumption (including for biofuels), stocks prices, and trade, as well as agricultural commodity speculation. This will help quickly detect any imbalances and facilitate swift responses. In this regard, IFPRI's excessive food price variability volatility early warning monitoring system is a useful tool.

With regard to countercyclical trade policy, the chapter rightly recognized that if countries engage in trade restrictions in the face of food price spikes, the payoff would be collectively low, as these measures reduce risk sharing between countries. Although export bans may help to secure domestic food supply, they lead to tighter markets for other exporting countries and induce panic purchases by food-importing countries, both of which lead to further price increases and volatility. In addition, eliminating export bans could benefit domestic food markets, since export bans tend to inhibit domestic production response, which could potentially exacerbate domestic supply problems.

The chapter also discusses in detail the important role that national public stock policies play in stabilizing food prices and the challenges surrounding them. Going beyond national public stocks, IFPRI has proposed for governments and international organizations to establish a global (or regional) emergency grain reserve to address the effects of food price crises for the most vulnerable. This reserve could be created through donations of grain stocks from large food exporters, such as the United States, Canada, and France, and large food producers such as China and India. The reserve could be owned and managed by an institution such as the World Food Programme, which already has a global food management system in place, including strong logistical capabilities. To some extent this process is already underway—the Association of Southeast Asian Nations plus China, Japan, and South Korea (ASEAN+3) emergency rice reserve is an example. A well-organized global emergency grain reserve system, with clear accumulation and release rules, could potentially be better at smoothing aggregate shocks than national public shocks that are highly susceptible to capture by farm lobbies.

Finally, the author acknowledged that biofuel policies in the United States and European Union contribute to the volatility of international and domestic food markets by diverting food from both domestic and global food markets. For example, about 40 percent of total maize production in the United States is currently used to produce ethanol. IFPRI recognizes this policy's negative impact on the poor and has consistently recommended that existing biofuels policies and subsidies should be curtailed and reformed in order to minimize impacts on food price volatility.

References

Fan, S., M. Torero, and D. Headey. 2011. "Urgent Actions Needed to Prevent Recurring Food Crises." Policy Brief 16. Washington, DC: International Food Policy Research Institute.

World Bank. 2012. "3 out of 5 People in Developing Countries Lack Safety Nets." Press Release 2012/380/HDN. Washington, DC: World Bank. http://go.worldbank.org/WLLWY0ACY0.

8

Food Price Spikes, Price Insulation, and Poverty

Kym Anderson, Maros Ivanic, and William J. Martin

Many countries have responded to spikes in international food prices such as those of mid-2008, early 2011, and mid-2012 by adjusting their agricultural trade barriers in an attempt to partially insulate their domestic markets from the price rises. Even when it may appear to each individual country that it has been successful, in the sense that its domestic price rose less than the international price for its food staples, this success is frequently more illusion than reality. The reason is that these policy responses—reductions in import protection or increases in export restraints—exacerbate the initial increase in the international price. Indeed, if both exporting and importing country groups happened to insulate to the same extent, domestic prices in both country groups would rise just as much as if no country had insulated (Martin and Anderson 2012). In reality, however, countries intervened to different extents, so that the impact of price insulation depends on both the actions taken by the country itself and the collective impact of interventions by all other countries.

The net effects on national and global poverty of such interventions could be favorable or unfavorable. On the one hand, if countries where the poor

Kym Anderson is the George Gollin Professor of Economics at the University of Adelaide and professor of economics in the Arndt-Corden Department of Economics at the Australian National University, Canberra. Maros Ivanic is a research economist with the agriculture and rural development team of the Development Research Group at the World Bank. William J. Martin is research manager of the agriculture and rural development team of the Development Research Group at the World Bank.

This chapter is a revision of a paper presented at the NBER conference titled "The Economics of Food Price Volatility" in Seattle, Washington, on August 15–16, 2012. Particular thanks are due to Signe Nelgen for assistance with the price distortions database. The chapter reflects the views of the authors alone and not necessarily those of the World Bank or any other organization. For acknowledgments, sources of research support, and disclosure of the authors' material financial relationships, if any, please see http://www.nber.org/chapters/c12818.ack.

are most adversely affected by higher food prices insulate more than countries where the poor are less vulnerable to or benefit from food price spikes, it is possible that such insulation reduces the number of people driven into poverty. A related possibility is that, if countries where producers and consumers are better able to deal domestically with such shocks transmit a larger portion of the increase in international food prices to their domestic markets, the adverse global poverty impact of the original shock will be less (Timmer 2010).

On the other hand, a more pessimistic possibility is that many of the countries that insulate against shocks to international food prices are countries for which the impacts on domestic poverty of higher food prices are minor or even pro-poor in the case where most of the poor are net sellers of food staples. High-income countries, for example, are well placed to absorb price shocks because of the small shares of farm produce in the expenditures of their consumers, their producers' access to risk-management tools such as futures and options markets, and their relatively well-developed social safety nets. Even so, some high-income countries continue to use insulating policy instruments such as variable import levies, or even just specific tariffs whose ad valorem equivalent varies inversely with the border price. Another example of this possibility is where large, poor, food-importing countries—for which insulation is more expensive because it turns their terms of trade against them—insulate less than would a small but otherwise similar country, and hence may not avoid adverse poverty outcomes because of inadequate domestic social safety nets.

It is clear from these examples that, other things being equal, alterations in trade restrictions could increase or reduce the national and global poverty impacts of higher international prices. Only by looking at data on the changes in agricultural distortions during periods of rapid increases in international food prices, and estimating the impacts of consequent domestic price changes on poverty in different countries is it possible to ascertain the net effects on national and global poverty.

This chapter begins by looking at data on the consumption patterns and income sources of low-income households in a sample of thirty developing countries, where three-quarters of the world's poor live, in order to assess which commodities are likely to be important in affecting poverty through changes in their commodity prices. We then turn to data on agricultural price distortions, and in particular on relative movements in domestic and international prices, to assess the extent to which countries insulated their domestic market from the changes in international food prices during 2006 to 2008.

With these data, we use a simple model to compare the actual changes in domestic prices with those that would have occurred in the absence of price-insulating policies. These price scenarios are then used to assess the impacts of food price changes on poverty both with—and in the absence of—price-insulating policy behavior. They allow us to make a much broader assessment of the impacts of price-insulating behavior on national and global poverty than has previously been available. The final section examines alternative policy measures at unilateral, regional, and multilateral levels which—together with complementary domestic measures—might more efficiently reduce the impact of future price spikes on poverty. The most cost-effective policy instrument for dealing with the poverty impacts of price rises is likely to be a domestic one—such as a well-targeted social safety net—that deals directly with the problem of poverty vulnerability.

8.1   What Price Changes Are Important for the Poor?

The direct short-run impact of food price changes on the well-being of a particular household depends on the proportional change in the real price of a particular food times the household's net purchases of that food (Deaton 1989). Since food typically makes up a large share of the spending of poor people, we would generally expect food price changes to have a large impact on the living costs of the poor. However, the vast majority of poor people are rural (three-quarters, according to Ravallion, Chen, and Sangraula 2007), and most poor rural people earn their living from agriculture. Hence food expenditure shares alone are insufficient for determining the impact of food price changes on poverty: account also needs to be taken of the shares of household income obtained from the sale of food to obtain the net expenditures on food by the household.

The first two columns of table 8.1 report the weighted-average shares of particular types of food in aggregate food expenditures and in total expenditures by the poor for the thirty developing countries for which we have detailed data on household expenditures and income sources.[1] Columns (3) through (9) of table 8.1 net out household production, and so are the most relevant for present purposes. Six countries' shares are shown as examples, together with the weighted average for all thirty countries. The top row reveals that, for our sample of thirty countries, food accounts for 61 percent of the gross expenditures of their poor. While we would like to consider all food expenditures, only a few of these products are homogenous enough to have reasonably representative international prices so we focus on four—rice, wheat, oilseeds, and maize—that account for 41 percent of those gross expenditures.

Table 8.1 also shows that the poor are, on average, net buyers of food in

---

1. The household survey years are Albania 2005, Armenia 2004, Bangladesh 2005, Belize 2009, China 2002, Côte d'Ivoire 2002, Ecuador 2006, Guatemala 2006, Indonesia 2007, India 2004, Cambodia 2003, Sri Lanka 2007, Moldova 2009, Mongolia 2002, Malawi 2004, Nepal 2002, Nigeria 2003, Nicaragua 2005, Niger 2007, Pakistan 2005, Rwanda 2005, Tajikistan 2007, Timor Leste 2001, Tanzania 2008, Uganda 2009, Vietnam 2010, Yemen 2006 and Zambia 2010.

Table 8.1   Food expenditures of people living on less than $1.25 per day, thirty developing countries, 2001–2010

	All countries gross share of food	All countries gross share of total consumption	All countries net share of total consumption	Average net share in expenditure of the poor, % of total							
				India	China	Bangladesh	Pakistan	Vietnam	Uganda	Tanzania	Indonesia
Total	100.0	60.8	37.0	59.7	26.2	26.1	37.8	−15.6	15.2	33.4	32.7
Rice (+ processed)	22.4	13.9	8.2	14.7	5.6	5.0	1.7	−9.3	0.1	2.8	2.6
Other food	15.6	9.7	7.6	9.9	7.5	7.7	4.4	3.5	1.6	7.9	18.9
Vegetables	15.3	9.3	4.5	11.0	0.5	4.6	6.2	−3.2	4.5	5.7	1.7
Meats	9.1	5.4	2.4	1.8	9.6	−0.3	1.3	−1.7	2.1	0.3	−0.6
Wheat (+ processed)	8.4	5.0	3.5	4.6	3.4	0.6	10.4	1.3	0.2	1.8	0.0
Oilseeds and edible oils	6.5	3.9	3.4	5.2	0.2	2.6	4.5	1.0	1.4	2.7	3.9
Fish and fish products	6.3	3.8	2.5	1.6	3.6	5.0	0.3	−1.7	2.1	3.3	2.7
Milk and dairy products	5.6	3.3	2.9	6.1	0.0	−0.3	3.4	0.7	0.3	−0.1	0.5
Maize and other grains	4.1	2.6	−0.5	1.5	−5.5	−0.1	0.2	−4.1	1.2	6.3	0.0
Fruits	3.9	2.3	1.1	0.9	1.4	1.0	1.0	−1.2	−0.5	−0.3	−0.6
Sugar	2.7	1.7	1.5	2.3	0.0	0.2	4.5	−0.9	2.3	3.1	3.5

Source: Authors' calculations.

Note: Weighted averages across the thirty developing countries are calculated using poor populations as weights. The $1.25 per day income level (2005 purchasing power parity) includes own-food consumption. Net share in expenditure refers to consumption of food less sales of food as a share of total expenditure, including own-food consumption. For the list of developing countries and their survey dates, see note 1 of the text.

most poor countries. In only one of the countries shown (Vietnam) are the poor, as a group, net sellers of the listed foods in aggregate, and there are only a few other cases where the poor are net sellers of particular foods. Over the full sample of thirty countries, column (3) shows that the poor are net buyers for all of the food items listed except maize. That column also reveals that rice, wheat, oilseeds, and maize account for 39 percent of the net food expenditures of the poor in our sample.

8.1.1   Extent of Domestic Price Changes, 2006–2008

The changes between 2006 and 2008 in domestic prices of each of these four key food items in each of the thirty sample countries for which we have information on both income sources and expenditure patterns are shown in table 8.2, together with changes in nominal nonfood prices as measured by the nonfood component of the consumer price index for each country.[2] Clearly domestic prices of these key foods generally rose considerably relative to nonfood prices during this period.

8.1.2   Impacts of Changes in Price Distortions on International Prices

To obtain an indication of the impact of the observed changes in trade restrictions on domestic prices, we need first to estimate their impact on international prices. That involves taking account of the changes in price distortions in countries that collectively account for a large share of world consumption. Following Martin and Anderson (2012), to assess the implications of price insulation on a homogenous product's international price, p^*, we begin with the global market equilibrium condition:

$$(1) \qquad \sum_i (S_i(p_i) + v_i) - \sum_i (D_i(p_i) + v_i) = 0,$$

where S_i is the supply in region i; p_i is the region's producer price; v_i is a random production shift variable for that region; D_i is demand in region i (assumed to be not subject to shocks from year to year); and p_i is the consumer price in region i. We assume that $p_i = (1 + t_p)p^*$ where t_p is the rate of distortion between the producer price and international price, and that $p_i = (1 + t_c)p^*$ where t_c is the rate of distortion between the consumer price and international price. With a focus on border measures, we can use a single variable for the power of the trade tax equivalent, $T = 1 + t$ where $t = t_p = t_c$.

Totally differentiating equation (1), rearranging it and expressing the results in percentage change form yields the following expression for the impact of a set of changes in trade distortions on the international price:

$$(2) \qquad \hat{p}^* = \frac{\sum_i H_i \hat{v}_i + \sum_i (H_i \gamma_i - G_i \eta_i) \hat{T}_i}{\sum_i (G_i \eta_i - H_i \gamma_i)},$$

2. Computed by using sample-average weights for food expenditures to remove the observed influence of the food CPI from the overall CPI numbers obtained from FAO.

Table 8.2   Changes in domestic food and nonfood prices, in nominal local currency terms, 2006–2008

	Rice (%)	Wheat (%)	Maize (%)	Edible oils (%)	Nonfood (%)
Albania	—	72.3	63.7	26	5.8
Armenia	—	84.5	—	—	11.1
Bangladesh	25.2	4.7	31.4	0.5	14.2
Belize	10.5	—	11.7	7.5	6.5
Cambodia	45.6	—	98	58.1	31.6
China	35.4	37.5	41.8	−17.9	1.4
Cote d'Ivoire	64	—	39.7	46.3	−0.8
Ecuador	76.4	124.5	140.3	18.5	7.4
Guatemala	75.6	—	29.6	—	10.9
India	48.9	26.6	14.1	36.8	9.4
Indonesia	22.7	—	22.2	80.1	4.8
Malawi	40.4	26.3	42.6	19.7	23.7
Moldova	—	72.8	53.6	43.3	25.2
Mongolia	—	111.3	—	—	22.1
Nepal	10.7	28	21.6	0.1	14.9
Nicaragua	34.1	—	41.7	7.7	14.3
Niger	26.8	28.1	28.4	27.4	4.7
Nigeria	22.8	39.6	57.4	29.4	17.1
Pakistan	−2.6	−9.3	−8.2	−2.3	21.1
Panama	45.5	—	57.5	—	7.5
Peru	118.1	100.5	54.4	37.2	6
Rwanda	−52.7	22.3	30.5	40.1	14.8
Sri Lanka	120.9	—	74.7	47	6.8
Tajikistan	−47.9	65.8	—	—	7.2
Tanzania	115.1	102.8	25	—	13.8
Timor-Leste	—	—	—	—	6.8
Uganda	22.2	—	33	—	16.3
Viet Nam	83.1	—	—	—	11.1
Yemen	—	61.3	50.2	—	15.5
Zambia	42.7	17.8	27.7	—	30.6

Sources: Authors' calculations based on the World Bank's Distortions to Agricultural Incentives database at www.worldbank.org/agdistortions, and the FAO's producer price data, CPI for all consumption and nonfoods, and its GIEWS survey data at www.fao.org.

where $\hat{p}^*$ is the proportional change in the international price; $\hat{v}_i$ is an exogenous stochastic shock to output such as might result from better or worse weather than average; η_i is the elasticity of demand; γ_i is the elasticity of supply; G_i is the share at international prices of country i in global demand; and H_i is the share of country i in global production. That is, the impact on the international price of a change in trade distortions in country i depends on the importance of that country in global supply and demand, as well as the responsiveness of its production and consumption to price changes in the country, as represented by γ_i and η_i. Note that if all countries alter their distortions by a uniform amount ($\hat{T}_i$ the same for all i), the elasticities of supply and demand are irrelevant to the impact on international prices, which will change by an exactly offsetting amount and so mean domestic prices rise as if no countries had insulated.

If we assume that output cannot respond in the short run and that inventory levels were low enough in this high-price period that stock adjustments have no effect, then $\gamma_i = 0$. If we further assume that the national elasticities of final demand (η_i) are the same across countries, then equation (2) suggests we can estimate the contribution to international price changes resulting from changes in national trade restrictions as simply the negative of the consumption-weighted global average of the $\hat{T}_i$s. To avoid dealing with interaction terms, we convert all proportional changes into log-change form and decompose the change in the domestic price in country i into the change in the world price and in the country's own protection:

$$(3) \qquad \Delta \ln p_i = \ln p_w + \ln T_i.$$

We are particularly interested in what the percentage change in the domestic price would be in each country if all countries had refrained from insulating. This is obtained by estimating the change in the international price that would result from all countries reversing their insulating actions, plus the change from reversing country i's own interventions. The proportional change in p from its initial level can be recovered by recalling that, if we set the initial price level at unity,

$$(4) \qquad \Delta \ln p = \ln(1 + \hat{p}).$$

If, for instance, all countries reduce the power of the protection rate applied in their market by 10 percent, the world price will rise by 10 percent. This means that a country that changes its national protection by less than the weighted average global change in trade taxation will experience a change in domestic prices that is larger than it would have experienced absent insulation by all countries.

Estimates of the impacts of price-insulating behavior on international prices are reported in the first column of table 8.3.[3] These are derived from annual protection changes estimated using domestic and border prices for those key food items in 103 countries that together account for more than 90 percent of the world market for each of rice, wheat, maize and edible oils. Most of those are obtained from the 82-country sample in the Distortions to Agricultural Incentives (DAI) database that was recently updated by Ander-

---

3. To test the sensitivity of those results, column 2 of table 8.3 reports the results if the supply elasticity is as high as unity instead of zero in each country and the common demand elasticity is set at –0.2. Clearly, using these different demand and supply elasticity assumptions makes little difference to the estimates (assuming still that those elasticities are uniform across countries). This result is not unexpected given that net trade is a small share of production and consumption of these food items in most countries, making each country's share of world output very similar to its consumption share.

Table 8.3   Impacts of domestic market insulation on international prices,
                     2006–2008

	Assuming no supply response	Assuming es = 1 and ed = –0.2. %	Share of world consumption covered, %	Share of world production covered, %	Number of countries included
Edible oils	30.9	25.5	95	97	96
Maize	18	17.3	93.8	97.2	103
Rice	51.9	50.5	91.8	93.9	82
Wheat	17.6	16.2	92.9	97.2	87

Source: Authors' calculations.

son and Nelgen (2013).[4] Because the DAI database does not include data for some of the smaller developing countries for which we have household data, we supplement the DAI data with estimates from other sources, particularly the FAO's domestic price and trade series. Details are provided in the appendix. The results in column (1) of table 8.3 suggest that the aggregate effect of all countries' price-insulating behavior during 2006 to 2008 was to raise the price in the international marketplace by 52 percent for rice, by 18 percent for both wheat and maize, and by 31 percent for edible oils.[5]

The extent of the contribution by each country to the changes in international rice, wheat, maize, and oilseed prices can be seen by the size of each country's rectangle in figure 8.1. In this diagram, the countries whose protection (measured by the proportional change in T) fell by more than the increase in the international price—also shown in figure 8.1 as the world price impact line—were effective in sheltering themselves from at least part of the increase in that price. Those countries where protection fell by less than the increase in the international price experienced a domestic price rise that was greater than would have occurred in the absence of insulation by all countries. Countries whose protection rate did not change experienced the full proportional increase in the international price—an increase that results from both the original shock and the additional effect of all countries' price insulation.

For rice, it appears that China, Indonesia, and Bangladesh reduced their protection enough to have a smaller domestic price increase than they would

4. For this study, a particularly important change from the version of the DAI used in earlier versions of this study was a move from using unit values to international indicator prices when updating changes in international prices. Of greatest importance for this study was the case of rice in India where the estimates of export prices in Pursell, Gulati, and Gupta (2009) were originally updated using export unit values and are now updated as an index to parallel the proportional increase in the Thai 5 percent broken rice price. For 2006–2008, the unit value of India's exports was strongly affected by a large increase in the share of much-more-expensive basmati rice exports.

5. These are slightly higher from the comparable estimates for the three cereals in Martin and Anderson (2012), because a larger sample of countries is used here.

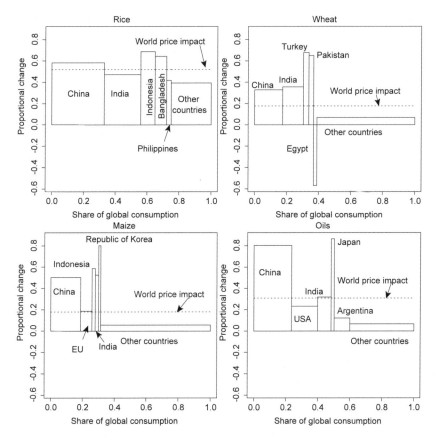

Fig. 8.1   Contribution of countries' insulation to global price changes

Source: Authors' calculations. Protection change is the negative of the proportional change in $(1 + t)$, estimated using the World Bank Distortions to Agricultural Incentives database, supplemented with data from FAOSTAT and FAO's GIEWS database. Global consumption shares at international prices are derived from the FAO's Commodity Balance Sheet database.

have experienced without insulation by any country. Other countries, such as India and the Philippines, insulated themselves to some degree from the increase in the international rice price, but not by enough to offset the price-increasing effect of all countries' collective action. That is, for these and other countries, their domestic rice price increased more than it would have done in the absence of their own and all other countries' insulation.

For wheat, the countries that insulated sufficiently that their domestic price rose by less than it would have in the absence of insulation by all countries include China, India, Turkey, Pakistan, and Japan. While most other countries insulated to some extent, they did not do so enough to reduce the increase in their domestic price below the increase that would have occurred in the absence of insulation. For maize, it appears that China, Korea, Indonesia, and India insulated enough to reduce the rise in their domestic price relative to the no-insulation scenario, while for edible oils China and Japan appear to have insulated enough to reduce the rise in their domestic price to less than the increase that would have occurred in the absence of insulation.

8.2   Changes in Protection in Our Sample Countries

For the developing countries for which household data are available, the 2006 to 2008 changes in protection to the four key crop products are detailed in table 8.4. The table suggests that protection in most developing countries fell during the observed period. The table also includes at the bottom, for comparison, several large countries for which suitable household data are unavailable: their changes in protection are broadly similar to the changes in protection in our sample countries, apart from Egypt and Russia, where protection rates appear to have increased for wheat and oils.

8.2.1   Domestic Prices with and without Insulation

We can now estimate the changes in domestic prices that that can be attributed to price insulation policies. These domestic price changes, reported in table 8.5, take into account two separate simulated price impacts: first, the impact of insulation by the country itself and, second, the insulation by the whole world. The first of these price changes is reported in table 8.4 while the second is the estimated change in world prices reported in column (1) of table 8.3.

The simulated domestic price impacts of removing insulation in all countries vary considerably across countries and commodities, depending on each country's level of insulation relative to the change in the international price. For example, the domestic price of rice would have fallen more in China as a result of own-country and rest-of-world insulation, but only by 5 percent: its own 37 percent reduction in protection lowered its domestic price relative to the international price, but the latter would have been 52 percent higher with global insulation. Overall for our sample of thirty countries, in 30 percent of cases the domestic price changed in the opposite direction to the country's own change in protection.

8.2.2   Distribution of Price Changes Due to Different Actions by Developing and Developed Countries

With different countries applying different changes in protection during 2006 to 2008, some countries achieved some degree of insulation of their domestic prices while others experienced higher prices than they would if no country had insulated. The countries that insulated the most vigorously "exported" price increases to the countries that insulated less. These "imports" and "exports" of price increases could have important consequences for poverty. Some advocates of price insulation argue that it can be

Table 8.4   **Observed change in protection, 2006–2008**

	Rice (%)	Wheat (%)	Maize (%)	Edible oils (%)
Albania	—	–21.5	–16.5	–39.2
Armenia	—	5.2	—	—
Bangladesh	–41.3	–38.3	–27.5	0.5
Belize	–40.7	—	–37.3	–30.1
Cambodia	–26.9	—	0.8	–17.6
China	–37.4	–23.5	–36.1	–52.2
Cote d'Ivoire	–23.1	—	–13.4	–17.2
Ecuador	–5.9	–2.9	23.7	10.1
Guatemala	–8	—	33.7	—
India	–30.2	–25.4	–37.7	–20.7
Indonesia	–44.1	—	–42.1	–13.1
Malawi	3.5	–29.6	145.6	–3.1
Moldova	—	–27	–21.4	0.4
Mongolia	—	6.2	—	—
Nepal	–60.5	–33.2	–10.7	–0.2
Nicaragua	–37.1	—	–22.6	–26.5
Niger	–7.7	–6.8	–14.5	–7.7
Nigeria	–42.4	–52.6	–14.1	–23.5
Pakistan	–54.3	–46.6	–49.8	–33.8
Panama	–8.7	—	–22.9	—
Peru	16.6	–8.3	–22.5	–4.6
Rwanda	–55.7	–31.6	161.1	–6.3
Sri Lanka	3.6	—	14.7	5.1
Tajikistan	–61.7	–48.7	—	—
Tanzania	0.9	19.5	–31.8	—
Uganda	–42.7	—	–27.4	—
Viet Nam	–15.9	—	—	—
Yemen	—	–39.9	–24	—
Zambia	–21.5	–32.2	67.7	—
Brazil	–21.6	–0.1	0.9	1.9
Egypt	–32.7	40.8	–24.5	31
EU	4.4	–0	–14.4	–5.1
Philippines	–26.7	—	–22	–8.9
Russian Federation	–18.1	6.7	–17.5	17.6
USA	–0.1	–0	–0	–15.1

Source: Authors' calculations.

used by developing countries to shift price increases to high-income countries, which are much better placed to manage such shocks. To see whether this was the case in 2006 to 2008, figure 8.2 shows the distribution of price changes due to countries' actions from two perspectives: developed versus developing countries, and within each of those country groups.

Consider first the impacts of the actions of developed and developing countries acting as two aggregate groups. The clear set of bars in each subfigure shows the magnitude of the value change transmitted between developed

Table 8.5   Implications of all countries' insulation for domestic prices, 2006–2008

	Rice (%)	Wheat (%)	Maize (%)	Edible oils (%)
Albania	—	–7.6	–1.5	–20.4
Armenia	—	23.8	—	—
Bangladesh	–10.9	–27.5	–14.4	31.5
Belize	–9.9	—	–26	–8.4
Cambodia	11.1	—	19	7.9
China	–4.9	–10	–24.6	–37.4
Cote d'Ivoire	16.8	—	2.1	8.4
Ecuador	42.9	14.2	46	44.1
Guatemala	39.7	—	–21.8	—
India	6.1	–12.3	–26.5	3.8
Indonesia	–15.1	—	–31.7	13.8
Malawi	57.2	–17.2	189.7	26.9
Moldova	—	–14.1	–7.3	31.4
Mongolia	—	25	—	—
Nepal	–40	–21.4	5.3	30.6
Nicaragua	–4.5	—	–8.7	–3.8
Niger	40.2	9.7	0.8	20.8
Nigeria	–12.6	–44.2	1.4	0.2
Pakistan	–30.6	–37.1	–40.8	–13.3
Panama	38.7	—	–9.1	—
Peru	77	7.9	–8.5	24.9
Rwanda	–32.7	–19.5	208	22.6
Sri Lanka	57.3	—	35.3	37.6
Tajikistan	–41.8	–39.6	—	—
Tanzania	53.2	40.5	–19.5	—
Uganda	–12.9	—	–14.3	—
Viet Nam	27.7	—	—	—
Yemen	—	–29.2	–10.3	—
Zambia	19.3	–20.2	97.8	—
Brazil	19	17.6	19	33.4
Egypt	2.2	65.6	–10.9	71.4
EU	58.6	17.6	1	24.3
Philippines	11.3	—	–8	19.3
Russian Federation	24.4	25.6	–2.7	54
USA	51.7	17.6	17.9	11.1

Source: Authors' calculations.

and developing countries. That magnitude is determined by the consumption share of each group (the *x* axis) and the size of excess insulation (over the international price change). As can be seen, in each case the actions of the developing countries lowered the extent of their own price rise at the expense of the developed countries. Only in the case of rice did the impact of the developing countries' actions not lower their own price rise much. This is because rice consumption in developed countries is a tiny share of world

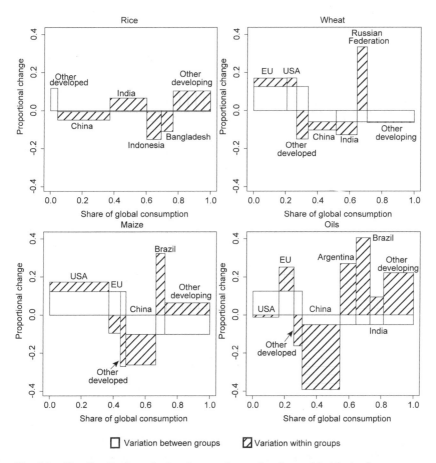

Fig. 8.2   The distribution of price changes due to the observed insulation between developed and developing countries (white) and among major developing and developed countries (diagonal lines)

Source: Authors' calculations.

consumption and hence little of the rice price increase could be exported to these countries.

Second, consider the level of coordination among developing countries' own actions, by focusing on the bars with diagonal lines, which show how much of the international price change was distributed within the group by group member actions. In the case of rice, for example, China, Indonesia, and Bangladesh insulated their markets much more than others, shifting the price increases onto the shoulders of other countries. A similar situation can be observed for the remaining crops, where China alone (plus India in the case of wheat) was successful in lowering the extent of its own domestic price rise—but, in doing so, it put upward pressure on prices in other countries.

8.3   Poverty Impacts

Using our sample of thirty developing countries, we can now evaluate the poverty impacts of the hypothetical price changes that would have been associated with the observed levels of price insulation in the period 2006 to 2008. To calculate poverty impacts, we follow the methodology of Ivanic, Martin, and Zaman (2012) who measure changes in poverty as a change in the number of people living on less than 1.25 US dollars a day in 2005 purchasing power parity (ppp) dollars. They do so by assuming household real income, B, depends on the expenditure required to achieve its initial level of utility, and on the income generated by any farm business it operates:

$$(5) \qquad B = e(p,w,u) - r(p,w),$$

where $e(p,w,u)$ is the cost of expenditure; $r(p,w)$ is the revenue from the farm firm (including that which is consumed by the household); p is a vector of prices; w is a vector of wage rates; and u is utility.

Differentiating gives Deaton's net consumption measure:

$$(6) \qquad dB = e_p dp - r_p dp = z_p dp,$$

where z_p is the household's net purchases of food. In contrast, with Hertel and Winters (2006) and Jacoby (2013), we consider the change in the revenue accruing to the household through the $r_p dp$ term, without allocating it into returns to labor and capital, because this allows us to assess the income effects of changes in individual food prices on farm households much more precisely. Because we consider such a short period, we assume that wage rates paid to labor sold outside the farm firms do not respond to changes in food prices. Most studies that allow for a dynamic path of response from commodity price changes to wages find quite small wage impacts in the first year or two (see, for example, Lasco, Myers, and Bernsten 2008).

This approach only considers the short-run impact of the changes in food prices on households' agricultural sales and food expenditures. That is, we ignore any quantity adjustments (increases in production or changes in consumption) because these are second-order impacts of the price changes. Because elasticities of demand for the staple foods considered are typically quite low, the inclusion of second-order impacts on demand is unlikely to have a large impact on the overall welfare impact. While the second-order impacts through changes in supply can be much larger, there is little scope to change quantities supplied in the short run.

Two simulations are reported in table 8.6. Starting from the hypothetical price levels representing the world with no insulation in each case, the first simulation shows the implications of the observed changes in trade distortions in all countries. The second scenario assumes that developing and developed countries insulated by the average observed level for that group. These simulations allow us to see whether developing countries were able to

Table 8.6   **Changes in poverty due to observed insulation, or from developing countries using a uniform rate of insulation, 2006–2008**

	Observed insulation		Uniform insulation in developing countries	
	Change in poverty headcount (%)	Change in number of poor (thousand)	Change in poverty headcount (%)	Change in number of poor (thousand)
Albania	−0.1	−2	−0.1	−2
Armenia	0.2	7	−0.1	−4
Bangladesh	0.8	1,235	−0.1	−146
Belize	−0.1	0	−0.2	−1
China	0.3	3,620	0.1	1,718
Cote D'Ivoire	1	194	−0.2	−35
Ecuador	0.6	89	0	1
Guatemala	−0.1	−16	−0.3	−42
Indonesia	0	104	0	−7
India	0.4	4,380	−0.4	−5,247
Cambodia	−1.7	−246	0.1	12
Sri Lanka	2.2	467	−0.2	−33
Moldova	−0.1	−3	−0.2	−8
Mongolia	1.2	33	−0.3	−8
Malawi	2.4	362	−0.3	−52
Niger	1	166	−0.1	−14
Nigeria	−0.7	−1,158	−0.1	−243
Nicaragua	−0.1	−5	0	−2
Nepal	−0.5	−150	−0.1	−22
Pakistan	−3.3	−5,898	−0.7	−1,273
Panama	0.3	11	0	−2
Peru	0.9	256	−0.1	−21
Rwanda	0.6	66	−0.1	−13
Tajikistan	−1.2	−86	−0.4	−25
Timor-Leste	0	0	0	0
Tanzania	0.6	292	−0.4	−169
Uganda	0	−2	−0.1	−18
Viet Nam	−0.4	−381	0.1	78
Yemen	−1.9	−483	−0.5	−127
Zambia	−1.9	−250	0	1

Source: Authors' calculations. In columns (3) and (4), developing countries insulate at the average rate observed in the sample while industrial countries insulate to the extent observed in the sample.

shift the price increases onto the industrial countries that are so much better placed to manage the effects of food price shocks, or whether the major redistributions of the price rises were between developing countries. Both sets of results are shown in table 8.6 in terms of percentage point changes in the initial poverty rates as well as the estimated absolute changes in the number of poor people.

According to the first pair of columns in table 8.6, the policy of insula-

Table 8.7   Sample coverage of the developing countries' $1.25 per day poor people, by region and income levels

		Region						
		East Asia & Pacific	Europe & Central Asia	Latin America	Middle East & North Africa	South Asia	Sub-Saharan Africa	World
Low-income	Poor population, mil	3.3	0.8	6.2	—	72.7	264.6	347.6
	Sample coverage, mil	3.3	0.5	0.0	—	72.7	69.8	146.3
	Sample coverage, share	100%	63%	0%	—	100%	26%	42%
	Weight	1.0	1.7	—	—	1.0	3.8	—
Lower-middle income	Poor population, mil	81.8	0.8	6.8	8.0	444.3	148.3	690
	Sample coverage, mil	59.6	0.1	2.7	4.3	444.3	124.5	635.5
	Sample coverage, share	73%	13%	40%	54%	100%	84%	92%
	Weight	1.4	10.7	2.5	1.8	1.0	1.2	—
Upper-middle income	Poor population, mil	175.8	1.4	22.6	3.7	—	19.1	222.6
	Sample coverage, mil	175.5	0.0	2.4	0.0	—	0.0	177.9
	Sample coverage, share	100%	0%	11%	0%	—	0%	80%
	Weight	1.0	—	9.6	—	—	—	—
World	Poor population, mil	260.9	3.0	35.6	11.7	517.0	432.0	1260.
	Sample coverage, mil	238.4	0.6	4.9	4.3	517.0	194.3	959.
	Sample coverage, share	91%	20%	14%	37%	100%	45%	76%

Source: Authors' calculations using World Bank income categories.

tion helped around half of the countries considered (thirteen of the thirty) to lower the poverty rate relative to the outcome from the initial exogenous international price shock. For many countries that insulated, however, the results in this table suggest that the combined effect of all countries' insulation was actually to raise poverty. Based on the second pair of columns, had all developing countries insulated by the average degree of insulation for developing countries, all but five of those thirty countries would have seen more of their people move out of poverty.

Based on the coverage of our sample of global poverty by region and income level, we extrapolate sample poverty changes into poverty estimates at the global, regional, and income-group level (low, lower-middle, and upper-middle income countries). To perform this extrapolation, we assign weights to the countries in the sample to make them represent all missing countries for the particular income group and region group. With the inclusion of China and India, our sample covers most of the regions and income groups with poverty and especially the "pockets of poverty" among lower-middle income countries of South Asia (SAR) and upper middle-income countries of East Asia (EAP) where our sample coverage is nearly complete, as shown table 8.7.

6. We use a standard normal distribution for convenience but the result will be invariant to the choice of variance.

Table 8.8   Extrapolated global poverty implications of insulation (in millions)

	Mean estimate	Standard deviation
Observed insulation	7.5	10.3
Uniform insulation in developing countries (and actual insulation in developed countries)	−7.2	8.4

The assigned weights for the countries included in our sample and knowledge of the weights of other developing countries for which poverty estimates are available allow us to evaluate the standard error associated with using our sample to estimate global poverty impacts. To do this, we perform a Monte Carlo simulation of 10,000 runs in which we simulate normally[6] and independently distributed poverty changes in a set of 109 developing countries. In each run, we calculate—using weights equal to each country's poor population share—the poverty change for the whole population and for our sample of thirty countries. We then measure the difference between the sample and the population mean in each period and calculate the variance of this difference over our 10,000 observations. Finally, we calculate the ratio of this variance to the weighted variance of the sample outcomes, which we find to be equal to 1.47 percent. This ratio means that the standard error of the estimates obtained from our sample is equal to 12 percent of the sample's weighted standard deviation.

The poverty results suggest that the observed level of price insulation most likely did not affect global poverty significantly. As a result of insulation, global poverty would not have changed significantly from zero since our mean estimate shows an increase of just eight million people with a standard deviation of ten million. Had all developing countries insulated identically at the average level, the overall global poverty change would still remain insignificantly different from zero with a mean estimate of minus seven million and a standard error of eight million (table 8.8).

Three partial indicators are also revealing. The first is the effect of the observed changes in domestic prices on poverty (table 8.9, second set of columns; table 8.10, first row). This measure suggests that the observed increases in domestic prices—using the approaches of this chapter—would have resulted in an increase in global poverty of eighty million people in developing countries living below the $1.25 per day poverty line (table 8.10) with a standard error of 19 million people. The second measure, which we term the apparent poverty reduction from price insulation, is the effect of altering trade restrictions on poverty assuming that the international price is unchanged by countries' interventions. This estimate is a reduction of poverty by eighty-two million people with a standard error of eighteen million people. It seems likely that policymakers—particularly in small countries— would focus on this latter measure (shown for individual countries in table 8.9) because it does not require a model of policy choice in a world of many

Table 8.9   Partial changes in poverty due to changes in domestic prices and in domestic protection in 2006–2008

	Insulation (assuming no implications for international prices)		Observed changes in domestic prices		Insulation (allowing for own impacts on world price)	
	Change in poverty headcount (%)	Change in number of poor (thousand)	Change in poverty headcount (%)	Change in number of poor (thousand)	Change in poverty headcount (%)	Change in number of poor (thousand)
Albania	-0.2	-7	0.6	18	-0.2	-7
Armenia	-0.1	-2	0.6	18	-0.1	-2
Bangladesh	-0.6	-842	-0.3	-434	-0.6	-902
Belize	-0.6	-2	0	0	-0.6	-2
China	-0.4	-5,710	0.3	3,967	-0.3	-4,442
Cote D'Ivoire	-1	-198	3.9	796	-1	-198
Ecuador	-0.1	-15	0.6	83	-0.1	-15
Guatemala	-0.5	-74	0.4	52	-0.5	-74
Indonesia	0.7	1,579	0.8	1,921	0.5	1,319
India	-4.8	-59,043	4.7	58,722	-4.3	-52,843
Cambodia	6.1	875	-1.7	-238	6.1	871
Sri Lanka	-0.3	-55	4.6	968	-0.3	-55

Moldova	−1	−37	1.2	43	−1	−37
Mongolia	−0.5	−14	4.4	123	−0.5	−14
Malawi	0.7	105	0.2	31	0.7	105
Niger	−0.5	−73	1	159	−0.5	−73
Nigeria	−2.7	−4,377	0.5	830	−2.7	−4,329
Nicaragua	−1.3	−75	0.2	9	−1.3	−75
Nepal	−1.3	−409	0	−12	−1.4	−413
Pakistan	−5.6	−9,936	−2.6	−4,600	−5.6	−9,845
Panama	−0.1	−4	0.2	8	−0.1	−4
Peru	0	−14	2.5	725	0	−14
Rwanda	0	1	0	4	0	2
Tajikistan	−1.8	−127	0.6	43	−1.8	−127
Timor-Leste	0	0	0	0	0	0
Tanzania	−0.9	−433	2.4	1,128	−0.9	−433
Uganda	−0.1	−38	0	8	−0.1	−38
Viet Nam	2.9	2,583	−0.1	−60	2.9	2,553
Yemen	−3.2	−799	2.7	682	−3.2	−796
Zambia	−1.5	−197	−0.1	−12	−1.5	−197

Source: Authors' calculations.

Table 8.10   Extrapolated global poverty estimates (in millions)

	Mean estimate	Standard deviation
Observed change in domestic prices	80.2	18.9
Insulation (assuming no implications for global price)	−81.6	18.4

countries, and does not require knowledge of the policy responses taken by other countries. For small countries, these numbers are the impact of the country's own price insulation on the poverty rate in their country. For large countries, they overstate the benefits of price insulating policies by failing to take into account the impacts of the country's own insulating policies on the international price. The results in this column highlight the nature of the collective action problem involved with price insulation. For many countries, including China and India, the apparent impact of insulation is to reduce poverty, while the outcome of price insulation by the world as a whole is to increase it.

The third partial measure, which we report in the final two columns of table 8.9, is the implications of each country's own insulation on its own poverty rate, both directly through its own price insulation and through the effects of that insulation on the world price. This table shows that while large countries' own insulation (mainly in India, China, and Bangladesh) has some adverse implications for poverty by pushing up international price, the size of this impact is generally dwarfed by the domestic impacts of their own insulation. This highlights the collective-action problem associated with this form of policy response—for individual countries, insulating frequently appears to make sense as a way to reduce the poverty impacts of world price increases even while it is collectively ineffective.

8.3.1   Some Policy Implications

Standard principles of economic policy suggest that the most effective approach in dealing with the poverty consequences of price volatility is via instruments targeted most directly at the problem. This suggests that a social safety net aimed directly at alleviating poverty is likely to raise more individuals out of poverty than an indirect policy that operates through market prices facing all consumers, and even more so than one at a country's border since that also affects producer incentives. In some settings pure safety net policies may not be feasible, and nations adopt or consider alternative policies. For example, Gouel and Jean (2012) find that targeted subsidies to domestic storage combined with trade policies achieve any given stabilization goal at lower cost than relying on trade or storage policies alone.

The apparent success of some countries in reducing the extent of increase in domestic prices might lead one to encourage or assist other developing countries to achieve the same high degree of price insulation. This would, however, run head first into the collective action problem: for commodities such as rice, where the market share of developed countries is small, equally successful insulation by all developing countries—both exporters and importers—would be very similar to no insulation at all.

What are the consequences of collective action problems for the effects of policies at different levels—national, regional, or global? If price stabilization were only attainable through price insulation, if all countries had the same responses to price volatility, and if all countries were small, then the collective action problem would need to be addressed at the regional or global level. Each country would, unilaterally, have an incentive to insulate to the same degree. Using rational storage policies as suggested by Gouel and Jean (2012) offers some possibility of diminishing the extent of beggar-thy-neighbor impacts than use of insulating trade policies alone. However, this proposal is very different from the policies observed in the 2008 crisis: global rice stocks—and stocks in most major developing countries—increased rather than decreased during 2007 to 2008, despite extraordinarily high prices.

The result that the largest developing countries tend to insulate their markets more than other countries raises important questions for their policymakers. That this occurred despite a higher cost to large importing countries than others of unilateral insulating action[7] is something of a puzzle. Are policymakers taking full account of the impact of their actions on international prices? In the case of food-exporting countries, their insulating action improves their terms of trade but risks alienating their trading partners. Perhaps part of the explanation is that the largest developing countries have historically been close to self-sufficient, and hence their policymakers are not overly worried about developing a reputation as an unreliable exporter—a goal that appears to have contributed to a pressure by farm interests, in such countries as the United States and Australia, against export restrictions.

At the regional level, there may be scope for policy commitments that reduce the adverse impacts of beggar-thy-neighbor policies. If, for instance, regional groups were able to make binding commitments to allow exports to flow even during times of shortage, then this may reduce the deep-seated concerns of policymakers in importing countries about the availability of sufficient importable food in times of crisis. Rice in Asia is the most obvious case in point.

It is understandable that countries depending heavily on the international food market worry that they might be vulnerable to export controls or taxes imposed by their suppliers. At the World Trade Organization (WTO), many importing countries have put forward proposals for disciplining export bar-

---

7. The welfare costs of unilaterally reducing the domestic price rise are higher in a food-deficit large country than a small one because such action by a large importing country causes the international price to rise and hence increases the welfare cost of achieving any given reduction in the extent of the rise in the domestic price.

riers (Congo 2001, Japan 2000, Jordan 2001, Korea 2001, and Switzerland 2000). Some of these proposals are far reaching. For example, the Jordan proposal is to ban export restrictions and bind all export taxes at zero. The proposal by Japan involves disciplines similar to those on the import side, with export restrictions to be replaced by taxes and those export taxes to be bound. Recognizing that importers' concerns about the reliability of supply might inhibit liberalization, some exporting countries have also advocated multilateral limitations on the right to use export restrictions. In the preliminary negotiations on agriculture held between 1999 and 2001 under Article 20 of the Uruguay Round Agreement on Agriculture, the Cairns Group (2000) and the United States (2000) put forward proposals for disciplines on export barriers and/or taxes.

The ability of importing countries to lower protection when prices rise is currently unconstrained by WTO rules. Countries with low initial tariffs have little scope to reduce their protection when world prices rise, but they can introduce import subsidies—as indeed some countries did in 2008. If exporting countries were to be restrained by WTO rules from introducing export barriers, however, there would be less reason for tariff reductions by food-importing countries.

8.4   Conclusions

In this chapter, we have analyzed the distributional and poverty impacts of the food price insulation that was observed in the period of 2006 to 2008 when prices of many staple food items increased sharply. For four major food items—rice, wheat, maize, and edible oils—which comprise nearly half of poor people's food expenditure, we have estimated how much the observed insulating actions of more than one hundred countries, taken as a whole and individually, affected international and domestic food prices and how much it alleviated an increase in global poverty.

As in other recent studies, we find that the observed patterns of price insulation resulted in such a rise of international prices, one which virtually completely offsets the benefits of insulation. We also find, however, that developing countries as a group insulated more than developed countries and, as a result, parts of the price increases were exported to developed countries. This pattern of insulation applies to all four commodities considered in this study, but least so in the case of rice because developed countries represent only a tiny portion of global rice consumption. Nonetheless, the price increase absorbed by developed countries was so small that its implication for global poverty appears negligible.

Our results highlight the seriousness of the problem of rapid increases in food prices in the 2006 to 2008 period. We find that the rise in poverty resulting from the increases in the domestic prices of the four commodities considered in this chapter was eighty million people. For many countries, price insulation appeared to be an effective policy for dealing with this challenge. We estimate that the changes in trade policies (mostly reductions in protection) would have reduced poverty by around eighty-two million if these policies had been adopted with no changes in international prices. However, the adoption of these insulating prices caused substantial increases in international prices, making them much less effective than they appeared in reducing the poverty impacts of the initial increases in world prices. These results highlight an extremely important collective action problem—policies of insulation that are effective for many individual countries are ineffective for developing countries as a group, because both exporters and importers so respond.

A number of caveats to this analysis need to be kept in mind. One is that we have examined the price effects for just four food items. Including all food items is unlikely to alter the main conclusions, though, because the four included items are so important within the set of traded food products for which price insulation plays a major role. Another caveat is that we have not taken account of any indirect effects on poor households that come via factor markets. In agrarian economies, with the vast majority of workers employed in agriculture, an increase in farm product prices may raise unskilled wages, although much of this effect may take longer than the short period we consider. That would lower the adverse impact on landless laborers of higher food prices (although we have not found this channel of effect to change the results substantially in earlier work in this vein—see Ivanic and Martin [2008], and Ivanic, Martin, and Zaman [2012]).

The literature suggests that social safety net policies can generate larger reductions in poverty, with fewer by-product distortions, than nth-best trade policy instruments that are used for social protection.[8] They could take the form of targeted income supplements to only the most vulnerable households, and only while the price spike lasts. The potential of these approaches is now much greater than it was just a few years ago, thanks to the digital information and communication technology (ICT) revolution. In the past it has often been claimed that such payments are unaffordable in poor countries because of the fiscal outlay involved and the high cost of administering such handouts. However, recall that in roughly half the cases considered above, governments reduced their trade tax rates or paid import subsidies, so even these trade interventions frequently required budget resources—as did the replacement in many cases of nonprohibitive export taxes with bans. In any case, the option of using value-added taxes in place of trade taxes to raise government revenue has become common practice in even low-income countries over the past decade or two (Besley and Persson 2013). Moreover, the ICT revolution has made it possible for conditional cash transfers to be

---

8. Indeed, conditional cash transfers can contribute not only to equity but can also enhance economic growth. See Alderman and Yemtsov (2013).

provided electronically as direct assistance to even remote and small households, and even to the most vulnerable members of those households (typically women and their young children). True, if those targeted have a greater propensity to spend on food than those being taxed to fund the transfers, they would boost the global demand for food and hence there would still be a beggar-thy-neighbor impact on international prices through income effects (as stressed by Do, Levchenko, and Ravallion 2013). Almost certainly, however, that would be far smaller than the impact generated by the much blunter approach of altering trade restrictions, which adds income effects on untargeted beneficiaries and substitution effects on both producers and consumers.

Appendix

The changes in domestic and border prices for the four key food items are compiled for 103 countries that together account for more than 90 percent of the world market for each of rice, wheat, maize, and edible oils. For the present analysis, data are required on changes in domestic and international prices for a set of countries that cover a very large fraction of world consumption, plus estimates of changes in protection in the set of countries for which we have detailed data on production and consumption of each food at the household level. The Distortions to Agricultural Incentives (DAI) database (Anderson and Nelgen 2013) provides annual estimates of agricultural price distortions in eighty-two countries that are most important in influencing world prices. Because the DAI database does not include data for some of the smaller developing countries for which we have household data, we supplement the DAI data with estimates from other sources, particularly the Food and Agriculture Organization of the United Nations (FAO)'s domestic price and trade series.

To assess changes in protection at the country level, we consider changes in international, domestic, and country-specific border prices of four key food items. Our estimates of the international price changes come from the World Bank's Global Economic Monitor (GEM) database. Because for most commodities the GEM reports a set of prices for specific varieties (e.g., US Hard Red Winter wheat, etc.), we calculate and use unweighted averages of all available international prices.

For domestic prices, we turn to the available DAI and FAO databases that usually contain a single price estimate for most agricultural commodities and countries. For edible oils, where a producer price index was not available, we calculated a weighted price index including several important oil seeds (soybeans, sunflower, groundnuts, rapeseed) in addition to palm oil.

In a very few cases where FAO producer price data were not available, we used the FAO GIEWS database to identify the changes in domestic prices using that source's most relevant price series available.

To get a sense of the extent of changes in trade restrictions during 2006 to 2008, we present below some summary material for each of the four food items.

Rice

Rice prices increased substantially between 2006 and 2008. The first part reports that the changes for three international indicator prices averaged close to 120 percent in nominal US dollars. National border price changes (shown in appendix table 8A.1 in US dollars) were generally smaller, with the median price increasing by 78 percent. Most of the border price changes that we observe range between 53 and 102 percent. The reasons they differ from the international reference price changes may include: contractual arrangements that delay adjustments in the prices of traded goods, differences between the types of rice traded, and freight costs that make the export prices that are quoted internationally more volatile than most border prices.

Changes in domestic prices of rice were more subdued than changes in the border prices. This is also shown in appendix figure 8A.1. The median price rise was only 44 percent, with half of the price increases in the 30 to 64 percent range. Because domestic prices generally rose less than international prices, we also observe a reduction in protection,[9] with a median change of −18 percent. Most countries' protection rates fell between 0 and 30 percent.

Wheat

According to the World Bank's Global Economic Monitor database, the price of wheat traded internationally increased substantially between 2006 and 2008, with US soft red winter wheat rising by 71 percent and Canadian Western Red Spring wheat rising by 110 percent. Using the data from the FAO database, however, we observe much greater variation in border price changes between countries (appendix table 8A.1). Some countries experienced negligible price changes while other countries experienced price increases of over 200 percent. For the majority of countries, the wheat border price rise was between 80 and 120 percent.

Domestic wheat prices rose much less than the large increases in border prices for most countries. The median domestic price change was 70 percent, and most countries experienced a price increase between 35 and 100 percent

---

9. Protection is defined as the ratio of the domestic price to the border price of a like product. If there are no other price-distorting policies than border measures, as assumed here, this is both the farmers' nominal assistance coefficient and an indicator of the distortion to the domestic consumer price. For some countries this indicator may be negative, usually because it is an exporting country with an export restriction, although in rare cases it indicates import subsidization.

(appendix figure 8A.1). Because domestic prices changed at very different rates from the border prices, there is a sharp reduction in protection. The observed median change in the protection index is only –0.1 percent, but most of the countries' protection fell between zero and 25 percent.

Maize

The international price of maize rose by 83 percent between 2006 and 2008 (appendix table 8A.1). The median change in border prices was 94 percent, with half the observations between 60 and 110 percent (appendix figure 8A.1). Domestic prices changed much less with a median price change of 49 percent and most countries experiencing increases in domestic prices between 30 and 85 percent. Corresponding to these differences in domestic and international price changes we observe a reduction in protection with a median fall of 17 percent and the majority of the cuts between 10 and 30 percent.

Edible Oils

Oilseeds and edible oils are much more complex to monitor than cereals because of the diverse set of commodities involved. To obtain at least a broad guide on price developments in this market, we examine three key oil products—palm oil, palm kernel oil, and soybean oil—to obtain the average changes in international prices shown in appendix table 8A.1, and the distribution of changes in border prices, domestic prices, and protection in appendix figure 8A.1. In order to measure the changes in domestic and border prices for edible oils, we consider a consumption-weighted price

Table 8A.1   Changes in international indicator rice prices between 2006 and 2008

	Price 2006, US$/t	Price 2008, US$/t	Change, percent
Rice, Thai, A1.special	220	482	120.0
Rice, Thailand, 5% broken	305	650	113.0
Rice, Vietnamese, 5% broken	260	567	118.0
Rice average, unweighted	262	566	117.0
Wheat, Canada WRS	217	455	109.7
Wheat, US, HRW	192	326	69.8
Wheat, US, SRW	159	272	70.8
Wheat average, unweighted	189	351	83.4
Maize	122	223	83.1
Palm oil	478	949	98.3
Palm kernel oil	581	1,130	94.4
Soybean oil	599	1,258	110.2
Oil average, unweighted	553	1,112	101.0

Source: World Bank Global Economic Monitor database.

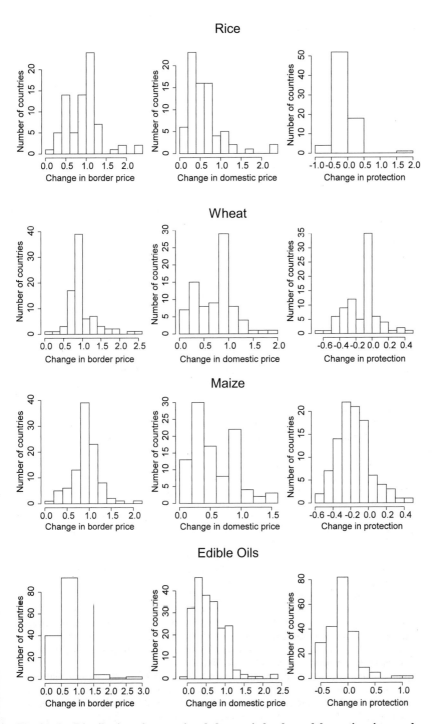

Fig. 8A.1   Distribution of proportional changes in border and domestic prices, and protection, 2006–2008

Source: Authors' calculations.

index for palm oil and major oil seeds (soybeans, cottonseed, soybeans, and groundnuts). We report a distribution of so-defined border prices in and find that the median border price change was 85 percent and that the majority of border price changes were between 55 and 110 percent. As with other commodities, domestic prices changed much less with a median price change of 54 percent and most of price changes between 30 and 80 percent. The median fall in protection was 12 percent, with half of the falls between 2 and 30 percent.

References

Alderman, H., and R. Yemtsov. 2013. "How Can Safety Nets Contribute to Economic Growth?" Policy Research Working Paper no. 6437, World Bank, Washington, DC, May.

Anderson, K., and S. Nelgen. 2013. "Updated National and Global Estimates of Distortions to Agricultural Incentives, 1955 to 2011." www.worldbank.org/ag distortions.

Besley, T. J., and T. Persson. 2013. "Taxation and Development." CEPR Discussion Paper no. 9307, January. Centre for Economic Policy Research.

Cairns Group. 2000. "WTO Negotiations on Agriculture—Cairns Group Negotiating Proposal: Export Restrictions and Taxes." World Trade Organization, 21 Dec G/AG/NG/W/93.

Congo. 2001. "Negotiating Proposals by the Democratic Republic of the Congo." 12 March. G/AG/NG/W/135. Geneva: World Trade Organization.

Deaton, A. 1989. "Household Survey Data and Pricing Policies in Developing Countries." *World Bank Economic Review* 3 (2): 183–210.

Do, Q.-T., A. L. Levchenko, and M. Ravallion. 2013. "Coping with Food Price Shocks: Trade versus Social Protection Policies." Policy Research Working Paper no. 6448, World Bank, Washington, DC, May.

Gouel, C., and S. Jean. 2012. "Optimal Food Price Stabilization in a Small Open Developing Country." Policy Research Working Paper no. 5943, World Bank, Washington, DC.

Hertel, T., and L. A. Winters. 2006. *Poverty and the WTO: Impacts of the Doha Development Agenda*. New York and Washington: Palgrave MacMillan and the World Bank.

Ivanic, M., and W. Martin. 2008. "Implications of Higher Global Food Prices for Poverty in Low-Income Countries." *Agricultural Economics* 39:405–16.

Ivanic, M., W. Martin, and H. Zaman. 2012. "Estimating the Short-Run Poverty Impacts of the 2010 Surge in Food Prices." *World Development* 40 (11): 2302–17.

Jacoby, H. 2013. "Food Prices, Wages, and Welfare in Rural India." Policy Research Working Paper no. 6412, World Bank, Washington, DC.

Japan. 2000. "Negotiating Proposal by Japan on WTO Agricultural Negotiations." 21 December. G/AG/NG/W/91. Geneva: World Trade Organization.

Jordan. 2001. "WTO Agriculture Negotiations: Proposal by Jordan." 21 March. G/AG/NG/W/140. Geneva: World Trade Organization.

Korea. 2001. "Proposal for WTO Negotiations on Agriculture." 9 January. G/AG/NG/W/98. Geneva: World Trade Organization.

Lasco, C., R. Myers, and R. Bernsten. 2008. "Dynamics of Rice Prices and Agricultural Wages in the Philippines." *Agricultural Economics* 38:339–48.

Martin, W., and K. Anderson. 2012. "Export Restrictions and Price Insulation during Commodity Price Booms." *American Journal of Agricultural Economics* 94 (2): 422–7.

Pursell, G., A. Gulati, and K. Gupta. 2009. "India." In *Distortions to Agricultural Incentives in Asia*, edited by K. Anderson and W. Martin. Washington, DC: World Bank.

Ravallion, M., S. Chen, and P. Sangraula. 2007. "New Evidence on the Urbanization of Poverty." *Population and Development Review* 33 (4): 667–702.

Switzerland. 2000. "WTO: Negotiations on Agriculture: Proposal by Switzerland." 21 December. G/AG/NG/W/94. Geneva: World Trade Organization.

Timmer, C. P. 2010. "Reflections on Past Food Prices." *Food Policy* 35:1–11.

United States. 2000. "Proposal for Comprehensive Long-Term Agricultural Trade Reform." 23 June. G/AG/NG/W/15. Geneva: World Trade Organization.

World Bank. 2007. *World Development Report 2008: Agriculture for Development.* Washington, DC: World Bank.

Comment   Marc F. Bellemare

Like most economists, I learned early on to view protectionism with suspicion. That is why the core finding in Anderson, Ivanic, and Martin's (hereafter, AIM) chapter—protectionist measures in times of high food prices can reduce poverty—was both unsurprising and interesting.

When global food prices start rising rapidly, there is almost always some discussion in the media of the protectionist measures adopted by developing countries to insulate themselves from high food prices. That discussion typically goes as follows: protectionist measures are bad because they exacerbate the problem of rising food prices. The implicit argument is thus that exacerbating already rising food prices can only hurt the world's poor, who were already facing high food prices to begin with.

In late 2011, for example, National Public Radio's *Planet Money* (NPR 2011) produced a podcast that recounted how rising rice prices led India and the Philippines to ban rice exports in 2008, thereby exacerbating a situation of high rice prices. Though the podcast did a good job of explaining how protectionist measures can compound the problem of high food prices, it included little to no discussion of the impacts of protectionist measures on poverty.

Marc F. Bellemare is assistant professor of applied economics at the University of Minnesota.

I thank Jean-Paul Chavas, David Hummels, and Brian Wright for inviting me to serve as a discussant at the conference. I am also grateful to the conference participants for several fruitful and enlightening exchanges. For acknowledgments, sources of research support, and disclosure of the author's material financial relationships, if any, please see http://www.nber.org/chapters/c12819.ack.

Does protectionism hurt the poor? In their chapter, AIM answer's is a qualified "yes." In other words, protectionist measures appear to increase poverty, and those same measures are almost always detrimental to other countries.

In this discussion, I would first like to use the AIM chapter as a springboard for my thoughts as to what I would like to see future researchers accomplish on this topic. Then, I wish to briefly extrapolate from the AIM chapter to speculate on the causes and consequences of food price protectionism.

Identification

As an applied microeconomist who came to the topic of food prices from development economics, most of my comments on the AIM chapter relate to the identification of the causal relationship flowing from protectionism to poverty. More accurately, my comments are what I would like to see future researchers do in order to refine our understanding of the relationship between protectionism and poverty and, ultimately, improve food policy.

The empirical relationship between poverty and protectionism is best represented by the equation

$$(1) \qquad Y_{it} = \alpha + \beta_i D_{it} + \sum_{j \neq i}^{J} \beta_j D_{jt} + \gamma X_{it} + \epsilon_{it},$$

where the subscripts i, and j denote countries i and j, respectively, subscript t denotes time period t, Y is a measure of poverty,[1] D_i denotes protectionist measures in country i, D_j denotes protectionist measures in country j, X is a vector of control variables, and ϵ is an error term whose mean is equal to zero.

The objective is to estimate the parameters β_i and β_j, which respectively measure the impact of protectionist measures in country i on the poverty rate in country i and the impact of protectionist measures in country j on the poverty rate in country i. One can respectively think of those effects as own and spillover impacts of protectionism. With J countries other than country i, the objective is to estimate $J + 1$ parameters.

As always, the problem is to identify the causal impact of D_{it} and D_{jt} on Y_{it}, a task that is made significantly difficult by the fact that poverty and protectionist measures are jointly determined. And although one can perhaps make the case that the protectionist measures adopted in country j are exogenous to poverty in country i, it can generally be the case that there is

---

1. Though AIM focus on the number of people living on less than a dollar a day, the measure of poverty retained for analysis need not be a headcount. Indeed, the dependent variable in equation (1) could be any of the higher-order Foster-Greer-Thorbecke measures of poverty, such as a measure of the depth of poverty (Foster, Greer, and Thorbecke 1984).

reverse causality between the protectionist measures adopted in country i and poverty in country i. Indeed—and as the next section briefly discusses—protectionist measures in theory depend directly on the level of development in country i.

The ideal data set to estimate parameters β_i and β_j in equation (1) would most likely be longitudinal and would follow a number of countries over time. Ideally, that data set would rely on monthly data in order to capture short-term movements in food prices and measure changes in protectionism as they happen.

The AIM findings are necessarily limited by data availability. In order to accurately estimate the impact of protectionist measures on poverty, however, future researchers should keep the following two things in mind.

Representativeness. To study the impacts of protectionist measures on poverty, AIM rely on household expenditures and income data for a convenience sample of thirty developing countries. Those data were collected between 2002 and 2010. It is difficult, however, to accurately estimate the impact of protectionist measures adopted between 2006 and 2008 without a representative sample of countries and without data that were collected at the same time. To make the study of the relationship between protectionism and poverty more systematic in the future, the World Bank should preselect countries where it would conduct rapid appraisals of how household incomes or expenditures have changed for a representative sample of households in response to food price spikes. As it stands, the data at our disposal are too spotty to accurately estimate the welfare impacts of food price spikes, let alone estimate the welfare impacts of the protectionist measures adopted in response to those food price spikes.

Timing of protectionism measures and planned versus emergency measures. Because the price data used by AIM cover the period 2006 to 2008, their findings can, in principle, encompass protectionist measures that were adopted up to a year and a half before the mid-2008 spike in food prices. To effectively identify the impact of those protectionist measures adopted *as a direct response to food price spikes*, however, it will be necessary to disentangle policies that are adopted before a price spike from those adopted afterward. Likewise, it will be necessary to distinguish policies planned long ahead of food price spikes from policies that are adopted as a response to food price spikes. In order to do this, researchers will have to come up with a precise definition of what constitutes a food price spike.

This is, of course, on top of ensuring that no important control variables are omitted and that the selected indicators do not suffer from measurement error. The latter problem is especially important when dealing with cross-country data, with each country potentially using slightly different variable definitions or reporting methodologies.

Causes: The Political Economy of Protectionism

Beyond looking at the impacts of protectionism on poverty, it is worth asking what might lead to the adoption of protectionist measures. Though this is not the place to develop a full-fledged model to account for the political economy of food price protectionism, I nonetheless wish to lay the foundations of what such a model might look like.

Assuming that protectionist measures actually work to reduce the price of food, the thirst for protectionism in a given country is presumably a function of the proportions of individuals who are net buyers of food $b \in [0,1]$, of individuals who are autarkic relative to food $a \in [0,1]$, and of individuals who are net sellers of food $s \in [0,1]$ in that country, with $b + a + s = 1$. For simplicity, I assume that there is a measure zero of individuals who do not depend on food markets for their subsistence, that is, $a = 0$. In practice, however, there certainly are cases where an individual or household remains autarkic relative to food, either because the individual or household consumes exactly what it produces or because of market failures.

I also abstract from dynamic considerations such as storage and buffer stocks (Williams and Wright 2005; Wright and Williams 1982) and general equilibrium effects, and I assume that rising food prices benefit net sellers of food but hurt net buyers of food (Deaton 1989). Everything else being equal, the former oppose protectionist measures, and the latter support them. Under a voting model, protectionist measures obtain when $b > s$. That is, when net buyers of food outnumber net sellers of food, politicians seeking reelection will have an incentive to enact protectionist measures, whose result is to lower the price of food.

Even in heavily agricultural, food-exporting countries, however, it will generally be the case that $b > s$; that is, net buyers of food outnumber net sellers of food. So why do we not observe protectionist measures everywhere?

The answer is likely because a pure voting model is not ideally suited to explain protectionism. Indeed, few developing countries have regular, open elections for their citizens to hold politicians accountable. Moreover, in most countries, food is but one issue voters care about. This is especially true in more developed countries: as a country develops and incomes increase, the budget share of food decreases, and so the price of food becomes an increasingly negligible concern. In such countries one might expect net sellers of food—farmers—to lobby politicians against protectionist measures (Bates 1981), simply because the gain to net sellers of doing so far exceeds the loss incurred by consumers because of higher food prices.

Indeed, as countries develop and their economies evolve from agrarian economies generating low incomes per capita to industrial economies generating higher incomes per capita, and then to service economies generating high incomes per capita, we can expect politicians to be increasingly unlikely to adopt protectionist measures. This is reinforced by Engel's law, which states that as countries develop and incomes increase, the budget share of food decreases for the average household, and so consumers care relatively less about the price of food. This progression of protectionist policies along the stages of development is similar in spirit to the "developmental paradox," according to which policies aimed at reducing the effects of food price volatility are more likely to be adopted as a country develops, as farmers become more likely to organize and lobby the state for price stabilization (Barrett 1999; Lindert 1991).[2]

Going back to developing countries, where food prices are of utmost importance to consumers because of high budget shares of food, though the voting model might not be terribly well suited to explain politics in developing countries, it is not clear that the lobbying model is either. Indeed, in developing countries, rural producers often lack the organizational capacity required to lobby politicians. In such countries, however, it is often the case that the threat of food-related social unrest (Bellemare, forthcoming; Rudé 1964) will provide politicians with enough of an incentive to adopt protectionist measures.

Consequences: Protectionism and Externalities

The foregoing focused on the likely causes of protectionist measures, but what about the consequences of such measures?

If protectionist measures decrease the price of food in country A but contribute to rising food prices elsewhere, there is an externality associated with those measures for country B.

Whether that externality is positive or negative depends once again on the distribution of households along the net buyer, autarkic, or net seller continuum in country B; that is, on the proportions b_B, a_B, and s_B. When $b_B > s_B$, protectionism in country A is a negative externality for country B. That is, for citizens in country B, the rest of the world overproduces protectionism. When $b_B < s_B$, however, protectionism in country A is a positive externality for country B. That is, for citizens in country B, the rest of the world underproduces protectionism, in which case politicians in country B should be willing to pay politicians in country A to adopt protectionist measures.

What politicians in country B do in response to the externality—that is, whether they encourage the politicians in country A to adopt (or disadopt) protectionist measures—however, depends on the political economy of food in country B, as discussed in the previous section. In other words, there might be a good case for country B to retaliate against or give preferential treat-

2. I distinguish between rising food prices (i.e., high food price levels) and food price volatility (i.e., the noise or uncertainty around the food price level), or between the mean and the variance of a food price series.

ment to country A in response to the latter's adoption of protectionist measures. In the limit, the externalities associated with food price protectionism can provide a rationale for intervention by global food policymakers.

Conclusion

The AIM chapter has explored the impacts on poverty of the protectionist measures adopted in response to rising food prices. In this discussion, I have outlined a possible agenda for future research aimed at understanding both the causes and consequences of such protectionist measures.

Specifically, by "causes," I mean the political economy of food price protectionism, and by "consequences," I mean the externalities that come with the adoption of protectionist measures. Understanding both the political economy of protectionism and the externalities arising from protectionist measures will help the design of global policy instruments aimed at mitigating the effect of high food prices.

References

Barrett, Christopher B. 1999. "The Microeconomics of the Developmental Paradox: On the Political Economy of Food Price Policy." *Agricultural Economics* 20 (2): 159–72.

Bates, Robert H. 1981. *Markets and States in Tropical Africa*. Berkeley: University of California Press.

Bellemare, Marc F. Forthcoming. "Rising Food Prices, Food Price Volatility, and Social Unrest." *American Journal of Agricultural Economics*.

Deaton, Angus. 1989. "Household Survey Data and Pricing Policies in Developing Countries." *World Bank Economic Review* 3 (2): 183–210.

Foster, James, Joel Greer, and Erik Thorbecke. 1984. "A Class of Decomposable Poverty Measures." *Econometrica* 52 (3): 761–6.

Lindert, Peter H. 1991. "Historical Patterns of Agricultural Policy." In *Agriculture and the State: Growth, Employment and Poverty in Developing Countries*, edited by C. P. Timmer. Ithaca, NY: Cornell University Press.

National Public Radio (NPR). 2011. "How Fear Turned a Surplus into Scarcity." *Planet Money*.

Rudé, George. 1964. *The Crowd in History*. New York: Wiley.

Williams, Jeffrey C., and Brian D. Wright. 2005. *Storage and Commodity Markets*. Cambridge: Cambridge University Press.

Wright, Brian D., and Jeffrey C. Williams. 1982. "The Economic Role of Commodity Storage." *Economic Journal* 92 (367): 596–614.

Trade Insulation as Social Protection

Quy-Toan Do, Andrei A. Levchenko,
and Martin Ravallion

9.1 Introduction

Over the last two centuries, there has been much debate about the role of trade policy in food crises. Governments of food-exporting but famine-affected areas have often been called upon by their citizens, and have often implemented, food export bans in the hope of protecting vulnerable people. Classical economists were influential in arguing against such policies in favor of free trade. For example, Aykroyd (1974) describes how the governor of Bombay in the early nineteenth century quoted Adam Smith's *The Wealth of Nations* in defending his policy stance against any form of trade intervention during the famines that afflicted the region. Various "Famine Commissions" set up by the British Raj argued against the trade interventions that were being called upon to help protect vulnerable populations. Similarly, Woodham-Smith (1962) describes the influence that Smith and other classical economists had on British policy responses to the severe famines in Ireland in the mid-nineteenth century. In modern time, free trade has been

Quy-Toan Do is an economist in the poverty team of the Development Research Group at the World Bank. Andrei A. Levchenko is associate professor of economics at the University of Michigan and a research associate of the National Bureau of Economic Research. Martin Ravallion is the Edmond D. Villani Professor of Economics at Georgetown University and a research associate of the National Bureau of Economic Research.

We are grateful to Jishnu Das; Alan Deardorff; Shantayanan Devarajan; Francisco Ferreira; Will Martin; Claudio Raddatz; Ron Trostle; an anonymous referee; Jean-Paul Chavas, David Hummels, and Brian Wright, editors of the present volume; and participants at the 2012 NBER "Economics of Food Price Volatility" conference for very helpful discussions. The findings, interpretations, and conclusions expressed in this chapter are entirely those of the authors. They do not necessarily reflect the views of the World Bank, its executive directors, or the countries they represent. For acknowledgments, sources of research support, and disclosure of the authors' material financial relationships, if any, please see http://www.nber.org/chapters/c12820.ack.

advocated as a means of stabilizing domestic food consumption in the presence of output shocks (World Bank 1986). Others have been less supportive. Sen (1981) and Ravallion (1987) pointed to the possibility that real income declines in the famine-affected areas can generate food export while people starved.[1] Regulated trade through taxes or even export bans may then be a defensible policy response in helping vulnerable groups relative to feasible alternatives (Ravallion 1997).

This debate resurfaced during the latest food price crises. Between 2007 and 2011 an estimated thirty-three countries resorted to restrictions on exports of grains and other food commodities (Sharma 2011). The international policy community mobilized itself against these practices. Then World Bank president Robert Zoellick, at the 2008 "High-Level Conference on World Food Security," advocated for "an international call to remove export bans and restrictions. These controls encourage hoarding, drive up prices, and hurt the poorest people around the world who are struggling to feed themselves."[2] Then US secretary of state Hillary Clinton echoes the same concerns in a 2011 speech on global food security: "We also saw how unwise policy also had an impact. Some policies that countries enacted with the hope of mitigating the crisis, such as export bans on rice, only made matters worse. . . . And that sounder approach includes . . . abstaining from export bans no matter how attractive they may appear to be, using export quotas and taxes sparingly if at all."[3]

This chapter revisits these claims and argues that trade policies are not necessarily the fundamental source of the macroeconomic amplification decried above. Rather, we show that an optimal *domestic* default social protection scheme would also take the shape of a "beggar-thy-neighbor" policy when beneficiaries of social transfers have a higher propensity to spend on food. Trade insulation policies are then mere second-best instruments available to policymakers that ought to be evaluated against policy alternatives. We therefore encourage a reassessment of food price policy responses that would not single out trade-based instruments but rather consider these together with the wide range of "second-best" options available to policymakers and evaluate the distortions specific to each of them (as suggested earlier by Meade [1955]).

To develop our argument, we analyze a two-country, two-sector endowment economy in which food price volatility is generated by endowment shocks. The endowment profile is such that some agents are net food sellers while others are net food buyers. Thus, there is some scope for insurance between the two types of agents: when food prices are high, net food sellers

---

1. Though in Ravallion (1987), the analysis of the time-series data for famines in British India indicated that the aggregate income effects were not strong enough to undermine the consumption-stabilizing effects of unrestricted trade in that specific period.

2. http://go.worldbank.org/BUEP7C3NC0.

3. http://www.state.gov/secretary/rm/2011/05/162795.htm.

have a positive income shock, while it is negative for net food buyers, and vice and versa. In an optimal social protection policy, the former would therefore transfer resources to the latter in times of food crisis, while the opposite would hold otherwise. Such domestic policy does not necessarily have any international implication unless agents also have heterogeneous preferences over items in their consumption baskets. In particular, when social protection payments during a crisis are being made to agents with a higher propensity to consume food, this will result in an increase in aggregate domestic consumption of food, with the associated implications for world food supply and, therefore, prices. Domestic social protection policies when agents have heterogeneous preferences therefore result in an amplification of supply shocks. Indeed, the insurance motive constitutes a countercyclical demand shock that exacerbates the effect of the output shock, thereby increasing overall food price volatility. When several countries engage in similar practices, policies are strategic complements, increasing the demand for insurance and resulting in even larger price increases.

It is in this context that we analyze trade insulation policies. In a world with limited commitment, the aforementioned social protection contract may not be feasible if one party can renege on her commitment and either sell to (resp. buy from) the international consumer (resp. producer). Trade insulation is then a government intervention to enforce an implicit social protection contract in times of high food prices. Agricultural subsidies, on the other hand, could then be viewed as compensations when food prices are low. While we have argued that trade-based instruments are not necessarily at the root of the amplification phenomenon described above, they admittedly distort consumption patterns across countries and result in additional upward pressure on food prices. Such distortion nevertheless decreases with the extent of preference heterogeneity among agents and eventually vanishes in the degenerate case.

This chapter builds on the literature that analyzes the interactions of international trade and domestic risk sharing. In a pioneering contribution, Newbery and Stiglitz (1984) showed that trade opening can reduce the de facto domestic risk sharing by making goods prices (and hence real incomes) less sensitive to supply shocks. Our chapter is closest to Eaton and Grossman (1985), who argue that when domestic insurance markets are incomplete, trade restrictions may improve welfare.[4] Unlike these contributions, we analyze the global implications of trade restrictions on the volatility of food prices. Our main argument is not so much that some trade restrictions are preferable to none. Rather, our point is that the optimal domestic policy would result in similar international outcomes as would export restrictions.

---

4. Dixit (1987, 1989) challenges the view that trade may reduce welfare, or that trade restrictions may increase welfare when domestic asset markets are incomplete, by modeling explicitly the sources of domestic market incompleteness through moral hazard and adverse selection.

Our chapter therefore relates to the literature on (ex post) food price stabilization policies (von Braun et al. 2008; Wright 2009; Gouel and Jean 2012) and departs from Martin and Anderson (2012) and Anderson (2012) in that we view trade restrictions as second-best implementation tools of a domestic social protection scheme. We therefore argue that international efforts to restrict trade-based instruments would make vulnerable populations at risk without necessarily mitigating food price volatility. More broadly, our chapter relates to the literature on the interplay between domestic and international risk sharing in the presence of domestic asset market frictions (Levchenko 2005; Leblebicioglu 2009; Broner and Ventura 2011). A repeated finding in this literature is that an increase in international risk sharing can lead domestic risk sharing to break down. In our model, it is greater domestic risk sharing that leads to increased volatility internationally.

The rest of the chapter is organized as follows. Section 9.2 lays out the foundation of the model and section 9.3 studies the optimal social protection policy. In section 9.4, we analyze trade insulation policies as government interventions to enforce an implicit social protection contract. Section 9.5 concludes. All the proofs are gathered in the appendix.

9.2   Setting the Stage

Let us consider a two-country, two-sector endowment economy. The two countries are labeled D and F for *Domestic* and *Foreign*, respectively. Agents have endowments of food and gold. There are two types of domestic agents: a representative net food sellers with an endowment $(\Phi_s, 0)$ of food and gold, respectively, and a representative net food buyers b with endowment vector $(0, \Gamma_b)$. On the other hand, the foreign country F is populated with one representative agent i with stochastic endowment $(\tilde{\Phi}_i, \tilde{\Gamma}_i) = (\Phi_i \tilde{\varepsilon}, \Gamma_i)$, such that $\tilde{\varepsilon} = \varepsilon^h$ with probability π and $\tilde{\varepsilon} = \varepsilon^l$ with probability $1 - \pi$, where $\pi \varepsilon^h + (1 - \pi)\varepsilon^l = 1$. For the purpose of the illustration, one can assume that π is large and ε^h is not much greater than 1, while ε^l is small and implies a large negative aggregate shock on food availability, hence triggering a food price crisis.

Timing and uncertainty. The economy consists of one single time period. At the beginning of the period, consumers and producers have the ability to sign contracts. Uncertainty about *Foreign* endowments is realized, and at the end of the period, payments—if any—are made, consumption takes place and agents die.

Preferences. For a given consumption bundle (f_k, g_k) of food and gold, respectively, agent $k \in \{s, b, i\}$ derives utility

$$V_k(f_k, g_k) = \alpha_k \ln f_k + (1 - \alpha_k) \ln g_k,$$

that is, agent k has log-linear preferences over composite good $f_k^{\alpha_k} g_k^{1-\alpha_k}$; preferences for food relative to gold are therefore allowed to vary from one individual to the other. Composite good $f^{\alpha_i} g^{1-\alpha_i}$ will henceforth be the numeraire. In the rest of the chapter, we will assume that $\alpha_b \geq \alpha_s$ to capture the idea that net food buyers are also putting a higher weight on food in their consumption basket. Thus, the two building assumptions of this chapter correspond to the case where (a) the poor spend a larger fraction of their income on food, and (b) they are net food buyers on average. The former assumption is Engel's law and has ample empirical support (see e.g., Houthakker 1957) while there is mounting evidence supporting the latter; Ivanic, Martin, and Zaman (2011) for example, find that the 2010 to 2011 surge in food prices has induced an increase in extreme poverty across the world. Thus, the difference $\alpha_b - \alpha_s$ that measures preference heterogeneity between net food buyers and net food sellers could be interpreted as the extent of inequality in the country; Engel's law implies that a larger wealth gap between the rich and the poor will translate into a larger gap in the share of food in their respective consumption baskets. We will henceforth refer to food consumers (resp. food producers) and the poor (resp. the rich) interchangeably.

Individual consumption, market clearing, and prices. As a benchmark case, agents are not allowed to contract at the beginning of the period; procurement of gold and food takes place on the international spot market at the end of the period. Prices for food and gold are denoted $(\bar{p}^\sigma, \bar{q}^\sigma)$ when $\tilde{\varepsilon} = \varepsilon^\sigma$ with $\sigma \in \{l, h\}$. Agent k dedicates a fraction α_k of her income to food consumption and the remaining to gold consumption. Since food consumption and food production equalize in equilibrium, the relative price of food to gold is therefore

(1)
$$\frac{\bar{q}^\sigma}{\bar{p}^\sigma} = \frac{(1 - \alpha_s)\Phi_s + (1 - \alpha_i)\Phi_i \varepsilon^\sigma}{\alpha_b \Gamma_b + \alpha_i \Gamma_i}.$$

Trade and welfare. Net food producing households therefore have welfare

$$\bar{V}_s^\sigma = (1 - \alpha_s)\ln\frac{\bar{p}^\sigma}{\bar{q}^\sigma} + \ln\Phi_s,$$

while consumers' is equal to

$$\bar{V}_b^\sigma = \alpha_b \ln\frac{\bar{q}^\sigma}{\bar{p}^\sigma} + \ln\Gamma_b.$$

Turning to the foreign representative agent, his utility is simply $\bar{V}_i^\sigma = \ln(\bar{p}^\sigma \Phi_i \varepsilon^\sigma + \bar{q}^\sigma \Gamma_i)$.

Subtracting total domestic consumption from total domestic food endowment (i.e., Φ_s) gives a net export level equal to:

(2)
$$\bar{X}^\sigma = \frac{\alpha_b \Gamma_b \alpha_i \Gamma_i}{\alpha_b \Gamma_b + \alpha_i \Gamma_i}\left(\frac{1 - \alpha_s}{\alpha_b}\frac{\Phi_s}{\Gamma_b} - \frac{1 - \alpha_i}{\alpha_i}\frac{\Phi_i}{\Gamma_i}\varepsilon^\sigma\right).$$

9.3   Social Protection

Focusing on domestic agents, we note that net food sellers and buyers face income uncertainty, and since a positive shock for one is a negative shock for the other, there is scope for mutual insurance. We will refer to the domestic insurance scheme as social protection. Although social protection programs often have a redistribution component built in so that payments are not necessarily state dependent, we restrict to the insurance part of these policies. Food voucher programs that are being implemented in times of crisis or the equivalent cash transfer programs, workfare programs in that they are being taken up when market wages drop below the program's proposed wage, would therefore fall into the category of schemes being considered in this analysis.

9.3.1   Arrow-Debreu Securities

We view a social protection program as the implementation of the allocation of resources that domestic agents would achieve if they were given the opportunity to purchase Arrow-Debreu securities at the beginning of the period. The price of an Arrow-Debreu security that pays out one unit of food in state of the world h (resp. l) is denoted πp^h (resp. $(1 - \pi)p^l$). Similarly, the price of an Arrow-Debreu security that pays out one unit of gold is denoted πq_h and $(1 - \pi)q^l$ in states h and l, respectively.

Domestic agents. Domestic agent $k = s,b$ chooses her consumption bundle $(f_k^\sigma, g_k^\sigma)_{\sigma=h,l}$ to maximize her expected welfare

$$W_k(f_k^h, g_k^h, f_k^l, g_k^l) = \pi V_k(f_k^h, g_k^h) + (1 - \pi)V_k(f_k^l, g_k^l)$$

subject to budget constraint

(3) $\pi(p^h f_s^h + q^h g_s^h) + (1 - \pi)(p^l f_s^l + q^l g_s^l) \leq [\pi p^h + (1 - \pi)p^l]\Phi_s$

for net food sellers, and similarly

(4) $\pi(p^h f_b^h + q^h g_b^h) + (1 - \pi)(p^l f_b^l + q^l g_b^l) \leq [\pi q^h + (1 - \pi)q^l]\Gamma_b$

for net food buyers.

Finally, at the heart of this chapter is the inability of aggregate risk to be smoothed, so that we require an additional trade balance condition, that is, for $\sigma = l,h$

(5) $p^\sigma(f_s^\sigma + f_b^\sigma) + q^\sigma(g_s^\sigma + g_b^\sigma) \leq p^\sigma \Phi_s + q^\sigma \Gamma_b.$

Foreign agents. Foreign agents do not have access to the insurance market, and therefore maximize their expected welfare

$$W_i(f_i^h, g_i^h, f_i^l, g_i^l) = \pi V_i(f_i^h, g_i^h) + (1 - \pi)V_i(f_i^l, g_i^l)$$

subject to budget constraint

(6)
$$p^{\sigma} f_i^{\sigma} + q^{\sigma} g_i^{\sigma} \leq p^{\sigma} \Phi_i + q^{\sigma} \Gamma_i$$

for $\sigma = h, l$.

9.3.2 Optimal Social Protection Policy

Equilibrium definition. An equilibrium is a price vector $\{(p^{\sigma}, q^{\sigma})\}_{\sigma \in \{h,l\}}$ such that consumption choices are the solutions to the maximization of agents' utilities subject to their respective budget constraints (3), (4), and (6). Furthermore, trade balance condition (5) holds and food and gold markets clear.

We now turn to the characterization of the equilibrium of the economy. For expositional simplicity, we can rewrite food sellers' budget constraint as a within-state-of-the-world budget constraint

(7)
$$p^{\sigma} f_s^{\sigma} + q^{\sigma} g_s^{\sigma} \leq p^{\sigma} (\Phi_s + \phi_s^{\sigma})$$

with a between-state-of-the-world budget constraint that ϕ_s^{σ} must satisfy, that is,

(8)
$$\pi p^h \phi_s^h + (1 - \pi) p^l \phi_s^l \leq 0.$$

Similarly for net food buyers, their budget constraint can be rewritten as

(9)
$$p^{\sigma} f_b^{\sigma} + q^{\sigma} g_b^{\sigma} \leq q^{\sigma} (\Gamma_b + \gamma_b^{\sigma})$$

where γ_b^{σ} verifies

(10)
$$\pi q^h \gamma_b^h + (1 - \pi) q^l \gamma_b^l \leq 0.$$

Transfers ϕ_s^{σ} and γ_b^{σ} could be interpreted as insurance payments made to or from agents in state of the world σ. For simplicity and without loss of generality, we henceforth assume that food sellers have insurance payments made in food, while food buyers have insurance payments made in gold. When conditions (8) and (10) are binding, insurance policies are actuarially fair.

The budget constraints then pin down to

(11)
$$p^{\sigma} \phi_s^{\sigma} + q^{\sigma} \gamma_b^{\sigma} \leq 0$$

for $\sigma = h, l$.

Consumer optimization and the demand for insurance. $\{(\hat{p}^{\sigma}, \hat{q}^{\sigma})\}_{\sigma \in \{h,l\}}$ refers to the equilibrium price vector. Consumer k spends a share α_k of her state-contingent, posttransfer income on food, and the remaining $1 - \alpha_k$ on gold, so that her budget constraint is binding. Furthermore, since insurance contracts are actuarially fair in equilibrium, for every equilibrium insurance policy schedule $(\hat{\phi}_s^{\sigma}, \hat{\gamma}_b^{\sigma})$, we denote $\hat{\phi} = -\hat{\phi}_s^l$ the premium paid by food sellers in times of a food crisis, and $\hat{\gamma} = -\hat{\gamma}_b^h$, the premium paid by food buyers in normal times so that $\hat{\phi}_s^h = [(1 - \pi)/\pi](\hat{p}^l/\hat{p}^h)\hat{\phi}$, and $\hat{\gamma}_b^l = [\pi/(1 - \pi)](\hat{q}^h/\hat{q}^l)\hat{\gamma}$.

Domestic agents' indirect utilities are therefore given by $\hat{W}_s(\hat{\phi})$ and $\hat{W}_b(\hat{\gamma})$, respectively, with

$$\hat{W}_s(\phi) = (1 - \alpha_s)\left[\pi\ln\frac{\hat{p}^h}{\hat{q}^h} + (1 - \pi)\ln\frac{\hat{p}^l}{\hat{q}^l}\right] + \pi\ln\left(\Phi_s + \frac{1 - \pi}{\pi}\frac{\hat{p}^l}{\hat{p}^h}\phi\right)$$

$$+ (1 - \pi)\ln(\Phi_s - \phi),$$

for net food sellers, and for net food buyers, we have

$$\hat{W}_b(\gamma) = -\alpha_b\left[\pi\ln\frac{\hat{p}^h}{\hat{q}^h} + (1 - \pi)\ln\frac{\hat{p}^l}{\hat{q}^l}\right] + \pi\ln(\Gamma_b - \gamma)$$

$$+ (1 - \pi)\ln\left(\Gamma_b + \frac{\pi}{1 - \pi}\frac{\hat{q}^h}{\hat{q}^l}\gamma\right).$$

Domestic agents choose their insurance policies to equalize their marginal utilities of consumption across states of the world, defining "demand for insurance" curves:

(12)
$$\begin{cases} \hat{\phi} = \pi\left(1 - \frac{\hat{p}^h}{\hat{p}^l}\right)\Phi_s \\ \hat{\gamma} = (1 - \pi)\left(1 - \frac{\hat{q}^l}{\hat{q}^h}\right)\Gamma_b. \end{cases}$$

As expected, the demand for insurance increases with the price difference between the two states of the world.

Market clearing, trade balance, and equilibrium insurance and price levels. Food market clearing implies that world food consumption and world food endowment equalize, that is,

$$\alpha_s\hat{\phi}^\sigma + \frac{\hat{q}^\sigma}{\hat{p}^\sigma}(\alpha_b\Gamma_b + \alpha_i\Gamma_i + \alpha_b\hat{\gamma}_b^\sigma) = (1 - \alpha_s)\Phi_s + (1 - \alpha_i)\Phi_i\varepsilon^\sigma,$$

and given the trade balance condition, $(\hat{q}^\sigma/\hat{p}^\sigma)\hat{\gamma}_b^\sigma = -\hat{\phi}_s^\sigma$, relative prices are thus

(13)
$$\frac{\hat{q}^\sigma}{\hat{p}^\sigma} = \frac{\overline{q}^\sigma}{\overline{p}^\sigma} + \frac{1}{\alpha_b\Gamma_b + \alpha_i\Gamma_i}(\alpha_b - \alpha_s)\hat{\phi}_s^\sigma.$$

When $\sigma = 1$, the world economy experiences an aggregate food shortage pushing food prices up. By shifting wealth from individuals who value food less to individuals who value food more, domestic insurance policies induce aggregate demand for food to increase, inducing an additional upward pressure on food prices as captured in equation (13). The general equilibrium effect is all the stronger than preference heterogeneity is more pronounced. For the rest of the chapter, we assume that $\alpha_b > \alpha_s$, so that net food buyers are also those who put a higher weight on food in their consumption basket.

Alternatively, interpreting $(\alpha_b - \alpha_s)$ as the extent of wealth inequality implies that the general equilibrium effect is stronger when wealth inequality is greater; a wealth transfer from the rich lowers their food consumption by less than it increases the poor's, and even more so than wealth differences are starker. To fully characterize the equilibrium of the economy, we need to solve for prices and insurance policies. To do so, we have the demand functions defined in equation (12), the market-clearing and trade balance conditions. The following proposition characterizes the equilibrium of the economy.

PROPOSITION 1: OPTIMAL SOCIAL PROTECTION. *The unique equilibrium of the economy is characterized by the following social protection policy: In times of food crises (i.e., $\tilde{\varepsilon} = \varepsilon^l$), net food producers transfer an amount*

$$(14) \quad \hat{\phi}_s^l = -\pi \frac{[(\bar{q}^h/\bar{p}^h) - (\bar{q}^l/\bar{p}^l)]\Phi_s}{[(\bar{q}^h/\bar{p}^h) + (\Phi_s/\Gamma_b)] - (\alpha_b - \alpha_s)[\Phi_s/(\alpha_b\Gamma_b + \alpha_i\Gamma_i)]},$$

of food to net food consumers, and in normal times (i.e., $\tilde{\varepsilon} = \varepsilon^h$), therefore receive

$$\hat{\phi}_s^h = (1 - \pi)\frac{[(\bar{q}^h/\bar{p}^h) - (\bar{q}^l/\bar{p}^l)]\Phi_s}{[(\bar{q}^l/\bar{p}^l) + (\Phi_s/\Gamma_b)] - (\alpha_b - \alpha_s)[\Phi_s/(\alpha_b\Gamma_b + \alpha_i\Gamma_i)]}$$

in return, where relative prices $(\bar{q}^\sigma/\bar{p}^\sigma)_{\sigma \in \{h,l\}}$ are defined in equation (1). Equilibrium prices adjust according to (13). ∎

The optimal social protection scheme is the intersection of a "demand for insurance" curve and a "food supply curve." The higher the price difference between the two states of the world, the larger the insurance motive. On the other hand, as agents insure themselves against food price shocks, the supply shock is exacerbated since *Domestic* demand is higher subsequently to a wealth redistribution from food producers (the rich) who value food relatively less to food consumers (the poor) who value food relatively more. Such additional effect further increases the optimal level of social protection as indicated in equation (14).

9.3.3   The n Country Case

We extend the analysis to the case of n identical exporting countries to a large foreign market, the size of which is also assumed to grow linearly with n. Among these n countries, we denote by $m \leq n$, the number of countries that actually implement a social protection policy as described above, and we denote $\theta = m/n$ the fraction of countries that implement a social protection scheme. Since agents are price takers, the demand for insurance remains identical and determined by equation (12). Relative prices are, however, changed and for expositional simplicity, we focus on prices in times of food crisis, that is, $\sigma = l$, and denote by $\hat{\phi}_\theta$ the optimal insurance policy when θn countries decide to implement a social protection scheme. Recall that $\hat{\phi}_\theta$ is the transfer made from net food producers in a given country to net food consumers of that same country and that transfers in other states of the world are defined by conditions (7) to (11) being binding. Prices are now equal to

(15)
$$\frac{\hat{q}^l}{\hat{p}^l} = \frac{\bar{q}^l}{\bar{p}^l} - \frac{\theta}{\alpha_b \Gamma_b + \alpha_i \Gamma_i}(\alpha_b - \alpha_s)\hat{\phi}_\theta.$$

How will agents in each country choose their social protection levels? As pointed out in Proposition 1, optimal insurance schemes depend on price levels that in turn depend on equilibrium levels of contingent transfers.

PROPOSITION 2: OPTIMAL SOCIAL PROTECTION WITH MULTIPLE COUNTRIES. *The optimal social protection policy* $\hat{\phi}_\theta$ *is given by:*

$$\hat{\phi}_\theta = \frac{\pi[(\bar{q}^h/\bar{p}^h) - (\bar{q}^l/\bar{p}^l)]}{[(\bar{q}^h/\bar{p}^h)(1/\Phi_s) + (1/\Gamma_b)] - [\theta(\alpha_b - \alpha_s)]/(\alpha_b \Gamma_b + \alpha_i \Gamma_i)}. \qquad \blacksquare$$

As the number of countries implementing social protection policies increases, the upward pressure applied on prices further increases the scope for insuring food consumers more. This pecuniary externality exacerbates the effect of social protection on food prices that increase more than linearly as the number of participating countries increases. To look at the welfare implications for domestic consumers of a given country as θ grows closer to 1, we assume that shocks are small enough so that second order effects are negligible. Formally, we notice that $\hat{\phi}_\theta$ converges to zero as the magnitude of the output shock goes to zero (i.e., ε^l gets arbitrarily close to 1), uniformly with respect to θ. Net food consumers' welfare levels

$$\hat{V}_b(\theta) = \alpha_b \ln\frac{\hat{q}^l}{\hat{p}^l} + \ln\left(\Gamma_b + \frac{\hat{p}^l}{\hat{q}^l}\hat{\phi}_\theta\right)$$

can be written as

(16) $\hat{V}_b(\theta) = \left[\alpha_b \ln\frac{\bar{q}^l}{\bar{p}^l} + \ln\Gamma_b\right] + \frac{\bar{p}^l}{\bar{q}^l}\frac{\hat{\phi}_\theta}{\Gamma_b}\left[1 - \theta\frac{\alpha_b\Gamma_b}{\alpha_b\Gamma_b + \alpha_i\Gamma_i}(\alpha_b - \alpha_s)\right]$

$\qquad + o(1 - \varepsilon^l),$

where $o(1 - \varepsilon^l)$ is a continuous function of $1 - \varepsilon^l$, such that $\lim_{\varepsilon^l \to 1} o(1 - \varepsilon^l)/(1 - \varepsilon^l) = 0$. As θ grows, net food consumers receive an increasing social protection payment $\hat{\phi}_\theta$, the welfare benefit of which is mitigated (or offset) by higher prices. The first term in equation (16) is the baseline welfare level, while the second term captures the income net of substitution effect. The following proposition establishes the conditions under which one effect dominates the other:

PROPOSITION 3: SOCIAL PROTECTION AND WELFARE. *As the number of countries* θ *implementing optimal social protection schemes increases, welfare of net food consumers in state of the world σ = 1 increases if and only if Domestic is a net food exporter, that is,*

$$\frac{1 - \alpha_s}{\alpha_b} \frac{\Phi_s}{\Gamma_b} > \frac{1 - \alpha_i}{\alpha_i} \frac{\Phi_i}{\Gamma_i} \varepsilon^l. \qquad \blacksquare$$

For food exporting (resp. importing) countries, as θ goes up, so does the price of food, inducing a positive (resp. negative) wealth effect. Thus, aggregate income increases in exporting countries, while it decreases in importing countries; for the poor in food exporting countries, the welfare gain from increased social protection transfers ends up exceeding the loss due to higher food prices. The opposite holds for the poor in food importing countries.

9.3.4   Discussion

Aggregate price volatility creates demand for insurance for domestic consumers. In the optimal social protection contract, wealth is transferred from net food producers to net food consumers in times of high food prices. However, such transfer might not be neutral in terms of aggregate consumption when agents have heterogeneous preferences over consumption goods. In particular, when resources are transferred to individuals with a higher propensity to spend on food, it results in an increase in aggregate food consumption, with the associated price implications.

The model therefore produces a countercyclical demand shock stemming from agents' insurance motive: the consequences of an aggregate supply shock are exacerbated by a concomitant demand shock due to the implementation of social protection policies that end up increasing the share of food in national consumption. Thus, under some parameter configurations— namely $\alpha_b > \alpha_s$—an optimal domestic social protection policy would qualify as a beggar-thy-neighbor policy in that it further reduces the quantity of food available on international markets. As expected, the amplification of price shocks is further enhanced as more countries engage in similar social protection policies. Finally, such countercyclical demand shock further results in an overall increased food price volatility, since in normal times ($\sigma = h$), the aggregate demand for food also drops, driving food prices further down.

9.4   Trade Insulation

The previous section characterized the optimal insurance contract that domestic agents are willing to sign in a world with perfect commitment and no transaction costs. If insurance contracts cannot be enforced, then one party has an incentive to renege depending on the realization of the output shock. The insurance market therefore collapses. Trade insulation can then be considered as a government-provided alternative enforcement of a social protection in states of the world where countries face a food crisis, that is,

$\tilde{\epsilon} = \epsilon^l$. Admittedly, such an instrument will come with distortions that are the focus of the analysis in this section. When on the other hand $\tilde{\epsilon} = \epsilon^h$, governments can resort to various forms of agricultural subsidies (input subsidies, credit) as the medium through which agricultural households, that is, net food sellers, receive compensations within the context of a broader social protection contract.

Note, however, that we are not arguing that trade insulation is a second-best policy since we are not considering the whole range of possible interventions. Rather, we study trade insulation in isolation, and compare it with the first-best benchmark, which is the optimal social protection scheme described in section 9.3.

9.4.1   Export Restrictions and Equilibrium Prices

We restrict ourselves to the case of food exporting countries and define X, the quota on exports from *Domestic* to *Foreign*. Alternatively, the analysis applies to importing countries, too, and the results are unchanged whether quantity or price restrictions are being put into place. There are now two sets of prices; international prices (prices paid by foreign consumers) ($\bar{p}^l$, $\bar{q}^l$), while domestic prices are denoted ($\bar{p}^l$, $\bar{q}^l$).

Looking at the foreign country, the trade balance and food market clearing conditions pin down the international price ratio, that is, $\bar{q}^l/\bar{p}^l = [(1 - \alpha_i)\Phi_i\epsilon^l + X]/\alpha_i\Gamma_i$, that we can rewrite

$$(17) \qquad \frac{\bar{q}^l}{\bar{p}^l} = \frac{\bar{q}^l}{\bar{p}^l} - \frac{1}{\alpha_i\Gamma_i}(\bar{X}^l - X).$$

The quantitative food export restriction affects the relative price of food in two ways: it both decreases the international supply of food, and at the same time, since trade should balance in equilibrium, it increases the international supply of gold, making food even more expensive relative to gold.

On the other hand, for a given export quota X, domestic food sellers have income $\bar{p}^l(\Phi_s - X) + \bar{p}^l X$. The domestic food market clearing condition can therefore be expressed as

$$\alpha_s(\Phi_s - X) + \alpha_s\frac{\bar{p}^l}{\bar{p}^l}X + \alpha_b\frac{\bar{q}^l}{\bar{p}^l}\Gamma_b = \Phi_s - X,$$

and since the prices of gold equalize across markets, the above condition pins down to

$$(18) \qquad \frac{\bar{q}^l}{\bar{p}^l} = \frac{(1 - \alpha_s)(\Phi_s - X)}{\alpha_s(\bar{p}^l/\bar{q}^l)X + \alpha_b\Gamma_b},$$

with the price ratio $\bar{p}^l/\bar{q}^l$ defined in equation (17).

9.4.2 Trade Insulation as Social Protection

To evaluate the ability of trade policy to act as a substitute for social insurance, let us consider the optimal social insurance policy $\hat{\phi}$, and choose a level of export quota $\hat{X}$ that keeps domestic food buyers at identical welfare level.

Trade insulation as social protection. Recall that under a social insurance contract, net food buyers have welfare

$$\hat{V}_b^l = -\alpha_b \ln \frac{\hat{p}^l}{\hat{q}^l} + \ln\left(\Gamma_b + \frac{\hat{p}^l}{\hat{q}^l} \hat{\phi} \right)$$

in times of high food prices. Considering small aggregate food shocks, that is $|1 - \varepsilon^l| \ll 1$, we can rewrite food buyers' welfare as

(19) $$\hat{V}_b^l = -\alpha_b \ln \frac{\bar{p}^l}{\bar{q}^l} + \ln \Gamma_b + \alpha_b \hat{\eta} \hat{\phi} + o(1 - \varepsilon^l),$$

where

$$\hat{\eta} = \frac{\bar{p}^l}{\bar{q}^l} \left[\frac{1}{\alpha_b \Gamma_b} - (\alpha_b - \alpha_s) \frac{1}{\alpha_b \Gamma_b + \alpha_i \Gamma_i} \right].$$

As we saw previously, any income transfer to a net food buyer translates into a commensurate welfare increase $(\bar{p}^l/\bar{q}^l)(1/\alpha_b \Gamma_b)$, but given general equilibrium implications, welfare is, however, reduced by higher food prices since $\alpha_b > \alpha_s$.

On the other hand, for a given export quota X, net food buyers have welfare level

$$V_b^l(X) = -\alpha_b \ln \frac{\hat{p}^l}{\hat{q}^l} + \ln \Gamma_b,$$

where prices are given by equations (17) and (18). Similarly to the case above, if we assume small output shocks, the scope for trade policy vanishes, so that we can write $o[1 - (X/\bar{X}^l)] = o(1 - \varepsilon^l)$. We can thus linearize domestic prices and write

$$\frac{\hat{q}^l}{\hat{p}^l} = \frac{\bar{q}^l}{\bar{p}^l}[1 + \dot{\eta}(\bar{X}^l - X)] + o(1 - \varepsilon^l),$$

with $\dot{\eta} = -(\bar{p}^l/\bar{q}^l)(\partial/\partial X)[(\hat{q}^l/\hat{p}^l)_{X=\bar{X}^l}]$. The derivation of $\dot{\eta}$ yields

$$\dot{\eta} = \frac{(1 - \alpha_s) + \alpha_s[1 - (\bar{p}/\bar{q})(\bar{X}^l/\alpha_i \Gamma_i)]}{(1 - \alpha_s)(\Phi_s - \bar{X}^l)}.$$

This implies, for net buyers' welfare,

(20) $$V_b^l(X) = -\alpha_b \ln \frac{\bar{p}^l}{\bar{q}^l} + \ln \Gamma_b + \alpha_b \dot{\eta}(\bar{X}^l - X) + o(1 - \varepsilon^l).$$

Equalizing equation (19) with equation (20) and henceforth omitting reference to smaller order terms, quota $\dot{X}^l$ verifies

$$(21) \qquad \dot{X}^l = \bar{X}^l - \frac{\hat{\eta}}{\dot{\eta}}\hat{\phi}.$$

In terms of the welfare of food buyers, $\dot{X}^l$ is the quota equivalent to the payment $\hat{\phi}$ they would receive from food sellers in times of food scarcity under the optimal social protection policy.

Beggar-thy-neighbor. We now look at what distortions are being induced by such trade insulation as opposed to an insurance contract. International prices are thus given by

$$\frac{\ddot{q}^l}{\ddot{p}^l} = \frac{\bar{q}^l}{\bar{p}^l} - \frac{1}{\alpha_i \Gamma_i}(\bar{X}^l - \dot{X}) = \frac{\bar{q}^l}{\bar{p}^l} - \frac{1}{\alpha_i \Gamma_i}\frac{\hat{\eta}}{\dot{\eta}}\hat{\phi},$$

while in the social insurance case,

$$\frac{\hat{q}^l}{\hat{p}^l} = \frac{\bar{q}^l}{\bar{p}^l} - \frac{1}{\alpha_b \Gamma_b + \alpha_i \Gamma_i}(\alpha_b - \alpha_s)\hat{\phi}$$

so that

$$\frac{\hat{q}^l}{\hat{p}^l} - \frac{\ddot{q}^l}{\ddot{p}^l} = \left[\frac{1}{\alpha_i \Gamma_i}\frac{\hat{\eta}}{\dot{\eta}} - \frac{\alpha_b - \alpha_s}{\alpha_b \Gamma_b + \alpha_i \Gamma_i}\right]\hat{\phi},$$

which, after plugging in the values of $\hat{\eta}$ and $\dot{\eta}$ and rearranging, pins down to

$$\frac{\hat{q}^l}{\hat{p}^l} - \frac{\ddot{q}^l}{\ddot{p}^l} = \frac{\alpha_b \bar{q}^l \Gamma_b + \alpha_s \bar{p}^l \bar{X}^l}{\alpha_i \bar{q}^l \Gamma_i - \alpha_s \bar{p}^l \bar{X}^l}$$

$$\times \left[1 - (\alpha_b - \alpha_s)\frac{\alpha_b \bar{q}^l \Gamma_b}{\alpha_s \bar{p}^l \bar{X}^l + \alpha_b \bar{q}^l \Gamma_b}\right]\frac{\hat{\phi}}{\alpha_b \Gamma_b}.$$

This leads us to the following proposition:

PROPOSITION 4: *Welfare loss from trade insulation. Comparing with an economy where Domestic implements an optimal social protection policy, the enforcement of export quota $\dot{X}^l$ as defined by equation (21) comes at a welfare loss*

$$\Delta V_i^l = \frac{\bar{p}^l}{\bar{q}^l}\frac{\alpha_i \bar{q}^l \Gamma_i - (1 - \alpha_i)\bar{p}^l \Phi_i \varepsilon^l}{\bar{p}^l \Phi_i \varepsilon^l + \bar{q}^l \Gamma_i}\frac{\alpha_b \bar{q}^l \Gamma_b + \alpha_s \bar{p}^l \bar{X}^l}{\alpha_i \bar{q}^l \Gamma_i - \alpha_s \bar{p}^l \bar{X}^l}$$

$$\times \left[1 - (\alpha_b - \alpha_s)\frac{\alpha_b \bar{q}^l \Gamma_b}{\alpha_s \bar{p}^l \bar{X}^l + \alpha_b \bar{q}^l \Gamma_b}\right]\frac{\hat{\phi}}{\alpha_b \Gamma_b}$$

to international consumers.

Furthermore, ΔV_i^l goes to zero as preference heterogeneity $(\alpha_b - \alpha_s)$ becomes arbitrarily close to 1. ∎

Trade insulation as a substitute for the optimal social protection scheme comes with a price distortion since *Domestic* and *Foreign* prices now diverge. This induces *Domestic* agents to overconsume food while *Foreign* agents underconsume. However, as preference heterogeneity increases, the relative loss to international consumers decreases and eventually vanishes in the extreme case where food buyers (the poor) only value food, and food sellers (the rich) only value gold; in such degenerate cases, the inefficiency disappears since there is no longer scope for the substitution effect to operate.

This last result carries an implication for the long-standing debate on trade and famines discussed in the introduction. People at the brink of starvation will spend everything they have on food. While saving lives will surely become the overriding policy goal, it is notable that in this extreme case the inefficiencies of trade intervention vanish. The intuition is as follows: the richer the rich are, the weaker the price effect stemming from trade insulation will be. Thus, their food consumption will be less distorted by the price subsidy, and so will aggregate domestic consumption. In other words, the greater the wealth inequality, the more attractive trade insulation is as a self-targeted social protection program.

9.5   Concluding Remarks

Critics of trade intervention for the purpose of protection from external price shocks have correctly pointed out that such a policy can exacerbate the problem of price volatility. However, in the absence of better options for aggregate intertemporal smoothing, the optimal nontrade social protection policy would entail transfers between net food producers and net consumers to coinsure, and this too would exacerbate the volatility. Given the symmetry between these policies, one cannot argue that the external trade intervention is necessarily an inferior form of social protection. We indeed argued above that trade insulation policies are not necessary to exacerbate food price shocks. Instead, trade policies are viewed as a mere instrument used to implement an underlying optimal social protection scheme. Such use of trade policy comes with some price distortions that need to be evaluated against distortions generated by alternative schemes. However, a priori there are no theoretical grounds for trade-based instruments to be systematically dominated by free trade alternatives from either domestic or international perspectives. Moreover, throughout the chapter, we have maintained the constraint that countries were not allowed to run a trade deficit, hence ruling out intertemporal smoothing. Relaxing such constraint would allow agents to diversify across states of the world instead. Efficiency gains could therefore be realized if countries were instead able to conduct countercyclical fiscal policies.

Appendix
Proofs

Proof of Proposition 1

Trade balance and the condition that insurance premia must be actuarially fair implies that in equilibrium

$$\frac{\pi}{1-\pi}\frac{\hat{q}^h}{\hat{q}^l}\frac{\hat{q}^l}{\hat{p}^l}\hat{\gamma} = \hat{\phi}.$$

Plugging in the equilibrium values of $\hat{\phi}$ and $\hat{\gamma}$ obtained from equation (12) implies

$$\pi\left(1-\frac{\hat{p}^h}{\hat{p}^l}\right)\Phi_s = \frac{\pi}{1-\pi}\frac{\hat{q}^h}{\hat{q}^l}\frac{\hat{q}^l}{\hat{p}^l}(1-\pi)\left(1-\frac{\hat{q}^l}{\hat{q}^h}\right)\Gamma_b$$

or

$$\frac{\hat{q}^h}{\hat{q}^l} = 1 - \frac{\hat{p}^h}{\hat{q}^h}\left(\frac{\hat{p}^l}{\hat{p}^h}-1\right)\frac{\Phi_s}{\Gamma_b}.$$

Furthermore, the following identity holds:

$$\frac{\hat{q}^l}{\hat{q}^h} = \frac{\hat{q}^l}{\hat{p}^l}\frac{\hat{p}^l}{\hat{p}^h}\frac{\hat{p}^h}{\hat{q}^h}$$

so that

$$\frac{\hat{q}^l}{\hat{p}^l}\frac{\hat{p}^l}{\hat{p}^h}\frac{\hat{p}^h}{\hat{q}^h} = 1 - \frac{\hat{p}^h}{\hat{q}^h}\left(\frac{\hat{p}^l}{\hat{p}^h}-1\right)\frac{\Phi_s}{\Gamma_b}$$

that we can rewrite:

$$\frac{\hat{p}^l}{\hat{p}^h} = \left(\frac{\hat{q}^h}{\hat{p}^h}+\frac{\Phi_s}{\Gamma_b}\right)\left(\frac{\hat{q}^l}{\hat{p}^l}+\frac{\Phi_s}{\Gamma_b}\right)^{-1}.$$

We can now plug in the expressions for the relative prices as given by equation (13)

$$\frac{\hat{p}^l}{\hat{p}^h} = \left(\frac{(1-\alpha_s)\Phi_s+(1-\alpha_i)\Phi_i\varepsilon^h+(\alpha_b-\alpha_s)[(1-\pi)/\pi](\hat{p}^l/\hat{p}^h)\hat{\phi}}{\alpha_b\Gamma_b+\alpha_i\Gamma_i}+\frac{\Phi_s}{\Gamma_b}\right)$$

$$\times\left(\frac{\hat{q}^l}{\hat{p}^l}+\frac{\Phi_s}{\Gamma_b}\right)^{-1}$$

$$= \left(\frac{(1-\alpha_s)\Phi_s+(1-\alpha_i)\Phi_i\varepsilon^h}{\alpha_b\Gamma_b+\alpha_i\Gamma_i}+\frac{\Phi_s}{\Gamma_b}+\frac{(\alpha_b-\alpha_s)[(1-\pi)/\pi](\hat{p}^l/\hat{p}^h)\hat{\phi}}{\alpha_b\Gamma_b+\alpha_i\Gamma_i}\right)$$

$$\times\left(\frac{\hat{q}^l}{\hat{p}^l}+\frac{\Phi_s}{\Gamma_b}\right)^{-1}$$

so that

$$\frac{\hat{p}^l}{\hat{p}^h}\left[1 - \frac{(\alpha_b - \alpha_s)[(1 - \pi)/\pi]\hat{\phi}}{\alpha_b\Gamma_b + \alpha_i\Gamma_i}\left(\frac{\hat{q}^l}{\hat{p}^l} + \frac{\Phi_s}{\Gamma_b}\right)^{-1}\right]$$

$$= \left(\frac{(1 - \alpha_s)\Phi_s + (1 - \alpha_i)\Phi_i\varepsilon^h}{\alpha_b\Gamma_b + \alpha_i\Gamma_i} + \frac{\Phi_s}{\Gamma_b}\right)\left(\frac{\hat{q}^l}{\hat{p}^l} + \frac{\Phi_s}{\Gamma_b}\right)^{-1},$$

which can be rearranged as

$$\frac{\hat{p}^l}{\hat{p}^h}\left[\left(\frac{\hat{q}^l}{\hat{p}^l} + \frac{\Phi_s}{\Gamma_b}\right) - \frac{(\alpha_b - \alpha_s)[(1 - \pi)/\pi]\hat{\phi}}{\alpha_b\Gamma_b + \alpha_i\Gamma_i}\right]$$

$$= \frac{(1 - \alpha_s)\Phi_s + (1 - \alpha_i)\Phi_i\varepsilon^h}{\alpha_b\Gamma_b + \alpha_i\Gamma_i} + \frac{\Phi_s}{\Gamma_b}$$

or

$$\frac{\hat{p}^l}{\hat{p}^h} = \left[\frac{(1 - \alpha_s)\Phi_s + (1 - \alpha_i)\Phi_i\varepsilon^h}{\alpha_b\Gamma_b + \alpha_i\Gamma_i} + \frac{\Phi_s}{\Gamma_b}\right]$$

$$\times \left[\left(\frac{\hat{q}^l}{\hat{p}^l} + \frac{\Phi_s}{\Gamma_b}\right) - \frac{(\alpha_b - \alpha_s)[(1 - \pi)/\pi]\hat{\phi}}{\alpha_b\Gamma_b + \alpha_i\Gamma_i}\right]^{-1}.$$

Taking the definition of benchmark no-commitment prices, we can write

(22) $$\frac{\hat{p}^l}{\hat{p}^h} = \frac{(\bar{q}^h/\bar{p}^h) + (\Phi_s/\Gamma_b)}{(\bar{q}^l/\bar{p}^l) + (\Phi_s/\Gamma_b) - [(\alpha_b - \alpha_s)(1/\pi)\hat{\phi}]/(\alpha_b\Gamma_b + \alpha_i\Gamma_i)}.$$

Equation (22) defines a "food price volatility" curve, while equation (12) defines a demand for insurance curve that we rewrite

$$\begin{cases} \dfrac{\hat{p}^h}{\hat{p}^l} = 1 - \dfrac{\hat{\phi}}{\pi\Phi_s} \\[4mm] \dfrac{\hat{p}^h}{\hat{p}^l} = \left(\dfrac{\bar{q}^h}{\bar{p}^h} + \dfrac{\Phi_s}{\Gamma_b}\right)^{-1}\left[\dfrac{\bar{q}^l}{\bar{p}^l} + \dfrac{\Phi_s}{\Gamma_b} - \dfrac{(\alpha_b - \alpha_s)(1/\pi)\hat{\phi}}{\alpha_b\Gamma_b + \alpha_i\Gamma_i}\right]. \end{cases}$$

Substituting:

$$\left(1 - \frac{\hat{\phi}}{\pi\Phi_s}\right)\left(\frac{\bar{q}^h}{\bar{p}^h} + \frac{\Phi_s}{\Gamma_b}\right) = \frac{\bar{q}^l}{\bar{p}^l} + \frac{\Phi_s}{\Gamma_b} - \frac{(\alpha_b - \alpha_s)(1/\pi)\hat{\phi}}{\alpha_b\Gamma_b + \alpha_i\Gamma_i}$$

$$\frac{\bar{q}^h}{\bar{p}^h} + \frac{\Phi_s}{\Gamma_b} - \frac{\hat{\phi}}{\pi\Phi_s}\left(\frac{\bar{q}^h}{\bar{p}^h} + \frac{\Phi_s}{\Gamma_b}\right) = \frac{\bar{q}^l}{\bar{p}^l} + \frac{\Phi_s}{\Gamma_b} - \frac{(\alpha_b - \alpha_s)(1/\pi)\hat{\phi}}{\alpha_b\Gamma_b + \alpha_i\Gamma_i}$$

$$\frac{\bar{q}^h}{\bar{p}^h} - \frac{\hat{\phi}}{\pi\Phi_s}\left(\frac{\bar{q}^h}{\bar{p}^h} + \frac{\Phi_s}{\Gamma_b}\right) = \frac{\bar{q}^l}{\bar{p}^l} - \frac{(\alpha_b - \alpha_s)(1/\pi)\hat{\phi}}{\alpha_b\Gamma_b + \alpha_i\Gamma_i}$$

$$\frac{1}{\pi}\hat{\phi}\left[\left(\frac{\bar{q}^h}{\bar{p}^h}\frac{1}{\Phi_s} + \frac{1}{\Gamma_b}\right) - \frac{(\alpha_b - \alpha_s)}{\alpha_b\Gamma_b + \alpha_i\Gamma_i}\right] = \left(\frac{\bar{q}^h}{\bar{p}^h} - \frac{\bar{q}^l}{\bar{p}^l}\right)$$

so that

$$\hat{\phi} = \frac{\pi[(\bar{q}^h/\bar{p}^h) - (\bar{q}^l/\bar{p}^l)]}{[(\bar{q}^h/\bar{p}^h)(1/\Phi_s) + (1/\Gamma_b)] - [(\alpha_b - \alpha_s)/(\alpha_b\Gamma_b + \alpha_i\Gamma_i)]},$$

which concludes the first part of the proof.

Plugging in the value of $\hat{\phi}$ to equation (12) yields:

$$\frac{\hat{p}^h}{\hat{p}^l} = 1 - \frac{\hat{\phi}}{\pi\Phi_s}$$

$$= 1 - \frac{(\bar{q}^h/\bar{p}^h) - (\bar{q}^l/\bar{p}^l)}{[(\bar{q}^h/\bar{p}^h) + (\Phi_s/\Gamma_b)] - (\alpha_b - \alpha_s)\Phi_s/(\alpha_b\Gamma_b + \alpha_i\Gamma_i)}$$

$$\frac{\hat{p}^h}{\hat{p}^l} = \frac{[(\bar{q}^l/\bar{p}^l) + (\Phi_s/\Gamma_b)] - (\alpha_b - \alpha_s)\Phi_s/(\alpha_b\Gamma_b + \alpha_i\Gamma_i)}{[(\bar{q}^h/\bar{p}^h) + (\Phi_s/\Gamma_b)] - (\alpha_b - \alpha_s)\Phi_s/(\alpha_b\Gamma_b + \alpha_i\Gamma_i)}$$

We can now substitute in the expression for $\hat{\phi}_s^h$:

$$\hat{\phi}_s^h = \frac{1-\pi}{\pi}\frac{\hat{p}^l}{\hat{p}^h}\hat{\phi}$$

$$= \frac{1-\pi}{\pi}\frac{[(\bar{q}^h/\bar{p}^h) + (\Phi_s/\Gamma_b)] - [(\alpha_b - \alpha_s)\Phi_s/(\alpha_b\Gamma_b + \alpha_i\Gamma_i)]}{[(\bar{q}^l/\bar{p}^l) + (\Phi_s/\Gamma_b)] - [(\alpha_b - \alpha_s)\Phi_s/(\alpha_b\Gamma_b + \alpha_i\Gamma_i)]}$$

$$\times\frac{\pi[(\bar{q}^h/\bar{p}^h) - (\bar{q}^l/\bar{p}^l)]}{[(\bar{q}^h/\bar{p}^h)(1/\Phi_s) + (1/\Gamma_b)] - (\alpha_b - \alpha_s)/(\alpha_b\Gamma_b + \alpha_i\Gamma_i)}$$

$$\hat{\phi}_s^h = \frac{(1-\pi)[(\bar{q}^h/\bar{p}^h) - (\bar{q}^l/\bar{p}^l)]\Phi_s}{[(\bar{q}^l/\bar{p}^l) + (\Phi_s/\Gamma_b)] - [(\alpha_b - \alpha_s)\Phi_s/(\alpha_b\Gamma_b + \alpha_i\Gamma_i)]},$$

which concludes the proof of Proposition 1.   ■

Proof of Proposition 2

The expression for the ratio of food prices is unchanged and equal to

$$\frac{\hat{p}^l}{\hat{p}^h} = \left(\frac{\hat{q}^h}{\hat{p}^h} + \frac{\Phi_s}{\Gamma_b}\right)\left(\frac{\hat{q}^l}{\hat{p}^l} + \frac{\Phi_s}{\Gamma_b}\right)^{-1}.$$

Since only aggregate endowment is affected, we can now plug in the expressions for the relative prices as given by equation (15)

$$\frac{\hat{p}^l}{\hat{p}^h} = \left(\frac{(1-\alpha_s)\Phi_s + (1-\alpha_i)\Phi_i\varepsilon^h + \theta(\alpha_b - \alpha_s)[(1-\pi)/\pi](\hat{p}^l/\hat{p}^h)\hat{\phi}_\theta}{\alpha_b\Gamma_b + \alpha_i\Gamma_i} + \frac{\Phi_s}{\Gamma_b}\right)$$

$$\times\left(\frac{\hat{q}^l}{\hat{p}^l} + \frac{\Phi_s}{\Gamma_b}\right)^{-1}$$

or, following the same steps as earlier in the proof of Proposition 1,

(23) $$\frac{\hat{p}^l}{\hat{p}^h} = \frac{(\bar{q}^h/\bar{p}^h) + (\Phi_s/\Gamma_b)}{(\bar{q}^l/\bar{p}^l) + (\Phi_s/\Gamma_b) - [\theta(\alpha_b - \alpha_s)(1/\pi)\hat{\phi}_\theta]/(\alpha_b\Gamma_b + \alpha_i\Gamma_i)}.$$

Similarly, equation (23) defines a food price volatility curve, while equation (12) defines a demand for insurance curve that we rewrite

$$\begin{cases} \dfrac{\hat{p}^h}{\hat{p}^l} = 1 - \dfrac{\hat{\phi}_\theta}{\pi\Phi_s} \\[3mm] \dfrac{\hat{p}^h}{\hat{p}^l} = \left(\dfrac{\bar{q}^h}{\bar{p}^h} + \dfrac{\Phi_s}{\Gamma_b}\right)^{-1}\left[\dfrac{\bar{q}^l}{\bar{p}^l} + \dfrac{\Phi_s}{\Gamma_b} - \dfrac{\theta(\alpha_b - \alpha_s)(1/\pi)\hat{\phi}_\theta}{\alpha_b\Gamma_b + \alpha_i\Gamma_i}\right] \end{cases}$$

to finally obtain

$$\hat{\phi}_\theta = \frac{\pi[(\bar{q}^h/\bar{p}^h) - (\bar{q}^l/\bar{p}^l)]}{[(\bar{q}^h/\bar{p}^h)(1/\Phi_s) + (1/\Gamma_b)] - [\theta(\alpha_b - \alpha_s)/(\alpha_b\Gamma_b + \alpha_i\Gamma_i)]},$$

which concludes the proof.   ∎

Proof of Proposition 3

Taking the derivative of $\hat{V}_b^l(\theta)$ with respect to θ gives

$$\frac{d\hat{V}_b^l(\theta)}{d\theta} = \frac{\bar{p}^l}{\bar{q}^l}\frac{\hat{\phi}_\theta}{\Gamma_b}\left\{\frac{\hat{\phi}_\theta'}{\hat{\phi}_\theta}\left[1 - \theta\frac{\alpha_b\Gamma_b}{\alpha_b\Gamma_b + \alpha_i\Gamma_i}(\alpha_b - \alpha_s)\right] - \frac{\alpha_b\Gamma_b}{\alpha_b\Gamma_b + \alpha_i\Gamma_i}(\alpha_b - \alpha_s)\right\}$$

$$\times \frac{\bar{p}^l}{\bar{q}^l}\frac{\hat{\phi}_\theta}{\Gamma_b}\left\{\frac{(\alpha_b - \alpha_s)/(\alpha_b\Gamma_b + \alpha_i\Gamma_i)}{[(\bar{q}^h/\bar{p}^h)(1/\Phi_s) + (1/\Gamma_b)] - [\theta(\alpha_b - \alpha_s)/(\alpha_b\Gamma_b + \alpha_i\Gamma_i)]}\right.$$

$$\left.\times\left[1 - \theta\frac{\alpha_b\Gamma_b}{\alpha_b\Gamma_b + \alpha_i\Gamma_i}(\alpha_b - \alpha_s)\right] - \frac{\alpha_b\Gamma_b}{\alpha_b\Gamma_b + \alpha_i\Gamma_i}(\alpha_b - \alpha_s)\right\}$$

$$= \frac{(\bar{p}^l/\bar{q}^l)(\hat{\phi}_\theta/\Gamma_b)[(\alpha_b - \alpha_s)/(\alpha_b\Gamma_b + \alpha_i\Gamma_i)]}{[(\bar{q}^h/\bar{p}^h)(1/\Phi_s) + (1/\Gamma_b)] - [\theta(\alpha_b - \alpha_s)/(\alpha_b\Gamma_b + \alpha_i\Gamma_i)]}$$

$$\times \left\{1 - \alpha_b\Gamma_b\left[\left(\frac{\bar{q}^h}{\bar{p}^h}\frac{1}{\Phi_s} + \frac{1}{\Gamma_b}\right)\right]\right\}.$$

Since

$$\frac{\bar{q}^h}{\bar{p}^h} = \frac{(1 - \alpha_s)\Phi_s + (1 - \alpha_i)\Phi_i\varepsilon^h}{\alpha_b\Gamma_b + \alpha_i\Gamma_i},$$

we have the following equivalence:

(24) $$\frac{\bar{q}^h}{\bar{p}^h} < \frac{(1 - \alpha_s)\Phi_s}{\alpha_b\Gamma_b}$$

if and only if

(25) $$\frac{1 - \alpha_s}{\alpha_b}\frac{\Phi_s}{\Gamma_b} > \frac{1 - \alpha_i}{\alpha_i}\frac{\Phi_i}{\Gamma_i}\varepsilon^h.$$

Thus,

$$\alpha_b \Gamma_b \left[\left(\frac{\bar{q}^h}{\bar{p}^h} \frac{1}{\Phi_s} + \frac{1}{\Gamma_b} \right) \right] < 1$$

if and only if equation (25) holds. Since equation (25) is a necessary and sufficient condition for *Domestic* to be a food exporter, this concludes the proof. ∎

Proof of Proposition 4

Welfare of the international consumer is driven by her total income, that is,

$$\hat{p}^l \Phi_i \varepsilon^l + \hat{q}^l \Gamma_i = \left(\frac{\hat{q}^l}{\hat{p}^l} \right)^{-(1-\alpha_i)} \Phi_i \varepsilon^l + \left(\frac{\hat{q}^l}{\hat{p}^l} \right)^{\alpha_i} \Gamma_i$$

$$= \left(\frac{\bar{q}^l}{\bar{p}^l} \right)^{-(1-\alpha_i)} \Phi_i \varepsilon^l \left(1 + (1 - \alpha_i) \frac{\bar{p}^l}{\bar{q}^l} \frac{1}{\alpha_i \Gamma_i} \frac{\hat{\eta}}{\hat{\eta}} \hat{\phi} \right) + \left(\frac{\bar{q}^l}{\bar{p}^l} \right)^{\alpha_i}$$

$$\times \Gamma_i \left(1 - \alpha_i \frac{\bar{p}^l}{\bar{q}^l} \frac{1}{\alpha_i \Gamma_i} \frac{\hat{\eta}}{\hat{\eta}} \hat{\phi} \right)$$

$$= \bar{p}^l \Phi_i \varepsilon^l + \bar{q}^l \Gamma_i + \bar{p}^l \Phi_i \varepsilon^l (1 - \alpha_i) \frac{\bar{p}^l}{\bar{q}^l} \frac{1}{\alpha_i \Gamma_i} \frac{\hat{\eta}}{\hat{\eta}} \hat{\phi} - q \Gamma_i \alpha_i \frac{\bar{p}^l}{\bar{q}^l} \frac{1}{\alpha_i \Gamma_i} \frac{\hat{\eta}}{\hat{\eta}} \hat{\phi}$$

$$= (\bar{p}^l \Phi_i \varepsilon^l + \bar{q}^l \Gamma_i) + [(1 - \alpha_i) \bar{p}^l \Phi_i \varepsilon^l - \alpha_i \bar{q}^l \Gamma_i] \frac{\bar{p}^l}{\bar{q}^l} \frac{1}{\alpha_i \Gamma_i} \frac{\hat{\eta}}{\hat{\eta}} \hat{\phi}$$

Since the international consumer is net importer of food, the second term is negative.

Under a social protection policy, the foreign consumer has total income

$$\hat{p}^l \Phi_i \varepsilon^l + \hat{q}^l \Gamma_i = (\bar{p}^l \Phi_i \varepsilon^l + \bar{q}^l \Gamma_i) + [(1 - \alpha_i) \bar{p}^l \Phi_i \varepsilon^l - \alpha_i \bar{q}^l \Gamma_i]$$

$$\times \frac{\bar{p}^l}{\bar{q}^l} \frac{1}{\alpha_b \Gamma_b + \alpha_i \Gamma_i} (\alpha_b - \alpha_s) \hat{\phi}$$

so that the income difference between the two regimes is

$$(\hat{p}^l \Phi_i \varepsilon^l + \hat{q}^l \Gamma_i) - (\hat{p}^l \Phi_i \varepsilon^l + \hat{q}^l \Gamma_i) \quad ,$$

$$= \frac{\bar{p}^l}{\bar{q}} [\alpha_i \bar{q}^l \Gamma_i - (1 - \alpha_i) \bar{p}^l \Phi_i \varepsilon^l] \left[\frac{1}{\alpha_i \Gamma_i} \frac{\hat{\eta}}{\hat{\eta}} - \frac{\alpha_b - \alpha_s}{\alpha_b \Gamma_b + \alpha_i \Gamma_i} \right] \hat{\phi}$$

that translates into welfare difference

$$\Delta V_i^l = \frac{\bar{p}^l}{\bar{q}^l} \frac{\alpha_i \bar{q}^l \Gamma_i - (1 - \alpha_i) \bar{p}^l \Phi_i \varepsilon^l}{\bar{p}^l \Phi_i \varepsilon^l + \bar{q}^l \Gamma_i} \left[\frac{1}{\alpha_i \Gamma_i} \frac{\hat{\eta}}{\hat{\eta}} - \frac{\alpha_b - \alpha_s}{\alpha_b \Gamma_b + \alpha_i \Gamma_i} \right] \hat{\phi}.$$

Plugging in the values of $\hat{\eta}$ and $\dot{\eta}$ gives

$$\frac{1}{\alpha_i \Gamma_i} \frac{\hat{\eta}}{\dot{\eta}} - \frac{\alpha_b - \alpha_s}{\alpha_b \Gamma_b + \alpha_i \Gamma_i}$$

$$= \frac{\alpha_b \bar{q}^l \Gamma_b + \alpha_s \bar{p}^l \bar{X}^l}{\alpha_i \bar{q}^l \Gamma_i - \alpha_s \bar{p}^l \bar{X}^l} \left[1 - (\alpha_b - \alpha_s) \frac{\alpha_b \bar{q}^l \Gamma_b}{\alpha_s \bar{p}^l \bar{X}^l + \alpha_b \bar{q}^l \Gamma_b} \right] \frac{1}{\alpha_b \Gamma_b}.$$

Hence the expression of ΔV_i^l in Proposition 4. As $\alpha_b - \alpha_s$ goes to 1, that is, α_b goes to 1 and α_s goes to zero, the expression in brackets goes to zero. ∎

References

Anderson, Kym. 2012. "Agricultural Trade Distortions during the Global Financial Crisis." Departmental Working Papers no. 2012-05, Arndt-Corden Department of Economics, Australian National University.

Aykroyd, Wallace R. 1974. *The Conquest of Famine.* London: Chatto & Windus.

Broner, Fernando, and Jaume Ventura. 2011. "Globalization and Risk Sharing." *Review of Economic Studies* 78 (1): 49–82.

Dixit, Avinash. 1987. "Trade and Insurance with Moral Hazard." *Journal of International Economics* 23 (3–4): 201–20.

———. 1989. "Trade and Insurance with Adverse Selection." *Review of Economic Studies* 56 (2): 235–47.

Eaton, Jonathan, and Gene M. Grossman. 1985. "Tariffs as Insurance: Optimal Commercial Policy When Domestic Markets Are Incomplete." *Canadian Journal of Economics* 18 (2): 258–72.

Gouel, Christophe, and Sébastien Jean. 2012. "Optimal Food Price Stabilization in a Small Open Developing Country." Working Papers no. 2012-01, CEPII Research Center, January.

Houthakker, H. S. 1957. "An International Comparison of Household Expenditure Patterns, Commemorating the Centenary of Engel's Law." *Econometrica* 25 (4): 532–51.

Ivanic, Maros, Will Martin, and Hassan Zaman. 2011. "Estimating the Short-Run Poverty Impacts of the 2010–11 Surge in Food Prices." Policy Research Working Paper Series no. 5633, World Bank, Washington, DC, April.

Leblebicioglu, Asli. 2009. "Financial Integration, Credit Market Imperfections and Consumption Smoothing." *Journal of Economic Dynamics and Control* 33 (2): 377–93.

Levchenko, Andrei A. 2005. "Financial Liberalization and Consumption Volatility in Developing Countries." *IMF Staff Papers* 52 (2): 237–59.

Martin, Will, and Kym Anderson. 2012. "Export Restrictions and Price Insulation during Commodity Price Booms." *American Journal of Agricultural Economics* 94 (2): 422–7.

Meade, James. 1955. *The Theory of International Economic Policy: II. Trade and Welfare.* London: Oxford University Press.

Newbery, David M. G., and Joseph E. Stiglitz. 1984. "Pareto Inferior Trade." *Review of Economic Studies* 51 (1): 1–12.

Ravallion, Martin. 1987. "Trade and Stabilization: Another Look at British India's Controversial Food Grain Exports." *Explorations in Economic History* 24 (4): 354–70.

———. 1997. "Famines and Economics." *Journal of Economic Literature* 35 (3): 1205–42.

Sen, A. 1981. *Poverty and Famines: An Essay on Entitlement and Deprivation.* Oxford scholarship online, Oxford University Press. http://www.oxfordscholarship.com /view/10.1093/0198284632.001.0001/acprof-9780198284635.

Sharma, Ramesh. 2011. "Food Export Restrictions: Review of the 2007–2010 Experience and Considerations for Disciplining Restrictive Measures." FAO Commodity and Trade Policy Research Working paper no. 32, Food and Agriculture Organization, Rome, May.

Von Braun, Joachim, Akhter Ahmed, Kwadwo Asenso-Okyere, Shenggen Fan, Ashok Gulati, John Hoddinott, Rajul Pandya-Lorch, Mark W. Rosegrant, Marie Ruel, Maximo Torero, and Te van Rheenen. 2008. "High Food Prices: The What, Who, and How of Proposed Policy Actions." Policy Briefs 1A. International Food Policy Research Institute (IFPRI).

Woodham-Smith, Cecil. 1962. *The Great Hunger: Ireland, 1845–9.* London: Hamish Hamilton.

World Bank. 1986. *Poverty and Hunger: Issues and Options for Food Security in Developing Countries.* Washington, DC: World Bank.

Wright, Brian. 2009. "International Grain Reserves and Other Instruments to Address Volatility in Grain Markets." Policy Research Working Paper Series no. 5028, World Bank, Washington, DC, August.

Comment   Ron Trostle

Introduction

As economists, we know that prices go up and prices go down. The market impacts of some of these price movements are reasonably well forecast and can be anticipated with considerable confidence. An example is the impact of a spike in livestock feed costs on future meat production. However, the causes of these price movements themselves tend to be almost completely unpredictable. An example is the severe drought and high temperatures in the United States and other adverse weather events in Russia, Ukraine, Kazakhstan, Turkey, southeast Europe, India, and parts of Africa that have led to the current jump in prices of certain crops.

The Do, Levchenko, and Ravaillion chapter compares two approaches to

Ron Trostle is an agricultural economist at the Economic Research Service, US Department of Agriculture.

For acknowledgments, sources of research support, and disclosure of the author's material financial relationships, if any, please see http://www.nber.org/chapters/c12821.ack.

mitigating the negative effects of a sharp increase in food prices; what the authors refer to as a "crisis." The two approaches are trade insulation and social protection.

Under the trade insulation approach to protecting consumers, an exporting country restricts exports in order to keep more food in the country. This action lowers prices in the country's domestic market—thus assisting consumers but at the expense of producers—but raises world prices; the approach is essentially transferring domestic price volatility to world markets. An importing country lowers import tariffs in an attempt to insulate its consumers from high world-market prices.

In the social protection approach, the authors analyze a social insurance scheme. Under the scheme, when prices are high, resource transfers (wealth) flow from net food sellers to net buyers, domestically and internationally. When prices are low, resource transfers flow from net food sellers to buyers.

The authors examine the impacts of each of the two approaches on net food sellers and net food buyers during a period of high food prices. The theory and math are elegantly set forth in the chapter, although one needs to appreciate the assumptions and limitations of the model when assessing its applicability to real world needs of policymakers. The conclusions about the impacts of the two approaches on food sellers and on domestic and international food buyers are what would be expected. In essence, in a crisis situation, the nature of the impacts of the social protection and trade insulation approaches are similar; that is, both approaches moderate the increase in food prices for net seller countries and reduce the impact of high food prices for net buyers. Under both approaches, domestic and world consumption and world food commodity prices are higher than would have been the case under a "do-nothing" approach.

The Policymaker's Dilemma

Since the impacts of the two approaches are theoretically similar, in the real world of the policymaker, which approach is preferred? Traditionally, countries have used trade insulation policies to deal with food price spikes. If you were a policymaker, how would this chapter help you?

If you are setting policy for an exporting country, this chapter might help justify your decisions to restrict or ban exports during a previous food commodity price spike. If you are a policymaker for an importing country, the chapter would help justify your past decisions to lower import taxes and subsidize consumers.

As a policymaker, one needs to determine: (a) Who are you trying to protect? (b) What are you trying to protect them from? (c) How much of the perceived risk are you trying to protect them from? and (d) Over what duration of time are you trying to protect them? That is, are you trying to protect producers and consumers from price swings that occur from week to week, from month to month, from season to season, from year to year, or over a multiyear period?

The Demand Side

The chapter focused on consumers—particularly on the impact on consumers with a high propensity to consume food. (The chapter does indicate that under the social insurance scheme, producers would receive resource transfers from consumers during periods of low prices, but the focus is on consumers.)

Historically over the last forty-five to fifty years, a food commodity price spike has occurred, on average, about every seven years. Conceptually, when prices are high (crisis), the social protection approach transfers resources from food producers in exporting countries to consumers in the exporting country and also in foreign importing countries. During the intervening six noncrisis years, under the authors' optimal social insurance scheme, transfers flow back to the producers. Under the trade isolation scheme, it is unclear that there are any flows back to producers, either from consumers within the exporting country, or consumers from importing countries.

As a policymaker you need to consider how the social insurance scheme will be implemented. How will the social insurance scheme function, either within a single country or within an international context? What kind of administrative bureaucracy will need to be established? How much will it cost to implement the scheme? Are there functioning examples in other countries that you could emulate?

A political concern would be how to manage six years of transfers from consumers to producers. Low-income consumers may not like transferring resources to producers over a six-year period of low and stable prices.

The authors assume away such implementation concerns. However, in considering these operational questions, one can see why policymakers in exporting countries have relied on export restrictions, and policymakers in importing countries have relied on reducing import tariffs and providing subsidies for food. Implementing such trade-insulating policies is relatively straightforward and would require less additional administrative support.

The Supply Side

The chapter addresses the demand side, but what about the supply side? Policymakers will likely be concerned about the impact of policy decisions on food production and prices in subsequent years.

In all cases of the at least seven distinguishable price spikes over the last forty-five years, production shortfalls played at least a minor role; and in most cases, sharply reduced global production was a primary factor. Generally, the production shortfall was caused by adverse weather in multiple-producing countries.

A spike has both an upside and a downside. After most of the past seven episodes of high prices, world food commodity prices declined abruptly and significantly. And they did so because global agricultural production responded to the incentives of high prices. Generally, the increase in production was primarily attributable to a large increase in the global area planted to crops.

Policymakers might want to adopt policies that encourage an increase in production in response to food crises. An exporting country that imposes export restrictions lowers domestic prices and incentives for future production. Not only do the export restrictions directly lower production incentives, they also increase farmers' uncertainties associated with decisions to be made about future production. In a dynamic sense, both the social protection (as defined by the authors) and the trade-insulation approaches reduce future production incentives compared to a do-nothing approach. At any rate, while a trade-insulation approach may have some benefits in an individual country context, it is unlikely to be a valid approach in a multilateral context. Insulation approaches reduce the role that global trade can play in reducing variation in world prices, and as such, are mutually self-defeating. For the net importing country, reducing import tariffs as a means to decrease domestic prices works only to the extent that there remain import tariffs to reduce.

The do-nothing approach brings me to my final comment. Even if there were to evolve sufficient international political clout to impose an international social insurance scheme (regardless of the difficulties and costs of implementation), why not instead adopt a prohibition against the trade-insulation policies of export restrictions and reducing import tariffs? Admittedly, if eliminating trade policy changes were the only response during high prices, there would be negative effects on low-income consumers, and possibly on producers with crop losses that likely contributed to the high prices.

To help mitigate the impact of large swings in food commodity production and prices on producers and consumers, exporting countries could rely on a crop insurance program to protect farmers from significant financial losses. Importing countries could protect low-income consumers through targeted subsidy programs. Using the authors' analytical framework, a country would have domestic insurance for net food sellers and domestic social protection programs for low-income consumers. Although this approach may not result in the theoretical optimum, it incorporates some of the concepts of the social insurance approach, and would appear to be much easier to implement (with less administrative bureaucracy).

Contributors

Philip Abbott
Department of Agricultural
  Economics
Purdue University
403 W. State Street
West Lafayette, IN 47907-2056

Julian M. Alston
Department of Agricultural and
  Resource Economics
University of California
Davis, CA 95616

Jock R. Anderson
Faculty of the Professions
University of New England Business
  School
Trevenna Road
EBL Building
University of New England
Armidale NSW 2351 Australia

Kym Anderson
School of Economics
University of Adelaide
Adelaide SA 5005, Australia

Nicole M. Aulerich
Cornerstone Research
1919 Pennsylvania Avenue NW, Suite
  600
Washington, DC 20006-3420

Marc F. Bellemare
Department of Applied Economics
University of Minnesota
1994 Buford Avenue
St. Paul, MN 55108

Steven T. Berry
Department of Economics
Yale University
Box 208264
37 Hillhouse Avenue
New Haven, CT 06520-8264

Eugenio S. A. Bobenrieth
Department of Agricultural
  Economics
Pontificia Universidad Católica de
  Chile
Vicuña Mackenna 4860
Macul, Santiago, Chile

Juan R. A. Bobenrieth
Department of Mathematics
Universidad del Bío-Bío
Avda. Collao 1202, Casilla 5-C
CP: 4051381, Concepción, Chile

Jean-Paul Chavas
Agricultural and Applied Economics
University of Wisconsin-Madison
427 Lorch Street
Madison, WI 53706

Quy-Toan Do
MSN MC3-306
The World Bank
1818 H Street, NW
Washington, DC 20433

Walter Enders
Department of Economics, Finance
    and Legal Studies
249 Alston Hall
University of Alabama
Box 870224
Tuscaloosa, AL 35487-0224

Shenggen Fan
International Food Policy Research
    Institute
2033 K Street NW
Washington, DC 20006

Philip Garcia
Department of Agricultural and
    Consumer Economics
University of Illinois
341 Mumford Hall
Urbana, IL 61801

Barry K. Goodwin
Agricultural and Resource Economics
North Carolina State University
Box 8109
Raleigh, NC 27695-8109

Christophe Gouel
INRA, Économie Publique
AgroParisTech
16 rue Claude Bernard
75005 Paris France

Derek Headey
International Food Policy Research
    Institute
2033 K Street, NW
Washington, DC 20006-1002

Matthew T. Holt
Department of Economics, Finance,
    and Legal Studies
248 Alston Hall
University of Alabama
Box 870224
Tuscaloosa, AL 35487-0224

David Hummels
Krannert School of Management
403 West State Street
Purdue University
West Lafayette, IN 47907-1310

Scott H. Irwin
Department of Agricultural and
    Consumer Economics
344 Mumford Hall
University of Illinois
1301 West Gregory Drive
Urbana, IL 61801

Maros Ivanic
The World Bank
1818 H Street, NW
Washington, DC 20433

Andrei A. Levchenko
Department of Economics
University of Michigan
611 Tappan Street
Ann Arbor, MI 48109

James M. MacDonald
Economic Research Service
US Department of Agriculture
355 E Street SW
Washington, DC 20024-3221

William J. Martin
The World Bank, MSN MC3-305
1818 H Street, NW
Washington, DC 20433

Philip G. Pardey
Department of Applied Economics
218j Ruttan Hall
University of Minnesota
1994 Buford Avenue
St. Paul, MN 55108-6040

Martin Ravallion
Center for Economic Research
Georgetown University, ICC 580
Washington, DC 20057

Michael J. Roberts
Department of Economics
University of Hawaii at Manoa
Saunders Hall 542
2424 Maile Way
Honolulu, HI 96822

Wolfram Schlenker
School of International and Public
    Affairs, Columbia University
420 West 118th Street, Room 1430A
New York, NY 10027

Aaron Smith
Department of Agricultural and
    Resource Economics
University of California
One Shields Avenue
Davis, CA 95616

Ron Trostle
Economic Research Service
US Department of Agriculture
355 E Street SW
Washington, DC 20024-3221

Brian D. Wright
Department of Agricultural and
    Resource Economics
207 Giannini Hall
University of California
Berkeley, CA 94720-3310

Author Index

Subject Index